Cubano Be
Cubano Bop

LEONARDO ACOSTA

One Hundred Years of Jazz in Cuba

Translated by Daniel S. Whitesell

Smithsonian Books
Washington and London

Copy editor: John Raymond

Designer: Brian Barth

Library of Congress Cataloging-in-Publication Data

Acosta, Leonardo.

    [Raíces del jazz latino. English]

    Cubano be, cubano bop : one hundred years of jazz in Cuba /
Leonardo Acosta ; translated by Daniel S. Whitesell.

      p. cm.

    Translation of the original Spanish edition (Barranquilla,
Colombia, c2001).

    Includes bibliographical references (p.) and index.

    ISBN 1-58834-147-X (alk. paper)

    1. Jazz—Cuba—History and criticism. I. Title.

ML3509.C88A2713 2003

781.65'097291—dc21   2003041446

British Library Cataloguing-in-Publication Data available

Manufactured in the United States of America

10 09 08 07 06 05 04 03   5 4 3 2 1

∞ The paper used in this publication meets the minimum
requirements of the American National Standard for
Information Sciences-Permanence of Paper for Printed Library
Materials ANSI Z39.48-1984.

Contents

Foreword

The Jazz Grotto

$\mathcal{I}$t was one of those luminous nights in Havana in the early Sixties, when our little gang of "Los Chicos del Jazz," cruising down Twenty-third Street, arrived at the nightclub La Gruta (The Grotto). We were going to listen to Free American Jazz, a group founded by pianist Mario Lagarde and saxophonist Eddy Torriente, two African Americans who had just established themselves in Cuba. It must surely have been Friday or Saturday, since the small club located in the basement of the La Rampa movie house was completely packed with jazz aficionados, or simply with curious people attracted by those musicians who had arrived from the mythical "Forbidden North." The rest of the quartet consisted of drummer Pepe "El Loco" and, on the contrabass, the composer Julio César Fonseca, a picturesque character of the bohemian Havana nights.

Down in the grotto, when we finally cut through the crowd and smoke, we found Eddy El Americano, seated on one of the high stools at the bar with a very cold beer in front of him: "Hey, Campeón del Mundo!" shouted the charming mulatto saxophonist, raising his frothy beer mug in the air. It was his signature salute to all those colleagues who came each evening to listen to his beat-up Conn alto sax, which he played in that old style inspired by his idol Paul Gonsalves.

Behind the bar, in the reduced space of the bandstand, and occupying Eddy's place next to his compatriot at the piano, there was a young, skinny man wearing glasses, looking somewhat like Paul Desmond. Hanging from his neck was an enormous silver-plated baritone sax made in Czechoslovakia. Mario Lagarde counted off a medium bounce tempo and, following a brief introduction of Pepe's Hi-Hat, the group began to play his composition "La Gruta Blues." The first solo was taken by the saxophonist, who immediately caught our attention, mainly because with the exception of the few Gerry Mulligan, Serge Chaloff, or Harry Carney recordings that my father or Amadito Valdés played at home, this was the first time that we heard a baritonist playing Be-Bop lines live! At that time I was almost a child and was fascinated with the musical language of that skinny guy with the enormous shiny saxophone that was none other than Leonardo Acosta.

"You are Tito's son! How is your old man doing? I haven't seen him in years," he said enthusiastically when I went to greet him at the end of the set. This was the beginning of a solid friendship that has lasted till today, and from then on I've deeply admired Leonardo's musical and literary labor. Along with Camille Saint-Säens, Artie Shaw, Nicolás Slonimsky, and a few others, Leonardo Acosta belongs to that select group of musicians who also possess the ability to communicate through the written word. That's why I've always thought he was the most appropriate person to tell the story of what happened in the past hundred years of jazz music on our island.

I hope you'll enjoy this new book of Leonardo's (which reads like a novel, as Nat Chediak would say) as much as I enjoyed his baritone solo on that far away evening in Havana at La Gruta Club.

PAQUITO D'RIVERA
New York
November 2002

Preface

The book you are about to read is the product of thirty years of research and active participation in the world of jazz in Havana by a highly distinguished Cuban musician, musicologist, writer, and literary critic. Leonardo Acosta was born in Havana in 1933 into an artistic family. His father was a notable graphic artist and his paternal uncle a major Cuban poet. Acosta undertook formal music studies from an early age and began a career in architecture, which he gave up quickly to dedicate himself to playing the love of his life, jazz, as well as Cuban popular music. In the 1950s he played saxophone (tenor, alto, and occasionally baritone) with all the important jazz groups in Cuba including the noted Armando Romeu orchestra.

In 1955 Acosta fulfilled a dream of his youth, traveling to New York for several months, where he was able to listen firsthand to his favorite jazz musicians: Coleman Hawkins, Dizzy Gillespie, Sonny Rollins, Phil Woods, Dinah Washington, Terry Gibbs, Dave Brubeck, Philly Jo Jones, Miles

Davis, George Shearing . . . but, in particular, Dr. Billy Taylor, with whom he talked at length about jazz on several occasions.

Upon returning to Havana, Acosta devoted himself to playing jazz but, in a demonstration of his versatility, joined for a while the Beny Moré band, at that time the premier Afro-Cuban dance band on the island, in which he and another jazz player, José "Chombo" Silva, were the two tenor saxophonists. Then, in 1958, Acosta and a few friends, among them Frank Emilio Flynn, Cachaíto López, Gustavo Mas, and Walfredo de los Reyes Jr., founded the Club Cubano de Jazz. The CCJ set out to bring, for the first time and on a systematic basis, notable jazz musicians from the United States to perform in Cuba. For the next three years the CCJ sponsored jazz concerts in Havana featuring invited U.S. jazz musicians such as Zoot Sims, Stan Getz, Philly Jo Jones, and others. The CCJ also organized jam sessions with Sarah Vaughan and her trio and with the American musicians that accompanied Nat King Cole and Dorothy Dandridge on their visits to Cuba. The CCJ fostered an interchange between jazz musicians in Cuba and the United States and provided an important stimulus to the development of jazz in Cuba.

In the 1960s and 1970s Acosta worked indefatigably as a jazz musician, as a leader of several jazz ensembles, and as a promoter of jazz performances in Cuba. He was the intellectual leader of a small nucleus of Cuban jazz "veterans" who consolidated Cuba's distinct jazz tradition and nurtured and inspired the new generation, the likes of Chucho Valdés and Paquito D'Rivera. Acosta also participated in an experimental modern music ensemble with distinguished musicians such as Leo Brouwer, Pablo Milanés, and Emiliano Salvador, and wrote the soundtracks for several documentaries and movies during this period.

By the late 1970s writing occupied most of Acosta's time, and he worked as a consultant on music programming for Cuban television. His articles on music and literature appeared in newspapers, journals, and anthologies in Cuba, Colombia, México, Argentina, the United States, Italy, Spain, France, England, and other countries. U.S. jazz aficionados first became aware of Leonardo Acosta's name, and of new developments in Cuban jazz, reading Acosta's liner notes to the 1978 Grammy Award-winning LP *Irakere* by the group of the same name.

A prolific writer, Acosta has published more than a dozen books on music and literary criticism as well as his own fiction and poetry. Internationally, his best- known works until now include *Música y Descolonización* (Havana, 1982), a theoretical analysis of the relationship between European art music and "other" musics of the world, and *Del tambor al sintetizador* (Havana, 1982), a critical account of the evolution of Cuban music that has been translated into French and Italian and, in condensed form, into English. Acosta justly acquired a reputation as an outstanding critic of Latin American art and literature as evidenced by his analysis of the Latin American baroque, the prose of Alejo Carpentier, and his incisive study of the poetry of José Martí.

Since 1998 Leonardo Acosta has served on the board of advisors of the Smithsonian Institution Traveling Exhibition Service (SITES) Latin Jazz project, which resulted in the exhibit "Latin Jazz: La combinación perfecta," currently traveling throughout the United States, and the book and CD of the same name published by Chronicle Books/SITES and Smithsonian Folkways recordings respectively. To all three Acosta contributed his advice, expertise, and writing.

The present book, *Cubano Be, Cubano Bop,* has been anticipated by numerous articles and conference presentations by Acosta over the last thirty years on the people, venues, and activities that make up the history of jazz in Cuba. There's no one better to write this history, immersed as he has been in the world of jazz and Latin jazz in Havana since the early 1950s. The book appeared in Spanish in two parts, the first published in Havana in 2000, and the second in late 2002. Another Spanish-language version, which was hastily produced, appeared in Barranquilla, Colombia, in 2001. The current English version incorporates corrections and revisions as well as updated materials beyond the Spanish editions. It includes more than sixty rare photographs documenting in their own way the evolution of jazz in Cuba. Leonardo Acosta, who reads and speaks English fluently, worked diligently and closely with translator Daniel Whitesell and myself to edit and complete the English text.

This thorough, and thoroughly enjoyable, history of jazz in Cuba is at the same time a valuable contribution to the history of Latin jazz and a welcome addition to the bibliography of jazz studies as a whole.

RAÚL FERNÁNDEZ
Los Angeles
January 2003

Introduction

*W*ithin roughly the last two decades, certain unknowns with respect to Cuban popular music have been clarified and significant historical and theoretical gaps have been filled in, the result not only of the work of Cuban researchers living on and off the island but also of the contributions of researchers from Colombia, Puerto Rico, Venezuela, the United States, Mexico, and other countries. Almost all of the varieties of our music have been dealt with in books, monographs, or essays that have appeared in anthologies or in specific-interest magazines. Nevertheless, there are very few studies about jazz in Cuba and the phenomenon of Afro-Cuban or Afro-Latin jazz—aside from occasional reviews and articles almost always dedicated to musicians of the last two decades, if not to the well-known ones of Afro-Cuban jazz that arose in New York in the Forties.

Consequently, there exists a vacuum of several decades in the history of jazz in Cuba, if we keep in mind that this music was performed since the beginning of the century and indeed flourished in the Twenties. This indicates that a development and a tradition existed, which in turn explains the prominence of Cuban jazz musicians in recent times, as well as the presence of Latin jazz, which was originally called Afro-Cuban jazz. It is this vacuum that I have attempted to fill in these pages, at least in part. In no way do I presume to have written a "history of jazz in Cuba," but rather just barely an outline of such; a sort of map or sketch from which more exhaustive research may be undertaken and which, on the other hand, will also help to eliminate certain simplified and overly repeated representations. In addition, this book could not be dedicated solely to jazz, but rather also to a variety of other musical manifestations, since for the most part our jazz musicians also played Cuban popular music—and continue to do so—and because many of them came out of military bands and symphony ensembles.

As something like an excuse for possible deficiencies in the present text, I should mention the difficulties I faced, which often seemed insurmountable. In the first place I was up against an almost complete lack of research bibliography and recording data; that is, I practically started from zero, without written or phonographic sources. Cuban musicians could hardly ever make jazz recordings, although they did record Cuban music, as well as some more or less "jazzed up" pressings within a quite commercial context, and sometimes they would go to the studio to record noncommercial singles strictly for home use. Only after the international hits of Irakere in the 1970s are jazz records made with some regularity by national musicians and groups. As for the bibliographic material, it suffices to say that only a brief history of Cuban jazz exists, which consists of some twenty-five pages, written by the late critic and disc jockey Horacio Hernández Sr. and never published in our country. As for the magazines covering the world of live performances, such as *Show, Radio-Guía,* or *Radiolandia,* and specialized sections of others such as *Carteles* or *Bohemia,* there is only material pertinent to a history of the stage, such as the one that Bobby Collazo undertook in a praiseworthy effort, but nothing of jazz.

This lack of information forced me to rely on direct testimonial sources almost exclusively; in other words, it has been the musicians themselves and some knowledgeable individuals who have made this history possible, through more than sixty interviews and with the help of my own limited memory, in my double role as witness and humble participant in this same history. The chapter on the emergence of Afro-Cuban jazz in New York in the Forties represents a separate case, for there exists ample documentation on the subject, mainly because of American authors. In this case I'm in debt to John Storm Roberts, Max Salazar, Larry Birnbaum, Marshall Stearns, and others, who are quoted throughout.

In its conception and first version, this book contained three aspects: the anecdotal, the theoretical, and the documentary. Because of the length, I decided to eliminate one part of the anecdotal material (which may fit in another context) as well as a considerable part of the theoretical material, especially all of what I had already included in *Música y descolonización* (1982) and later works. In this way the text gains fluidity by limiting itself to the descriptive testimony and the strictly historical. The important thing in the first place is to get to know—even if only in a broad sense—the names of many musicians forgotten today, and to learn which bands and groups, soloists and jazz styles existed in Cuba and when. It's also important to know the places where they played, whether as part of their work or as part of that world of the jam session so important for the very existence of jazz, as Francis Newton pointed out in his *Sociology of Jazz* (1961). I share this view absolutely, which has been fundamental with respect to writing this book, the only modification being that in Cuba the jam session became our *descarga.*

Once the book was finished, I had the chance to read the Spanish-language edition of *Jazz: The Theme Song of the United States,* by James Lincoln Collier (1995), and what I found of great interest was his exposition on the bands that preceded the big bands of swing between 1910 and 1925, and which, unlike the typical Dixieland ensemble, incorporated instruments such as the saxophone and the violin. It was precisely this type of ensemble, influenced by the vaudeville bands—according to Collier—that proliferated in Cuba at about the same time, with distinct formats, and whose presence was also felt in theater possibly before invading the cabaret and the ballroom, although it's necessary to research this parallelism carefully.

Acknowledgments

$\mathcal{F}$irst of all, I must thank Horacio Hernández for having provided me with a copy of his work on jazz in Cuba, which, despite its brevity, served as a guide to continue researching the topic: the essential clues were there to follow so that, by filling in the gaps, a history in danger of being lost could be reconstructed. The same work showed me what my next step should be: to go to the maestro, Armando Romeu, one of the primary unifying threads of this history and the only active Cuban jazz musician from the Twenties through the Nineties. I thank him for support similar to that of Horacio's, for lending me his autobiographical outline and authorizing me to use the necessary passages.

Likewise, I am indebted to the veteran saxophonist Amadito Valdés and his son Amadito Jr., a distinguished percussionist, for valuable information. Other musicians whose contribution to this book proved to be essential were Rolando Baró, Luis Rodríguez, Frank Emilio Flynn, Guillermo Barreto,

Luisito Palau, Osvaldo Urrutia, and Felipe Dulzaides, as well as many others that I include in my interview list. A special mention goes to trumpet player Jorge Varona, who provided me with the most detailed information on Irakere. Also to the percussionist and photographer Manolo "Cala" Armesto, who provided me with most of the graphic material, and to Dulce María Betancourt, for her information and historical photos of the first Cuban jazz bands.

I cannot leave out Max Salazar, Vernon Boggs, and other Puerto Rican, North American, and Cuban friends living in the United States. And with respect to information about the world of live performance in Cuba, I will be forever in debt to the writer Eduardo Robreño, the choreographer Luis Trápaga, and the great Afro-Cuban singer Merceditas Valdés. To all of them—many of whom have already passed away—I dedicate this book.

1
Cuban Music and Jazz

First Encounters

$\mathcal{A}$ lot has been written about the music of
African origin in the Americas and in general about what the German
Jeinhanz Jahn calls "neo-African cultures" of the New World—which we prefer to call African American, with the term America or the Americas desig-
nating a whole that includes the South as well as the North.[1] The African
presence in the music of various American countries—particularly the United
States, Cuba, Brazil, Haiti, and more recently Jamaica and other English-
speaking Caribbean islands—has also been studied extensively and pro-
foundly.[2] The essential "Africanness" of Cuban popular music has been shown
to the point of exhaustion by *Don* Fernando Ortiz and his followers, and for
the United States and jazz specifically there exists a voluminous bibliography
on the topic. A decisive musicological contribution in our opinion is Gunther
Schuller's book *Early Jazz: Its Roots and Musical Development.*[3]

Based on this affinity and common background of Cuban music and jazz, and given the geographic proximity of Cuba and the United States and their close though sometimes conflicting relations of all kinds over the last two centuries, it is quite understandable that reciprocal musical exchanges and borrowings have created a real fusion that has come to be known as Latin jazz. Two factors have a strong bearing on the process that would lead to this fusion: (1) the interinfluences between one type of music and the other, which at times we might consider confluences; (2) the parallelism in the development of both forms of expression, linked to a certain historical parallelism evident primarily in the nineteenth century, in spite of all the obvious differences in the political, economic, and social developments of the two countries.

Among the historical events that had a strong influence on these processes are the following: the official abolition of slavery in Cuba in 1886 and the subsequent exodus of free black Cubans to New Orleans; the Spanish-American War, in which battalions of U.S. African American soldiers participated, some of whom remained on the island; the American intervention, which lasted from 1898 to 1902; and the existence of an important community of Cuban exiles in New York and other American cities during the wars of independence. In all of these more or less migratory movements, professional and amateur musicians from one region or another took part. Two conditions are of particular relevance and interest: the presence of Cuban musicians and musicians of Cuban origin in New Orleans during the formative years of jazz, and the visit to Havana by North American minstrel companies, which without a doubt exercised a certain influence on Cuban comic theater, an either unknown fact or one that has been silenced until now by historiography and brought to light by the musicologist Robin Moore.[4]

The phenomenon that we have designated as parallelism implies a similar and sometimes coincidental development between two types of music and between some of their determinant social factors, and it is a phenomenon that we could also demonstrate between Cuba and countries such as Mexico and Brazil, to mention just two other cases. In the concrete case of Cuba and the United States, we have some typical examples of this parallelism, one of which is the economic and social situation of blacks after the abolition of slavery and the end of the bloody wars that both countries suffered. In the United States, on incorporating into civil life after the war, blacks found themselves excluded from better-compensated occupations. Just as in Cuba, many lived off music, a skill that they usually combined with others such as the tailor's trade and carpentry. According to Zutty Singleton, whom Marshall Stearns cites, the New Orleans musicians worked by day as bricklayers, carpenters, cigar/cigarette makers, and plasterers; others had small businesses such as charcoal and firewood or vegetable stores, and some worked in the cotton industry or as train porters.[5]

We also find strictly musical parallelisms. For example, many musicians of both jazz and Cuban popular music have come out of brass bands like those that were so common and still exist in New Orleans and their Cuban equivalents, the military bands, particularly those of the mulatto and black battalions that were organized by the Spanish government. We cannot forget the parallelism between the first jazz groups and the typical *danzón* bands, particularly in the incorporation of instruments such as the clarinet, the cornet, and the trombone (sometimes the *figle* in Cuba), as well as a main percussion instrument (drums in jazz, the tympani or timbales in danzón). The typical Cuban band was ahead of its time in using the double bass as a rhythmic instrument of accompaniment; jazz bands didn't incorporate it until the 1920s, as a substitute for the tuba, which filled the same function.[6]

Of special importance in this whole process is the role that New Orleans played. In this active port city, which had belonged to both France and Spain, French—and to a lesser extent Spanish—customs prevailed, with a greater tolerance for music of African origin than in the rest of the United States. This made possible the emergence of a Creole music similar to that of Haiti or Martinique, with musical influences from Haiti. On top of all this were the aforementioned Cuban migrations that began in 1886. We still lack precise information about the presence of Cuban musicians among the first jazz musicians of New Orleans, but the number of Spanish surnames—comparable to the number of French ones—that are found among them is noteworthy. The best known are those of Manuel Pérez, Lorenzo Tío, Luis Tío, Willy Marrero, Paul Domínguez, Florencio Ramos, Alcides Núñez, Perlops Núñez, and Jimmy Palau.

We know for sure that the cornet player Manuel Pérez was Cuban; born in Havana in 1863, he has become a true jazz legend. Between 1890 and 1898 he played in different bands until forming his own, first the Imperial Band and then the Onward Band. Later he traveled to Chicago and other northern cities and returned to New Orleans at the beginning of the twentieth century.[7] The case of Luis and Lorenzo Tío has been studied by John Storm Roberts in his

classic book *The Latin Tinge.* They were Cuban-Mexicans, part of an important colony of Cuban refugees in Mexico, in Mexico City, the Yucatan, and
Veracruz. The Tio brothers traveled to New Orleans in 1884 with the Eighth
Regiment band of the Mexican cavalry, which included in its repertoire various Cuban *danzas* (some were *contradanzas* and *habaneras*). Both of them settled in New Orleans, where Lorenzo was the mentor of some of the best jazz
clarinet players of the period. Florencio Ramos arrived in the same military
band and likewise settled in the populous city on the Mississippi.[8]

Roberts is the first researcher who expressly cites the Cuban origin of various musicians, among others Alcides Núñez (who had a Mexican father and
a Cuban mother), Perlops Núñez, and Jimmy Palau, who played in the band
of the legendary cornet player Buddy Bolden. I assume that Palau was a white
Cuban musician, because he played in white as well as black ensembles, and
in all probability is related to many other Palau musicians of Catalan origin
who settled on the island in the nineteenth century. Among them were Felipe
Palau, organist for the Havana Cathedral, professor and composer, and his
brother Rafael Palau, bandleader and composer who was popular in comic
theater. The next generation of this family of musicians would organize the
famous Palau Brothers jazz band, in which jazz musicians such as the sax
player Rafael "Tata" Palau and the drummer Luisito Palau (of whom we shall
speak in the following chapters) got their start. Returning though to the first
stages of jazz in New Orleans, John Storm Roberts has found more than two
dozen musicians with Spanish surnames among the first jazz musicians, who
played in black, white, and mixed ensembles. To find out how many of them
were of Cuban origin would require an extensive study. In any case, the perspective of a Cuban musician such as Frank Grillo ("Machito") is interesting: "When Cuba was a colony of Spain there were many supporters of independence who escaped to New Orleans, among them many musicians; that's
why New Orleans was always so important."[9]

In the history—or "prehistory"—of musical exchange between Cuba and
the United States there is a special case that, although it doesn't fit very well
in such a history, is important to mention: the continued presence of Louis
Moreau Gottschalk in Cuba in the middle of the nineteenth century.
Originally from Louisiana, Gottschalk—perhaps precisely because he was
from Louisiana—was particularly talented at assimilating African American
music and incorporating it in his works. According to Alejo Carpentier, his

most significant contribution lies "in having been the first European-edu-
cated musician who recognized, in a general way, the richness of Cuban,
Puerto Rican and African rhythms."[10] We know that many works of
Gottschalk are based on themes and rhythms from Louisiana, Cuba, Puerto
Rico, and Brazil, and today there is a renewed interest in the works of this
composer and piano virtuoso. What was not so easy to determine was
whether the rhythms he took from Cuban music had an influence on other
American musicians, considering that his work was long forgotten. Today
the enigma is being solved, as we shall see.

The "Spanish Tinge": Tango-congo, Ragtime, and Blues

The statements of old jazz musicians from New Orleans, reproduced by jazz
researchers and historians, provide us with a clearer picture. Today, all recognize the presence of what they called the "Spanish tinge" and the "tango
rhythm" in many pieces of that time, and consider them typical jazz characteristics. The most quoted statement on the subject comes from Jelly Roll
Morton, who would affirm that jazz came "from Italy, from France, from
Spain, from Cuba and from my own invention."[11] The ragtime pianist and
composer, a key figure in the history of jazz, frequently made reference to that
"Spanish tinge," which was actually Cuban, and which Marshall Stearns and
others considered a "tango rhythm." This rhythmic pattern, which is called
tango-congo in Cuba, constitutes the basic rhythmic cell of the *contradanza,*
danza, and *habanera* accompaniments, and, according to Argentinean musicologists such as Carlos Vega, it spread to the Argentinean *milonga* and tango.
In Gunther Schuller's history of jazz, there are good examples of these rhythmic cells in ragtime and especially in the rhythm of the so-called cakewalk.[12]
    John Storm Roberts has presented numerous examples of "Latin" influ-
ences in American music and particularly in New Orleans, from as far back
as the nineteenth century. He demonstrates that these influences come over-
whelmingly from Cuba, whose music circulated in printed form in New
York in the 1850s, and then by way of Louis Moreau Gottschalk, who in his
very extensive work maintains as a constant the utilization of rhythmic patterns and other elements of Cuban music that he assimilated in his frequent
visits to the island. Roberts has provided us with other keys that have barely

been researched, and his work supports some of the conclusions at which I had arrived in this study. For example, when he refers to the Spanish American War, he points out that black regiments from the United States fought in it, and many soldiers who were musicians or who knew about music "presumably acquired some first-hand experience with Cuban music." Expanding on Roberts's precise deduction, we know that there were also U.S. African Americans who stayed to live on the island, communicating their knowledge of blues and jazz to Cubans and learning popular Cuban genres such as *son* and bolero.

A case that has been proven is that of Santiago Smood, a black American musician who arrived in 1898 and lived in Santiago, Cuba (hence the nickname "Santiago"). He sang the blues and played the banjo, and in Oriente he learned to play the *tres* (a guitar with three double-strings) and to sing in Spanish. He moved to Havana, where he formed a duet with "El Gallego" Menéndez that was called El Blanco y el Negro, which performed at the Bodegón La Sambumbia (at Monte and Cienfuegos). In 1921 he formed another duet with the great *trovador* and *sonero* Graciano Gómez, with whom he worked in the cafe and bar Dos Hermanos in the Havana port (at San Pedro and Sol). This "Cubanized" African American, Santiago Smood, died in Havana in 1929, and is a symbol for us of the mixture that would be produced when the two types of music came together. At the beginning of the century (ca. 1910) a group of musicians would get together in a house on Chávez Street (a block from Belascoaín) in Havana to participate in the first of what would come to be known as jazz and blues jam sessions in Cuba. The musicians were Hugo Siam (guitar and banjo), Pucho Jiménez (tres), José Dolores Betancourt (bass), César Arjona (drums), and the pianist Bienvenido Hernández, who was nicknamed "El Americano." Would they have known Santiago Smood? Might they have learned from him and others like him? It's possible.[13]

The "tango rhythm," for its part, had an influence on the blues when W. C. Handy used it in 1912 in "Memphis Blues" and in 1914 in "St. Louis Blues." This famous U.S. African American composer, Roberts points out, visited Cuba with a band in 1900, that is, during the U.S. occupation of the island. Handy returned to the United States with a copy of our national anthem, which he orchestrated by adapting it to the instrumentation of his band. But Handy also made interesting observations, such as mentioning musical street groups that he had listened to in Havana and that had made a profound impression on him. In his words, "These fascinated me because they were playing a strange native air, new and interesting to me. More than thirty years later I heard that rhythm again. By then it had gained respectability in New York and had acquired a name: the Rumba."

Roberts suggests that what Handy saw and heard was a *son* group. Nevertheless, there are no clear indications that the son had arrived in Havana from Oriente by such an early date; still, it is a time of great musical ferment in the old Havana barrios (neighborhoods), which were predominantly black and in which many famous *rumberos* were born. We are inclined to believe, therefore, that Handy was right and that what he heard was probably a *guaguancó*, a variety of rumba that includes singing, dancing, and percussion, and in whose texts appear repeatedly the words "rumba" and "rumbero." In his autobiography, Handy makes various allusions to the presence of Cuban rhythms in (U.S.) African American music of that time, on which Roberts comments. Handy's band would play numbers that had a "Latin flavor" for black dancers, and he saw how they responded and quickly assimilated these rhythms. Among the pieces of his repertoire were the famous *habanera* "La paloma" by Sebastián Yradier, as well as "Maorí" by William Tyers, who according to Roberts incorporates a syncopated 2/4 bass beat reminiscent of the rumba, while Handy considered it a habanera rhythm. These contradictions will occur time and again with respect to Cuban rhythms.[14]

In "Beale St. Blues" and in the other previously mentioned pieces of his, Handy introduced what he called "*tangana* rhythm," a term that comes from tango and that is without a doubt of African origin, according to Fernando Ortiz.[15] Aside from W. C. Handy and Jelly Roll Morton there were other composers who incorporated Cuban rhythms at this time, such as William Tyers, who in addition to "Maorí" composed the now classic "Panamá" and "La Trocha," subtitled "danza cubana," which had a contradanza habanera rhythm. Roberts mentions quite a few of these composers and performers, among them important names such as Eubie Blake, Jesse Pickett, Henry Lodge, and Scott Joplin. Of course, not all of the ragtimes had the "habanera rhythm"; perhaps most of them retained a heavier and more monotonous rhythm that some refer to as "European rhythm." Roberts states, "The habanera influence may have been part of what freed [American] black music from ragtime's European base."[16] Another interesting development is the mixture of Afro-Latin elements with the blues (aside from Handy), such as "The Dream" by Jesse Pickett. Roberts comments, "And the blending with blues is significant of the way in which Latin ingredients have always melted into U.S. music."

The history of American music has shown this to the point of exhaustion: There can scarcely be found a type or a style of popular music in the United States without at least a trace of this Afro-Latin element. These rhythms have become a part of ragtime, blues, jazz, Tin Pan Alley, Broadway, Hollywood, rhythm and blues, rock, soul, and disco. The ease with which these two types of music mix is explained to a large extent by the common roots of their rhythmic patterns and other elements (melody, harmony, pitch). But it is probable that another part of the explanation lies in the "suspicion" expressed by Roberts that "the Latin ingredients in early New Orleans jazz are more important than has been realized."

The Decisive Decade of the Twenties

The Twenties constitute the decisive decade for the development and expansion of jazz and other types of African American music throughout the entire world: tango, son, rumba, and samba spread in popularity. I have expressed my difference of opinion about the deeply seated notion that this decade was the "Jazz Era." I believe rather that it was the "Dance Era," as Roberts suggests, for what caught on everywhere were the new dance styles, three examples of which are the son, the tango, and the Charleston. Other events of incalculable consequence were the advent of radio and the consolidation of the record industry. And if indeed it's true that jazz became known in the world thanks primarily to these technological revolutions, the boom in the United States of Latin American musical styles originating from Cuba, Mexico, Brazil, Argentina, and Puerto Rico also begins at this time. In Cuba, this decade is abundant in musical achievements, as well as in political, social, and cultural events in general, and has been studied extensively.[17] But before we get to the Twenties, let us look briefly at what happened in Cuba from the time of W. C. Handy's 1900 visit to the decade in question.

Starting with the U.S. military occupation in 1898 and even after withdrawal in 1902, the island was practically inundated with every type of American music and dance. The United States had come to almost totally control the economy of the country, including businesses such as tourism and entertainment that were then relatively small. It's only natural that the success of U.S. businesses on the island would lead to the emergence of a community of U.S. citizens in Cuba, while at the same time the number of visitors arriving from North America (either for business or for pleasure) would increase. New hotels were built, many of them owned by American citizens, and there appeared numerous places of entertainment capable of satisfying the tastes of the average American, in which music and dance played an important role.

In the long run, music as well as cinema and many other elements of American popular culture took root in Cuba as they have in no other Latin American country. This has created between both countries that particular "love-hate" relationship that extends to the present, in which the Cuban population has practically divided itself into two parts, which don't always correspond to class divisions. Since the beginning of the century, nationalist politicians and intellectuals condemned the first "invasion" of foreign cultural products. Patriotic feelings, inflamed during the war, were now turned against the United States, which replaced Spain as "the enemy." Afro-Cuban rhythms such as danzón, which in the 1800s was condemned as being "lascivious" and "wild" by the white dominant class in Cuba, were accepted in the early 1900s as an emblem of "Cubanness" by the same people who rejected it before, only because they now faced an "invasion of foreign rhythms" that they felt compelled to oppose with something accepted by the Cuban people.

The hypocrisy of any racist dominant class such as the Cuban one, at any time in history, often produces the most paradoxical results. At the beginning of the twentieth century, composer Eduardo Sánchez de Fuentes and other ideologues of the white middle class maintained that danzón did not contain any African elements and it became the "national dance" (a claim that was absurdly validated in the Sixties, when it had not been danced in Cuba for more than thirty years). Jazz, nevertheless, was a "foreignizing" influence because it was black. In reality, the same dominant class that solicited the collaboration of blacks to fight against Spain was now denying them rights, and above all, participation in positions of power. And to counter the black and mulatto population (close to 40 percent of the population of the island), the same people that once fought against Spain now favored Spanish immigration (440,000 Spaniards entered Cuba from 1898 to 1916) to "whiten the country," a unique policy among Latin American countries after independence. With respect to the United States, many of the "nationalists" who opposed its presence and its customs were happy for the United States to reinforce the already prevalent racism, and there was no delay in sharing their interests.

What is paradoxical is that these contradictions, inconsistencies, and hypocritical attitudes have favored the acceptance of danzón first and then son, and later it was precisely danzón that would be the first type of Cuban music to assimilate American influences, by including entire passages of Broadway and Tin Pan Alley numbers, without sacrificing a bit of its Cuban flavor. From that point on, just as Cuban music permeated practically all of the North American musical styles, so did American music and more specifically jazz permeate various types of Cuban music, from danzón to ballroom rumba, and from the "feeling" type of song to mambo and salsa. This phenomenon—call it transculturation, fusion, or crossover—has been a positive one and has enriched the music of both countries.

The years from 1902 to what has been called "the critical decade" of the 1920s (some specify the period from 1923 to 1933) were for the most part years of national frustration, political corruption, military insurrections, foreign economic domination, poverty and unemployment for the majority, and a worsening of the racial situation, which had taken a backseat during the wars against Spain. This resurgence of racism was manifested in its most vulgar form in three ways: the repression of the largely black and mulatto popular movement in 1906, followed by a new American intervention until 1909; the assassination of the independence general Quintín Banderas, already seventy years old at the time, as well as the assassination or marginalization of other black and mulatto generals and officials; finally, the Little War of 1912, unleashed by President José Miguel Gómez as a reprisal for the formation of the Independent Colored Party, a war that culminated in the massacre of some 4,000 blacks and mulattos, mostly country people from Oriente Province. This shameful episode in our national history, as well as the formation of racist groups such as the White League of Cuba and the Order of Knights, conceived in the mode of the Ku Klux Klan in the United States, are pages that almost all historians continue to leave out even in the present, and show an interesting parallelism with North American social history.[18]

One of the most significant developments of the Twenties in Cuba is the formation of an intellectual and artistic movement that will take an active part in politics and will promote a kind of "new awakening" of national consciousness. Driven by a number of influences—such as our folklore, the European artistic vanguard movements, Marxist thought, and the legacy of José Martí and the Mexican Revolution—intellectuals and artists began to come together and enter the arena of public debate for the first time in twenty years of republican control. Their attitude manifests itself in the Protest of the Thirteen, which was headed by Rubén Martínez Villena in 1923 and directed against the government of Alfredo Zayas, and in the Anti-Imperialist Manifesto of 1927, as well as in the pages of the magazines *Social* and then *Revista de Avance*. Starting in 1923, student, union, and political organizations began to emerge that ten years later would do away with the dictatorship of Gerardo Machado. Also at this time the first union organization of musicians is created, Solidaridad Musical (precursor of the National Federation of Musicians formed in 1933), whose first leaders included Fernando Anckermann and Antonio Andraca.[19]

Perhaps the most significant development from a musical (and, in general, artistic) point of view is the movement known as *afronegrismo*, a real appreciation by the Cuban cultural vanguard for the black contribution to national culture, in which music plays such an important role. The principal theoretical foundation for afronegrismo can be found in the works of *Don* Fernando Ortiz, who was well educated in practically all areas of human knowledge, and whose books opened the way to the study of music, dance, religion, and other manifestations of Afro-Cuban culture. Together with the Brazilian Nina Rodrigues and the Haitian Jean Price Mars, Ortiz was the originator of Afro-American studies in Latin America and its greatest champion.[20] In addition, Ortiz founded a number of important magazines and presided over the Society of Afro-Cuban Studies and the National Association Against Racial Discrimination, which included outstanding representatives of literature, the arts, science, and politics.[21]

Havana's Grupo Minorista, which contained distinguished intellectuals from other provinces, included the best writers and artists of the period. Without policies or directives, the Group was able to foster the latest advances in the arts through magazines, manifestos, expositions, and concerts. Its foremost proponents were: in politics, Rubén Martínez Villena; in historiography, Emilio Roig de Leuchsenring; in sociology and ethnology, Fernando Ortiz. The artists of the Group decidedly supported afronegrismo in music, literature, and the plastic arts. Afronegrista poetry included eminent writers such as Ramón Guirao, José Z. Tallet, and Emilio Ballagas, and culminates in the works of Nicolás Guillén. In the realm of fiction, the most prominent writer was Alejo Carpentier, who also wrote musical criticism. In music, the major exponents were Amadeo Roldán and Alejandro García Caturla, with a vast production of symphonic, chamber, theater, and popular music.

In the works of Roldán and García Caturla, for the first time practically all of the modalities of Cuban popular music—including the ritual music of African origin such as *yoruba* and *abakuá*—were integrated in the symphonic domain. Both composers achieved an authentic fusion of the Afro-Cuban tradition and "pure" European sounds, making use of the most advanced technical and aesthetic arsenal of the time. From our jazz-based focus, the band innovations of the 1950s in this area (by George Russell, Gil Fuller, Pete Rugolo, Johnny Richards, and Chico O'Farrill) had in part already been done by Roldán and Caturla, although outside the language of jazz. But if these composers didn't explicitly use jazz in their scores, they were not ignorant of it.

As we will see further on, Amadeo Roldán was a violinist in jazz groups, and Alejandro García Caturla formed and led various jazz bands: one at the University of Havana, the jazz band Caribe (in which he played the piano, the violin, and the saxophone), and another in Caibarién. Jazz formed part of the aesthetic preferences of Grupo Minorista, one of whose members, Alejo Carpentier, became not only the leading exponent of afronegrismo in Cuban music, in Havana and Paris, but also the first Cuban jazz critic.[22]

From the Symphonic to the Popular,
and from Xavier Cugat to Ignacio Piñeiro

In this same decade our first symphonic organizations were created in Havana: the Symphonic Orchestra that Gonzalo Roig founded in 1922 and the Philharmonic Orchestra, which began in 1924 under the direction of the Spanish musician Pedro Sanjuán and was later conducted by Amadeo Roldán. Also emerging in these years were the Sociedad Pro-

Arte Musical, which until 1958 would be the primary proponent of concert music, and such prestigious conservatories as the Hubert de Blanck, Alberto Falcón, Benjamín Orbón, Eduardo Peyrellade, and González-Molina. The Havana Philharmonic rapidly achieved prominence, performing a substantial part of the production of Roldán, García Caturla, and the vanguard in world music. The Symphonic Orchestra represented a more conservative artistic direction, but it is nevertheless very important with respect to our music, for among the composers whose works were played we find Ernesto Lecuona, Rodrigo Prats, Gonzalo Roig, and Eduardo Sánchez de Fuentes, all of whom were drawn more to song composition and lyric theater, although Lecuona also excelled in piano works. Paradoxically, their music was more "popular" but less "black" than that of García Caturla and Roldán.[23]

Within the practice of songwriting, these composers successfully entered into the realm of the "Afro-song," the *pregón*, and a sophisticated rumba that frequently had only the name in common with the original rumba, and which caught on rapidly in the United States and in Paris, while their works for lyric theater are known today by certain fragments and arias that are performed as songs. In these genres, Eliseo Grenet, Moisés Simons, and Margarita Lecuona (author of "Babalú" and "Tabú") were also successful, with hits that reached international popularity. "Blackness" in the works of all of these authors is rather diluted, but it may be for this same reason, and for the genres they cultivated, that they were a major factor in the gradual introduction of our music and rhythms in the United States, where interestingly our leading "musical ambassadors" were initially two Catalan musicians: Enrique (Enric) Madriguera and Xavier Cugat.

Both were in Cuba, but the Xavier Cugat "case" is filled with obscurities that Cugat himself created, at least two of which we can clear up. It is said that his family arrived in Havana in 1905, and he affirmed that at eight years of age he played the violin in Havana cafes and was part of a trio that accompanied films in the movie theater, with Moisés Simons as pianist. J. S. Roberts adopts a wise attitude of systematic doubt—which we share— with respect to the contradictory news about his life, which almost always comes from interviews and from his own writings. But we can clearly refute his claim that he had played the violin in "the Havana Symphonic." In the first place, his name doesn't appear in any of the organization's compilations or documents. Then there are the two versions about his departure for New York, which was (according to him) on the encouragement of Enrico Caruso. One of the versions says 1921 (the year Caruso died) and the other, 1915. If either one of these two versions is correct, Cugat could not have played in the Symphonic, founded in 1922, or in the Philharmonic (1924). On the other hand, Oscar Luis López provides us with an interesting fact about Cugat's stay in Cuba, saying he studied violin in the Havana Conservatory González-Molina (at San Lázaro and Escobar), from the violinist Joaquín Molina and his wife, pianist Matilde González.[24]

The decade of the 1920s in Havana (without Cugat) represents above all the explosion and definitive triumph of *son oriental* and of its greatest singers, the Miguel Matamoros Trio. But the son undergoes transformations in the capital, where the formats of the sextet and then the septet are introduced. Sextet groups began to flourish right away: the Sexteto Habanero, the Sexteto Occidente of María Teresa Vera, the Sexteto Nacional (later, Septeto) of Ignacio Piñeiro, and others as well, which emerged across the island. Of particular importance is the Sexteto Habanero, formed in 1919. In 1923 it becomes the first to introduce the double bass, in place of the *botijuela* or the *marímbula,* as well as the first to record, in 1925 in Havana and in 1926 in New York. Also of importance is the Sexteto Enriso, formed in 1927 by Nené Enriso and the first to incorporate a wind instrument, the clarinet, played by Amadito Valdés, who would later become a distinguished jazz saxophonist. And above all we must emphasize the emergence of the Sexteto Nacional (1926) of Ignacio Piñeiro, a master of the sonero movement in the eastern part of the country and one who represents a synthesis of son up to 1939 or 1940.[25]

Ignacio Piñeiro becomes the first to achieve an association between the two popular basic genres: rumba (from Occidente) and son (from Oriente), both representative of grassroots elements of the island. Piñeiro therefore becomes, if not the father, the grandfather of salsa, for this synthesis and fusion; not, incidentally, for having coined the term in his famous tune "Echale salsita" ("Put a little salsa on it"). Born in 1888, Piñeiro worked with amalgams such as the *afro-son,* the *guaguancó-son,* the *rumba-son,* and the *tango-son.* Just as decisive for the subsequent evolution of son was the incorporation of the piano, the double bass, and finally the trumpet in the sonero arrangement. These innovations turn out to be similar to those introduced at the same time in jazz, in which the guitar and the bass replace the banjo and the tuba. And more importantly for us, with this new parallelism between jazz and a popular Cuban genre, a broader foundation was laid, which would make possible, twenty years later, the fusion of Afro-Cuban music with jazz.

We have already pointed out the similarity in band composition between jazz groups and the typical *danzoneras,* with the latter having the advantage of already using the double bass in the era of Miguel Faílde, around 1870, whereas jazz incorporated it around 1925. But with the impact of son and the new septets, there was a general decline of danzón and of *danzonera* orchestras, of the typical ones primarily, which were gradually supplanted by the so-called *charanga francesa.* By utilizing mainly flutes and violins, without clarinets or brass, the *charanga* became widely popular because of radio, as its sound quality was much better suited to the new medium, taking into account the technical limitations of the period. In time, the actual charangas came to be called "typical," creating a confusion that would last to the present.

Despite the "*son* craze" and the growing popularity of American rhythms, danzoneras survived, the typical ones as well as the charangas. The latter would prevail in the 1930s, a decade that would see the emergence of *danzonete* and then of the "new rhythm *danzón*" of Orestes and Cachao López. The danzoneras survived in the Twenties particularly within the "recreation societies," which still maintained danzón as a "national dance." There were white, black, and mixed or integrated danzonera groups and they played, without discriminating, in both white societies and in societies "of color." Among the main groups, with varying formats, were those of Antonio María Romeu, Félix González, José Belén Puig, Pablo Valenzuela, Enrique Peña, Domingo Corbacho, Ricardo Reverón, Tata Pereira, and Neno González. Some, like that of Antonio María Romeu, still maintained their immense popularity and their music would be recorded in New York, just as the sonero groups were recorded. In the Thirties there emerged two important danzoneras: Belisario López's and Antonio Arcaño's. From these ensembles, as well as from the military bands and the theater and symphonic orchestras, would come almost all of the first Cuban jazz musicians, and with them a long tradition of musicians capable of performing any type of Cuban or foreign music. And the first American jazz and "society music" bands had already arrived in Cuba.

2
The Twenties and the First Jazz Ensembles

One of the toughest problems in researching a historical development is the question of origin. In trying to determine which was the first jazz group or professional jazz band in Cuba, or whether the first ones were American or Cuban, I continue to uncover contradictions and conflicting evidence. The most logical assumption is that the first jazz ensembles were American groups that came to perform in Havana, but from the information available, nothing can be confirmed with certainty. Even the primacy of Havana, a seemingly indisputable fact, could be questioned, and so to affirm it would be to commit the sin of "capital city centrism."

The doubt increases when there are jazz bands in almost all of the country's provinces in the 1920s. The most extraordinary case seems to be that of Pedro Stacholy, a Cuban musician who went to New York to continue his studies at the beginning of the century and then returned a few years later to his hometown, Sagua la Grande (in the former province of Las

Villas), where he put together a band, presumably a jazz band. Can we consider him the indisputable pioneer of jazz in Cuba? I don't think so, because we still don't know very much about him. Judging from an old photograph, his is a typical jazz band of that era, composed of eight musicians, among them a cornet player, a saxophonist, a trombonist, and a drummer (at an American-style drum set). But an uncertainty arises: When was the photo taken? It is very likely that it was taken in the 1920s, since it was published in 1928. With all of this, let us forget for the moment the question of who came first and limit ourselves to presenting a general panorama of the situation and the time.

We know that the first U.S. groups and bands began to arrive in Cuba around 1920 and probably before. The first phonographic recording of jazz had already been made by 1917, and in Europe jazz had made a strong impression, especially among musicians. In Cuba, or more specifically in Havana, these bands responded to an increasing demand from U.S. citizens who were residents on the island, from a booming tourism, and from an upper class linked to American interests that had the eagerness of the new rich to experience foreign novelties, especially if they came from *"el Norte."* The economic situation had improved along with the price of sugar in the age of "fat cows," and after a subsequent age of "thin cows" there was a new recuperation in the middle of the decade, during the first years of the later despised Gerardo Machado regime. Moreover, with Prohibition in the United States, tourism and as a result the musicians continued to enjoy a sort of bonanza, thanks to the wave of thirsty tourists that arrived on our shores.

During the Twenties, a variety of cabarets, luxury hotels, casinos, and sumptuous clubs of the new middle class emerged. It was at places such as the Jockey Club—in the Marianao Race Track—the Gran Casino Nacional, the Plaza and Sevilla Biltmore hotels, and other similar places, often managed by American businessmen, where the first Cuban jazz bands, as well as various American ones, performed. But we should question to what extent these bands really played jazz, for by that time many white U.S. musicians had incorporated elements of black music to create so-called society music, and dance variations like the one-step, the two-step, the Charleston, and the fox trot were being invented, dances that were the true trademark of the mislabeled "Jazz Age," an age lamentably lacking in real jazz creators.

The ones who really made money and took advantage of this period were the society bands of Guy Lombardo, Ted Lewis, Rudy Vallee, Abe Lyman, Hal Kemp, Jan Garber, Ted Weems, Paul Tremaine, Vincent López, and others who have already been forgotten. The case of Paul Whiteman, of whom it is constantly repeated that "he brought jazz to the concert hall" by conducting works of George Gershwin—which, by the way, were not specifically jazz—deserves a special mention. Whiteman (whose name may be taken as symbolic, "white man") acquired so much money and fame that, in a field in which it is almost impossible to maintain a large band, he eventually had twenty-eight "secondary" or branch bands. At a time when a jazz musician was doing well if he earned two dollars a day, Whiteman enjoyed annual earnings of more than a million dollars. At the end of the decade, one of his bands worked in Havana, in the Hotel Presidente, while Vincent López worked in the Sevilla Biltmore.

Horacio Hernández, in his historical outline of Cuban jazz, refers to American violinist Jimmy Holmes as a "pioneer" in the field; he informs us that Holmes's group consisted of a violin, two saxophones, a banjo, drums, and percussion, and that he began to perform in the La Verbena cabaret (in Marianao) around 1925. It might seem strange that this jazz group would be using a percussion instrument (a Cuban one) at such an early date, but this was normal when Cuban numbers were included in the repertoire: normally a *güiro* (a percussion instrument made of a dried gourd) was used to accompany the danzones. Apparently Holmes used different combinations, as other sources indicate that in the same La Verbena cabaret (Forty-first and Twenty-sixth Avenues, to be more exact) he incorporated musicians such as Antonio Vidal, Prisciliano Almeida, trumpet player Remberto "El Chino" Lara (whom we will see years later in New York with the Antonio Machín quartet), the also "historic" trumpet player Lázaro Herrera, and the American pianist Chuck Howard. We don't know the exact date of Holmes's arrival in Cuba, but if it was 1925, he can't be considered a jazz "pioneer" because several Cuban jazz bands already existed. On the other hand, Holmes was involved in other musical scenes, more specifically occupying a seat as a violinist in the Philharmonic Orchestra.[1]

Jimmy Holmes was not the only North American violinist who led a jazz ensemble in 1920s Havana. The great writer Alejo Carpentier assures us that another violinist, Max Dolin, became the first jazz musician to lead a band in Cuba. Carpentier doesn't give an exact date as Hernández did, but fortunately we have more information on Dolin. The researcher Cristóbal Díaz Ayala places Dolin in Havana leading a charanga-type band that performed Cuban music; this is corroborated by the fact that in New York Dolin recorded various pressings of Cuban numbers for RCA Victor in the mid-Twenties.[2] John Storm Roberts confirms that among the pieces recorded we find "La golondrina" (which is Mexican) and "Si llego a besarte," by Luis Casas Romero, explicitly identified as "Cuban bolero." He also recorded, with the so-called Novelty Orchestra, Latin American classics such as "Cielito lindo," "Quiéreme mucho," "Morena mía," and the danzón "Teléfono a larga distancia," written by Aniceto Díaz. So Dolin appears as a sort of "musician bridge," transmitting music from the two countries in both directions, and we will find further examples of this type of musician.

At any rate, during the same period there were other American bands performing in Havana, such as Ted Naddy's and Earl Carpenter's. The great Cuban jazz musician Armando Romeu informs us that in 1924, working as a flutist at the Jockey Club in the charanga band of his father, Armando Romeu Marrero, they alternated with Ted Naddy's orchestra. During the breaks, Armando listened to the American band and became familiar with live jazz, for at the time not only were there recordings available but U.S. radio broadcasts of jazz could also be heard. Coincidentally, Armando Romeu Marrero (brother of Antonio María Romeu) was also a pioneer in radio and musical recordings in Cuba. So Armando Romeu Jr. could hear the best jazz bands of the age, in direct broadcasts from Chicago's Grand Terrace. Up to that time Armando had played the flute in the Regla Municipal Band and with his father's charanga band; from Ted Naddy's jazz band he discovered the possibilities of the saxophone and he bought his first tenor sax from a musician in this orchestra. Later Armando would play the tenor sax in Naddy's band. He recalls: "I had been exposed to American jazz and soon I got used to the style. And I began to play dances with the first jazz orchestras to appear in Cuba. Many American bandleaders would come during the summer to hire Cuban jazz musicians."[3]

Here two interesting factors come to mind: first, something that is somewhat common among Cuban musicians is their ability to assimilate jazz, thanks to their previous command of the different types of popular Cuban music, which are linked to jazz by African roots and in which improvisation is common; second, Armando's observation that many bandleaders from the United States came to hire Cuban jazz musicians. As he himself explains, "The Cuban musicians were very good readers." This comment takes me to Marshall Stearns, who pointed out that the white bands of the Twenties and Thirties liked to have one or two jazz soloists who were good improvisers and a black arranger whom neither the public nor the promoters needed to see. As a representative case he mentions the thirty-six arrangements by Fletcher Henderson that Benny Goodman had in 1934. The counterpart of this situation was—according to Stearns—that many talented jazz musicians either didn't know how to or didn't want to read music, and they made fun of those who could only read and not improvise. He cites Wingy Manone, who said he knew how to read the notes but not how to separate them, and he would joke that the key signature with five flats looked like a bunch of grapes.[4]

Among the Cuban musicians this attitude didn't exist, that is, if we exclude son and rumba players with their typical instrumentation. Because jazz arrived in the form of already written arrangements, our first jazz musicians were men with a more or less academic education and with experience in genres that required an ability to read music, such as danzón or military band music. Armando Romeu, the most important Cuban jazz bandleader of all time, passed through both schools. Once he had taken up the saxophone, Armando played for a time in a duo with the pianist Nacho Alemany in the Céspedes cinema in Regla, and then was a member of another American jazz band, Earl Carpenter's, at a cabaret that for three decades was the most exclusive in Havana: the Casino Nacional. Of the time he put in as a saxophonist in Earl Carpenter's band, Armando Romeu would later say that it was "a good experience" for his career as a jazz musician.

However, maestro Romeu forgot something that we consider important: If on the one hand it's true that Cuban musicians were and are good readers, there is another reason why American bandleaders began to hire local musicians. This factor was an economic one: Cuban musicians were good and turned out to be less expensive, and the costs of round-trip tickets and lodging were spared. In the beginning they were discriminated against by American promoters who, according to the saxophonist Manolo Castro, claimed that Cuban musicians were "unreliable and drunkards." Later, when they realized the advantages of hiring them, "American managers would cheat Cuban musicians," Castro adds.

A North American Musician
in the Bohemia of Havana

Another American musician that lived in 1920s Havana was pianist Chuck Howard, who worked at the La Verbena cabaret with Jimmy Holmes, at the Tokio nightclub (Blanco and San Lázaro), the most important jazz venue of the period, and later at the Montmartre cabaret (P Street between Twenty-third and Humboldt). Like Jimmy Holmes and Max Dolin, Chuck Howard has been only an obscure legend that is now being brought to light. We don't know if it was coincidental, but Howard was associated with the Grupo Minorista, which, as we have seen, had an artistic, political, and social presence, were promoters and defenders of the afronegrismo movement, and showed an interest in jazz. But we lacked a dimension, the bohemian one, similar to that of Paris and even more so to that of Madrid at the beginning of the century, which Ramón Gómez de la Serna has immortalized in his *Retratos contemporáneos, Pombo,* and other books.

The magazine *Social* and other publications of the time indicate that the Group would get together on Saturdays to have lunch in the Lafayette Hotel (in Old Havana) and in other places, and that they organized concerts and expositions as well as banquets for a wide range of contemporary artists and celebrities, such as the boxer Kid Chocolate, the Mexican philosopher Antonio Caso, or the North American aviator Eddie Rickenbacker. It was this bohemian aspect of at least a part of the Group with which the pianist Chuck Howard came in contact. In addition to frequenting the Lafayette Hotel, the Automobile Club, the law office of Emilio Roig de Leuchsenring, and various Havana cafes, some *minoristas* would get together in a spacious apartment on the corner of San Lázaro and Manrique (two blocks from the Tokio Cabaret), with a view of the Havana Malecón from the back side of the apartment. This house was rented by two founders of the group: the sketcher, illustrator, and photographer José Manuel Acosta and the journalist and historian José Antonio Fernández de Castro. Chuck Howard rented them a room with a piano, and the other room was rented by the Japanese painter Tetsuo Hama, who covered the walls of the house with murals; it became known as the "Little

Republic." Among the regular visitors were Alejo Carpentier and the poet José Zacarías Tallet, both journalists and night owls. All those who visited the apartment were committed advocates of afronegrismo and jazz; for example, Tallet wrote the famous poem "La rumba," the text of which Alejandro García Caturla would use for a concert piece; Carpentier was writing his novel *¡Ecue-Yamba-O!*; and Acosta had illustrated works by Fernando Ortiz and later in New York he would paint portraits of great black cultural figures such as Louis Armstrong, Bill Robinson, and Katherine Dunham.

As Alejo Carpentier tells us, it was there that García Caturla first presented the piano version of one of his masterpieces, *Three Cuban Dances,* and that Amadeo Roldán first presented the versions of his ballets *La rebambaramba* and *El milagro de Anaquillé,* which both included librettos from Carpentier. With respect to the "Little Republic," Alejo has also made reference to the presence of personalities that visited the country such as the dancers Ted Shawn and Ruth Saint Denis and the Russian pianist Evgueni Helmer, as well as the performances by different pianists of works by vanguard composers such as Stravinsky, Satie, Ravel, Milhaud, and Prokofiev. Did Chuck Howard attend these sessions? Of course he did, and he surely became acquainted with García Caturla and Roldán. It also makes sense that he would have organized some jam sessions with other musicians that worked at the Tokio Cabaret, only two blocks away and the center of jazz at that time. On occasion, Chuck, who also worked at the new Montmartre cabaret, would organize parties in which American models from the Montmartre would participate. That the neighbors never complained about the ragtime and blues music that came from the house every night seems to indicate that the Havana locals had already developed an appreciation for this type of music.[5]

Armando Romeu provided me with additional information about Chuck Howard that is very interesting. The pianist traveled frequently to the United States, probably to Florida, to get printed music, whether it was the latest Tin Pan Alley hits or arrangements for jazz bands, and Armando as well as other jazz musicians and Cuban bandleaders would buy music from him or have him buy music for them so that they could keep their repertoires up to date. In this way Howard can be seen as another one of the "musician-bridges" between Cuban and American jazz musicians. However, even with the limited information that we have about Howard and about James Holmes, Max Dolin, Ted Naddy, or Earl Carpenter, it is necessary to at least reflect on the real situation of jazz in Cuba. Up to now we have discovered various indisputable facts: (1) the majority of musicians and bands that came from the United States were white, hired by predominately American clubs and hotels; (2) the repertoires were based on printed music and for the most part included more society music than authentic jazz; and (3) many groups were headed by violinists, a characteristic of society music, while in the genuine "hot jazz" of the Twenties and Thirties the inclusion of violinists—such as Eddie South, Joe Venuti, or Stuff Smith, and Ray Nance in his occasional solos with Duke Ellington's band—was the exception.

All of these facts lead us to the conclusion that Cuban jazz musicians depended on records, radio, and occasional trips to the United States to become very fluent in the language of jazz and to hear the music of their main idols, a topic to which we will return later on. Meanwhile, by looking at other Cuban jazz groups of the era we see that the "cafe group" tradition of society music was continued, and thus the violin still played an important role. And so it was with the quartet of Teddy Henríquez, who—following the norm—was violinist and conductor; the rest of the group was made up of a saxophonist, a pianist, and a drummer. In 1926 they played at the Cabaret Royal, a central location on the corner of Prado and Neptuno, a now famous corner because it was there in 1950 that the sounds of the *chachachá* rhythm could be heard for the first time in an upper-level ballroom. We don't know the name of the saxophonist, but two leading figures in the history of Cuban jazz distinguished themselves in that quartet: the vocalist and drummer Alberto Jiménez Rebollar and pianist Célido Curbelo, considered by Horacio Hernández to be "the best jazz pianist that Cuba had in many years," while Armando Romeu is of the opinion that "he was thirty years ahead of his time." With respect to Teddy Henríquez, he later left for Paris as a contrabassist in the Justo Aspiazu band, known first as the Havana Casino and then by the surname of its leader, *Don* Aspiazu. This band enjoyed great success in Paris, where a community of Cuban musicians began to form, of which Teddy Henríquez was a part, while *Don* Aspiazu would become a legend in New York.

The Best of the Decade

Between 1927 and 1928 the septet led by Hugo Siam, who played the typical American banjo at the time, worked in the El Pirata Cabaret. The cabaret was located in the nearby coastal village of Cojímar, the same fishing village that Ernest Hemingway would make famous some three decades later with his novel *The Old Man and the Sea*. In Hugo Siam's group the great flutist Alberto Socarrás distinguished himself and in 1928 traveled to the United States, where he recorded the first flute solo in the history of jazz and then earned a top spot in Latin jazz and salsa. In Siam's septet we also find violinist Jesús Pia, who is considered by Horacio Hernández as "one of our greatest jazz artists," an opinion shared by the great saxophonist Amadito Valdés.[6] Another prominent musician in this group was René Oliva, the first Cuban jazz trumpeter. Somewhat short and commonly known by his nickname "El Jiníguano" ("peasant" or "hillbilly," a nickname usually given to someone from the countryside), Oliva was the first among the island's trumpet players to create real jazz improvisations. As a drummer and vocalist we come back to Alberto Jiménez Rebollar, who will prove to be the best exponent on his instrument in Cuba for two decades. The same could not be said of Cuban saxophonists, for at that time a handful of sax players such as Amadito Valdés, Germán Lebatard (then in the Almendares Hotel band), Armando Romeu (in the Casino Nacional), and Luis López Viana (in the Hotel Sevilla band) began to shine.

Perhaps the best jazz group in Cuba in the 1920s was the one that played at the Tokio Cabaret through 1929 and 1930, a group that included some of the aforementioned musicians. I'm referring to the octet of José Antonio Curbelo, an excellent violinist from a distinguished family of musicians. In the Twenties the Curbelo jazz band would play at the Tokio in the winter and in the summer at the Summer Casino, which was located across from the Casino Nacional, in Marianao. The pianist of the group was his brother Célido Curbelo, whom we saw with the Teddy Henríquez quartet; on trumpet was René Oliva ("El Jiníguano"); on alto sax Amadito Valdés, who later became the most sought-after lead in the history of Cuban jazz; the drummer was the incomparable Alberto Jiménez Rebollar. Members of this octet also included the tenor sax player Heriberto Curbelo and a banjo player whose last name was Casuso; we don't know the name of the bass player. This ensemble also worked at the Montmartre, where two very important figures of jazz and Cuban music joined them: Armando Romeu on tenor sax and the then clarinet and alto sax player Mario Bauzá, to whom we will return in Chapter 5.

During the five years from 1925 to 1930, Cuban jazz bands multiplied not only in Havana but also in many different cities and provinces. In the capital, native ensembles slowly replaced the American ones, partly because of the aforementioned reasons, and in the midst of an economic crisis that had begun even before the 1929 bank failures. But what is important is that Cuban bands gradually come to prominence and in the following decades the number of American bands in Havana dropped off. We should clarify that these jazz bands looked very little like the big bands of the 1930s, which had from twelve to as many as sixteen musicians. The ensembles we are dealing with—which were similar to Dixieland or Chicago bands—had an average of seven musicians, and among the best known were Curbelo's, Arturo Guerra's (said to have been started in 1920 at the Trianón Theater), and the Palau Brothers Band, led by Gerardo Palau, which was started in 1922 and included in its long history the second- and third-generation Cuban musicians of this family. Originally organized under the name Los Califate, in the beginning this jazz band was an ensemble that specialized in jazz and tango, in addition to Cuban music, and was made up of the following musicians: Genaro Palau (piano and accordion), Edmundo "Mundito" Palau (various saxes and clarinet), Rafael (tenor sax and contrabass), Felipe (violin), Luciano (organ and bass sax), and Lorenzo Palau Carballosa (drummer). These five brothers and one cousin were joined by Félix Guerrero on guitar, and the vocalist was Germán Pinelli, who later became a popular actor and television entertainer. This versatile band worked at the Plaza, Sevilla, and Almendares hotels and at the Casino Nacional, Summer Casino, and Sans Souci cabarets. Also, the first Cuban jazz bands to work on radio were those of the Palau Brothers and Alfredo Brito. The Palaus would later appear in musical films such as *Mi tía de América* (1936) and *Estampas habaneras* (1939). In Hollywood they took part in the film *Cuban Love Song*, which was titled *El manisero* (The Peanut Vendor) in Spanish. From the beginning of the 1930s the Palaus adopted the format of the American big bands of swing. Countless jazz soloists worked with them, and even in their early years they included such important musicians as trombonist Angel Mercado, trumpet player Alfredo Hernández ("Bocachula"), drummer Atilano Arango, and alto sax player Manolo Castro, who would soon form his own "family" band and use the big band format before the Palaus did.

Another very popular jazz band of the time was the violinist Froylán Maya's Los Diplomáticos de Maya, which included talented musicians such as Mario Bauzá, Armando Romeu, and Leonardo Timor Sr., a pianist who also played tuba and bass and was later leader of the Havana Casino and other bands. Earlier, the very same Froylán Maya, Armando Romeu, and Manolo Castro had been together in the jazz band of the pianist Rogelio "Rojito" Barba, who enlivened dances at Las Playitas, El Progreso (in El Vedado), and the Círculo Militar (in Marianao), and also at the Hollywood cabaret (Twenty-third and P streets, Vedado). Rogelio Barba, as we will see, was a member of the group of Cuban musicians that emigrated to Paris in the early 1930s.

Froylán Maya, of Jewish origin like several other Cuban jazz musicians, was an intelligent businessman who had a store next to the radio station CMQ (then at Monte and Prado) and an imaginative man, who thought of putting electric lights on the instruments to light up the band more. Froylán Maya's Diplomáticos has been forgotten today, but it would produce such prominent jazz bandleaders and arrangers in our musical history as Leonardo Timor Sr., Armando Romeu, and Mario Bauzá. The same would happen with Manolo Castro, saxophonist and founder of the Castro Brothers together with Juan (piano), Antonio (trombone), and later Andrés Castro (trumpet). This jazz band would be important for at least two reasons: (1) In 1929 and 1930 it was the first to have sections of three brass instruments and three saxophones; in other words, it became the country's first real big band in the style of the "Age of Swing" bands that became so popular in the United States in the 1930s, and (2) A few years later musicians from this band would put together two jazz bands that are considered two of the most popular that the country has had: the Casino de la Playa band and later the Riverside Orchestra.

Jazz Bands Spread

Fortunately, we have some information on jazz bands that were formed at this time in different parts of the country, such as the one that Maestro Gatell conducted in Cienfuegos and that usually performed at the Prado Theater. This band consisted of a violin, two saxes, a cornet, piano, banjo, double bass, and drums (eight musicians). We have less information on the Camagüey Jazz Band: it usually performed in the Sociedad Popular Santa Cecilia (patron saint of Cuban musicians), at the Tennis Club, and in the Sociedad El Progreso, and its leader was Alberto Noriega de Varona, a student of Luis Casas Romero who played clarinet, flute, and saxophone. In Ciego de Avila a band was put together that performed regularly at the Teatro Principal and interpreted jazz and Cuban music; it included its leader and pianist, maestro Borrego, Virgilio Domínguez (violin), Oscar Domínguez (alto sax), Bernardo Sariol (bass), J. A. Rodríguez (timbales), Fidel Díaz *(güiro)*, and Juan Rayo *(claves)*. In Cárdenas another jazz band was organized that featured José del Valle (leader and piano), Raúl del Valle (cornet), Ismael Ortega and Miguel Torriente (saxophones), José María Casals (violin), Manuel Fonte (bass), and Alberto Damas (drums).[7]

In the heart of the country, where cabarets and tourist hotels were hard to find, jazz bands would work mainly for theaters and leisure societies, which could be white or "colored" and might also represent different social levels and classes. Often many of these musicians also belonged to the local town brass band. Another ensemble with these characteristics was the Sagua Jazz Band, whose leader and pianist Pedro Stacholy we referred to earlier. We know very little about him: He studied in Cuba with maestro Antonio Fabre and then studied in New York for three years, a segment of his life for which we have no information, such as the school he attended, who his teachers were, which musicians he associated with, or even the exact dates of his stay in New York. We have reason to believe that his band, founded in 1914, played jazz, but we don't know its setup or the names of the members. We do know, on the other hand, that around 1926 his jazz band included Pedro Stacholy (leader and piano), Hipólito Herrera (trumpet), Norberto Fabelo (cornet), Ernesto Ribalta (flute and sax), Humberto Domínguez (violin), Luciano Galindo (trombone), Antonio Temprano (tuba), Tomás Medina (drums), and Marino Rojo (güiro)—a total of nine musicians, and once again the presence of the violin as well as the tuba.

A very unusual case was that of Thomas Aquinto, an Italian who emigrated to the United States as a French horn virtuoso and whose history is somewhat different from that of other foreign musicians—predominantly North American and Spanish—that lived in Cuba. In the United States Aquinto learned to play the typical banjo and apparently learned a bit of the new language of jazz. In Havana he put together an ensemble of seven musicians that in 1928 performed at the most exclusive community of the Havana bourgeoisie, the Country Club. Aquinto's jazz band performed as well in the Plaza and Royal Palm hotels, and it consisted of a violin, two saxophones, a piano, a banjo, a contrabass, and drums. Aquinto later enlarged his group and changed the format, because we know that trumpet player Pedro Mercado and trombone player Antonio Castro worked with him.

An interesting jazz band was the one that Moisés Simons, composer of the very popular "El manisero," conducted in the Roof Garden of Havana's Plaza Hotel starting in 1924. The band consisted of piano, violin, two saxes, banjo, bass, drums, and timbales. The pianist was Moisés Simons; the violinist was Virgilio Diago, first violin in the Symphonic Orchestra and the father of the great Cuban painter Roberto Diago. The great Alberto Socarrás played alto sax and flute, and Simons's band also included bassist Pablo O'Farrill and tenor saxophonist José Ramón Betancourt. Simons was still playing the Plaza Hotel in 1928 when he hired trumpet player Julio Cueva, who was later a successful composer and bandleader and enjoyed, as did Simons, considerable international success (both would soon be in Paris).[8] In passing we should mention that this was one of the highest-paying gigs for a musician at that time: eight pesos (dollars) per night.

In 1925 Eliseo Grenet, another famous songwriter with his "Mama Inés" and other songs, organized a jazz band that performed at the Montmartre cabaret and at the Jockey Club. It featured Manolo Castro on alto sax, José Ramón Betancourt on tenor sax, Pedro Mercado on trumpet, and for a brief period on piano, Jorge Bolet, later a well-known concert pianist residing in the United States; Enrique Santiesteban, who would later become one of the most popular Cuban radio, film, and television actors of the 1940s, participated as a vocalist and drummer. At that time Grenet had already made a number of recordings of Cuban music for the Brunswick label, with a group consisting of two violins, flute, clarinet, tenor sax, piano, and a güiro. The flutist was José María Arriete, the saxophonist was José R. Betancourt, and the pianist was Emilio Grenet, brother of Eliseo. Many of the authors of Cuban songs that would become famous worldwide in the Thirties had played in or led jazz bands, such as those of Grenet and Moisés Simons. To these names we must add that of Rodrigo Prats, a well-known zarzuela composer whom we find playing the violin in the Cuban jazz band started by his father Jaime Prats in 1922 as well as in the bands of Eliseo Grenet and

Rogelio "Rojito" Barba. Alberto Socarrás (sax and flute) and the trombonist Pucho Jiménez also played with Jaime Prats.

In 1929 a jazz band led by Mario Suazo appeared at the Chateau Madrid (on the Arroyo Arenas highway); it included Joaquín del Río (violin), Pepín García (trumpet), Angel Mercado (trombone), Luis González (tenor sax), Mario Guas (drums), violinist José A. Curbelo, and pianist Pedro Menéndez. Another unusually large ensemble for those days was the Orquesta Cuba (ten musicians), composed of a cornet, trumpet, and trombone (three brass instruments), two saxes, a banjo, a tuba (a brass rhythm instrument), and drums. In the group we find already familiar names such as René Oliva (cornet), Pedro Mercado (trumpet), Angel Mercado (trombone), Primitivo Quesada and José Ramón Betancourt (alto and tenor sax), Tellería (banjo and guitar), Luis Fernández (tuba), and Merito Reyes (drums).

Already in 1930, Armando Romeu Marrero had changed his charanga danzonera format and formed a jazz band of eight musicians: a violin, trumpet, two saxes, piano, banjo, tuba, and drums. Romeu Sr. was the pianist, and the band featured Alfredo Hernández ("Bocachula") on trumpet, Reinaldo Godínez on alto sax, José R. Betancourt on tenor sax, and drummer Ernesto Romeu, who would later play trombone in Armando Romeu Jr.'s great band. Another band of the era that is of special interest was the one organized by the bassist Fernando Anckermann to perform in the Sevilla hotel, where there was an American ensemble that became mixed after four Cubans—Manolo Castro among them—joined it. Anckermann, as a union leader, helped to bring about this type of band in which Cubans and North Americans played together for the first time.

There emerged other jazz bands at the time, such as Primitivo Quesada's and Jesús Solomo's, which performed in 1929 and 1930 at the cabaret El Infierno (different sources put its location at Industria and San José or at Amistad and Barcelona). Solomo was the trumpet player, and he had as his violinist the great composer and symphonic conductor Amadeo Roldán; his saxophone players were Prisciliano Almeida (alto) and José R. Betancourt (tenor); and rounding out the band were pianist Dr. Amador Banderas, symphonic bassist Pablo O'Farrill, and drummer Enrique Santiesteban. Rarely did such diverse personalities get together as they did at this exclusive cabaret. One of their members, José Ramón Betancourt, later formed the Betancourt Orchestra, which performed at the Bristol Hotel and included Enrique

Ramírez (trombone), Pedro Mercado (trumpet), Lázaro Hernández and the conductor (saxes), Juan Betancourt (drums), and three instrumentalists whom I have not been able to identify and who played violin, piano, and bass.

In contrast to Amadeo Roldan's part-time work in jazz bands, Alejandro García Caturla was a real jazz enthusiast. In the jazz band Caribe, which he organized at the University of Havana, he proved to be a versatile instrumentalist, playing the piano, the saxophone, and the violin. The other members, who never worked professionally in music, were Fidel Requejo (piano), Gaspar Betancourt (violin), José Luis Justiniani (trombone), and Gonzalo Alfonso (drums). They graduated from college and became lawyers or judges, as did García Caturla himself. Nevertheless, according to various accounts Caturla also led professional jazz ensembles, one of which included saxophonists Alfredo Brito and Manolo Castro. The latter would comment half a century later, when asked about García Caturla: "He was crazy; what chords he would play!"

In the early Thirties, as we will see, there emerge in Cuba dozens of bigger and bigger bands, with individual styles and some shared characteristics, such as their versatility in playing any kind of music, whether it be Cuban or North American, Spanish and Caribbean or Latin American. But in contrast to what occurred traditionally in Cuban popular music and in the United States with jazz, in Cuba more than half of the original jazz professionals were white. This is explained by the fact that the places where American music—and jazz, by extension—was played were exclusive locations of the white middle class of European descent and of Americans, residents on the island and tourists. In spite of all this, we see black and mulatto musicians from the very beginning and even more in the Thirties, in the capital and in provinces, as well as black orchestras and others in which racial integration was a very normal thing, something still quite uncommon in the United States at the time.

Nightlife Map: Cabarets, Hotels, and Theaters

In the 1920s Havana, like seldom before or after, was the scene of an artistic and cultural life that drew artists and performers from all over the country and from abroad; those from overseas considered Havana to be the first obligatory stopover in "doing America," as was expressed particularly by Spaniards, and as Cuban writer Eduardo Robreño reminds us.[9] Except for a few changes, this Havana remained almost the same during the following two decades, and so here we will give priority to describing what the capital was like in that seminal decade, while in other chapters we will cover the most important changes, primarily in the Fifties. If we are to locate the center of the city, we have to look in the direction of Acera del Louvre, which had been a prominent focal point of Havana's social life since the nineteenth century, even when the political and economic centers or the residential areas changed. The cafe El Louvre had been famous since the nineteenth century, and so its name came to designate that whole side of the street (Prado between Neptuno and San Rafael), across from Havana Central Park. Next to this cafe was the Hotel Inglaterra, and in the same area the main theaters of the capital could be found.[10]

Forming part of the sizable Centro Gallego building, on the next block, was the Teatro Nacional (on Prado between San Rafael and San José), a short distance from the Capitolio Nacional. This grand theater as well as the Auditorium in El Vedado were the homes of the Symphonic and Philharmonic Orchestras. In turn, during these years the Payret (also on Prado), which was founded in 1877, held symphonic concerts, operas, zarzuelas, and variety shows. In 1926 Ernesto Lecuona presented at the Payret the first performance in Cuba of George Gershwin's *Rhapsody in Blue*, two years after the world premiere in New York's Aeolian Hall, led by Paul Whiteman. Armando Romeu took part as a saxophonist in the Payret performance.

Also at the Teatro Nacional, all kinds of shows were presented, and to one side of the Nacional was the Campoamor theater (at San José and Industria), smaller than the others but with excellent acoustics, today in ruins. Likewise, near Paseo del Prado was the historic Principal de la Comedia (at Animas and Zulueta), built in 1921 and gone in the Forties. At Zulueta and Dragones one could find the Teatro Martí (where the Irijoa theater was in the nineteenth century), one block from the Capitolio, across from which were the attractive open-air cafes, "Los Aires Libres," where the famous female orchestras such as Anacaona and Ensueño performed starting in the Thirties. As far back as the nineteenth century travelers would compare this stretch of Havana, from the open-air cafes to the Acera del Louvre, with Paris. At the Teatro Martí there were zarzuelas, reviews, variety and vaudeville shows, until it was closed in the 1970s; although today it is in ruins, like the Campoamor, it is now being restored.

The also historic Teatro Alhambra (at Consulado and Virtudes) represented, from 1900 to 1935—the year the building collapsed—the heart of Cuban popular or vernacular theater, featuring genres such as the *sainete costumbrista* (a one-act farce on local customs and manners), the *sainete lírico* (a lyric one-act farce), the *sainete de solar* (a one-act tenement farce), and musical reviews. It was the truest inheritor of the already classic *teatro bufo cubano* (Cuban comic opera) from the previous century. Two top-notch musicians, Manuel Mauri and Jorge Anckermann, were successively musical directors of this theater.[11] On the site where the Alhambra used to be, the movie theater Alkázar was built, which became Havana's Teatro Musical in the 1960s, which to a certain extent renewed the tradition; then it was closed again, with the building in poor condition. During the 1930s and 1940s a nearby theater gained musical importance, the Encanto (on Neptuno between Industria and Consulado), where the Bruguera Brothers orchestra and the Lebatard Brothers jazz band worked for years. A number of musicians as well as the pianist and conductor Armando Oréfiche would come out of these bands to make up the famous Lecuona Cuban Boys. In the 1940s, the most successful jazz band from Mexico, Luis Arcaráz's, performed at the Encanto Theater. The theater was demolished in the 1950s to make way for a shopping center. Around the same time, musicals were presented at the Teatro Fausto (Prado and Colón), which was converted to a movie theater in the 1950s.

With respect to hotels, many were to be found in the area surrounding Acera del Louvre: the aforementioned Inglaterra (right on Acera), the Sevilla Biltmore (at Prado and Trocadero), the Plaza (Monserrate and Neptuno), the Royal Palm (Industria and San Rafael), the Bristol (on Amistad between San Rafael and San José), the Lincoln (Galiano and Virtudes), and the Saratoga (on Prado across from Fraternity Park, one block from the Teatro Martí). Many cabarets were also concentrated in this same area as the hotels and theaters, such as the Eden Concert (Monserrate and Virtudes), a short distance from the Plaza Hotel, and later the Zombie Club; the French Casino (Prado and San Rafael), next to the Teatro Nacional; the Tokio (San Lázaro and Blanco); the Royal (Prado and Neptuno); and the already mentioned El Infierno. Well within Old Havana were the Miami (Santa Clara and San Pedro), the Jiggs (across from the Muelle de Luz), and the Kursaal (Oficios and Teniente Rey). From about 1928, the most exclusive cabarets gradually moved further and further from the center of the city. The age of the automobile was in full swing, and the Montmartre (previously Molino Rojo) appeared in El Vedado as did two luxury hotels, the Nacional ("O" and Twenty-first streets) and the Presidente (Calzada and "G" streets). Even farther away, in the municipality of Marianao, were the Jockey Club, the Casino Nacional, and the Summer Casino, as well as the Sans Souci in the Country Club Park development. With a different character, that of the people and the popular classes, the Marianao Beach zone became another focal point for Havana nightlife, with the cabarets La Playa, Las Fritas, the Paraíso, and later the Pennsylvania, the Rumba Palace, the Choricera, the Panchín, and the Niche.

Dance and the Recreation Societies

Aside from the cabarets, theaters, and hotels, we mustn't forget the primary function of the musicians in Cuba: dances. Almost all of our popular music is for the purpose of dancing, unlike jazz after the Swing Era. On the island, dance is a deeply rooted form of recreation, a topic on which the colonial-period chronicles provide us with information: there was dancing in the slaves' living quarters, in the country *guateques,* in high-class ballrooms, and in the *bailes de cuna* of free blacks and mulattos. Later there was dancing above all in the "leisure societies," which outlived the colonial period and became even more firmly entrenched during the period of the republic. The study of these societies is highly instructive for understanding the island's somewhat complex social and racial stratification, to say nothing of the "balkanization" that could be seen in the regional Spanish societies during the republic.

The dances of this era were held primarily within the so-called recreation societies, in public ballrooms and in the open, in the *academias* (sometimes linked with prostitution), and, of course, in the cabarets. Not only was there dancing in reduced spaces—in private houses and tenements *(solares)*—but also on the immense grounds of the Tropical and Polar breweries. In the center of the city were the dance halls Sport Antillano (Zanja and Belascoaín), La Galatea (across from Albear Park), the Encanto (Zanja and Gervasio), and La Fantástica (for blacks, at Galiano and Barcelona), as well as the Marte and Belona academies (Monte and Amistad), Havana Sport (Galiano and San José), Rialto (Neptuno between Consulado and Prado), and many others.[12]

There were also the salons of regional societies and labor union halls, particularly Spanish ones such as the Centro Gallego and the Centro Asturiano (on both sides of Central Park), the Centro de Dependientes (on Prado), the Asociación Canaria, the Centro Vasco, and many others. The recreation societies, which represented almost all classes as well as social and racial strata, in part followed the caste model created by the colonial system and strengthened by the republic with its policy of large-scale Spanish immigration to "whiten" the country. Furthermore, a middle class of blacks and mulattos emerged, and "colored" citizens were divided according to their income and by the shade of their skin, and there also were attempts to divide them according to their region of origin, reviving the old nation councils (*cabildos de nación:* Congo, Lucumí, Carabalí) from the colonial period. The Spanish grouped in regional societies, while the Chinese, the Arabs, and the Jews formed their own. The North Americans, naturally, created their own societies such as the American Club (at Prado and Virtudes) or the Community House (on Miramar), as they mingled with the Cuban well-to-do in the Havana Biltmore Yacht & Country Club, with a private beach, pool, and bowling facilities, golf courses, tennis courts, equestrian centers, and, of course, parties as well as teas that included dancing.

The "colored" societies generally included blacks and mulattos indiscriminately and were distinguished above all according to income and social position; so, the Atenas Club had a more aristocratic character than the Unión Fraternal or the Jóvenes del Vals. Other popular societies that were known for their dance parties were the Sport Antillano, the Sociedad El Pilar, and the Club Danzario. Comparing the black and white middle-class societies we find a paradoxical yet explainable phenomenon. In the Atenas Club it got to the ridiculous point that the orchestras were obligated by a disciplinary commission to play foxtrots, waltzes, danzones, or boleros, but they were forbidden to play rumbas, sones, or mambos. Meanwhile, the whites of "proper society" would go crazy dancing to black music, even though they generally hired white bands. In addition, it became customary to end parties with a street conga, in which everybody would wind around in single file, a custom that passed to the United States.

The aristocratic white clubs usually owned a stretch of beach on the coast (except the most exclusive of all, the Country Club), in addition to sports facilities, a bar, a cafeteria, a restaurant, and places to dance, open as well as covered. Hierarchically, after the Country Club and the Havana Yacht Club came the Havana Biltmore and the Vedado Tennis Clubs; then, new societies formed by members of the liberal professions (doctors, lawyers, architects) sprang up like mushrooms, societies such as the Miramar Yacht Club and the Club de Profesionales, while other clubs would group diverse social strata, such as the Círculo Militar or the Casino Español (which admitted white Cubans from the small bourgeoisie). Other societies had a trade union character, such as the Club de Ferreteros or the Cubaneleco, from the "workers aristocracy" of the Cuban Electric Company. Without a beach but always with dance halls, there were societies of sales clerks, bus drivers, and on and on without end.

Some of the newly wealthy decided to establish, on their own or with a few partners, their own clubs, which would include the always desired stretch of beach, such as the Swimming Club and the colorful Senator Hornedo's Casino Deportivo, which (for unknown reasons) was the favorite of the Jews, whose other places did not have a beach. The blacks didn't have access to the Havana beaches either, except the democratic Balneario Universitario, which was for students of a university that blacks could enter on an equal basis. The situation changed somewhat when the Atenas Club acquired the grounds of the Marbella Club on Guanabo Beach, to the east of the capital. For their part, the Club Náutico and La Concha, on Marianao Beach, were open to all who paid their dues, although they maintained racial discrimination. In all of these societies Cuban and American music was performed at the dances. Occasionally societies such as the Atenas Club and the Casino Deportivo would present jazz groups and organize jam sessions in the 1940s, as did the "colored" society Juan Gualberto Gómez, from the nearby municipality of Regla, a decade later.

The Beginning of Mass Media

I've only just alluded to the onset in the 1920s of three forms of mass media that will be very important to music: records, radio, and cinema, primarily the first two. The first radio broadcast on the island is from 1922 and was made by PWX of the Cuban Telephone Company. In that same decade Cuba held the lead in Latin America with respect to the number of radio stations and radios per capita; in 1933 there were no less than sixty-two radio stations including large and small companies. As one would imagine, music played an important role in broadcasting, and among the most popular genres were danzón and lyric songs, as were later on the love ballad *(trova),* the son, and the danzonete, although concert music was also broadcast.[13] With respect to jazz, thanks to Horacio Hernández, we have a very interesting piece of information: In 1927 our first live radio broadcast of jazz was made, directly from the site of the Tokio cabaret, in which Alberto Jiménez Rebollar proved to be a precursor of vocal jazz performance on the island. The group was José A. Curbelo's, previously mentioned.[14] As we will see later on, in the following decades many jazz programs emerged, some of which were live with Cuban jazz musicians, while others played the latest jazz recorded in the United States.

Regarding records and recorded music, our jazz musicians were not involved at all in this area at that time, if we overlook the extraordinary case of Alberto Socarrás, who recorded in the United States. Similar cases would be repeated in the future when the tenor saxophonist Gustavo Más would record with Woody Herman's band or José "Chombo" Silva with Cal Tjader's group, because the Cuban jazz musicians could only record as jazz artists (and in very few cases) in the United States, particularly when they had lived in that country. So, as might be expected, the recording industry of the 1920s and '30s was never interested in "Cuban" or "Latin jazz," but only in exploiting our own music, which caused such a commotion in the world and produced greater profits than jazz itself. We should also remember that in the United States at that time black music was being recorded and sold in the form of "race records" by companies that took advantage of the limited but secure market within the big city ghettos.

With the lack of recordings of the first Cuban jazz, one might ask, "How do we fill an almost complete vacuum in the island's jazz history, if we don't know what our jazz musicians accomplished?" We can only guess as to the style of the individual soloists, or repeat what those who listened to them say, except for the ones who stayed active in the following decades, thereby giving us the chance to hear them personally. "How did they play and what were their repertoires?" These are the questions that arise. Or perhaps, looking for the easier route, "Who were their influences?" From what we know, some of the best were Duke Ellington, Earl Hines, Red Nichols, Louis Armstrong, Fletcher Henderson, Bix Beiderbecke, Syd Catlett, Coleman

Hawkins, and shortly thereafter Jimmy Lunceford, Benny Goodman, Fats Waller, Art Tatum, Bunny Berrigan, Cozy Cole, Gene Krupa, Johnny Hodges, Benny Carter, whom they could hear on records or on the radio, or live if any of the orchestras or musicians traveled to the United States. Also there were the unavoidable influences of blues performers, ragtime pianists, groups such as the Original Dixieland Jazz Band, the Chicago school (which helped to popularize the saxophone as a jazz soloist instrument), as well as the white commercial orchestras of Paul Whiteman, Fred Waring, Rudy Vallee, or Horace Hayes.

A typical example might have been Armando Romeu, who as an arranger and orchestra leader was an unconditional admirer of Duke Ellington; as a tenor saxophone player, without overlooking Coleman Hawkins and Ben Webster, he always expressed a particular partiality for a musician in Ellington's band, Paul Gonsalves. Nevertheless, Armando was also interested in what Paul Whiteman was doing, and attended his performance in the Hotel Presidente. As we have seen, it was one of Whiteman's twenty-eight branch bands; and when Armando Romeu would go every day to listen, interested primarily in the arrangements, the orchestra conductor was his colleague and friend Alfredo Brito, another very distinguished Cuban musician. Brito had studied flute with Armando's father; then he studied the piano, the clarinet, and the saxophone, and studied with the maestro Pedro Sanjuán, becoming a brilliant arranger, composer, and bandleader. His first steps were as a flutist in Antonio María Romeu's danzonera orchestra, and he wrote such classic danzones as "The Magic Flute" and "El volumen de Carlota." He was also a member of Justo *(Don)* Aspiazu's orchestra, and it was Alfredo Brito who did the arrangement of "El manisero" for Aspiazu, which not only made its author Moisés Simons, *Don* Aspiazu, and the singer Antonio Machín famous, but also initiated the Cuban music boom in New York in 1930 (it sold a million records, an impressive figure for the time). Brito composed cinema and symphony music as well, led a jazz band in the Eden Concert cabaret, and formed the Siboney orchestra, with which he traveled to Europe.

Where the Jazz Artists Are From

Just like Armando Romeu and Alfredo Brito, other Cuban saxophonists who emerge as jazz pioneers on the island began as flutists in charangas, or also as clarinetists and saxophonists in military and municipal bands, the same as trumpet and trombone players. Another musician who began in danzonera orchestras was Alberto Socarrás, whose career after 1928 would develop in the United States. And from the danzón orchestras would come excellent jazz pianists such as Pedro Jústiz ("Peruchín") and Rubén González, and bass players such as Israel López, the now world-famous "Cachao," and his nephew Orlando López ("Cachaíto"). However, the principal source of wind-instrument musicians was the military bands, which had a long tradition, begun by the Spanish during the colonial period. The same as in New Orleans with the brass bands, in Cuba the bands became a school for future members of the Cuban big bands. To get a rough idea of the significance of these bands in the musical life of the country, it will suffice to point out that we have been able to identify about eighty, not including student and children's bands, for there were few schools that didn't have at least a drum and bugle ensemble.

A crucial factor was that these bands, starting in the nineteenth century, began adapting popular Cuban pieces to their format; in the repertoires we find contradanzas, danzas, danzones, *guajiras,* and *criollas.* The parallel with New Orleans is evident, but also with Mexico. Of special importance in the Cuban band tradition was the formation, by the colonial regime, of the mulatto (Pardos) and black (Morenos) battalions, since from them emerged the orchestras of some ten musicians that enlivened dances and parties with that popular repertoire now adapted to the new format. Many of the "brown and colored" members (mulattos and blacks, that is) who were graduates of the bands formed these orchestras, which were later called *típicas* and achieved, in the words of Odilio Urfé, a real "re-creation of the *contradanza,*" from which the danzón would be derived.[15]

Each branch of the military (the Army, Navy, Police, Artillery, Infantry, Firemen, Scouts) and each military district had its own band. Then there were the municipal bands, which existed in towns that are still small today. The list would be endless. As well, we find bands that belong to conservatories and music schools, and musical instruction, public or private, was second to none, which made possible the high quality of our musicians. Instrumentalists that fed our jazz orchestras began their education in these bands, some of which included among their founders or conductors eminent Cuban musicians.

For example, the Banda Municipal de Colón had as its conductors Carlos and Leonardo Timor Sr. and the Banda de Infantería had José Marín Varona. The Havana Municipal Band was organized by Guillermo Tomás in 1899 and then Gonzalo Roig conducted it; the Remedios Municipal Band had as its leader Alejandro García Caturla, and Trinidad had Julio Cueva. Among the originators of the Navy Band (1914) are José Ramón Betancourt and Pedro Mercado; in the Regla Municipal Band we will find Armando Romeu Jr., in Sagua la Grande the Temprano brothers, in Remedios the Patinos, and in Guanabacoa the Castros; in Jovellanos, Santiago Peñalver Sr. and Emilio Peñalver. An unusual case is the Banda Invasora which, organized in 1895 by the *holguinero* Jesús Avilés, accompanied General Antonio Maceo in the War of Independence, and which has survived until now as the Hermanos Avilés jazz band.

Cuban musicians were known for their versatility, and they played just as well in a band, *conjunto,* or charanga as they did in a symphonic ensemble. We've already mentioned Amadeo Roldán and Alejandro García Caturla, both of whom were founders of the Havana Philharmonic. The exceptional case is that of García Caturla, who aside from his concert work formed jazz groups, sang in Cuban lyrical works, composed danzones, and led the Remedios band, for which he adapted numerous symphonic and popular works. Jazz musicians also participated in the symphonic orchestras, whether they were soloists or regular musicians in the jazz bands. Among the violinists we can name José A. Curbelo, Alberto Iznaga, Guillermo Portela, Virgilio Diago, Amadeo Roldán, and Alejandro García Caturla. Among the bassists were Tomás Barrenechea, Pablo O'Farrill, and later the virtuoso Orestes Urfé and the López brothers: Pedro, Israel ("Cachao"), and Orestes ("Macho"). Among the flutists were the virtuoso Roberto Ondina, who conducted orchestras for radio and TV, and Pedro Guida, a saxophonist in many jazz bands; among the clarinetists, Roberto Sánchez López, Prisciliano Almeida, the virtuoso Juan Jorge Junco, and the great Mario Bauzá; among the trumpeters, Jesús Solomo, Pedro Mercado, and René Patzi (and in a later period Luis Escalante, Alejandro Vivar, Julio Cueva, and Marcos Urbay); as trombonists, Florencio and Humberto Gelabert, Angel Mercado, Alejandro Onésimo, Enrique Ramírez, and José Serio. Among the pianists were Pedro Menéndez and José Urfé. So we see that the symphonic orchestras were another productive source of jazz and popular musicians. The high technical level of these musicians comes guaranteed by the quality of the symphonic ensembles, above all the Havana Philharmonic Orchestra, whose resident conductors, after Pedro Sanjuán and Amadeo Roldán, were Juan José Castro, Massimo Freccia, Erich Kleiber, Igor Markevich, Artur Rodzinski, and Frieder Weissman. As if this were not enough, among the guest conductors who led the Philharmonic are the following: Sir Thomas Beecham, Ernest Ansermet, Carlos Chávez, Antal Dorati, Herbert von Karajan, Georges Enescu, Serge Koussevitzky, Pierre Monteux, Eugene Ormandy, Nicolás Slonimsky, Leopold Stokowski, Igor Stravinsky, Joaquín Turina, Heitor Villa-Lobos, and Bruno Walter.[16]

3
The Big Bands and the Contradictory 1930s

*I*t is common practice to divide everything into groups of ten, and when dealing with historical events, we usually count by decades and centuries. For the most part, we will follow this standard here, but we must point out its drawbacks and its schematism. Almost all of the jazz histories carry this schematism to the extreme and define each decade with one or two styles. For example, in Joachim E. Berendt we have: "Pre-history" (before 1890); "Ragtime" (1890s); "New Orleans" (1900s); "Dixieland" (1910s); "Chicago" (1920s); "Swing" (1930s); "Bebop" (1940s); "Cool Jazz and Hard Bop" (1950s); "Free Jazz" (1960s). The following decades still resist classification, although the terms "Fusion," "Electronic Jazz," and others are commonly used.[1] The desire to categorize is justified in part for practical reasons. However, in the case of jazz in Cuba this approach is even more problematic: It's almost impossible to establish a precise line of division between the 1920s and 1930s; the same occurs with the 1940s and 1950s, so that we prefer to view these decades more in terms of continuity than as separate periods.

The 1930s in Cuba present a very contradictory panorama. On the one hand, the country's political and economic situation is chaotic. The struggle against the Machado dictatorship until his fall in 1933, the failure of the 1930–33 revolution, the ephemeral provisional governments, and the enthronement of Batista as a strongman (backed by the U.S. government) are steps in a process that negatively influences the country's social and cultural life, and ultimately its music. Unemployment and low wages accelerate the emigration of Cuban musicians to New York, Mexico, South America, and Europe, especially Madrid and Paris, and they often settle permanently in one or another of these countries. A musician's pay in a cabaret averaged about two pesos a day, and in outdoor places or interior patios, like the Eden Concert, if it rained they didn't get paid. During the years of struggle against Machado the cabarets sometimes looked like Western saloons because of the armed confrontations between revolutionaries and *porristas,* the dictator's paramilitary men. Armando Romeu recalls that Curbelo's jazz group was practicing in the Montmartre while just two blocks away the biggest shootout of the era was taking place: It was September 30, 1930, when the police attacked a university protest and student leader Rafael Trejo was killed.[2]

Many cabarets closed and a number of others opened, sometimes only for a few months. Nonetheless, many were able to make it, thanks in part to Prohibition in the United States. While this was in effect, North American tourists continued to come and even improved their consumption habits, for in Havana they had a wide selection to choose from: Cuban rum, Spanish cognac, Scotch whiskey, English gin; in short, something better than whatever the smugglers had to offer at home. The shootouts and police violence didn't cause too much concern for people visiting from a country in which the likes of Al Capone were so prominent. And if Prohibition was paradoxically so beneficial for Cuban musicians, another development had occurred that would favor them as well: the rapid growth of Cuban radio. Radio offered "work" only indirectly, as it didn't yet pay the musicians, but it did allow them to become known. This new and extraordinary publicity translated into contracts to play dances that were organized by the numerous recreation societies throughout the country. It became customary for the orchestras, in their live radio programs, to announce their upcoming tours, town by town.

Toward the end of the decade the economic situation improves, the capitalist countries continue to recover from the banking collapse, the threat of war in Europe increases, and the price of raw materials rises. As usual, Cuba comes out of the wars and crises intact, possibly even benefiting from them. And now cinema arrives to compete with radio: Hollywood movies play an important role, but so do those from Mexico and Argentina, and there are countless Cuban businessmen who boldly set out to create a national commercial cinema at decade's end. Singers and actors, *vedettes* as well as Cuban orchestras will appear not only in national productions but also in Mexican and even American cinema. This, because Cuban music, which had been slowly entering the United States, practically invades that country beginning in 1930 and becomes the essential ingredient or "Latin tinge" that will liven up musical life, whether on Broadway, for Tin Pan Alley, in Hollywood or Harlem—as John Storm Roberts has so clearly stated.[3]

This "invasion" has two sides: on one side is the Afro-Cuban music that slowly takes hold among the Spanish-speaking and African-American populations, and which later would have a strong influence on jazz; the other side represents the more commercial direction that proved to be decisive when it came time to familiarize the diverse sectors of the U.S. public with our music. This direction is based first and foremost on the popularization of songs by Ernesto Lecuona, the Grenet brothers, Sánchez de Fuentes, Gonzalo Roig, Nilo Menéndez, and other composers. Cuban rhythms and dances such as the "rumba" and the "conga" are also popularized, being simplified and adapted to the taste of the white middle class in the United States by orchestras such as Xavier Cugat's, Enric Madriguera's, and many other Cuban orchestras, from the Lecuona Cuban Boys to *Don* Aspiazu.

To this is added the high interest shown by producers, editors, and some renowned American composers for "Latin" motifs and rhythms, from the first great names on Broadway such as Victor Herbert and Sigmund Romberg to Irving Berlin and George Gershwin, all of whom visited the island, and also others such as Cole Porter or Rodgers and Hart. John Storm Roberts has thoroughly researched this development and has shown the confusion that existed among the producers and the Broadway composers with regard to the different Latin American rhythms and genres, predominantly those of Mexico,

Argentina, Brazil, Puerto Rico, and Cuba. Nevertheless, Roberts is correct when he states that despite the watering down and commercialization of "Latin rhythms" in the United States, this process of "Latinization" of North American music was certainly a positive one for both sides, because the contact and hybridization between musical cultures generally has a revitalizing effect. The "invasion" of Cuban music during the 1930s also contributed to the greater acceptance of Afro-Cuban jazz in the 1940s.

Cuban Musical Life and the Great Bands

What is ironic about this decade is that while Cuban music establishes itself in Europe and particularly in the enormous North American market, cultural activity in Cuba declines considerably in all areas; artistic organizations and movements disappear and the enthusiasm of the avant-garde cools off, in music as well as in literature and the fine arts. Many artists and performers emigrate for economic reasons or because of frustration and skepticism brought on by the political situation. This situation particularly affected symphonic music, which is dependent on major art patrons who provide the necessary financial support for such expensive ensembles. Despite all of this, the Philharmonic was able to survive with great sacrifices from its musicians and its conductor Amadeo Roldán (its first conductor, the Spaniard Pedro Sanjuán, moved to California).

In 1931 María Muñoz de Quevedo successfully established the Havana Choral Society, a feat comparable to the one she had accomplished in 1928 together with her husband Antonio Quevedo (both Spaniards) with the publication of the journal *Musicalia.* In 1932 the Chamber Orchestra Society was created, directed by the Catalan musician José Ardévol. But the premature deaths of Amadeo Roldán (1939) and Alejandro García Caturla (1940) darkened the national musical scene—already in crisis—and were a premonition of the stagnation of Cuban concert music, which will have a brief resurgence in the following decade with the presence of Erich Kleiber as conductor of the Philharmonic and the resurgence of the Grupo de Renovación Musical, which our best composers joined.

The everyday musicians could now present themselves and gain popularity through radio, although more than one talented *trovador* or *sonero* found themselves having to wander through the bars of the Havana port area to earn a few pesetas by singing, playing, and passing the hat. Dancing continued to be—along with gambling, politics, and baseball—one of the ingrained passions of the Cuban people, and the recreation societies throughout the country managed to continue hiring orchestras, whether they were charangas (which reemerged with the new *danzonete,* created by Aniceto Díaz) or jazz bands, which were acquiring a growing predominance. But these jazz bands no longer resemble the ones from 1920 or 1928, similar to the Dixieland or the vaudeville theater ensembles in the United States, but rather the big bands of the Swing Era whose foundations were laid by Fletcher Henderson, Don Redman, Duke Ellington, and then Benny Goodman, Jimmy Lunceford, and Count Basie.

Although the first big band was the one that Manolo Castro organized, others were formed at once. Saxophonist Manolo Castro and his brothers Juan, Antonio, and later Andrés had an excellent band in which pianist Anselmo Sacasas and the popular Afro-Cuban singer Miguelito Valdés excelled. Countless important musicians passed through the Castro Brothers orchestra over the span of three decades, as it lasted until 1960. In the beginning, the Castro Brothers worked in the Campoamor theater, and later went on tours throughout the country as well as on a transatlantic liner. They traveled to New York in 1932, then to Venezuela, where they performed in the Club Tropical and on Radio Cultural, and to Puerto Rico. They also appeared in the Warner Brothers film *Havana Cocktail.* In Cuba they performed on Radio Salas and other stations, in cabarets, hotels, and recreation societies, and recorded often. Five members of the Castro Brothers would be the founders of the Orquesta Casino de la Playa in 1937: the pianist Anselmo Sacasas, violinist Guillermo Portela, singer Miguelito Valdés, trumpet player and bolero singer Walfredo de los Reyes (senior), and the alto sax player Liduvino Pereira, who led the band.

The Casino de la Playa orchestra, which would surpass the Castro Brothers in renown, also had Alfredo Sáenz (tenor sax soloist), Evelio Reyes and Carlos González (saxes), Luis Rubio and Plácido Pereira (trumpets), José Manuel Peña (trombone), Ernesto de la Vega (percussion and guitar), Antonio González (bass), and Luis Suao (drums), as well as other members of the original band. Taking its name from the cabaret in which it began, this orchestra performed until the 1950s, at which time it played primarily in the Montmartre cabaret. The Casino band recorded more than six hundred records, and participated in five short films for American television and in Cuban movies. Two of its original members emigrated to the United States in the 1930s: Anselmo Sacasas, who became part of the Latin circuit in New York and recorded with his own orchestra for RCA Victor, and Miguelito Valdés, the Afro-Cuban singer par excellence in the United States along with Frank Grillo ("Machito"). Meanwhile, the Casino band continued along the road of success in the 1940s with the acquisition of Dámaso Pérez Prado as pianist and arranger and Orlando Guerra ("Cascarita") as a singer.

Another group of musicians coming from the Castro Brothers orchestra created the Riverside Orchestra in 1938, one of the longest lasting Cuban jazz bands in terms of popularity. One of its organizers was pianist José Curbelo, who the following year decided to emigrate to New York, where he formed his own band in 1941. The first conductor of the Riverside Orchestra was Enrique González Mantici (conductor of the National Symphonic from 1959 to 1974). This jazz band adopted a cooperative type of organization, a common practice within the country and one that Orestes Aragón would follow the next year when he created the famous charanga Orquesta Aragón in Cienfuegos. The Riverside Orchestra played primarily on the radio during its first stage, as accompaniment to singers. Starting in 1947 it was directed by saxophonist Pedro Vila and reached its highest popularity in this period until the end of the 1950s, with singer Tito Gómez. Like many other Cuban jazz bands, the Riverside never really played jazz, except for Glenn Miller-type American band arrangements, very popular at dances. The importance of these bands lies rather in the adaptation of the American jazz band sound to Cuban music, accomplished by arrangers such as the Riverside's Pedro Jústiz.

Returning to the beginning of the 1930s, we should acknowledge one of those orchestras already forgotten because of their short life: the jazz band directed by the violinist Alberto Dolet in the Hotel Presidente, in which the two best jazz and improvisational saxophonists of the time appeared: Germán Lebatard on alto sax and Armando Romeu on tenor sax. Germán, together with Gonzalo, Julio, and Luis Lebatard, later organized another one of the top Cuban jazz bands of the following decades, the Lebatard Brothers Orchestra, which Germán directed until the end of the 1940s. In the Thirties the Lebatard Brothers played in the Encanto Theater, the

Montmartre, the Sans Souci, and then the orchestra focused primarily on dances. It was one of the bands that consistently included jazz numbers in its repertoire, and it featured good jazz players such as bassist Reinaldo Mercier and his brother, trumpet player Wichy Mercier.[4] Another "family" orchestra, active since the 1920s as we have already seen, is the Palau Brothers Orchestra, which became a big band in the 1930s; it included performers such as singer Orlando Guerra ("Cascarita"), trumpet player and composer Julio Cueva, and jazz musicians such as trumpeter Luis Escalante, saxophonist Rafael "Tata" Palau, and drummer Luisito Palau.

The "Conquest" of Europe

Two Cuban orchestras take on particular importance at the outset of the decade: Alfredo Brito's Siboney Orchestra and the Havana Casino Orchestra founded by Justo Aspiazu. Around 1930 Brito organizes the Siboney Orchestra, not to be confused with the Siboney, which was led by violinist Alberto Iznaga in New York and in which Dizzy Gillespie played. Brito was hired by the exclusive Country Club. The band included his brother Julio Brito, a multi-instrumentalist (he played sax, xylophone, guitar, and drums) and popular author of songs such as "Mira que eres linda" and "El amor de mi bohío," and who subsequently turned to directing radio studio orchestras. The following members rounded out the Siboney jazz band: Paquito Isla (piano); Antonio Argudín and later Enrique Aparicio Velvert (guitar); Manuel Godínez (violin); Luis Fernández Nodone (bass); Armando López and the Bolivian René Patzi (trumpets); Angel Mercado (trombone); Mario Alvarez, José Fernández, and Armando Romeu (saxophones).

In 1932 the band was hired to go on a European tour that would begin in Madrid, with a "Cuban-Spanish" show consisting of the Matamoros Trio, the Spanish ballerina Granito de Sal, the *rumbera* Yolanda González, and Enrique A. Velvert as a tap dancer (as well as a guitarist in the band); the promoter *(empresario)* was Isidro Rivas, former world champion billiards player who specialized in trick shots. On arriving in Madrid, they found Ernesto Lecuona, who upon hearing of the Siboney's success once again showed his business talent and convinced his promoter Velazco to organize a similar type of "band-show." He telephoned pianist and composer Armando Oréfiche in Havana, who had worked with him in theater companies and was at that moment a pianist in the Encanto Orchestra. Previously Lecuona had attempted to hire the Havana Casino, without Aspiazu, but the offer was declined. Oréfiche rounded out his ensemble and left for Spain with the brand new Lecuona Orchestra and several other performers such as the lyrical singers Miguel de Grandy and Mercedes Menéndez. For some time they were on tour in Spain competing with the Siboney, but without much success. When Lecuona gave up the venture, Oréfiche asked him for authorization to keep his name and, shortly thereafter, at the request of a European manager, he renamed it the Lecuona Cuban Boys. And thus was born the band that would remain for half a century the "ambassador" of Cuban music throughout the world.

This story has pleasant and unpleasant aspects. The two Cuban orchestras competed in their respective tours through Spain and when one of the groups would arrive at a location, they would find in the dressing rooms a sign saying that the other had already been there. However, once when Isidro Rivas signed a contract to perform in Paris with the Siboney, upon arriving he discovered that the contract had been rescinded in order to sign the Lecuona Boys. On the other hand, it should be clarified that Ernesto Lecuona never played in this orchestra, which only used his name for publicity purposes. Made up almost exclusively of white musicians, the orchestra-show had more similarities with Xavier Cugat's band than with other popular Cuban ensembles, even though some records of the first Casino de la Playa (1930s) bring to mind that same "cosmopolitan" style. With respect to the Lecuona Cuban Boys, in 1947 the name would change again, to Havana Cuban Boys, although later in the United States a new version of the LCB was formed, which I saw in Caracas, Venezuela, in 1957 with percussionist Cándido Camero as the featured attraction.[5]

Nevertheless, the Lecuona Cuban Boys had excellent musicians and some great jazz players, for the band performed in the best venues, paid its members well, and traveled continually through North and South America, Europe, and Japan. It included jazz musicians such as trumpeter Luis Escalante, bassists Rafael or Orlando "Papito" Hernández, and drummer "El Gordo" Machado. But the key ingredient was provided by musicians who were real showmen, such as trumpet player Carlos Arado, singer and saxophonist "Chiquito" Oréfiche, conga and maraca player Rogelio Darias, and bongo player "Manteca" (Lázaro Plá).

Another band that has caused a certain amount of confusion is the Havana Casino Orchestra, which was put together around 1924 by Justo *(Don)* Aspiazu and which in 1932 was divided into two: the orchestra of *Don* Aspiazu, which had great success in Paris and New York, and the one that remained in Havana under the original name Havana Casino, organized as a musical cooperative since then. The story goes like this: Justo Aspiazu (not yet *Don*) formed the band and worked in the Gran Casino Nacional; shortly thereafter he was performing in New York in the summer and in Havana during the winter. The first big international breakthrough for "*Don* Aspiazu y su Orquesta Havana Casino" occurred in Broadway's Palace Theater, April 26, 1930, primarily with the incredible success of "El manisero" ("The Peanut Vendor"), written by Moisés Simons, sung by Antonio Machín, and arranged by Alfredo Brito. In 1931 *Don* Aspiazu returned to New York and proceeded with his distinguished career, which is admirably related by J. S. Roberts in his aforementioned book.

At that time Aspiazu was able to put together a band of top rank personnel, which included "Jiníguano" René Oliva and Pepín García (trumpets), Luis López (trombone), Miguel Dubrocq and Ramón González (alto saxes), Armando Romeu and Luis González (tenors), Hugo Siam (guitar), Leonardo Timor (bass), and Tirso Sáenz (drums). The pianist was Aspiazu, but Leonardo Timor, also an arranger, substituted for him on the more difficult numbers. Their agent in the United States was the brother of *Don* Aspiazu, Eusebio, later known as "*Don* Antobal." This particular character had been a secretary of Mario G. Menocal, the president of Cuba from 1913 to 1921, and it was rumored that he had to flee to the United States after having swindled the astute politician out of one hundred thousand dollars. Whatever may have occurred, in 1931 Antobal got a new contract for his brother, this time a European tour, which would start in Monte Carlo. Most of the musicians, however, decided to stay in Cuba, and *Don* Aspiazu formed a new orchestra. As a consequence, drummer Tirso Sáenz registered the original band under the name Havana Casino, which hadn't been registered by *Don* Aspiazu.[6] Now directed by Leonardo Timor, the Havana Casino remained at the Casino Nacional and later went on to the radio station RHC. Pedro Menéndez joined as a pianist for Timor, who continued exclusively as a bandleader, and guitarist Hugo Siam switched to bass. In a subsequent period, the orchestra was directed by saxophonist Ramón González.

In Paris, *Don* Aspiazu repeated his New York success; once again he arrived at the right moment at a place where people were beginning to take an interest in—and enthusiastically embrace—Cuban music. So, *Don* Aspiazu alternated between Paris and New York, until he decided to remain in the United States. The orchestra that he presented in Monte Carlo and Paris in 1931–32 included José Pereira (vocals), Emilio Hospital (violin), Francisco González (clarinet and sax), Pedro Guida (clarinet and sax), Julio Cueva and Pedro Via (trumpets), Lozano Morejón (piano), José "Chepín" Socarrás (guitar), Teddy Henríquez (bass), Pedro Tellería (drums), and Alvaro de la Torre (bongo); along with them the dancer Alicia Parlá performed, under the name of "Mariana." As early as 1929 Alejo Carpentier, who wrote a series of articles on Cuban music in Paris, predicted that the "providential" moment had come for the triumph of Afro-Cubanism.[7]

This same year Afro-Cuban music was being played in several Parisian theaters and cabarets in the Montmartre and Barrio Latino districts, and a community of Cuban musicians similar to the one in New York developed, although it has not been nearly as well known and its history has not yet been written. According to Carpentier, the orchestra of pianist Rogelio Barba, whom we saw years before leading a jazz band in Havana, was performing at that time at the Palermo cabaret, on Rue Fontaine; in Bateau Ivre (Latin Quarter) they would announce our music as "Cuban jazz," and in the Concert Mayol, French performers put on the revue *Bajo el cielo de Cuba*. In the Palace Theater they were presenting the popular Cuban singer Rita Montaner, and in the Sala Wagram of the so-called Club de Fauburg, Carpentier himself was presenting Moisés Simons and the orchestra of Cuban saxophonist Filiberto Rico. In 1931 Cuban symphonic music had its turn, with pieces that represented afronegrismo: works by Amadeo Roldán, Alejandro García Caturla, and Pedro Sanjuán were performed in two festivals of North American, Mexican, and Cuban music that were put on by Nicolás Slonimsky, who also conducted pieces by Charles Ives, Edgard Varèse, and Henry Cowell, among others. The concerts were celebrated in the Salle Gaveau and in the Salle Pleyel.

In 1932 Moisés Simons and the Barreto Brothers Orchestra appear at Melody's Bar; Don Aspiazu and his orchestra at the Empire Theater and at the Plantation cabaret on the Champs Élysées, and Filiberto Rico's orchestra at La Coupole. Don Aspiazu's successful orchestra takes part in the filming of *Orquídeas negras,* a movie starring Argentina's mythical tango singer Carlos Gardel that begins with Julio Cueva's trumpet playing Simons's "El manisero." In that same year Don Aspiazu performs in Brussels, at the Palace Hotel and the Pingouin cabaret, and in London at the Lester Square Theatre, then returns to Havana and New York, while Julio Cueva remained in Europe, joining in 1933 the jazz band of Snow Fisher and his Harlomarvels, with which he then traveled to Switzerland and Spain. In 1934 Julio Cueva returns to Paris. The Cuban musical scene continues to flourish: the Théâtre des Bouffes Parisiens presents Moisés Simons's operetta *Toi c'est moi* (1934–35) and a new cabaret dedicated to Cuban music opens, La Cabaña Cubana, where singer Fernando Collazo appears as its main attraction. This cabaret will become a meeting spot for Cuban musicians, who in the early morning hours enjoyed "jam sessions" or *descargas,* although they weren't called that yet. Carpentier offers us an interesting piece of information: Among the regulars at these sessions was the famed American comedian Buster Keaton.

In 1934 a Cuban-Arab businessman opens a new cabaret in Paris, which he names La Cueva, in honor of the already famous trumpet player and bandleader Julio Cueva; Cueva organizes a new orchestra that includes the also famous Eliseo Grenet on piano and his brother Ernesto on drums. Later Cueva will travel with different groups to Tripoli, Beirut, Lisbon, and finally to Madrid. He will stay in Spain as a fighter in the Civil War until 1939, at which time he returns to Havana.[8] Meanwhile Justo Aspiazu will travel to New York again at the end of the decade and then in the early 1940s. However, the "Latin" musical scene had changed a lot, and the man who had taken Afro-Cuban music to the United States was practically forgotten. Don Aspiazu died in 1943 in Cuba, where few remembered him. And in this sense the parallel with Julio Cueva turns out to be rather striking, except that Cueva recorded his biggest hits in his own country and in the 1940s, after returning from Europe. Nevertheless, in the 1950s he was persecuted for being a communist and at one time had to pawn his own trumpet. And the worst was that after 1959, under a communist government, he could only find a job as a file clerk with a salary of 101 pesos and then a pension of sixty pesos. He died in 1975, unknown and forgotten.[9]

Another important occurrence related to the great Cuban jazz bands was the appearance after 1932 of numerous bands composed of women, the most complete and famous of which was the Anacaona. These bands performed for many years in the Aires Libres, the cafes located on the esplanade opposite the Capitolio, contributing to the unique character and touristic attractiveness of this place, from the 1930s through the 1950s, until its disappearance in the 1960s. The Anacaona orchestra was started by eight sisters: Concepción Castro (conductor and saxophonist), Argimira (drums), Xiomara (trumpet), Ada (trumpet, violin, and *tres*), Alicia (clarinet, sax, and bass), Ondina (trumpet), Olga (clarinet, sax, flute, and maracas), and Caridad (bass). Rounding out the ensemble were Hortensia Palacio (piano) and the singer Graciela Pérez, sister of Frank Grillo ("Machito"), who would later become the outstanding female Cuban singer in New York for more than three decades.

The Anacaona traveled throughout Latin America, the United States, and Europe, and in Havana they also did very well on the radio. In that same decade of the Thirties a number of bands emerged: the Ensueño Orchestra, led by Guillermina Foyo (later Orbe); the Social, the Alvarez Sisters, the Herrera Sisters, the Imperio Orchestra, Renovación, the Indias del Caribe, and the septet Las Trovadoras del Cayo (put together by the pianist and composer Isolina Carrillo), and the Sexteto Occidente, which was led by Maria Teresa Vera. Singer Paulina Alvarez also led her own band. This is a unique development in our musical history: the proliferation of female orchestras, whether they were jazz bands or not, was a trend that inexplicably died out and has not been regenerated even at times when women's liberation and the fight against male chauvinism (the typical Latin American *machismo*) are so persistently pursued. Today a new version of Anacaona has been created, perhaps to remind us that at one time there were more female musical groups in Cuba than in the United States, where only Ina Ray Hutton's band achieved national popularity, as Cristóbal Díaz Ayala has shown.[10]

Of the jazz bands that played within the country and did not travel abroad, the following stood out: Mariano Mercerón and Chepín Chovén (led by Electo Rosell) in Santiago de Cuba; the Avilés Brothers in Holguín; Jorge González Allué and Joaquín Mendivel in Camagüey; the Valdés Brothers in Sancti Spíritus; and the Cienfuegos Orchestra, which included pianist René Hernández and trumpet players Raúl Hernández and Alberto Jiménez ("Platanito").

The Jazz Bands of
Armando Romeu and René Touzet

Until now I have referred to a series of great Cuban jazz bands (jazz bands in format) from the 1930s, which as I previously pointed out played little jazz, with only a few exceptions. In cabaret shows, on radio, or on recordings, these orchestras performed basically Cuban music of all sorts. Some of the musicians and bandleaders were themselves composers of songs, boleros, sones, rumbas, and *guarachas*. Jazz was only present—and sometimes very watered down—in the dance sets these bands played at nightclubs or for recreation societies. And of course, the influence of jazz was reflected not only in the format of the band but also in the way music was arranged for such a format—when standard American arrangements weren't used—and sometimes in the phrasing of a jazz soloist. With Armando Romeu Jr. the situation changes drastically.

In 1932 Armando traveled to Spain with the Siboney Orchestra of Alfredo Brito, who subsequently moved to Paris and performed in the Empire Theater together with Maurice Chevalier, although the band only remained in France for one month because of pressure from the country's musicians' union. It appears that the invasion of Cuban bands was a very unsettling development for the French musicians. In Great Britain the Siboney couldn't even work because of union opposition. Cuban musicians, in spite of their success—or because of it—constantly suffered this type of treatment by unions of other countries, the same in Europe as in North or South America, while Cuba opened its arms to any foreign musician who wanted to work or even live on the island. On his return from the European tour, Armando Romeu decided to form his own band and made his debut in the Eden Concert cabaret, with a show that included Rita Montaner, Dinorah (a tango singer), the rumba couple René and Estela, and choreographer Henry Bell's dance troupe.

This typical "mixed salad" would be the formula for cabaret shows in Cuba until the arrival of the super-productions of the Tropicana and its competitors at the end of the 1940s and in the 1950s. In the days of Eden Concert, the musicians' salaries remained at two pesos a day "if it didn't rain." Leonardo Timor Sr. has stated that in 1931 he earned three pesos a day at the Campoamor theater in Havana with a group that played for silent films, and saxophonist Alfredo Sáenz recalls having earned from forty cents to one peso and forty cents in the movie theaters, on average. There were exceptions: Manolo Castro was able to earn eighty pesos a week at the Hollywood cabaret (which didn't last long) with the Rogelio Barba orchestra, and Moisés Simons paid Julio Cueva eight pesos a day at the Plaza. It's interesting to compare this situation with that of American jazz artists. In the 1920s Jelly Roll Morton was able to earn up to eighteen dollars a day in the famous Lulu White brothel in the Storyville quarter (New Orleans), while the cabaret musicians were earning an average of two dollars per night. As far back as 1936, Count Basie was earning about twenty-one dollars a week and his musicians eighteen, according to Marshall Stearns. In both countries, it was a pittance.[11]

Getting back to Armando Romeu, he was returning as a bandleader to the same Eden Concert where he had once played tenor sax with Alfredo Brito's orchestra, the same one that he was now leaving. Armando's first band right away will include three trumpets, a trombone, four saxes, and the rhythm section (piano, guitar, bass, and drums), the classic format of big bands, which were so popular at that time in the United States. This is where Armando's association with musicians such as the alto sax player Amadito Valdés begins. The band included a singer and master of ceremonies who was none other than our well-known drummer Alberto Jiménez Rebollar. At the time, singers still had to rely on a manual megaphone; the "Age of the Microphone" had not yet arrived.

The following year (1933), in the middle of the crisis that caused many venues to close, Armando had no alternative but to disband. He continued as a tenor saxophonist in different groups and in the middle of the decade he received an offer that could have changed his career as a musician as well as the history of jazz on the island, which would have lost out: the offer came from Charlie Barnet, a saxophonist and leader of one of the best white jazz bands in the United States who had visited Cuba at that time. Armando traveled to New York to join Barnet's band, but once again he found himself rejected by a union, the well-known Local 802. And this wouldn't be the last of this sort of adversity for him in foreign countries, a factor that might have weighed in his decision not to emigrate but to pursue almost his entire career in Cuba. In 1936 Armando Romeu reorganized his band with many musicians from the previous one and appeared at the Mitsuko cabaret, which took over the old Tokio place. According to Horacio Hernández, "his group had become stronger with the addition of Emilio Peñalver on tenor saxophone, Jesús Pia, who played violin and tenor sax, and Luis Escalante, considered since then the most versatile trumpet player in Cuba."[12]

This band lined up the following musicians—trumpets: Luis Escalante, Antonio Temprano, and an unidentified musician; trombones: Ernesto Romeu and Emilio Temprano; saxes: Amadito Valdés, Jesús Pia, Emilio Peñalver, and A. Gelabert; piano: Juanito Castro; drums: Merito Reyes (we haven't been able to identify the bassist). The singer was once again Alberto Jiménez Rebollar. This band had four top-quality jazz soloists: Luis Escalante, Jesús Pia, Emilio Peñalver, and Armando Romeu. After working at the Mitsuko, where jam sessions were held on a regular basis and in which musicians from other bands would take part, Armando Romeu's orchestra started playing dances at clubs and society functions, and that same year of 1936 they played the winter season at the Nacional Hotel. Next they set out on a tour of South America, which encompassed Peru, Chile, and Argentina, with saxophonist and singer Tico Viada joining the band. In Lima they worked at the La Cabaña cabaret; in Chile they performed together with the Matamoros Trio and the dance pair of Julio Richards and Carmita Ortiz. Because of union problems (again!) they couldn't perform in Argentina, but on the positive side Armando stayed in Buenos Aires for a few months while he was hired as a tenor sax soloist in the band of Paul Wyer, an old associate of W. C. Handy, who had singer Elsie Day in his group.

New problems arose with the Argentinean union and Armando Romeu returned to Havana, where he joined a new jazz band: that of pianist and famous songwriter René Touzet. This band, which appeared at the Taberna Cubana and the Casino Nacional in 1938, brought together a constellation of Cuban jazz stars: trumpets: José Patiño, Armando López, and Arturo "Chico" O'Farrill (later to become the most brilliant Cuban arranger of jazz); saxophones: Pedro Vila, "El Cabito" Quesada, Armando Romeu, and Hugo Yera; (we don't have the names of the trombone players); violin: José Andreu; guitar: Isidro Pérez; bass: E. Andreu; drums: Alberto Jiménez Rebollar. The pianist was René Touzet and the singer René Márquez, prominent later with Antonio Arcaño, Julio Cueva, and as a composer of boleros and guarachas. With this band Touzet recorded the number that would make him famous, "No te importe saber," in the voice of René Márquez, even though the song had already been recorded by Miguelito Valdés with the Casino de la Playa orchestra and would become a hit in the United States ("Let Me Love You Tonight"). In 1944 Touzet moved to Los Angeles, California, where he had a group that included such important American "West Coast" jazz musicians as altoist Art Pepper.

Another important orchestra that emerged at the end of the decade was the Cosmopolita, created by Vicente Viana in 1938, which was led after 1944 by pianist and composer Humberto Suárez. Vicente Viana, saxophonist and clarinetist, for years devoted himself to teaching and showed a true philanthropic spirit toward his colleagues and students, who would come to him even to borrow an instrument, according to Manolo Castro. In the Cosmopolita there were musicians of the stature of Osvaldo Estivil (piano), trumpet players Raúl Hernández and Alejandro Vivar, sax players Tito Zayas and Leopoldo Junco ("Picolino"), and singer Vicentico Valdés. But already by decade's end Armando Romeu stands out as the most important Cuban jazz bandleader of all time, whose work on the island could only be compared to that of Mario Bauzá in New York. But unlike Bauzá, Armando decided to give up his instrument almost entirely, to focus on leading the band, composing, and arranging. Perhaps Armando is being excessively modest when he insists that he made the decision to give up the tenor sax when he heard Gustavo Más in a jam session in which Gustavo "dethroned" him as the best tenor saxophonist in Cuba.[13] Más, who had previously worked with the Casino de la Playa and René Touzet, would be the tenor soloist in Armando Romeu's next orchestra, the Bellamar, the best Cuban jazz band up to that time, according to all accounts.

The Bellamar and the Inception of "Latin Jazz"

In growing competition with the Casino Nacional, in 1940 the luxurious Sans Souci hired this Bellamar orchestra, which Armando Romeu directed until 1942. The band was the result of initiative on the part of Armando and trumpet player Luis Escalante, two musicians whose collaboration would produce, twenty-five years later (1967), the Orquesta Cubana de Música Moderna, the last great Havana jazz band. Armando left René Touzet's band in 1939, while Luis Escalante had left the Palau Brothers to join—for only a brief period—the Lecuona Cuban Boys. The trumpet player suggested to Armando that they form an "all star" orchestra with the best jazz musicians to play at the Sans Souci, whose manager Daniel Vila had been the promoter at the old Tokio cabaret and then the Montmartre. When they showed him a list of musicians, Vila responded skeptically and threw out a challenge: "If you can get all of them together, I'll hire them." Suffice it to say that the Bellamar Orchestra lined up the following instrumentalists: trumpets: Luis Escalante, José Patiño, and Armando López; trombone: Leopoldo "Pucho" Escalante; saxophones: Amadito Valdés, Edilberto Escrich (altos), Gustavo Más, Armando Romeu (tenors); piano: Antonio Núñez; guitar: Félix Guerrero; bass: Tomás Barrenechea; drums: Ernesto Grenet. As a singer they hired Manolo Suárez. Besides the presence of Luis Escalante and Armando Romeu, this band had the two best altos of the time (if we don't count Germán Lebatard) and the two top tenors. The brass section was perfect, and no less important was the acquisition of Pucho Escalante (brother of Luis), who for two decades or more remained the best jazz trombonist in Cuba and a top-quality arranger. Also very important was the presence of Félix Guerrero, instructor to almost all the Cuban arrangers of the time.

As the 1940s begin, it would be difficult to say that there existed a Cuban jazz with specific characteristics that were more or less defined. Our musicians would play jazz just as they would any type of Cuban music, but there still didn't exist an integration of the two languages. As might be expected, Cuban jazz musicians took as their reference the styles of American jazz instrumentalists, orchestras, and arrangers. It is also difficult to determine precisely what the repertoires of ensembles at this time were like with respect to American music, whether we're dealing with the authentic jazz production or with the Tin Pan Alley song arsenal, which was later added to jazz in the United States as well as in Cuba.

Thanks to the instantaneous aspect of radio and to geographic proximity, which allowed a rapid exchange of records and printed music, pieces from the American repertoire would arrive in a surprisingly short time. The lapse of time from the release of a record or printed musical edition in the United States to its first performance by a Cuban band was a question of weeks. Of course, found in the repertoires of our most up-to-date bands were the numerous rags, stomps, blues, shuffles, and jumps that character- ize jazz at that time. And shortly after their appearance in the United States, many popular numbers were performed in Cuba: numbers such as "Whispering," "Basin Street," "Alexander's Ragtime Band," "After You've Gone," "Broadway," "Honeysuckle Rose," "Blue Skies," "Mood Indigo," "Sometimes I'm Happy," "One O'Clock Jump," "Stompin' at the Savoy," "Pennies from Heaven," "Chicago," "Louise," "I've Got Rhythm," "Solitude," "Royal Garden Blues," "I Can't Get Started," "Twelve Street Rag," "I've Found a New Baby," "Sweet Georgia Brown," "Caravan," "Avalon," "What's New," "What Is This Thing Called Love," "Margie," "Someday Sweetheart," "Ida," "Fine and Dandy," "Sweet Sue," "Tickle Toe," "Body and Soul," "Take the A Train," "Topsy," and many more.

It would be a mistake to look for traces of what would subsequently be called Afro-Cuban jazz in the music that the Cuban bands were playing in the 1920s and 1930s. They performed, without a doubt, the Cuban gen- res (son, danzón, guaracha, rumba) as well as jazz and society music. And imperceptibly these bands, like the ones that were performing in New York, were gradually laying the foundations for the explosion of Afro-Cuban jazz in the following decade. The decisive fusion of the two languages occurs in New York, and not simply because of the renown of its performers and the greater exposure that this movement enjoyed (records, radio, press), but primarily because of the awareness that its creators had of what was hap- pening and its eventual importance for jazz and Afro-Cuban music. On the island there was a tendency to mix both types of music, although nobody seemed to realize it or give it any thought, except for a few musicians who mastered both and were drawn to experimentation and fusion.

It's also true that decisive economic factors, which cannot be overlooked, played an important role on the island; for example, the big U.S. record labels were not the least bit interested in Cuban groups that played jazz. At that time Cuban music was a hot product on the international market. They were interested in selling the music of the Matamoros Trio, Ignacio Piñeiro, or María Teresa Vera because these artists were seen as more or less "exotic" treasures, and even more so the songs of Lecuona, Grenet, or Simons, which, without losing their exotic quality, were already being created by profes- sionals who had an excellent Western musical training. Neither musical experimentation nor "fusion" of any sort were of interest at that time. The prevailing attitude in the United States was that Cuban musicians should stick to playing their own music, in which they were considered "experts," because there were more than enough jazz musicians in North America.

On the other hand, to speak of authentic jazz in Cuba one has to go back to the jam sessions that the musicians themselves would organize after (or before) their regular jobs for their own enjoyment, whether it be at someone's home, a cabaret, or any other spot. In the United States as well as in Cuba, jazz musicians always lived in two different worlds, and at certain times in jazz history the one most important and favorable to creativity and the development of the musicians themselves has been that "other world" of the jam sessions, as the British sociologist Francis Newton has intelligently suggested.[14] But because our jazz musicians have been so strongly rooted and well trained in the Cuban (or Afro-Cuban) tradition, three things would gradually and almost imperceptibly occur with respect to their understanding, assimilation, and interpretation of jazz: (1) The soloists, on wind as well as string instruments and piano, would progressively come to master the phrasing, diction, and rhythmic sense of both types of music, until they gradually combined the two into one common language. (2) Cuban percussion would slowly adapt itself to jazz arrangements and occasionally it would be the other way around, and the arrangements were written using the polyrhythmic elements of our music as a base. An exceptionally important role would fall to the drummers, who gradually "invented" a new way of playing their instrument that would better fit the Cuban rhythms. (3) The arrangers would incorporate elements taken from jazz into their orchestrations of Cuban numbers of all genres and into their own compositions.

In a word, "Latin" or "Afro-Cuban" jazz developed gradually and simultaneously in New York and Havana, with the difference that here (in Cuba) it was a silent and almost natural process, practically imperceptible; nobody was seeking to create a new style of fusion and even if somebody had attempted to create one, there wasn't the slightest possibility of receiving support or promotion. Ultimately, here as well as in New York conditions were developing that would lead to the sudden "explosion" of the 1940s with the fusion of bebop and Afro-Cuban music.

4
The Forties

Bebop, Feeling, and Mambo

$\mathcal{T}$he 1940s was a decade of economic bonanza for Cuba, because of the high prices for sugar during the Second World War. In 1940 the Constituent Assembly met in Havana and the nation's new constitution, popularly referred to as the Carta Magna, took effect; then a coalition government was formed in which the Partido Socialista Popular (Communist party) participated for the first time. These were the years of Franklin Roosevelt's Good Neighbor Policy and the Anti-Fascist Front. And with the legalization of the communists the radio station Mil Diez appeared, which would be of great importance particularly for music. Mil Diez would broadcast a wide variety of music, emphasizing national music, and would promote as well programs dedicated to jazz and tango. But above all, it was at this radio station where a movement of Cuban arrangers came together, of which Félix Guerrero will be the indisputable leader.[1]

It is also through Mil Diez that the new style of songwriting and singing known as the "feeling" movement will find its outlet; partly influenced by jazz, it included in its ranks some outstanding jazz musicians. Mil Diez's jazz program (from 1 P.M. to 1:30 P.M. daily), directed by Norman Díaz, would disseminate the latest jazz records from the United States, and was the first to introduce by way of Cuban radio the creators of bop, such as Charlie Parker and Dizzy Gillespie. This station was not, however, the vehicle for Cuban jazz musicians, who played live jazz, for the first time at a set place, on the station CMQ, then at Monte and Prado. CMQ's program "El Club del Swing" broadcast an hour of jazz on Saturdays, and included, among others, tenor saxophonists Armando Romeu and Gustavo Más, trumpet player Luis Escalante and trombonist Pucho Escalante, alto saxophonist Rafael "El Cabito" Quesada, and jazz vocalist Delia Bravo. Radio station RHC, which under the direction of Amado Trinidad was becoming CMQ's main competitor, presented, among other groups, pianist Luis Mendoza's American Swing, which included two tenor saxes, Gustavo Más and Emilio Peñalver, drummer Evelio Quintero, and trumpet players Alejandro "Coco" Barreto and Raúl Hernández—who was better known as "Cootie Williams," for playing in the unique style of that great trumpeter from Duke Ellington's band. Raúl Hernández was the brother of René Hernández, who would later be the pianist and arranger for Machito and his Afro-Cubans.

In this group of Luis Mendoza, we find two important singers of our jazz movement: Delia Bravo and Dandy Crawford, of Jamaican origin. Dandy was very much connected with the feeling movement and was also the first Cuban singer to get involved in scat vocalizing. In Cuba, at the beginning of the decade the big swing bands were still at their height of popularity; the arrival of bebop was delayed because of the recording ban beginning in 1942, which set back the release of bop recordings until 1945.[2] The first Cuban bop group was organized in 1947, made up of musicians who just shortly before were playing in the swing style, but who adapted very quickly to the new language. Nevertheless, it's clear that swing and bop coexisted for many years in Cuba (as well as in the United States), and although bop came to dominate in the end, it's significant that the image of jazz as "swing" would remain, even to the point that a magazine with the title *Swing Makers* would be published at that time in Havana.[3] Another example: In 1940 two of our first bop musicians, drummer Guillermo Barreto and pianist Bebo Valdés, formed a Benny Goodman style trio with Roberto Barreto as the clarinetist.

The work that Mil Diez did to attract a mass audience was important, as was its ability to find talent and its excellent organization and programming, but just as important, if not more, was the competition between the major commercial radio stations, primarily CMQ and RHC, for Mil Diez paid very low salaries. This competition was very beneficial for musicians, who began to receive higher and higher salaries in a medium that just in the previous decade had served solely as a way to gain exposure. Together with this, and as a result of the economic boom, in the late 1940s the competition intensified among increasingly bigger nightclubs capable of holding more than a thousand people and of putting on supershows that became more and more expensive. The immenseness of the cabarets, a trend begun by the Gran Casino Nacional and the Montmartre, increased with the Sans Souci and the Tropicana, and brought on a relative decline of small cabarets such as the Tokio, the Eden Concert, the Infierno, or the Mitsuko, although nightclubs of this type would experience a comeback in the 1950s.

In 1942 the Sans Souci cabaret closed its doors until the end of World War II in 1945, which caused the dissolution of the Bellamar Orchestra. Its conductor, Armando Romeu, was then hired to form an orchestra at the Tropicana, where he would remain for the next twenty-five years, except for a brief interlude. Romeu's fourth jazz band now had four trumpets, three trombones, and five saxes, plus a rhythm section that included the great guitarist Isidro Pérez. Singer Delia Bravo also joined the band, and in the future a series of Cuban percussion stars would join the orchestra.

The lineup of Armando's brilliant band was as follows: trumpets: Arturo "Chico" O'Farrill, César Godínez ("Piyú"), Alberto Jiménez ("Platanito"), and Dagoberto Jiménez ("Rabanito"); trombones: Miguel Reina, Ernesto Romeu, and Generoso Jiménez ("Tojo"); saxophones: Amadito Valdés, Enemelio Jiménez (altos), Emilio Peñalver and Roberto Romero (tenors), and Orlando Fernández Walpole ("Macanta") or Ñico Romero (baritone); piano: Pedro Jústiz ("Peruchín"); guitar: Isidro Pérez ("Isito"); bass: Enrique "Kiki" Hernández; drums: Daniel Pérez. The singer Delia Bravo, unjustly forgotten today, was married to Armando Romeu. This orchestra not only surpassed the Bellamar but would in turn be surpassed by the bands to follow that Romeu put together in the very same Tropicana during the Fifties.

It's important to point out not only the power of the trumpet section, in which the Jiménez brothers could divide up the lead with "Piyú" Godínez, our first specialist in high notes, and in which Chico O'Farrill would perform the improvised jazz solos, but also the presence of Generoso Jiménez in the trombone section, later a key member of Beny Moré's band and the first trombonist to create a Cuban style of improvisation. Improvising on sax were Enemelio Jiménez (brother of Generoso), tenor Emilio Peñalver, and the baritone "Macanta." The rhythm section was the best that had been put together to that point, with the great "Peruchín" on piano, creator of his own "Latin jazz" style, with Isidro Pérez on guitar mastering the styles of Charlie Christian, Django Reinhardt, and later Billy Bauer and Barney Kessel, and two musicians as technical as they were imaginative on bass and on drums, Kiki Hernández and Daniel Pérez.

Armando Romeu had built an extensive jazz repertoire with the best arrangements of the bands of Duke Ellington, Count Basie, Fletcher Henderson, and Woody Herman, which he would transcribe note by note from recordings, in addition to his own compositions and arrangements. But in this band the presence of Chico O'Farrill now as an arranger is very important, as he contributed original scores that were ahead of their time. According to Horacio Hernández,

> In 1942, Arturo "Chico" O'Farrill began his career as an arranger in the orchestra that Armando Romeu conducted at the Tropicana cabaret, an orchestra in which the most famous musicians of the time were concentrated. Around 1945, when the first bop recordings arrived in Cuba, O'Farrill was one of the first to understand the innovations of that style, and in very little time his command of the orchestration and his knowledge of jazz allowed him to work in the bands of Benny Goodman, Dizzy Gillespie, and Stan Kenton.[4]

Jazz Groups: From Swing to Bop

In 1945 a group called the Swing Racketeers was formed, featuring Arturo O'Farrill (trumpet), Roberto Sánchez Ferrer (clarinet), José Alvarez (piano), Rafael Mola (guitar), Rafael ("Felo") Hernández (bass), Fausto García Rivera (drums), and Ana Menéndez as singer. Chico O'Farrill, who appears in this swing group, will organize a bop group two years later. Along with him, we find Felo Hernández, the oldest of three bass-playing brothers who are of great importance in Cuban jazz; the second, Kiki, will be in O'Farrill's next group and with Armando Romeu's band, and later Orlando ("Papito") Hernández will make his appearance. The drummer Fausto García Rivera forms part of a trio of musicians along with Daniel Pérez and Walfredito de los Reyes who will take instrumental technique to a much higher level than had been previously heard in Cuba, and who will prove to be essential for the Cuban jazz scene in this decade and the next. Roberto Sánchez Ferrer will subsequently turn to orchestral composing and conducting, particularly in the lyrical and operatic genre. Ana Menéndez pursued a parallel career as an opera soprano and the two were married for a period of time.

Meanwhile, bebop was gradually taking hold and was being assimilated by a good many musicians. In 1947 Chico O'Farrill would create the group Los Beboppers, with whom he appeared on the *marquesina* at the Saratoga Hotel. It consisted of O'Farrill on trumpet, Edilberto ("Eddy") Escrich (alto sax), Gustavo Más (tenor sax), René Urbino (piano), Kiki Hernández (bass), and Daniel Pérez (drums). With these and other musicians, O'Farrill made some recordings that I would categorize as "homemade"; they were paid for by the musicians using an independent recording studio and were then passed out among themselves and a few jazz-fan friends. It's hard to forget Gustavo Más's tenor sax solo in the standard classic of tenor players, "Body and Soul," in a style that owes a lot to Lester Young.[5] I also remember several bop tunes in the string of recordings that Red Rodney and Neal Hefti made with their respective groups and which were brought together on the album *Be-bop* on the Mercury label. These and other recordings of Cuban jazz from that period are today not only collector items—they've practically disappeared.

Around 1946 another station, Radio Capital Artalejo, began to broadcast a Sunday spot on jazz, the "Club de Música," produced by Orlando Battle and Rafael Simón Jr. The studios were the property of another important Cuban radio promoter, Arturo Artalejo, and were located on F Street between Third and Fifth (Vedado). It was here that a jazz group described as "way ahead of its time" by Horacio Hernández appeared: it included César "Piyú" Godínez (trumpet), Pedro Chao (tenor sax), Agustín "Tico" Mercier (piano), Orlando "Papito" Hernández (bass), and Daniel Pérez (drums). At about the same time another group appeared at the Rívoli Theater (corner of Twenty-seventh and Twenty-sixth streets, La Sierra district); some sources cite them as New York Swing while others refer to them as Los Newyorkers; it included Chico O'Farrill (trumpet), Gustavo Más and Emilio Peñalver (tenor saxes), Kiki Hernández (bass), Diego Iborra (drums), and a pianist who may have been either Agustín Mercier or Mario Romeu.

Another interesting development in this decade was the impact of the quintet Hot Club de France on Cuban musicians, with its legendary guitarist Django Reinhardt and the violinist Stephane Grapelli, another jazz legend. A similar group, which would perform a large part of the Hot Club's repertoire, was formed in Havana, although primarily they would get together to play at Kiki Hernández's house. It included three of the best jazz guitarists in Cuba: Isidro Pérez, Rafael Mola, and Manolo Saavedra. The outstanding Isidro Pérez would lead in those days one of the country's best jazz bands, which performed at the Montmartre cabaret. The violinist of the "Cuban Hot Club" was Manolo Triana, and the bassist was Kiki Hernández. This group is another illustration of the "coexistence" of swing and bop among the same congregation of Cuban jazz musicians.

Along with the big cabarets, smaller ones emerged, and some made room for jazz. In 1948, for example, an excellent bop group played for a time at the High Seas (at Monserrate and Empedrado); it was led by an American musician, Harry Johansson, who played trumpet, valve trombone, and vibraphone. He lived for a few years in Havana and on two occasions was part of Armando Romeu's band, in this decade and the following. The group enlisted two tenor saxophonists who were beginning to shine at that time, Rafael "Tata" Palau and Pedro Chao; the pianist was Agustín "Tico" Mercier; the bassist was José Manuel Peña (also a trombonist); and the drummer was Fausto García Rivera. The High Seas was another one of those nightclubs that became a center for jam sessions, which attracted musicians from a number of orchestras; among those who participated were bassist Reinaldo Mercier and trumpet player Wichy Mercier, brothers of the pianist Agustín Mercier, one of the first and most outstanding interpreters of bop on his instrument. More on the swing side, the Red Devils appeared regularly at the Casino Deportivo and included musicians of the stature of Juan Jorge Junco (clarinet), the veteran Célido Curbelo (piano), Eddy Sastre (violin and conductor), and tenor saxophonist José "Chombo" Silva, later very successful in the United States as well as in Cuba. Founded in the Thirties, this group also included singer Miguelito Valdés, pianist Emilio Eguiluz, and tenor saxophonist Leopoldo Junco ("Picolino").

Jazz Bands and the Supershows

Although the 1940s can be considered the "Age of Conjuntos" because this was when the format created by Arsenio Rodríguez reached its peak, the jazz bands remained active and new ones emerged. An exceptional jazz band was organized by Chico O'Farrill and the great guitarist Isidro Pérez in 1947; it performed in the Montmartre cabaret and played very advanced arrangements, written primarily by O'Farrill. "Isito" lined up an impressive number of top musicians: trumpets: Dagoberto Jiménez ("Platanito"), Armando López, and Chico O'Farrill; trombone: Pucho Escalante; saxophones: Edilberto Escrich and Osvaldo "Mosquifín" Urrutia (altos), Gustavo Más and José "Chombo" Silva (tenors), and Pedro Ruiz (baritone); piano: Mario Romeu; guitar: Manolo Saavedra; bass: Kiki Hernández; drums: "El Gordo" Machado. The singer was Ray Carson, with a voice very much like Bing Crosby's. In addition to conducting, Isito would play the guitar solos, while Saavedra would play the accompanying guitar. Tenor player Pedro Chao also joined the band at times.

This orchestra of Isidro Pérez's was replaced at the Montmartre by a new version of the famous Casino de la Playa, although now without some of its great names. Alto saxophonist Liduvino Pereira conducted it and tenor soloist Alfredo Sáenz remained with the band. A group of its musicians had come from Isito's band, such as altoist Eddy Escrich, saxophonist "Mosquifín" Urrutia (who switched to baritone sax), and trumpeter Alberto Jiménez (who became lead in the brass section). Meanwhile, at the Tropicana, which was already becoming the primary competitor of the Sans Souci and the Montmartre (the Casino Nacional had closed its doors), changes were occurring not only in orchestras and show directing but with promoters as well.

The great Tropicana productions begin in this decade, although the nightclub situated in Villa Mina or Mansión Truffin (corner of Forty-first and Seventy-second, Marianao) still lacked the extravagance that it would later acquire. Perhaps the show that inaugurated this era was *Congo Pantera* (1940 or 1941), which presented Rita Montaner, Julio Richards, Carmita Ortiz, Ignacio Villa (Bola de Nieve), and the great drummer, composer, and singer

Chano Pozo. This supershow, which is of interest to us here because of the participation of Chano, was in part the result of pure chance, because of the presence of the great ballet choreographer David Lichine in Cuba. He had come with Colonel Basil's Russian Ballet, which in spite of its fame went bankrupt, leaving its members on their own. Hired to do this show, Lichine took the two leading figures from the ballet, Tatiana Leskova and Paul Petrof, and part of the colonel's dance corps; but he also found a number of "colored" chorus dancers to fulfill the demands of an international tourism eager to see "tropical exoticism," all of this with a distinctive Afro-Cuban music and original choreography, to which Julio Richards contributed, along with all of the spectacular resources of staging, lighting, and wardrobe.

Congo Pantera turned out to be historic for various reasons, which can be reduced to the encounter of three such dissimilar performers as David Lichine, Chano Pozo, and an individual who also participated as an assistant to Lichine and Richards, whose name was Roderico Neyra, later internationally famous as *Rodney*. This encounter Lichine-Rodney-Chano Pozo would be for the world of show business in Cuba as important as the one between Chano and Dizzy Gillespie was for Afro-Cuban jazz or Cubop some years later. The life of Rodney is one of those stories that Hollywood just loves, the poor individual who makes it big, especially in show business. Roderico Neyra started out playing small roles and sketches at the Shanghai Theater, in Havana's Chinese Quarter, then at the Actualidades Theater and at cabarets as a chorus dancer, and he was still unknown when he worked alongside Lichine in *Congo Pantera*. In 1945, known as Rodney by then, he organized the show "Las Mulatas de Fuego," a big hit in Cuba and Mexico, and he would then be successful as an artistic director for shows at the Sans Souci, the Tropicana (where he stayed for fifteen years), and even for a few seasons at the Waldorf Astoria in New York and the Flamingo in Las Vegas. Rodney produced the shows that gave international prestige to the Tropicana, among them *Omeleikó, Voodoo Ritual, Carabalí, Mayombe, Carnaval Carioca, Copacabana, Tambo,* and *Sun Sun Babaé* (which sold out the Flamingo in Las Vegas). And Rodney's shows included such artists as Josephine Baker, Nat King Cole, Tongolele, Carmen Miranda, Beny Moré, Maurice Chevalier, Xavier Cugat, and Liberace.

When Chano Pozo was hired for *Congo Pantera* he had already become an important figure in the Cuban musical scene, contrary to the commonly held notion that he was just another drummer who happened to get a lucky break. The musical history of the era tells us that Luciano Pozo was more than just a well-known *rumbero* from the Africa *solar*, in the Cayo Hueso barrio, or La California of the Belén barrio, and in other rumbero barrios such as Atarés, Jesús María, or Pueblo Nuevo. He was in addition a popular songwriter of hits such as "Blen blen," "Nagüe," "Ariñáña," "Pin pin," "Anana boroco tinde," "Parampampín," and the theme song of the *comparsa* Los Dandys de Belén, a comparsa in which he danced with other celebrities such as Rita Montaner and songwriter-entertainer Bola de Nieve. He was a prominent member of the Sociedad de Autores Musicales, which Ernesto Lecuona presided over at the time. He was also well known for playing with the Orquesta Azul, from the station RHC Cadena Azul, and the Havana Casino jazz band. But what is of more significance to us is the fact that Chano Pozo had performed as a soloist in a show presented at the Alkázar theater with Mario Santana's jazz quartet, which included Santana on piano, bassist Luis "Pellejo" Rodríguez, drummer César Sánchez, and the bongo player Panchito Bejerano. This means that Chano Pozo had an understanding of jazz and that he had played with jazz groups in Cuba before traveling to the United States, which enabled him to quickly pick up what Dizzy Gillespie was doing with his new band.

With respect to the Tropicana, a new era was beginning when its promoter Víctor Correa brought to Cuba in 1949 the Spanish orchestra-show Los Chavales de España, formed specifically to perform in our country, an interesting analogy—although inverted—to the history of the Lecuona Cuban Boys seventeen years earlier. And to complete the parallel, Los Chavales played in a "Spanish-society" style equivalent to the "Cuban-society" style of the Cuban Boys (aside from the fact that "chavales" is a translation of "boys"). But there are secondary aspects of this history of the "best cabaret in the world" as well: the promoter Correa, because of personal and family favoritism and some kind of trouble involving women, decided to remove Armando Romeu so that he could name as leader of the Tropicana orchestra the Spaniard Adolfo Araco.

By then Romeu's orchestra had changed: the trumpet section included José Patiño, Harry Johansson, Wichy Mercier, and Pedro "El Guajiro" Rodríguez; on trombone was the Spaniard Alberto Martí and on sax Amadito Valdés and Santiaguito Peñalver (altos), with Roberto and Ñico Romero on tenor. The bassist was Fernando Vivar ("Yuca") and the drummer was Guillermo Barreto. Dandy Crawford was involved as a singer. When Adolfo Araco arrived as the new leader, the rhythm section remained—almost intact—as did Crawford for some time. Other musicians joined, among them the trumpet player Alejandro "Coco" Barreto and the Catalan pianist León Borrell, who would excel in Cuban jazz in the following decade.

At that time Ernesto Grenet, having returned from abroad, simultaneously led and performed as a drummer in the Tropicana's second orchestra. Among his musicians were the veteran bassist Tomás Barrenechea, the saxophonists Juanito Barrenechea and Osvaldo Urrutia ("Mosquifín"), and trumpet players José Patiño and Evelio Martínez ("El Manquito"). A little bit later the Tropicana had the wisdom to bring in, to the satisfaction of jazz purists who detested the Spanish orchestra-show, a group formed by Woody Herman with a constellation of jazz stars, whose performance will be covered in another chapter. Meanwhile, Adolfo Araco, on the advice of drummer Guillermo Barreto, over a period of time brought in pianist Bebo Valdés, trumpeters Alejandro "El Negro" Vivar and the brothers Alberto and Dagoberto Jiménez, as well as the alto saxophonist Rafael Quesada ("El Cabito"), son of Primitivo Quesada, and tenor saxophonist Pedro Chao. Thanks to these musicians, and particularly to outstanding bop soloists such as Bebo Valdés, Barreto, Pedro Chao, and "El Negro" Vivar, the Spaniard Araco all of a sudden found himself conducting an excellent jazz band that included an extensive repertoire of bop numbers, which were usually transcribed by Guillermo Barreto from records. But despite everything, Tropicana had to call back Armando Romeu.

In addition to the competition among the big nightclubs, but also because of it, the Tropicana needed somebody really talented at putting together original compositions and arrangements for supershows, which were becoming more and more complex. The sensational show provocatively titled *Cocaína,* presented in theaters and cabarets, was a great success in Havana, with the Uruguayan dance couple Siccardi and Brenda as the main attraction. The music was written by Armando Romeu, and once again Romeu was called upon to lead the Tropicana's first orchestra. But now the person who was besieged by problems was the promoter Victor Correa, because others who were more powerful and driven decided to take over the business, which was becoming more and more profitable. The trio formed by

Martín Fox, Oscar Echemendía, and ex-dealer Alberto Ardura (in charge of the shows from that point on) now had control of the cabaret's casino, and Correa, under pressure because of his gambling debts, found himself forced to sell. Businesses related to cabarets, hotels, casinos, shows, and music itself were beginning to enter into the realm of "la Cosa Nostra," and so we begin to see characters, seemingly Hollywood-type creations, such as Santo Trafficante, Frank Sinatra, George Raft, Lefty Clark, or Meyer Lansky during the "golden decade" of the 1950s.

The competition among the Sans Souci (reopened in 1945), Tropicana, and Montmartre would eventually turn into a "fraternal emulation," in the sense that these three giants of Havana's nightlife were being gradually transformed into domains under the control of a few "families" with similar interests. Around 1950 the Sans Souci orchestra was led by pianist Rafael Ortega and included trumpeters "Coco" Barreto and Walfredo de los Reyes (senior), saxophonists Amadito Valdés, Orestes Barbachán, Juanito Martínez, and Charles Rodríguez, and trombonists Ernesto Romeu and José Manuel Peña, whom we saw as a bassist at the High Seas. Ortega also hired drummer Guillermo Barreto, who would subsequently return to the Tropicana with Armando Romeu.

Jazz Bands in the Conjunto Era

One might imagine that the great popularity of the *conjuntos* during the 1940s would have negatively affected the jazz bands, but that wasn't the case. The groups that suffered because the prominence of the conjuntos were, once again, the danzonera orchestras, which would reemerge once more in the following decade with the tremendous popularity of *chachachá.* Jazz bands stayed around because of their ability to play any type of music, and demand for them increased thanks to cabaret, theater, and later television shows. With a conjunto or charanga format it was impossible to play American or Spanish music or to accompany singers from Mexico, Argentina, Italy, France, Spain, and the United States who performed frequently in Havana, for starting in 1945 our capital was quickly becoming the great tourist and musical destination that would define it in the ensuing decade. And by that time son, danzón, and other Cuban rhythms had already been adapted to the jazz band format by the arrangers. But we must emphasize that the only bands that really played the best jazz and gave plenty of room to the soloists were those of Armando Romeu and Isidro Pérez, the Bellamar (Romeu-Luis Escalante), and occasionally Germán Lebatard's band. Aside from these and a few other exceptions, the Cuban bands, it must be said, didn't get any further than Glenn Miller or Tommy Dorsey, even though they did have a number of jazz musicians.

The Palau Brothers orchestra, for example, reached the height of its popularity in the 1940s, through radio programs on which they played Cuban music and with singers such as Orlando Guerra ("Cascarita"), Francisco Cova ("El Indio"), or Manolo Manrique ("El Morito"). Great instrumentalists passed through the Palau Brothers orchestra. For example, we find trumpet players such as Luis Escalante, José Patiño, Julio Cueva, Leonardo Timor (junior), Eddy Martínez, "El Loco" Medina, and Manuel Duchesne Cuzán (future conductor of the National Symphonic Orchestra); saxophonists such as Vincente Viana, Pedro Guida, "El Cabito" Quesada, Miguel Sánchez, Pedro Ruiz, and Virgilio Vixama; and trombonists such as Alejandro Onésimo. In addition to the generation of the Palau family that founded the orchestra in 1922, a younger generation played in the band in the 1940s; it included saxophonists Rafael "Tata" Palau and Enrique Palau, trumpeter Tony Palau, and drummer Luisito Palau. Working in this band as well were pianists Mario Santana and Orlando Arango ("Maíno"), bassists Luis Rodríguez and Felo Hernández, drummer Merito Reyes, percussionist Marcelo "El Blanco" González, and the subsequently famous singer Rolando Laserie. Among the arrangers, Muñoz Bouffartique and Félix Guerrero stood out. A trumpet player with strong ties to the Palau brothers was Julio Cueva, who organized an orchestra when he returned from Europe that featured, among others, trombonist Alejandro Onésimo, trumpet player Remberto "El Chino" Lara, saxophonists José Pérez Cedeño ("Bebo") and Enemelio Jiménez, pianist Felo Bergaza, and the great *guarachero* "Cascarita" as singer.

At the breakup of this band, Julio Cueva and Cascarita joined the Palau Brothers, which worked several seasons at the Sans Souci nightclub. When the radio station Mil Diez was created, Julio Cueva organized a new jazz band that included saxophonists Mario Menéndez and Bruno Guijarro (altos), José Pérez Cedeño and Miguel Sánchez (tenors), as well as trumpet player Alberto Jiménez ("Platanito"), bassist Salvador ("Bol") Vivar, percussionists Marcelo González (bongo) and Oscar Valdés (conga), and the singers Reinaldo Valdés ("El Jabao") and Juan Antonio Jo Ramírez ("Fantasmita"), who had performed with the Palau Brothers. The pianist this time was the great René Hernández. At the end of this decade Cueva's band would split up, as would the Lebatard Brothers band. After the breakup, Germán Lebatard worked in different orchestras, then formed a jazz group and after that moved to Miami, where he conducted the Hotel Fontainebleau orchestra.

Meanwhile, the renowned Casino de la Playa band started to fade when it lost Dámaso Pérez Prado and "Cascarita." Despite the acquisition of Julio Gutiérrez, who was also a pianist and composer, the Casino was no longer the same, and Gutiérrez would leave in 1948 to form his own orchestra. In spite of everything, this famous jazz band was never without excellent musicians and jazz soloists, something that unfortunately we will never be able to prove based on its recordings. Led by Liduvino Pereira, the Casino played long seasons at the Montmartre, as we have already seen, with Ray Carson as singer and a repertoire that included jazz numbers in the dance sets. Among the musicians in the band, along with the founders and those already mentioned, were trumpet players Dagoberto Jiménez, Alberto Jiménez, and "El Loco" Medina, a high note specialist; alto saxes Eddy Escrich and Miguelito Franca; tenor saxes Alfredo Sáenz and Gustavo Más; baritone sax "Mosquifín" Urrutia; bassist Carlos Villa; pianist Luis Franca; and valve trombonist Alberto Giral ("El Men"), an excellent jazz improviser.

Radio, growing rapidly in the 1940s, favored the hiring of big orchestras, sometimes enhanced with string sections. They were our first "studio orchestras," which guaranteed new sources of steady work for musicians. Gone were the difficult days when an orchestra could consider itself fortunate to perform live on the radio one night just to promote itself for upcoming dances. The main stations were CMQ and RHC, but a number of others soon began to form their own orchestras. Radio Cadena Suaritos, a strictly musical station that became very popular, hired as its orchestra leader the great flute virtuoso Roberto Ondina, who brought to the studio a "small symphonic ensemble" to accompany the many foreign singers—particularly Spanish singers—whom Suaritos would hire on an exclusive basis. And in 1943 RHC-Cadena Azul created "la Orquesta Gigante," with Rodrigo Prats as conductor, which alternated with a second orchestra, the Havana Casino conducted at that time by Leonardo Timor Sr.

Mil Diez organized an orchestra with thirty musicians, capable of performing any type of music: it was basically a jazz band, but with a string section (eight violins, two violas, two cellos), a woodwind section (flute, oboe, bassoon, clarinet), and a Cuban percussion section. Sometimes large concertinas *(bandoneones)* were added for Argentinean music or a small tambourine *(pandereta)* and castanets for Spanish music. As conductors they had Enrique González Mantici, Félix Guerrero, Roberto Valdés Arnau, and Adolfo Guzmán, who became the station's musical director. And a team of arrangers worked under the direction of Félix Guerrero: Francisco Melero, Rafael Ortega, Pepe Bravo, Bebo Valdés, Osvaldo Estivil, Rey Díaz Calvet, Humberto Suárez, and Adolfo Guzmán.[6] But Mil Diez also featured such distinguished bands as Arsenio Rodríguez's conjunto, Los Jóvenes del Cayo, Julio Cueva's orchestra, the Rigual Brothers trio, the Matamoros Trio, and the Conjunto Matamoros, with which Beny Moré started his impressive career. And among all of the singers of different styles who became known through Mil Diez we should mention Miguelito Valdés, Orlando Guerra ("Cascarita"), Olga Rivero, Zoila Gálvez, Alba Marina, Pepe Reyes, Miguel de Gonzalo, Elena Burke, Reinaldo Henríquez, Berta Velázquez, Celia Cruz, and Olga Guillot. As we shall see, the feeling movement was well represented in the broadcasts of Mil Diez.

In 1948 RHC hired Julio Gutiérrez, pianist and composer, to conduct the station's orchestra. The jazz band that Julio conducted at RHC lined up a good group of jazz musicians: trumpet players Alejandro "El Negro" Vivar and Nilo Argudín (both later played with Armando Romeu at the Tropicana and with Machito in New York); alto saxes Eddy Escrich and "Mosquifín" Urrutia and tenors Emilio Peñalver and Rubén Morales ("Perro Chino"), excellent improvisers; pianist René Urbino; bassist Fernando Vivar (and then his brother Salvador); the great drummer Daniel Pérez and percussionists such as Oscar Valdés and Rogelio Darias. A few years later Gutiérrez along with some of these musicians would go on to Channel 4 television, while Roberto Ondina would go on to Channel 2, and Channel 6 (CMQ-TV) would absorb the rest of the musical personnel from the defunct Mil Diez, hiring Adolfo Guzmán and Roberto Valdés Arnau, among others.

Cuban jazz bands stayed at the very height of their popularity in the 1940s, and even in the following decade, even though it is at the end of the 1940s in the United States when talk of the "decline of the big bands" begins; they were becoming economically untenable and thereby opening the way for the predominance of smaller groups, coinciding as well with the consolidation of bebop as a style. In 1955 none other than Woody Herman would tell Bill Coss, a critic from *Metronome* magazine, that since 1948 the whole big band business had gone to pieces, and that he himself had lost $175,000 "which he didn't have," and as a result had to dissolve his band and form the very group (an octet) that he brought to Havana in 1950.[7] So we find ourselves dealing with two totally independent processes, for in Cuba the decline and essentially the complete disappearance of jazz big bands occurred in the 1960s.

As radio reaches its highest point in the Forties, so too do the attempts to create a national cinema, undertaken in the preceding decade under conditions similar to those of Mexican commercial cinema and sometimes in collaboration with it. In the twenty or so films that were made, music played the key role in this fledgling movie industry, as the titles indicate: *La última melodía* (1939), *Cancionero cubano* (1939), *Siboney* (1939), *La canción del recuerdo* (1946), *Oye esta canción* (1947), *Música, mujeres y piratas* (1950), *Cuba canta y baila* (1950), and many others. Singers, *vedettes,* and orchestras worked in these as well as in Mexican and American films. But these two motion picture industries were too much competition for the bold pioneers of a Cuban national commercial cinema, which finally succumbed after 1950 because of the rapid development of commercial television in Cuba, which was among the best in the world and attracted all of the support.[8]

The Conjuntos: Son, Feeling, Bop, and El Niño Rivera

The conjunto evolved from the enlargement of the old son septet, and its most obvious characteristic at a glance is that instead of a single trumpet it employs two, three, and even four, and in the rhythm section a conga is added to the bongo. The creator of this format was Arsenio Rodríguez, the great *tres* player and composer, but there exists a precursor for the incorporation of the conga drum, as musicologist Jesús Blanco informs us: the Sexteto Afrocubano, formed by the great rumbero Santos Ramírez, from El Cerro barrio, incorporated the conga into the son in 1936, four years before Arsenio.[9] The conjuntos caught on among the public, basically in two genres: son

and bolero, as well as guaracha with a son rhythm. But now Arsenio
Rodríguez was using rhythmic variations, which he called *diablo,* that would
later give rise to mambo. With the triumph of mambo around 1950, the conjuntos experimented with a successful hybrid, bolero-mambo. The conjuntos achieved success not only through their performances at dances, cabarets,
and on radio, but they were the primary beneficiaries of the new market for
Victrolas (jukeboxes), which spread like wildfire throughout the country,
with more than ten thousand by 1954 just in Havana.[10]

A large part of the conjunto's popularity lay in its singers, something that
happened only on rare occasions with jazz bands (in the cases of Miguelito
Valdés, Tito Gómez, Cascarita, or Beny Moré). The excellent sonero and
bolerista Miguelito Cuní enjoyed great success first with Arsenio and then with
Félix Chapottin. Roberto Faz, Roberto Espí, Agustín Ribot, Nelo Sosa, and
Orlando Vallejo sang in the Conjunto Casino, which became the most pop-
ular and sought-after conjunto in the country. La Sonora Matancera—which
represents a third style as distant from Arsenio as from the Casino—included
Bienvenido Granda and Celio González, although it specialized more in
accompanying singers such as the *boricua* Daniel Santos, Dominican Alberto
Beltrán, and Cuban Celia Cruz. In the Gloria Matancera conjunto Roberto
Sánchez stood out, as did Faz, Vallejo, and Carlos Querol in Alberto Ruiz's
Kubavana. Other popular conjuntos were Nelo Sosa's Colonial, with pianist
and composer Pepé Delgado as musical director, and the conjunto of Roberto
Faz, who upon leaving the Casino would work with the pianist, arranger, and
musical director Rolando Baró, later a member of various jazz groups.

The conjunto trumpet soloists maintained the tradition of *sonero* improv-
isation with its characteristic Cuban phrasing, and some of these trumpet
players were also excellent jazz soloists or leads in jazz band brass sections.
José Gundín ("El Fiñe"), Alberto "Mazorca" Armenteros, and Manuel
Mirabal ("El Guajiro") were with Conjunto Casino. On bass, we have
Cristóbal Dobal and Luis "Pellejo" Rodríguez, who worked with the best
jazz bands and ensembles. Among the percussionists we should mention
Carlos "Patato" Valdés, who was later famous in the world of New York
Afro-Latin jazz. Pianist Yoyo Casteleiro worked with Conjunto Kubavana.
Another percussionist who also worked with different conjuntos was
Armando Peraza ("Mano de Plomo"), subsequently renowned in jazz with
George Shearing's group and with Cal Tjader.

Even though the conjuntos never played jazz and didn't include saxophones and trombones, in them the sonero styles of improvisation that later became characteristic in Latin jazz and salsa were developed. Among the trumpet players, "El Negro" Vivar, Alfredo "Chocolate" Armenteros, "El Guajiro" Mirabal, Jorge Varona, and others took this style to the top. Along with the charanga flutists, this style and phrasing was assimilated by saxophonists, such as Chombo Silva and Virgilio Vixama, who fused it with jazz improvisation. Even more so could this be said of the jazz pianists who worked in conjuntos or emerged from them; here it will suffice to mention Rolando Baró, Adolfo Pichardo, Bebo Valdés, Frank Emilio Flynn, Pedro Jústiz ("Peruchín"), Rubén González, Yoyo Casteleiro, and Samuel Téllez.

On the other hand, I must point out the contributions to our popular music made by Arsenio Rodríguez, whose influence will be decisive in the fusion styles that emerge from the Forties to the present. Arsenio kept the tres as a primary instrument (for accompaniment and solos) in his conjuntos, but the new format that he created has various implications that should be noted:

1) The consolidation of the piano as a primary harmonic instrument, in place of the guitar;

2) The addition of the conga to the bongo, a combination that will also become standard in Cuban jazz bands (only Sonora Matancera always used *pailas,* which came from the danzonera orchestras);

3) The presence of an arranger (necessary for the consolidation of a section of three or even four trumpets), who could integrate the typical jazz band harmonizations—although because they were dealing with a different music and format, arrangers would contribute their own innovations. Here El Niño Rivera will play an important role.

The combination of percussion instruments used from the Twenties to the Forties also changes. For example, traditional son has only the bongo and traditional danzón has timbales (or *pailas*), while the congas were limited to the separate world of rumba. Subsequently, Antonio Arcaño incorporates the conga in charanga and in danzón as well, shortly after Arsenio had done so in the realm of son. Meanwhile Cuban jazz bands, which in the beginning only employed the drum set, gradually added the conga and the bongo to perform the Cuban numbers, before the existence of a fusion music. Later

Machito and His Afro-Cubans will introduce the conga-timbales-bongo combination, without drums, in what will be the standard layout in later salsa ensembles. For his part, Dámaso Pérez Prado appears with two congas, a bongo, and pailas with a top cymbal. Of course, the following instruments should be added to these combinations: claves, güiro, and maracas, which come from the sonero sextet and are normally played by the singers, as well as the "cow-bell" *(cencerro)*, generally played by the *bongosero* or the *timbalero*.

Getting back to harmonic and orchestral aspects, in 1934 we see that the tres player Andrés Echeverría, better known as El Niño Rivera, has recently arrived in Havana from his birthplace, Pinar del Río, and is playing with sextets such as the Bolero, Gloria Habanera, and the legendary Sexteto Boloña. Coming from a sonero background, El Niño begins to assimilate other genres and musical styles, and he gets to know Arsenio Rodríguez as well as several jazz musicians and members of the future "feeling" movement, which will renovate Cuban *canción* and bolero. He works with the conjunto Los Astros, which René Álvarez conducted, and with the Modelo. He takes guitar and harmony classes with Vicente González Rubiera ("Guyún"), who had incorporated classic technique and contemporary harmony in popular Cuban guitar playing. This allows El Niño to bring more advanced harmonies to the tres, surpassing Arsenio as he creates a new scope for sound for this typical Cuban instrument. El Niño also studies orchestration with Félix Guerrero, listens to the best in jazz, and creates his own conjunto, Rey de Reyes, as he becomes involved in the "feeling" movement. In a recent book on this movement we read: "The rhythmic-harmonic renewal of *son* has two great innovators: Arsenio Rodríguez and El Niño Rivera. It could be said of El Niño that he represents the live bridge that connects feeling with *son*. It was his arrangements for *conjunto* and jazz band which brought the feeling style to dance *conjuntos* such as the Casino, Roberto Faz's and his own."[11]

Feeling was a movement centered on canción and bolero, but it also encompassed other genres and, surprisingly, shows a certain parallel with bebop, primarily an instrumental movement, which emerged in Harlem a few years before. Although bop (including in its sung variety, scat vocal) tends to convert the human voice into an instrument, which doesn't happen with feeling, the first two scat singers in Cuba came out of this movement: Dandy Crawford and Francisco Fellove, the creator of a scat style with Cuban phrasing. If it's possible to draw a parallel between what was happening in jazz (bop) and Cuban music in the 1940s, the point of reference cannot be our instrumental music and much less our jazz movement (what our jazz musicians did in that era was assimilate the language of bop). On the other hand, the feeling movement is one of renovation within Cuban music, which implies not only another style or a new form of making or "saying" but a change of attitude toward musical creation and interpretation. It was a call not only for "sentiment" (feeling) but for experimentation and innovation with respect to the different musical parameters and in song texts, as well as a rejection of conventionalism and the typical rhetorical lyrics.

A parallel between bop and feeling can be established in spite of the logical differences between a song movement and a predominantly instrumental one. Similarities exist in the anti-racist motivations of both, in their shared rejection of commercialism, and, musically, in an apparent affinity in the treatment of the melodic-harmonic material, which sometimes is manifested by an almost obsessive interest in "harmonic progressions." One time Charlie Parker said that bop basically consisted of "searching for the pretty notes." Of course bop was much more than that, and nobody knew it better than Bird. But taking this line for what it is, a nice metaphor, what else did the creators of bop and their feeling contemporaries do? Both opened the way to a higher expressivity in melodic phrases, unusual intervals, original sequences, richer harmonic progressions, and internal rhythm, all of which moved away from conventional practices, stale recipes, and the affectation of certain old styles and especially their more commercial versions.

For their part, Cuban jazz musicians incorporated into their repertoire the bop classics, sometimes orchestrated for band and obligatory in jam sessions. Numbers such as "Now's the Time," "Anthropology," "Salt Peanuts," "Minor Walk," "A Night in Tunisia," "Lady Bird," "Manteca," "Algo Bueno," "Yardbird Suite," "Robbin's Nest," "Ornithology," "Ool-Ya-Koo," and others from Bird, Dizzy, Monk, Bud Powell, Tadd Dameron, Gil Fuller, Johnny Mandel, and other boppers. There were also the Broadway and Tin Pan Alley numbers that jazz musicians have always incorporated step by step, turning them into standards according to preferences that change with the times—it's not uncommon for a jazz musician to revive an old, almost forgotten standard. The boppers, starting with Charlie Parker, chose their own standards, although usually only the harmonic structure of these standards would be preserved and the original melody discarded and replaced by a sinuous melodic line of their own invention. At that time, in the 1940s and early 1950s, Cuban jazz musicians adopted these same numbers, such as "How High the Moon," "Perdido," "I've Got Rhythm," "Indiana," "I'll Remember April," "Darn that Dream," "All the Things You Are," "Lady Be Good," "Out of Nowhere," "The Song Is You," "Cherokee," "Strike Up the Band," "Just Friends," "Tangerine," "Sweet Georgia Brown," "Lady in Red," "East of the Sun," "Stella by Starlight," and so many others, some of which had been around since the days of swing. A little later they would assimilate numbers from the cool style musicians, as well as those of George Shearing, the Lennie Tristano school, and those of Sonny Rollins, Horace Silver, Benny Golson, Art Blakey, and the rest of the great hard boppers.

Cuban jazz musicians such as Arturo O'Farrill, Bebo Valdés, and Armando Romeu wrote their own numbers, but even more important was the incorporation of tunes written by feeling composers into the repertoire of Cuban jazz musicians, some of whom were very much into the movement. In this way we begin to have our own standards, consisting of ballads, boleros, sones, and guarachas, and then mambos composed in the feeling style. Among these numbers are "Delirio," "Noche cubana," "Nuestra canción," and others by César Portillo de la Luz; "Quiéreme y verás," "Si me comprendieras," "Decídete," by José Antonio Méndez; "Tony y Jesusito" and "Mi ayer" by Ñico Rojas; "El jamaiquino" by Niño Rivera; and "Mango mangüé" by Francisco Fellove. And contrary to what had occurred in North America, Cuban jazz musicians were extending their repertoire of national numbers from the present to the past, incorporating into their "jazzed up" repertoire the most treasured numbers of our traditional song collection.

Fusion, Feeling, and the World of Jam Sessions

The fusion styles that have rejuvenated popular music so much in recent years (Latin jazz, jazz-rock, salsa, Latin rock, bugaloo, and so on) have their roots in the fusion that was taking place in Havana in the 1940s between jazz and different genres of Cuban music. Feeling is a crucial moment in this process, and involved in it we find, for example, three of the most important pianists in the history of jazz (particularly Latin jazz) in Cuba—Frank

Emilio Flynn, Bebo Valdés, and Peruchín Jústiz—who became involved in the fusion of jazz, son, danzón, and mambo. It is also within the feeling movement that a Cuban musician, Niño Rivera, attempts a fusion of bebop and our music, which can be seen in his arrangements for the conjunto Rey de Reyes. El Niño calls his new style Cubibop, and in it he would blend elements of son, danzón, mambo, feeling, and bebop. Cubibop emerges totally independently from New York Cubop, which will gain world fame and bring together performers such as Dizzy Gillespie, Mario Bauzá, Machito, Chano Pozo, and Charlie Parker. And in contrast to what occurs in New York, El Niño develops his new concepts based on the conjunto format, not that of the jazz band or the bop quintet, and utilizes vocal groups. The problem was that Cubibop, like Bebo Valdés's *batanga* rhythm afterward, lacked any promotion, or perhaps it didn't surface at the right time and place, and in fact it didn't even become popular on the island. It represented, nevertheless, a stimulating experience for the Cuban musicians who continued to work in this line of fusion.

The feeling movement was for two decades a subject of controversy, which seems to still exist. The very name "feeling" (sentiment), which the movement (and the style) acquired years after its inception, was a "lightning rod for trouble" for many who would object to it for selfish reasons or racial prejudices and label it "foreignizing." From our point of view, that same controversial name is further proof of its relationship with jazz. According to one of its originators, Luis Yáñez, the name came up when they heard the number "I gotta feeling" sung by Maxine Sullivan, at the home of saxophonist Bruno Guijarro, who was then with Alfredo Brito's orchestra. At about that time, as in previous decades, the musicians who would later create feeling would get jazz records by way of black American sailors, in the bars around the Havana docks, and preferably "race records."[12] Thanks to these contacts, the young musicians of feeling were introduced to Horace and Fletcher Henderson, Al Cooper, Chick Webb, Ella Fitzgerald, Jimmy Lunceford, Cab Calloway, Sarah Vaughan, Billy Eckstine, Nat King Cole, the Ink Spots, and the Mills Brothers. It's not surprising that around the same time, as critic Max Salazar informs us, Puerto Rican musicians living in New York's Barrio district had identical preferences: Nat King Cole, Billy Eckstine, Cab Calloway, the Ink Spots . . .[13]

A musician who had a particularly strong influence on feeling was Nat

King Cole, more as a singer than as a pianist, although he left his mark on various Cuban pianists, especially those who were involved in feeling. Nat King Cole, even after his more jazzy stage with his classic trio and as his career was in full swing (1950s), maintained a style, a resonance, a diction (in other words, we would say that it was a particular "way of saying") that were characteristic of the best feeling singers such as Miguel de Gonzalo, Pepe Reyes, Reinaldo Henríquez, and particularly Leonel Bravet, who when singing in English sang just like Nat King Cole. A special admirer of Nat Cole was José Antonio Méndez, the leading exponent of feeling along with César Portillo de la Luz. José Antonio started the routine of calling every musician or singer who impressed him "King," using the nickname as synonymous with quality, which in the long run resulted in everybody calling him "The King."

Like other varieties of our popular urban music, feeling was born in private homes or rooms of different *solares* or neighborhood houses, where *trovadores* and other musicians would get together for the now historic jam sessions ("descargas"). Of these meeting places the most well known today is the home of the trovadores Tirso and Angel Díaz in Callejón de Hammel, in the Cayo Hueso barrio and close to the strategic corner of Infanta and San Lázaro Streets. But the feeling group would meet at other barrio houses such as composer Rolando Gómez's (from the Yáñez and Gómez team) or Pepito Franco's (son of the historian José Luciano Franco), in the home of composer and singer Jorge Mazón (Marqués Gonzáles between Salud and Jesús Peregrino), and Eva and Estela Martiatu's (San José between Lucena and Marqués González). They also met in other neighborhoods such as Belén, Atarés, Párraga, Jesús del Monte, or El Cerro; for example, at the house of Aida Armenteros and "Papo" Morúa in Jesús del Monte, at Niño Rivera's house in Párraga, and at Silvia and Gloria Consuegra's (Infanta and Pedroso) in El Cerro.

Something noteworthy that up until now has passed unnoticed is that while the movement was given an English name, "feeling," the group itself "Cubanized" the term "jam session" by replacing it with *descarga*. For it was at the feeling sessions, starting in the late 1940s, that they began using the terms *descarga* and *descargar*. These terms would then be taken up by Cuban jazz musicians, who would in turn incorporate them into Latin jazz and salsa, after the series of records made by Israel "Cachao" López, Peruchín

Jústiz, Walfredito de los Reyes, and others under the common designation "Descargas." These albums were recorded between 1957 and 1959 and important Cuban jazz musicians such as Chico O'Farrill, Gustavo Más, Walfredito de los Reyes, Bebo Valdés, and José "Chombo" Silva, as well as those already mentioned, worked on them. From this, critics and Latin musicians from New York have inferred that the descarga as a concept and as a musical form (improvisations on Cuban themes and rhythm) originates with these records. They've even gone so far as to distinguish Cachao as "the creator of the *descarga.*" The truth is something quite different.

As a concept and as a form, a descarga was nothing more than a jam session, an informal, spontaneous musical encounter; the only difference was the Cuban expression. And this Cuban term was originally used as a verb, *descargar,* with the multiple meaning "to fight, to reproach, to talk too much, to chat, to talk about one's own problems, to let it out / get it off your chest." And it's more or less this sense of letting it all out or expressing what one feels inside that applies to music, and basically to musical improvisation or to the performance of any music that might contain an "air of improvisation," as Fernando Ortiz would say about our music and about all music of African descent.[14] That is, for us *descargar* meant to improvise in the sense that American jazz musicians say "to jam" or "to blow." But *descarga* as a substitute for the term jam session was an "invention" of the creators of feeling, from whom Cuban jazz musicians, many of whom were closely associated with feeling, took the term. All of this was ten years before the famous records by Cachao and his brilliant fellow musicians, and undoubtedly before the 1960s when the term *descarga* would mean for the Palmieris, Ray Barreto, or Tito Puente the equivalent of a session (or a number, or a record) with improvisations based on *montunos* and on Afro-Cuban rhythms.

I myself heard the word *descarga* more than once from José Antonio Méndez, Frank Emilio, César Portillo, Luis Yáñez, Francisco Fellove, and others in the late 1940s, and in those descargas feeling numbers were played for the first time, be they canciones, sones, or guarachas, and jazz improvisations would often be played on top of them. Shortly thereafter the term became common in jazz sessions, and at one jam session around 1950, when somebody from the audience requested a popular commercial number, the saxophonist Gustavo Más responded: "Sh**! I came to jam *(descargar)!*" With respect to improvisations to montunos and Afro-Cuban rhythmic patterns, they always existed in one form or another in all of our main genres, whether it be danzón, rumba, or son. Getting back to the historic 1956–59 recordings, it's not just a coincidence that two of them would be designated *Cuban Jam Sessions*, and that Cachao himself, who used the term *Descarga* for three albums, would record a fourth with the very descriptive title *Jam Session con Feeling*.[15]

Participating in the jam sessions of "los muchachos del feeling," as they were paternalistically called in the beginning, were first and foremost the trovadores José Antonio Méndez, César Portillo de la Luz, Jorge Mazón, Rosendo Ruiz Quevedo, Angel Díaz, Armando Peñalver, Roberto Jaramil, Enrique Pessino, Luis Yáñez, Rolando Gómez, Giraldo Piloto, and others such as the great guitarist and composer Ñico Rojas, whose contribution to the renewal of the guitar in popular Cuban music can only be compared to that of *el maestro* Guyún (Vicente González Rubiera). Other guitarists who followed this course of innovation were Elías Castillo, Manuel Herrera Dreke, and Octavio Sánchez ("Cotán"). Among the pianists associated with feeling and dedicated to the jam sessions (descargas) were Frank Emilio Flynn, Bebo Valdés, Isolina Carrillo, Enriqueta Almanza, Aida Diestro, Marcelino Guerra ("Rapindey"), El Niño Rivera, Vicentico Valdés (a singer in Vicente Viana's Cosmopolita orchestra at the time), Miguelito Valdés ("Mr. Babalú"), and Pacho Alonso. An immediate forerunner to these sessions were the "descargas de jazz y son" that the composer and pianist Isolina Carrillo would organize, in which Paulina Alvarez, Dandy Crawford, saxophonist Virgilio Vixama, and bassist Alfredo León also took part.[16]

Groups, Arrangers, and Singers

Among the arrangers who dedicated the most time to orchestrating feeling numbers, whether for records, radio, or TV, to accompany a singer, or in an instrumental version for a jazz band, we find several who are involved in jazz and "Latin jazz," such as Bebo Valdés, Peruchín Jústiz, El Niño Rivera, Félix Guerrero, René Hernández, and Chico O'Farrill. It's worth remembering that René Hernández was later, as a pianist and arranger, one of the pillars of the band of Machito and His Afro-Cubans, and that Chico O'Farrill included on his records three instrumentals based on numbers of feeling songwriters: "El jamaiquino" by El Niño Rivera, "Mango mangüé" by Francisco Fellove, and "Delirio" by César Portillo, with an extraordinary solo by trumpet player Art Farmer. But perhaps more telling than the work of the arrangers in the jazz-feeling relationship would be the mention of some of the groups created by musicians of the movement, which invariably included jazz numbers in their repertoires.

Some of the groups—or combos—of feeling included saxophone, trumpet, or electric guitar, in addition to piano, bass, drums, and Cuban percussion. The best known, and a precursor of the rest, was founded in 1946 and was called significantly Loquibambia Swing. Its leader was José Antonio Méndez, who played lead guitar, and it also featured Alberto Menéndez (second guitar), Eligio Valera and Leonel Bravet (singers), Oscar ("Kiko") González and then Isauro Hernández (bass), Frank Emilio Flynn (piano), and a little bit later Omara Portuondo, who distinguished herself as a singer of jazz and feeling. El Niño Rivera and guitarist Froylán Amézaga often worked with Loquibambia Swing, as did at times the trumpet player Edelburgo ("Wichy") Mercier. The group, like others organized by the members of the movement, would adopt different formats and personnel according to the circumstances because sometimes a few members would get steady work in nightclubs and on radio and others would substitute for them. For example, on one occasion I played in a group consisting of José Antonio Méndez (electric guitar), Rosendo Ruiz (acoustic guitar), Dandy Crawford (jazz singer), Luis Yáñez (vocalist and maracas), Francisco Fellove (vocalist and conga player), Isauro Hernández (bass), Frank Domínguez (piano, substituting for Frank Emilio), and Leonardo Acosta (alto sax, substituting for trumpet player Wichy Mercier).

In 1951 Frank Emilio Flynn formed his own group, which included two excellent singers: the great balladeer Pepe Reyes and the guarachero and *bibosero* Francisco Fellove, initiator of a typically Cuban scat; rounding out the group were José Antonio Méndez (guitar), Isauro Hernández (bass), and percussionists Augusto Barreto and Oliverio Casanova (half-brother of Miguelito Valdés). El Niño Rivera and his conjunto Rey de Reyes, employing three trumpets, would experiment with bop passages. One of the three was César "Piyú" Godínez, jazz improviser and high-note specialist, an ability that El Niño made use of by writing passages in which Piyú would play an octave above the lead voice. Another feeling group was Los Leoneles, led by the singer Leonel Bravet, "the Cuban Nat King Cole"; it included

Roberto Lausán (piano), Froylán Amézaga (guitar), Ernesto Cordobés (bass), and Alberto Menéndez (güiro and cencerro/cowbell). When Cordobés left the group, Froylán Amézaga switched to bass and the great composer César Portillo de la Luz came in as a guitarist. This group worked at the Sans Souci, Chez Merito (in the Hotel Presidente), Calypso Club, and Pigalle, a club that jazz musicians would frequent later on.

With feeling, a new way of singing emerges as well, closer to that of jazz singers than to the lyric and operatic voices of the 1920s and 1930s or to that of the soneros and first bolero singers, with their typically Cuban nasal voice. Although creators or trovadores of feeling sing or "say" their own songs, formidable performers appear in the 1940s, such as Berta Velázquez, Olga Rivero, Elena Burke, Pepe Reyes, Reinaldo Henríquez, Leonel Bravet, Moraima Secada, Aurelio Reinoso, Omara Portuondo, and the most consummate of all, Miguel de Gonzalo, one of the most versatile singers that Cuban popular music has produced. Other singers outside of the movement were attracted to it and contributed to its dissemination. I've already mentioned the bolero singer Roberto Faz; I should also mention Vicentico Valdés, who while living in New York was able to popularize many feeling numbers, as Fernando Alvarez, Pacho Alonso, and the multifaceted Beny Moré did on the island.

Along with feeling and within the movement itself vocal quartets proliferated, in which there is obviously a jazz influence in the way the voices are harmonized and in the phrasing that moves away from the traditional son duos and trios as well as the "Mexican style" trios, which were numerous ever since the success of Los Panchos. The only trio linked directly to feeling was that of the Rigual Brothers, which established itself successfully in Mexico, popularizing feeling classics such as "Contigo en la distancia" by Portillo de la Luz. The only Cuban group to precede feeling in its approximation to North American vocal groups was the Marvel Sisters trio, who performed in several Hollywood films and lived for a long time in the United States as the De Castro Sisters. Perhaps one of the secrets of the De Castro Sisters was that their arranger for years was Armando Romeu. Performing with Tito Puente in New York in 1952, the sisters recorded the first mambos to have English lyrics.

A number of vocal quartets were led by renowned songwriters such as Orlando de la Rosa, Facundo Rivero, and Bobby Collazo; from these normally mixed groups (two men and two women), as later from Aida Diestro's female quartet, came excellent soloists, all within the feeling style. With more jazz elements and a repertoire that included American numbers, the Cuban Pipers quartet was inspired primarily by groups such as the Ink Spots and the Mills Brothers. Gilberto Valdés led the group, and rounding it out were Regino Tellechea, Hermes Goicochea, and Tony Suárez Rocabruna, whose home on Lealtad Street was another center for jazz and feeling jam sessions. Various members of the Cuban Pipers were university students, including the pianist and arranger Virgilio "Yiyo" López. After this quartet split up, Gilberto Valdés (who was also a trombonist and a drummer) created in the 1950s a similar group, Los Cavaliers, which included himself, Regino Tellechea, Ramiro de la Cuesta, and Rafael "Felo" Brito, with Radamés Díaz joining later when Tellechea started his career as a soloist, one of the best to come out of Cuban jazz. The pianist and arranger for Los Cavaliers was Adolfo Pichardo, and the quartet performed at the Sans Souci, the Tropicana, the Hotel Sevilla, and the Las Vegas club, as well as on radio and television.

Mambo and Jazz

It's not easy to specify the most outstanding events of this decade, which is so decisive for jazz, Cuban popular music, and its confluences. Some important developments are: the peak of the conjuntos in Cuba; the continuity on the island of the great jazz bands, at cabarets and on radio stations; the formation of a school of Cuban arrangers who are fluent in the language of jazz; the emergence of the feeling movement; the formation of vocal quartets with a new harmonic concept; different combinations in Cuban percussion; the development of important Cuban jazz soloists, some of whom very quickly assimilate the language of bop; and experimentation that will lead to new rhythms and styles. In this last line, I must mention the revolution that mambo caused in Afro-Latin music.

The world arrival of mambo had as its indisputable central figure Dámaso Pérez Prado, even though his primacy is always called into question by those in Cuba who invoke the names of Arsenio Rodríguez, Orestes "Macho" López, and Israel "Cachao" López, and by those in the United States, or more specifically in New York City, who invoke the names of Machito, Tito Puente, and more recently Cachao López. The controversy began in the

1950s when Arsenio reclaimed paternity of the "new rhythm," which he had called "diablo"; in the 1960s and 1970s the danzón "Mambo" from 1937 or 1938 by Orestes López made a strong comeback. In New York Machito was seen as the creator of mambo, and on and on ad infinitum. The truth is that the mambo *rhythm,* as it was used by Orestes and then Israel López with the orchestra of Arcaño y sus Maravillas, and Arsenio with his conjunto, came from a syncopated motif that was very common among the tres players of the son conjuntos. But to speak of a new genre or modality, we should be able to indicate at least the presence of various "new" combined elements, such as: (1) rhythm or rhythmic patterns; (2) the melodic-harmonic dimension; (3) the orchestration style and the general scope of the sound, and (4) the form or structure. And in spite of all the influences that he may have received, Dámaso Pérez Prado is the one who best fits these requirements.[17]

Before leaving for Mexico, the country that would return mambo to Cuba in a boomerang effect, Dámaso Pérez Prado had attempted to "launch it" in Havana, where he recorded two demo numbers for a record company, "Mambo Caén" and "Só caballo." For these recordings, Pérez Prado used, among others, alto saxophonist Germán Lebatard and other musicians from his orchestra such as baritone saxophonist Osvaldo Urrutia, bassist Reinaldo Mercier, and the great guitarist Vicente González Rubiera ("Guyún"). But apparently, Cuba wasn't interested in any innovations, and the Matanzas musician had the same fate as El Niño Rivera and Bebo Valdés did a bit later. And yet, Peréz Prado had already laid down his fundamental ideas for mambo, as the Casino de la Playa recordings from the 1940s demonstrate with his arrangements and with singer Orlando Guerra ("Cascarita"). These recordings contain the same rhythmic figures and treatment of saxes and brass as his successful recordings in Mexico, where the *matancero* initially established himself with the help of bongo player Clemente "Chicho" Piquero, the actress and *vedette* Ninón Sevilla, and other friends.[18]

Above all, we must point out the work of Pérez Prado as an arranger, or better yet composer and arranger, and his clear influence on most other Cuban arrangers from then on. It has been repeated time and again that Pérez Prado achieved his particular style by mixing Cuban rhythms with the jazz format and orchestration, which in fact doesn't say anything. This argument, accepted or at least repeated by even the sharpest critics and historians of jazz and

Cuban music, covers up Pérez Prado's real achievements. Cuban musicology also errs when it endlessly repeats that mambo comes from danzón, or worse yet, from a supposed "danzón" complex. In the last analysis, Pérez Prado might have taken precisely *the last part* of the "new rhythm *danzón*" introduced by "Macho" López and originating from son, with the result that mambo is more an outgrowth of son than of danzón, even though it retains some characteristics of the latter in its use of timbales or *pailas* and some rhythmic figures. All of this becomes obvious in the slower variety *(mambo caén)*, while the more up-tempo one *(mambo batiri)* carries the stamp of rumba. Pérez Prado achieved in this way a great rhythmic variation, since two congas, a bongo, and pailas can assume different functions: the bongo, for example, can play the part of the *quinto* in the rumba, and the pailas with the addition of the top cymbal can take on the function of the drum set.

In addition to son, danzón, and rumba, there are elements of *guajira* and jazz in Dámaso's mambo. In this last aspect, however, it's false what critics from here and there maintain when they mechanically convert Pérez Prado into a follower of Stan Kenton and his arrangers, or of the tendencies of jazz arrangers at the time. A thorough analysis is not necessary to see essential differences between the bands of Kenton and Pérez Prado. At the very time when Kenton increases the trombone section to four and then five, Dámaso employs a single trombone, and this for effects such as pedals, rhythmic accentuations, or "growls" similar to the "jungle sounds" of Duke Ellington. The trumpet section does go to five, but the Cuban employs it constantly in passages in unison and in response to the saxophone section, which for its part is reduced from five to four, with the elimination of a tenor sax, and is also employed almost always in unison and in the low register. Of course there are exceptions, such as the duo of altos in "La chula linda" or the alto solo in "Mambo in Sax." Finally, the phrasing of trumpets and saxes responds completely to the polyrhythm that the percussion, bass, and piano establish.

In summary, the dominant tendency in jazz since the 1930s was to increasingly combine the sound of the bands, blending instruments from different sections—a tendency accelerated by Kenton, Pete Rugolo, and Bill Russo, and which will reach its peak in Gil Evans. Pérez Prado does the opposite and establishes different planes with two basic registers: one high register with the trumpets and one low one with the saxes, both in constant counterpoint and contrast, also making the function of the sections more *melodic-*

rhythmic than *melodic-harmonic*. The musical impact of Pérez Prado was felt immediately among Cuban arrangers, for whom the acceptance of mambo by the greater public had a liberating effect. Now even the most conservative promoters were prepared to accept more advanced orchestrations that they would have rejected shortly before, which encouraged Cuban arrangers to do what they wanted to more often.

The mark of Pérez Prado is present in original mambos by the best Cuban composers-arrangers of the period, such as Bebo Valdés ("Güempa," "Rareza del siglo," "Rimando el chachachá"), Peruchín Jústiz ("Mamey colorao," "España en llamas," "Semilla de marañón"), or Armando Romeu with his "Mambo a la Kenton," which provoked a long battle over authorship because Pérez Prado put it under his own name. It may have been precisely this number by Armando Romeu, who employs Kenton's theme song "Artistry in Rhythm," which confused the critics. Whatever the case, Armando was indeed influenced by Stan Kenton's band, many of whose numbers he transcribed for his own orchestra. And surely Stan Kenton, when he recorded "Viva Prado!" in tribute to the "King of Mambo," was not aware of the wrong that he was committing, while the number should have been titled "Viva Romeu!" or "Viva Armando!" And it's not surprising that Beny Moré, in whom Pérez Prado found the only singer who would be able to match and even surpass Cascarita, would use Dámaso's sound in his band, even though his three primary arrangers (Eduardo Cabrera, Peruchín, and Generoso Jiménez), like others mentioned before, followed their own paths in orchestration.

The same could be said of the course that mambo followed in New York, with the three most representative big bands of the "Age of Mambo" in that city: Machito, Tito Rodríguez, and Tito Puente, and arrangers such as Mario Bauzá, René Hernández, and Chico O'Farrill, among others. It should be remembered that in the experimental stage preceding the birth of mambo, the López brothers and Arsenio weren't the only ones experimenting in this sense, at the same time that Pérez Prado was; we also have El Niño Rivera, Bebo Valdés, and René Hernández, who took mambo from Havana directly to Machito's band. As I have pointed out in different articles, all of these musicians knew each other and mambo was something that "was in the air."[19]

With respect to the birth of Afro-Cuban jazz, which we address in the following chapter, *el maestro* Armando Romeu has explained in his own way what I'm trying to prove here: that so-called Latin jazz emerged not only in New York and as a product of the genius of a few musicians who were without a doubt exceptional, but also in Cuba, where the foundations of this fusion music were gradually being laid, over the course of decades, primarily between jazz on the one hand and son (and then mambo) on the other. On the topic, Romeu states:

> We [Cuban musicians] were not unaware of the technical-stylistic evolution of jazz in all of its parameters, and much less of Cuban music. From the very beginning excellent jazz musicians emerge in our country, who would perform in North American jazz bands as well as in the first [Cuban] ones, which started to emerge in the Twenties. These bands did not play exclusively jazz, but also incorporated Cuban rhythms, thus contributing to enrichment through the new acoustic, harmonic and expressive solutions that were required.
>
> This is an example of the interrelation between jazz and Cuban music. But this process didn't have an instant effect; it required time to internalize the essential aspects of both genres and stimulate its stylistic synthesis.[20]

Orquesta Cine-Teatro Prado, Havana

José Ramón Betancourt's Orquesta Cuba (Betancourt is the second from the left with tenor saxophone)

Moisés Simons (standing by piano), the composer of "The Peanut Vendor," with his jazz band in the Roof Garden of the Hotel Plaza, Havana, 1928

Armando Romeu Sr.'s
Orchestra

Thomas Aquinto (seated)
and his jazz band

Armando Clapera's Villa
Clara jazz band, Santa Clara

Cárdenas Jazz Band, led by
pianist José G. del Valle

Orchestra, Teatro Principal, Ciego de Ávila

Camagüey Jazz Band, led by Alberto Noriega de Varona

Pedro Stacholy (seated, first from left) and his jazz band Sagua, founded in 1914

Orquesta Bellamar, led by Armando Romeu Jr., in the Sans Souci cabaret, Havana, 1942

Armando Romeu, in the middle, surrounded by some musicians from his 1950s Tropicana cabaret orchestra. From left to right: Isidro Pérez (guitar), Pucho Escalante (trombone), Nilo Argudín (trumpet), Kiki Hernández (bass), Bebo Valdés (piano, wearing a hat), and Guillermo Barreto (drums).

Guitarist and bandleader Isidro Pérez

Pedro Chao

Tata Palau (tenor sax) and El Negro Vivar (trumpet)

Osvaldo ("Mosquifín") Urrutia

Benny Goodman and drummer
Guillermo Barreto at the Tropicana

Vinnie Tanno, invited by the Club Cubano de Jazz,
Havana, 1958

Guest trombonist Lon Norman and all-star orchestra
organized for a Club Cubano de Jazz concert

Gustavo Más and three U.S. musicians invited by the CCJ. Standing,
Gustavo and Eddie Miller; seated,
Vinnie Tanno and Lon Norman. At
the Hotel Nacional, Havana.

Eddie Miller

Roy Haynes (drums) and Richard
Davis (bass), in a jam session in
Havana, when they traveled there
(with pianist Jimmy Jones) as part of
Sarah Vaughan's trio

Kenny Drew, guest of the CCJ, in
Havana

Zoot Sims in Havana

Gustavo Más

Gustavo Más (tenor sax) accompanied by Chico O'Farrill on piano

Jimmy Casal, at the Havana 1900, the CCJ's main venue

Bill Miller, from Kenny Drew's quartet, with radio announcer and jazz critic Horacio Hernández

Pianist and arranger Don Ippolito at the Havana 1900

Bill Barron, from Philly Joe Jones's Sextet

The Bebo Valdés Trio, Roof Garden of Hotel Sevilla: Delia Bravo (vocalist), Orestes Urfé (bass), Guillermo Barreto (drums), and Bebo Valdés (piano)

The first Latin R&B group, the Hot Rockers, with Manolo Armesto on Cuban percussion

Philly Joe Jones in Havana, invited by CCJ, 1960

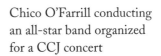

Chico O'Farrill conducting an all-star band organized for a CCJ concert

The Bodegón de Goyo, meeting place for Cuban jazz musicians, during a tribute to Chico O'Farrill and his wife Lupe Valero

Zoot Simms with Cuban friends at the Bodegón de Goyo

Luis Escalante (trumpet) with the Noneto of his brother, trombonist Pucho Escalante

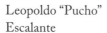

Leopoldo "Pucho" Escalante

Pucho Escalante's Noneto in recording session

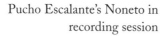

Guitarist, composer, and arranger Juanito Márquez

From left to right: Papito Hernández (bass), Chucho Valdés (piano), Emilio del Monte (drums), Leonardo Acosta (alto sax), and Carlos Emilio Morales (guitar), 1966

Pianist, composer, and arranger Rafael Somavilla

Ricardo Abreu ("Papín"), leader of group "Los Papines"

Arístides Soto ("Tata Güines")

Veteran pianists Felipe Dulzaides (left)
and Frank Emilio Flynn in the 1980s

Chucho Valdés (piano), Billy Cobham (drums), and
Carlos del Puerto (bass) in the EGREM recording
studios, 1978

Jorge Varona (trumpet),
Carlos Emilio Morales
(guitar), and Manolo
Armesto (bongos)

Chucho Valdés

Enrique Plá, Irakere's
drummer

Carlos Emilio Morales,
Irakere's guitarist

Carlos del Puerto

Juan Munguía, trumpet
player, Irakere

Arturo Sandoval

José Crego, "El Greco"

Singer and multi-instrumentalist Bobby Carcassés

Saxophone Quintet led by Manuel Valera (center)

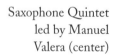

Germán Velazco

José Luis Cortés ("El Tosco"), currently the leader of N. G. La Banda

Ronnie Scott, a mainstay of the Jazz Plaza festivals in Havana

Jiri Stivin at the Jazz Plaza festival

Max Roach during his first appearance at a Jazz Plaza festival

Max Roach with the Irakere rhythm section

Gonzalo Rubalcaba

Chucho Valdés with the author, in front of the headquarters of the National Union of Writers and Artists of Cuba (UNEAC)

5

The Explosion of Cubop or Afro-Cuban Jazz

$\mathcal{W}$ hile jazz becomes firmly rooted and the revolutionary language of bop is taken up in 1940s Havana, at the same time that the feeling movement emerges and mambo takes over, in New York the onset of bop at the beginning of the decade prepares the way for the fusion explosion of bop with Afro-Cuban rhythms. Musicians from both countries participate and three Cuban artists achieve world renown: Frank Grillo ("Machito"), Mario Bauzá, and Luciano "Chano" Pozo. But these weren't the only Cuban musicians who contributed to the mutual fertilization between jazz and our popular music, since—as we have seen—it was a long process, which started almost at the beginning of the twentieth century.

A social development of great importance in the fusion of jazz and Afro-Cuban music, precisely in the city of New York, was the establishment of an important Puerto Rican community in the so-called Barrio Latino (later simply El Barrio). This community included many *boricua* (Puerto Rican) musicians who would play our rhythms just as well as they played their own (both already closely related) at the same time that they assimilated black American jazz. The exodus of Puerto Ricans to New York began in 1917, the year they were granted North American citizenship. The first immigrants settled in the Red Hook district, in Brooklyn, but the majority went to live in East Harlem, at that time the home of Jews and Italians and in the immediate vicinity of the most important African American ghetto in the country, which already in the 1930s was beginning to flourish as the world capital of jazz. The result was an impressive mixture of African Americans, Cubans, Puerto Ricans, Jews, and Italians, which characterizes the history of jazz, Latin jazz, and salsa.[1]

The first Cuban to organize an orchestra in New York was Vicente Sigler in 1926, and he gains popularity with "Rumba de medianoche," recorded by Victor.[2] In 1927 a very important Cuban musician settles in New York, the flutist and saxophonist Alberto Socarrás. The first flute solo recorded in the history of jazz took place on February 5, 1929, and the number that he performed was "Have You Ever Felt that Way," for Clarence Williams's QRS label. (Williams, as a musician, accompanied performers of the stature of Bessie Smith and Sidney Bechet, and led his own quintet, the Clarence Williams Blue Five.) A few months later, Socarrás and Puerto Rican trumpet player Augusto Coen, who also had a long and rewarding career, traveled the country with a show put on by American black performers, Lew Leslie's Blackbirds Revue. They subsequently worked with another black revue company, Rhapsody in Black, with which they traveled to Europe.[3]

In the second half of the 1920s there were Cuban and Puerto Rican bands in New York that were already playing for a growing Hispanic population. Another record company, Columbia, created a department of "Latin music" that Joseph La Calle directed and in whose studios Alberto Socarrás and pianist Nilo Menéndez worked, earning up to $150 a week. Menéndez was soon to become world famous for his song "Aquellos ojos verdes," composed in 1929. Vicente Sigler remained for ten years with his orchestra in luxury hotels such as the Waldorf Astoria, the McAlpin, and the Astor, and with him Caribbean musicians of the stature of Socarrás, Augusto Coen, and Cuban violinist Alberto Iznaga would work. Nilo Menéndez also formed his own orchestra, which would play Cuban shows in the Harlem Opera House, and in which Alberto Socarrás was featured as a soloist. It was around this time that two violinists and conductors of Catalan origin, Enric Madriguera and Xavier Cugat, were beginning their successful careers, with their mixture of South American, Mexican, and Caribbean rhythms.

Don Aspiazu and Alberto Socarrás

An important event for Cuban music in New York was the sold-out performance on April 26, 1930, at the Palace Theater on Broadway, of *Don Aspiazu's* orchestra, which incorporated for the first time before an American audience a rhythm section complete with typical Afro-Cuban instruments such as the conga (or *tumbadora*), the bongo, timbales (or *pailas*), maracas, claves, and güiro. No less important was the first performance of Eliseo Grenet's "Mama Inés" and Moisés Simons's "El Manisero," presented for the first time in 1927 in Havana and a classic of world popular music since 1930. A month later Don Aspiazu recorded "The Peanut Vendor" for RCA Victor, and by 1931 it became a national hit in the United States, in spite of the negative predictions of Guy Lombardo, the successful orchestra leader of "society" music. Another detractor of "El Manisero" was columnist Walter Winchell, who out of ignorance arrogantly stated that it was a plagiarism of Maurice Ravel's "Bolero," a work composed four years later and based on the Spanish bolero, which has nothing to do with the Cuban bolero.[4]

The singer who popularized "El Manisero" with Aspiazu was Antonio Machín, who had distinguished himself in Havana with a son quartet in which he was the leader and sang lead vocals, with Daniel Sánchez (second voice and guitar), Alejandro Rodríguez ("Mulatón") on tres, and Norberto Fabelo on trumpet. In addition, Machín was the first black to sing in Havana's Casino Nacional, with Aspiazu's orchestra. As I have already pointed out, Alfredo Brito did the arrangement of "El Manisero." Meanwhile, Moisés Simons's great hit was being popularized in Cuba and throughout Latin America by Rita Montaner. That same year Machín left Don Aspiazu's band to put his quartet back together in New York, acquiring trumpet player Remberto "El Chino" Lara from the same Aspiazu orchestra. And as luck or destiny would have it, "El Chino" Lara decided to return to Cuba and Machín had to replace him—although only for a brief period—with Mario Bauzá, who picked up the trumpet again for these circumstantial reasons, just as he had done in Havana with José A. Curbelo's jazz band. This sim-

ple occurrence would have incalculable consequences for Latin jazz. In turn
Machín would decide to leave for Europe and settle for good in Spain, where
he became an ambassador of Cuban music and is to this day an idol and a
legend. Meanwhile "El Manisero," like all great musical hits, followed its
own course. After conquering Broadway and spreading throughout the country on record, Hollywood would use it as a theme song in the movie *Cuban
Love Song,* in whose cast we find Jimmy Durante, Lupe Vélez, baritone
Lawrence Tibbett, and a Cuban jazz band, the Palau Brothers.

Don Aspiazu's orchestra went on tour throughout the United States in
1931, increasing his popularity even more. "Chiquito" Socarrás had replaced
Machín as a singer, but the real discovery was Marion Sunshine, who was
married to Eusebio Aspiazu (*Don* Antobal) and had been a successful music-
hall singer in the Twenties. Sunshine dedicated herself to providing English
lyrics for the biggest hits from Cuba and all of Latin America, and her versions were performed by the most important jazz vocalists. For good reason, Chick Webb called Marion Sunshine "The Rumba Lady."[5]

A prominent figure is the flute virtuoso Alberto Socarrás. Born in
Manzanillo in 1903, in the Twenties he worked in Havana in the orchestras
of the Campoamor, Cubano, and Fausto Theaters, as well as in hotels such as
the Plaza. After touring with the aforementioned black musical revue companies, in 1934 he organized a group that could play jazz and blues, as well as
all of the Cuban genres, which makes this great musician a precursor of the
fusion styles that will appear later in New York, not to mention his future
renown in the world of salsa. Socarrás's orchestra played jazz and blues at
places in Harlem such as Small's, Connie's Paradise, and the historic Cotton
Club and Savoy Ballroom, and Cuban music at the Club Cubanacán, the Park
Palace, the Campoamor Theater (of New York), and other centers of Afro-
Latin music. The following year (1935), the subsequently famous Puerto Rican
pianist Noro Morales joined him, although only for a short time. During
the 1930s Alberto Socarrás made a living playing jazz and Cuban music not
only with his own orchestra (particularly at the Cubanacán, opened especially
for him) but also playing with important jazz musicians and groups. In 1933,
for example, for a few months he was with the band headed by the great alto
saxophonist and multi-instrumentalist Benny Carter, who also hired the
boricua pianist Nicolás Rodríguez to replace Teddy Wilson, who would gain
well-deserved recognition with the groups of Benny Goodman.

In 1934 Socarrás also played with New Orleans clarinetist Albert Nicholas and saxophonist Gene Sedric in Sam Wooding's orchestra. Socarrás's own band performed a number of times at Harlem's Apollo Theater, alternating with the legendary blues singer Bessie Smith and participating in one of those famous "battle of the bands" with the orchestra of the unjustly forgotten Luis Russell, a black musician of Panamanian origin. From 1937 until 1940 Socarrás's orchestra played as the house band at the famous Cotton Club, where they alternated with three of jazz's greatest: Duke Ellington, Louis Armstrong, and Cab Calloway. John Storm Roberts says without reserve: "Socarrás in the 1930s and Machito in the 1940s were among the more experimental musicians of their time, and both men were Cuban."[6]

For his part, Don Aspiazu, who was ahead of Cugat in using American singers and lyrics in English for Cuban pieces or Spanish language songs in general, was a pioneer in a number of areas. The initiator of the first "invasion" of genuine Cuban music in the United States, he was also the first bandleader who dared to challenge the color barrier in Cuba as well as in the United States, before Benny Goodman or Artie Shaw. He holds the honorable distinction of having hired musicians for his orchestra regardless of whether they were white or black, which caused him innumerable problems. In 1932 he returned to Cuba after his triumphant European tour, and at the end of the decade he returned to New York, where he appeared at the Rainbow Room alternating with the Casa Loma orchestra, and he also made various recordings, one of which was an excellent original version of Joseph La Calle's "Amapola." John Storm Roberts has a clear understanding of the injustice committed against Don Aspiazu; his misfortunes and the oblivion to which he has been relegated in the United States as well as in Cuba are sometimes attributed to bad luck and at other times to his unwavering character in a hypocritical and hostile environment.

With respect to Don Aspiazu's character, trombonist Angel Mercado provides us with an invaluable account of his stay in Monte Carlo. In the cabaret where they were going to debut, Aspiazu realized that the name of his orchestra appeared in second place among the show's performers on the marquee. He immediately protested to the manager, stated that his orchestra was the main attraction and advised him that if they didn't put his name in the top spot, the orchestra wouldn't perform. The promoters had to give in. In the United States he faced other problems having to do with racism. One time in

St. Louis they informed him that the black musicians in his band would have to use the service elevator, to which he responded: "My band will use the main elevator, or I won't play here tonight." And his booking at the Rainbow Room ended abruptly when they demanded that he play only Cuban music and that he leave the American numbers to the Casa Loma Orchestra, the famous swing band that produced so many white jazz stars. Aspiazu flatly refused. Around 1940 he returned to Cuba, where in 1943 he died in obscurity. Referring precisely to the Rainbow Room incident, John Storm Roberts in his often-cited book dedicates an eloquent paragraph, which is worth reproducing:

> That incident underlines a more general problem faced by many Latin musicians in the States. Not unreasonably, American impresarios regarded them as Latin experts; but they were often at least as interested in creative fusions. Sammy Kiamie believes that "Don Aspiazú was 25 to 30 years ahead of his time in his styling." Raúl Aspiazu adds that his father always liked to play American music, and "always had it in mind that Cuban music would intermarry with American music, as it happened later with the mambo."[7]

This observation by Roberts turns out to be extremely important for all Latin American musicians and particularly for those of us from Cuba, who had to put up with the same attitude of promoters not only in the United States but also in Cuba, where American as well as Cuban impresarios— with few exceptions—only allowed Cubans to play American music in cabarets and tourist hotels (almost 100 percent North American tourism), and we're talking about a music that was almost always of the "society" or commercial type. In the record industry, however, there wasn't the slightest chance of recording anything that sounded like jazz.

The Latin Scene in New York

During the Thirties and Forties, dancers from Harlem would attend the Savoy Ballroom matinees to dance jazz and swing, and then at 7 P.M. would go to the Park Palace Ballroom at 110th Street and Fifth Avenue to dance rumbas, boleros, guarachas, and danzones. Among these dancers there were native Spanish speakers and African Americans who didn't understand the lyrics of the songs, but would dance as if they were Cubans or boricuas, and gradually a community was formed that enjoyed Caribbean music just as well as jazz. In the schools and on the streets of East Harlem they listened to rhythm and blues along with guarachas and *plenas*. This was the atmosphere that was developing uptown, ideal for fusion and interweaving. At the same time in the downtown luxury hotels and nightclubs frequented by white middle- and upper-class North Americans, Cuban and American music gradually started mixing, although at a more superficial level and with certain concessions to the preference for the latest popular songs and "cocktail music."[8]

By 1930 East Harlem had already developed a good part of the infrastructure for a flourishing musical scene of its own. The first great dance hall, the Golden Casino, was created in 1930 by a Puerto Rican civic association. Soon El Barrio had its own radio program on WABC, where local artists would appear. The Jewish theaters slowly became "Latinized": the Photoplay turned into the San José and the Mount Morris into the Campoamor. Then the Teatro Hispano emerged at 116th Street and Fifth Avenue, where Augusto Coen's band and Noro Morales's combo played. At the end of the decade the Cuban Casino club appeared. As we have seen, Cuban musicians began to arrive in the 1920s, and immigration went up in the following decade and particularly in the 1940s. Some of these musicians and singers are practically unknown today in Cuba, which is just as unfair and absurd as the ignorance in the United States with respect to others who remained in Havana. For example, Luis del Campo is considered one of the pioneers of Afro-Cuban jazz; he arrived in New York to work with Xavier Cugat, and then formed his own orchestra. In the 1940s he hired jazz musicians such as saxophonist Frankie Sokolow, trumpet player Red Rodney, and arranger Johnny Mandel, who also worked in Los Angeles with René Touzet. Today, not many people remember Luis del Campo because of his early death in 1950.

One generally underrated musician is the boricua pianist Joe Loco (José Estévez), who joined a number of groups and played alongside the best performers of jazz and Caribbean music. At the head of different groups, Joe Loco was known for playing American numbers with Cuban rhythms, an important aspect of the fusion process between both musical languages and interestingly the opposite of the approach taken by many Cuban jazz musicians, who would frequently perform numbers of our composers with a jazz rhythm. An important Cuban musician at this time was violinist Alberto Iznaga, whom we saw in Havana in the 1920s, and whose Siboney orchestra would play boleros, rumbas, and danzones in New York. At the end of the 1930s Iznaga was playing at the Half Moon, and in 1940 he formed a group that included a singer who would later become world famous: Machito. Another legendary musician who worked with Iznaga was Dizzy Gillespie.

At that time singer Miguelito Valdés and pianist Anselmo Sacasas, two of the founders of the Casino de la Playa, arrived from Cuba. Shortly thereafter pianist José Curbelo, who had helped found the Riverside orchestra in 1938 and emigrated the following year, reached New York. Two years later Curbelo would organize his own orchestra in New York, which would include two Puerto Rican musicians who would be among the most exceptional of the following decades: Tito Rodríguez and Tito Puente. Miguelito Valdés, who had sung in Cuba with María Teresa Vera's Sexteto Occidente and the Castro Brothers band before moving on to the Casino de la Playa, worked in the United States with Xavier Cugat, before going independent as a soloist. But the musician who would play a crucial role in this history had gone to the United States in 1932: Mario Bauzá.[9]

Mario Bauzá: The Father of Afro-Cuban Jazz

By 1940 the ground had been prepared for the emergence of the band that would revolutionize the jazz and Afro-Caribbean scene in New York, resulting in a consolidation of the fusion between the two types of music: we are referring to Machito and His Afro Cubans, which had Mario Bauzá as its driving force, arranger, saxophonist, trumpet player, and musical conductor. Another precursor whom we presented earlier, Alberto Socarrás, was enjoying a first for a black Cuban musician: His orchestra alternated with Glenn Miller's at the aristocratic Glenn Island Casino, in New Rochelle, where never before had a "colored" orchestra performed. After that, he appeared with equal success at the Beachcomber in Boston, and soon he would be renowned as one of the great flute virtuosos of any style. But the impact of Mario Bauzá on jazz and Afro-Latin music would be much greater in the long run.

There are many surprising things in Mario's musical life and work, but there are two that are almost unexplainable: first, the almost complete ignorance that has existed and still exists in Cuba about the one man in the last century who has done more to spread the legacy of our popular music throughout the world; and second, the late although definitive recognition that he received in the United States, where for four decades his name was subordinated to those of Machito and other musicians whose contributions, as important as they are, do not surpass those of Bauzá.

Among Mario's achievements we have, of course, his leading role in the creation of Afro-Cuban jazz, later called Cubop and finally Latin jazz; and as if that were not enough, Mario Bauzá launched the stellar careers of four performers who are today almost mythological in the history of one or both musical languages: Ella Fitzgerald, Dizzy Gillespie, Machito, and Chano Pozo. Although historiography and the critics have pointed out these facts, they haven't always related them. What unique talent did Mario Bauzá possess that allowed him to recognize a great figure almost immediately? For it was on his urging that Chick Webb, skeptical at first, added Ella Fitzgerald to his band. He was the one who kept on insisting that Cab Calloway accept the eccentric Dizzy as a trumpet soloist. Mario was also the one who brought his brother-in-law Frank Grillo to New York and put him at the head of a band that he himself had organized, a band that made history. And finally, it was his weighty opinion that immediately convinced Dizzy Gillespie to hire Chano Pozo, a decision that led to one of the great moments in jazz history.

In spite of all this and his talents as an instrumentalist, composer, and arranger, Mario stayed behind the scenes for decades, respected and admired by musicians, but scarcely given any serious attention by most critics, disc jockeys, promoters, or musicologists. The only explanation for this second inexplicable fact is the mediocrity of many critics, disc jockeys, and others who were unable to appreciate the greatness of performers such as Charlie Parker, John Coltrane, or Thelonious Monk in their day, at the historic moment in which they arrived to revolutionize the U.S. musical scene. But there is also another reason: Mario Bauzá was an incredibly modest and generous person, always ready to launch someone's career or help anybody who was talented and needed a hand, but unwilling to engage in "self-adulation," reluctant to be in the spotlight, and not at all interested in a fame that didn't always come to the best and which tended to be deceiving and ephemeral.

There is no better example of Mario's modesty and good judgment than his response to the question of what were the most successful and important events of his career. He cited three: (1) when he graduated from the conservatory in Havana as one of the most distinguished students; (2) when Chick

Webb put him in charge of conducting his orchestra in 1934, and (3) when Machito's band was accepted on Broadway, that is, when they succeeded in breaking the racial barrier between blacks and whites. But history will say something else in response to the question of Mario Bauzá's numerous successes, such as: the composition of "Tanga," considered the first Afro-Cuban jazz piece, in 1943; his participation in four of the great jazz bands of all time (Chick Webb, Don Redman, Fletcher Henderson, and Cab Calloway); the recordings of the 1940s with Charlie Parker, Flip Phillips, Buddy Rich, and other jazz greats with Machito's band and arrangements by Mario, John Bartee, and Chico O'Farrill; the award for his contributions to art and culture that Mario received in 1984 from the mayor of New York City; the formation in 1986 of the "Mario Bauzá and his Afro-Cuban Jazz Concert Orchestra"; the tribute in his honor in 1991 at Symphony Space, New York, with a performance by his band and special guests such as Dizzy Gillespie, or the success of his latest LPs such as *Tanga* and *My Time Is Now*.[10] In reality Mario enjoyed many achievements in his prolific musical career.

But sometimes legends are built around great individuals, and one such myth is that Mario, after arriving in New York as a saxophonist, learned to play the trumpet in only fifteen days, and shortly thereafter was the lead trumpet in Chick Webb's band. According to the legend, when Remberto "El Chino" Lara returned to Cuba, Antonio Machín asked Mario if he could find a substitute and he responded: "Get me a trumpet and see if I can play it." And in fifteen days he was playing it. Of course it should be understood that Mario has contributed to the legend with his silence; the truth is that Mario had learned to play the trumpet in Havana when he was working in José Curbelo's band at the Montmartre cabaret, but nevertheless, he did learn to play it in record time. The mystery was whether he did so only by using a method or whether he had learned at least the basics of the instrument (embouchure, positions) with another musician. The answer is that Mario learned the "ABCs" of the trumpet with Lázaro Herrera, who was from Ignacio Piñeiro's Sexteto Nacional and one of the sonero trumpet players par excellence.[11]

Two other questions about Mario Bauzá that haven't been fully explored are: first, why he decided to leave Cuba in 1930 after having visited New York for the first time in 1926, and second, why he never returned to the island after 1957. On the first point there is some evidence. Mario left Cuba not because he was "fascinated" by New York on his first visit but rather as a rejection of the racism that was prevalent on the island, particularly in the world of the arts. One might ask: "And the United States isn't racist?" Of course it is, but the exposure of racism in the long run led America on a different course than that of Cuba or Brazil, where racism has always been more subtle, paternalistic, and hypocritical. Getting to know New York in 1926, Mario discovered that blacks had their own musical circuit, with nightclubs, theaters, records, and radio stations or programs.

In Havana at this time, and for decades later as well, the best jobs available for a musician were in hotels and cabarets dedicated to North American tourism, where the conductors and the majority of the musicians had to be white. More than once Mario heard the statement "What a shame that you're black!" as a pretext to deny him a job. If he joined José Curbelo's group it was because José was one of the exceptional individuals, like Justo Aspiazu and, let's face it, also Xavier Cugat, whose sins didn't include that of racism, as Mario Bauzá himself stated. Aware of similar cases—Chano Pozo's among them—Mario Bauzá, even though he was one of the best musicians in Curbelo's band, could no longer stand being referred to by the promoters and their followers as the orchestra's *negrito*.[12]

There remains another unknown: Why didn't Mario ever return to Cuba after the visit that he and Machito made to Havana in the 1950s? Mario told me that in the 1960s while he was in Peru on a South American tour that he attempted to travel to Havana when he learned of the seriousness of his adoptive mother's health. He couldn't return because he was denied a Cuban visa. Since then he swore that he would never go back to his country.[13] A case such as this reflects the incomprehensible paradox of a country that on the one hand shows so much pride in its cultural heritage but on the other has at times shown an extreme insensitivity to individuals who have done so much for national culture and art. That such outstanding musicians as, for example, Arsenio Rodríguez, Miguelito Valdés, Machito, and Mario Bauzá, have never been invited to Cuba is as unexplainable as it is ridiculous that a ban on music and even the simple mention of names of Cuban performers who left the country after 1959 was put into effect.

All of this has had something to do with the misunderstanding that exists on the island about Mario Bauzá, the man and his work. But there are other reasons, for in the heyday of Machito and His Afro-Cubans (1940s and '50s) very little of his music and his renown reached the island. In my opinion, a factor contributing to the obscurity of this band was the deficient distribution of the first labels (except Decca) on which Machito and Mario Bauzá recorded, as opposed to others such as RCA Victor, which helped bring about the immediate success of Pérez Prado, for example. In addition, one has to keep in mind the proliferation in Cuba of orchestras, charangas, and conjuntos of great popularity at this time: Palau Brothers, Riverside, Beny Moré, Casino de la Playa, Julio Cueva, Conjunto Casino, Sonora Matancera, Orquesta América, Aragón, Melodías del 40, and so forth. Many of them increased their popularity thanks to national radio or North American or Cuban labels, particularly Panart.

What did exist uninterrupted until the 1950s was the contact between Cuban musicians in Havana and New York. Miguelito Valdés would visit Havana often, for example, and Machito as well as Tito Puente and other Latin bandleaders living in New York would frequently hire musicians from Havana. A common connection for these conductors was Armando Romeu, who for more than twenty years as leader of the Tropicana orchestra would receive frequent visits from New York colleagues coming to ask him for advice, as they did in New York with Mario Bauzá.[14] Another result of these contacts among musicians was that some Cuban orchestras would popularize Machito's numbers such as "Sopa de pichón" and "Rumbantela." It's worth remembering here that there didn't always exist this type of open collaboration between Cuban and Puerto Rican bandleaders. Mario Bauzá has spoken out about his confrontation with Cuban bandleaders in New York such as Juanito Sanabria, Eddie Le Baron, Chiquito Socarrás, Panchito Riset, Enric Madriguera, and Rafael Audinot who considered themselves discriminated against by the U.S. Association of Musicians. Mario accused them in turn of being racist, for they wouldn't hire black Cuban or Puerto Rican musicians for their orchestras under any circumstances.[15]

With the severing of ties between Havana and New York there suddenly occurred an almost complete isolation, and only recently has anything been heard or written about the great Cuban musicians living in New York, and particularly about the top creator of Afro-Cuban jazz, Mario Bauzá. This has been influenced by factors such as the trips abroad by Cuban orchestras, research and reporting by musicologists and journalists, and the work of a few informed disc jockeys. But we are always left with the crucial question: Was Mario Bauzá really the creator of Afro-Cuban jazz, Cubop, or Latin jazz? I'm convinced that no one creates anything on one's own, and that—as we have been demonstrating up to this point—in general everything arises from a process in which there certainly could have been a primary figure, as is the case here with Mario Bauzá.

Max Salazar has done the most to recover the figure of Mario Bauzá, which is entirely justified, but perhaps he goes too far when he states with almost mathematical precision that Afro-Cuban jazz was created on the night of Monday, May 28, 1943, in the La Conga cabaret, at the moment in which the basic idea of "Tanga" arose.[16] For the most part we accept Salazar's statement, although to me there is something more important than the genesis of "Tanga" in attributing the paternity of Afro-Cuban jazz to Mario Bauzá. That is, Mario Bauzá was just about the only one who for years strove consciously and tenaciously to fuse jazz and Afro-Cuban music, who had a deep understanding of both languages and the necessary patience to successfully carry out his plan. We should remember that when Mario left Cab Calloway's band he would often get together with Dizzy Gillespie to search for a way to achieve this productive fusion, which would revitalize both types of music. We can therefore say that Afro-Cuban jazz "was born" with the recording of "Tanga" (at least officially) in 1943, but since the beginning of the 1930s it had been germinating in the mind of various musicians, particularly in that of its main creator, Mario Bauzá.

Important Dates in the Life of Mario Bauzá

1911   On April 28 Mario Bauzá is born in the Cayo Hueso barrio of Havana.

1926   He travels to New York with the danzonera orchestra of Antonio María Romeu, with whom he records a number of danzones.

1927   He graduates from the Conservatorio Municipal de la Habana, turns down a scholarship to study in Milan, Italy, and begins to play the bass clarinet in the Havana Philharmonic. He also works with José A. Curbelo's jazz band.

1928   Together with Francisco Grillo (Machito) he forms a group.

1929   He works with Froylán Maya's jazz band, Los Diplomáticos.

1930   He returns to New York, for good this time, and records with Antonio Machín's Cuarteto.

1931   He joins Noble Sissle's orchestra as an alto saxophonist.

1932   Mario joins Chick Webb's band as first trumpet.

1933   He is named the musical director of Chick Webb's band, with which he will remain until 1937.

1935   After seeing an amateur contest at the Apollo Theater in Harlem, won by the young Ella Fitzgerald, Mario brings her in to Chick Webb's band. When Webb dies some years later, Ella will lead the band for a period of time.

1936   Bauzá travels to Cuba and returns to New York married to Estela Grillo, Machito's sister.

1937–39 Mario Bauzá joins the jazz bands of Don Redman and Fletcher Henderson.

1938   He joins Cab Calloway's band, and convinces Cab to hire the young trumpet player Dizzy Gillespie.

1940   He leaves Calloway's band to form, together with his brother-in-law Frank Grillo, the band Machito and His Afro-Cubans.

1943   Mario Bauzá composes "Tanga," the classic of classics in Afro-Cuban jazz.

1948   The height of Cubop; Mario writes "Cubop City."

1950   Mario composes "Mambo Inn" with René Hernández and Bobby Woodlen; it is recorded by Count Basie and becomes a classic.

1970s   Mario creates new orchestrations for Machito's band and brings in soloists such as Cachao and Chocolate Armenteros.

1975   The album *Afro-Cuban Jazz Moods* is recorded, with new arrangements by Chico O'Farrill and with Dizzy Gillespie as a soloist. This same year Mario Bauzá separates from Machito's band after twenty-five years together. The singer Graciela also leaves the band.

1984   Frank Grillo (Machito) dies in London, on a European tour. Mario Bauzá takes part in the tribute that the city of New York organizes for Machito. On November 27 Mario Bauzá receives the City of New York Mayor's Award of Honor for Arts and Culture.

1986   Mario and Graciela record the album *Afro-Cuban Jazz,* which includes musicians such as Paquito D'Rivera, José Fajardo, and

Daniel Ponce. He also organizes his Afro-Cuban Jazz Concert Orchestra.

1991   Another tribute to Mario Bauzá for his 80th birthday. His new orchestra performs in New York's Symphony Space, with Dizzy Gillespie.

1992   Mario records his album *My Time Is Now*.

1993   On July 11 Mario Bauzá dies at 82 years of age, in his house in New York.[17]

Machito Arrives on the Scene

Frank Grillo, Machito, was, together with Mario Bauzá, the Cuban who had the biggest influence on different currents of popular music in the United States, from jazz and rhythm and blues to salsa. Unfortunately, he is hardly known in his own country, as is the case with Mario Bauzá, Alberto Socarrás, Alberto Iznaga, José Curbelo, Don Aspiazu, and other artists mentioned here who are known only by a small group of musicians and enthusiasts of our music. Nevertheless, jazz historians such as Marshall Stearns in the United States and Joachim E. Berendt in Europe have called him "the Count Basie of Afro-Latin music."[18] And it's undeniable that Machito led for more than forty years the best and most important orchestra of Afro-Cuban (or Afro-Antillean or Latin) music in the United States, and with it he traveled the whole world, from Europe to Japan to Latin America, with the very regrettable exception of Cuba, his native country.

Francisco Grillo was born in Marianao (Havana) on December 3, 1909, that is, the day of Santa Bárbara or the *orisha* Changó, or more precisely on the eve, when the most important celebration of Afro-Cuban worship takes place. Starting in 1928 Machito began to play in nationally recognized sonero groups: María Teresa Vera's Sexteto Occidente; the Conjunto Agabama, in which he sang second voice along with Abelardo Barroso; the Pic-Nik conjunto, which he also formed with Barroso; the Sexteto Universo; and Ignacio Piñeiro's Sexteto Nacional, with which he performed in the Montmartre cabaret. When the new danzonete genre arrived from Matanzas, Machito was the first to sing it in Havana, with the orchestra of Gerardo Pérez ("Calabaza") in the dance hall of the Sport Antillano society (Zanja and Belascoaín). It was during this period of his life that

Machito met Mario Bauzá, who, already living in New York since 1930, helped Machito to emigrate in 1937.

Machito sang in numerous ensembles, such as Estrellas Habaneras, the orchestra of Alfredito Valdés (brother of Vicentico) at the Habana Madrid cabaret, alternating with the then Septeto Anacaona in which his sister Graciela sang; with the Cuarteto Caney; the Conjunto Moderno (with which he recorded in 1938 for Decca and Victor); the Hatuey orchestra; and the orchestra of the trumpet player Augusto Coen. His association in 1939 with violinist Alberto Iznaga's Siboney orchestra was more stable. He recorded with the Puerto Rican pianist Noro Morales, already well known in the Hispanic and North American circles of New York. He also recorded eight pieces, as singer and maraca player, with Xavier Cugat's orchestra, who was at that time looking for more Cuban and boricua musicians to give more authenticity to the Latin American mélange of his first era.[19]

Machito's beginnings in New York were therefore quite promising. In the "Latin world" Miguelito Valdés, "Mr. Babalú," was already a star and together with Machito was one of the singers who carried the Afro-Cuban sound to the United States. Also in the New York metropolis, with its growing Spanish-speaking community, there were a number of outstanding orchestras and groups such as those of Alberto Socarrás, Johnny Rodríguez, Pupi Campo, Noro Morales, José Curbelo, Alberto Iznaga, Anselmo Sacasas, and many others, Cuban and Puerto Rican. These ensembles prepared the way for the appearance of the Afro-Cubans, although some maintained a style and a sound that would be more characteristic of the trend that has been called "Latin society" (a la Madriguera or Cugat). These orchestras performed in grand hotels and exclusive cabarets such as the Chateau Madrid, Fontainebleau, or Caesar's Palace, but they are important because of the Caribbean repertoire that they introduced and because of the excellent musicians that came out of them.

Machito and Mario Bauzá exchanged ideas and worked on plans to form a Cuban music band in New York; Mario's experience in jazz would be combined with Machito's expertise in all genres of Afro-Cuban music, and in 1940 the dream would come true in the form of Machito and His Afro-Cubans, whose debut was scheduled for the cabaret La Conga. But their debut had to be postponed, and José Curbelo's band performed in their place. On this occasion the violinist (and arranger) Alberto Iznaga was to perform with the Afro-Cubans, but with the postponement, Iznaga and Bauzá continued in their respective jobs. Finally they were given another opportunity, most of the musicians were brought back together, and Machito debuted at La Conga on December 20, 1940. This first band of Machito's featured, among others, Mario Bauzá and Bobby Woodlen (trumpets), Johnny Nieto and José "Pin" Madera (saxes), Frank Gilberto Ayala (piano), Julio Andino (contrabass), Tony Escollés (timbales), Bilingüe (bongo), and Machito (vocals and maracas). Mario Bauzá and John Bartee, also an arranger for Cab Calloway, were in charge of the arrangements.

The New Afro-Cuban Sound

Machito and His Afro-Cubans caught on quickly, and what was so surprising was that they did so playing for a wide range of audiences: black and white, Latin and American, demanding jazz fans as well as the most demanding dancers of Afro-Cuban rhythms. John Storm Roberts considers the formation of Machito's band "the single most important event of the decade for Latin music's development as an autonomous U.S. substyle."[20] The early success of Frank Grillo as a songwriter was largely due to hits such as "La paella" and "Sopa y pichón," but he also recorded pieces written by other Cuban composers for Decca, such as "Tingo talango" (by Julio Cueva), "Llora timbero" and "Nagüe" (by Chano Pozo), "Chacumbele," "Que vengan los rumberos," and "El niche." Until 1942 Machito's repertoire was strictly Cuban; experimentation with jazz begins with "Tanga" in 1943. Just as we have seen in the bands of this decade and the previous one in Havana, Machito's band started out with two or three trumpets and three or four saxes, and gradually the sections became larger. In the same way, the rhythm section grew, and a key moment in this process was the addition of Carlos Vidal on conga, who along with José Mangual on bongo for many years formed the "rhythmic engine" of Machito's formidable orchestral apparatus.

The orchestra maintained basic structures in sones, guarachas, and other Cuban genres, with rhythms, vocal improvisations, and chorus refrains, piano style in octavas and montunos, *guajeos,* and mambos. The basic structure of the numbers continued to be theme-montuno—improvisation (vocal and instrumental)—refrain-mambo. At the same time, Mario Bauzá, with his valuable collaborator John Bartee, incorporated jazz concepts into the harmonic and orchestral aspects. The band soon had a greater harmonic density, with three trumpets, two trombones, and five saxophones, just like what happened in Cuba with the bands of Armando Romeu, the Bellamar, Isidro Pérez, the Castro Brothers, and others. The only difference was that some of Machito's jazz soloists were American. In this way jazz and Afro-Antillian elements were gradually fusing, just as they were in Havana. Since the music of Machito and Mario Bauzá was blacker than the other bands that performed in New York, and also more vibrant and advanced, its relationship with jazz and its musicians was more natural and spontaneous.

After the band's performances at La Conga (Fifty-third between Seventh Avenue and Broadway), Machito and His Afro-Cubans played at the Park Plaza (110th and Fifth Avenue), at the Beachcomber (Broadway), at the Concord hotel, at jazz clubs such as the Royal Roost, Bop City, Birdland (all in the vicinity of Fifty-second and Broadway), at Harlem's Savoy, and at Blen Blen, named by Machito after the title of Chano Pozo's number. They played for all types of audiences with the same success, and they were back and forth between luxury hotels and cabarets, jazz clubs downtown and in Harlem, and the favorite spots of the Spanish-speaking community. But the indisputable center for Machito and His Afro-Cubans was the already historic Palladium Ballroom, at Broadway and Fifty-third, a dance hall with room for a thousand couples in which the band played almost without interruption from 1947 to 1966, and which turned out to be the center of Afro-Latin music in New York for this entire period.

After the first hits, recorded for Decca in 1941, the band recorded again, this time accompanying Miguelito Valdés. Machito and Mario Bauzá also made some valuable personnel acquisitions for the Afro-Cubans, including the multifaceted Tito Puente on timbales and the pianist Joe Loco. This created an exceptional rhythmic combination, which included three virtuosos—Tito Puente, Carlos Vidal, and José Mangual—in a percussion section that was the first of its kind in New York. Just as—if not more—important for the evolution of the Afro-Cubans was the acquisition of the pianist and arranger René Hernández (replacing Joe Loco), who popularized in a definitive way the Cuban piano style in the United States and influenced such notable jazz pianists as George Shearing.[21] Aside from his role as a pianist, René Hernández became one of the most important Afro-Latin jazz arrangers, and his and Bobby Woodlen's composition "Killer Joe" was the one that gave the bold impresario Norman Granz the idea of bringing together the best jazz soloists of the era to perform with Machito and Mario's band.

Joining the orchestra in 1943 was the singer Graciela Pérez, Machito's sister, who shortly before had performed with the female orchestra Anacaona and arrived in New York after a European tour. From 1943 to 1947 the Afro-Cubans recorded for the Clef, Coda, and Continental labels, and traveled to Los Angeles, Miami, and other U.S. cities with large Latin populations. These were the years of consolidation for Machito and His Afro-Cubans, even though there were other excellent Afro-Latin orchestras, most of them led by Cubans and Puerto Ricans. Among these orchestras we should remember the one led by Marcelino Guerra ("Rapindey"). He arrived in the United States in 1945 as an arranger for Robbins Music Company and then formed his band, which recorded for the Verne label and in which various jazz soloists played, such as trumpeter Doc Cheatham. Rapindey's band alternated at the Palladium with Machito, Tito Puente, and others.

A Cuban who had a strange but successful career in the United States was René Touzet, primarily as a composer of romantic songs, but also as a conductor of orchestras and combos. The composer of "No te importe saber" ("Let Me Love You Tonight") was involved in jazz, particularly in 1946 when he led a group in the Avedon Ballroom in Los Angeles; he hired drummer Jackie Mills who in turn brought in trumpet player Pete Candoli, alto saxophonist Art Pepper, and arranger Johnny Mandel, who according to Marshall Stearns was the composer of the first "Latin blues," titled "Barbados," a subsequent classic of Bird's, which explains why many mistakenly considered Charlie Parker to be the composer of the number. Mandel continued to be involved in Afro-Latin jazz, worked in 1949 with Luis del Campo, and is one of the musicians who is credited with having coined the term "Cubop."[22]

José Curbelo arrived in New York in 1939 and worked for a time with Xavier Cugat. He formed his own orchestra in 1942, with two trumpets, three saxes, piano, bass, and timbales, with the boricua Polito Galíndez as singer. He alternated with Machito at La Conga and worked at various luxury hotels, as well as at cabarets on the Broadway circuit. In 1946 three top percussionists played with Curbelo: Tito Puente on timbales, Carlos Vidal on conga, and "El Chino" Pozo (no relation to "Chano" Pozo) on bongo, and the orchestra's singer was none other than Tito Rodríguez. From that year to 1947 Curbelo made recordings that are a good example of the mixture of different Cuban genres with calypso, samba, and boogie-woogie. Later, José Curbelo formed a quintet that included tenor saxophonist Al Cohn, one of the great *cool* style saxophonists.[23]

Machito, Bauzá, Dizzy, and Chano Pozo

A number of bop creators such as Dizzy Gillespie, Bud Powell, Charlie Parker, and drummers Max Roach, Kenny Clarke, and Art Blakey were interested from the beginning in Afro-Cuban music, just as—among others—Cab Calloway and Duke Ellington had been before them, and as the trumpet player Fats Navarro, tenor saxophonist Sonny Rollins, pianist Horace Silver, and arrangers such as Tadd Dameron, Johnny Mandel, and many more would do after them. The focal point of this music in New York would be more or less wherever Machito and His Afro-Cubans were playing. Dizzy Gillespie was one of the first to participate in Cuban descargas along with Mario Bauzá, Noro Morales, and others, and he also worked one or two weeks with Alberto Iznaga's orchestra. When Machito's band was formed, Dizzy would often go to the Park Plaza not only to visit his old friend Mario Bauzá but also to sit in and play with the band's musicians. Drummer Kenny Clarke, the man who revolutionized the way his instrument was played at the outset of bop, has mentioned his frequent visits to the Palladium to play with Latin bands, among them Machito's. Elsewhere I have suggested that a large part of Clarke's innovative focus was the result of his assimilation of the rhythms and sound of Afro-Cuban percussion.[24] Other jazz musicians would frequent the Palladium, and the famous photo in which a strange coincidence has Charlie Parker and Stan Getz sharing a table at a nightclub may be explained by the presence of Machito and Mario Bauzá along with them.

The scene and the conditions were prepared for Luciano "Chano" Pozo's arrival in New York, at the height of mambo and Afro-Latin music in 1947. Machito had met Chano in Havana when the latter was only eight years old. Miguelito Valdés in the United States and Rita Montaner in Cuba encouraged him to continue in New York his successful career as a composer, *tamborero*, singer, and rumba dancer, which had reached its peak in Havana. Finally, Mario Bauzá put him in contact with Dizzy Gillespie, who not only was organizing the best bop jazz band of all time but also was looking for the right percussionist to make Cu-Bop a reality. The history of Chano Pozo has already become legend and is the object of innumerable polemics, which we're not going to cover here. The one who has probably done the best job of telling the life and musical legacy of Chano has been Max Salazar, in a number of articles for the magazine *Latin Beat.*[25]

Gillespie and Pozo played Carnegie Hall in 1947 performing the *Afro-Cuban Drum Suite,* and their collaboration has been preserved in the recordings of other classics: "Manteca," "Tin Tin Deo," and "Algo Bueno" (or "Woodyin' You"), both by Chano and Dizzy, and other numbers such as "Cool Breeze," although the finest example of Chano's artistic mastery is probably found in the Afro-Cuban jazz suite *Cubano Be, Cubano Bop,* composed by George Russell. Since then much has been written about Chano Pozo, particularly because of his tragic death, and just as much in Cuba as in the United States erroneous and even absurd versions of his life and death have been repeated ad nauseam; the same character has been presented alternatively as "hero" and "antihero." One example is the version that Chano had revealed "toques secretos" of the Afro-Cuban society *abakuá.* This is impossible by the very rules of that society—which in addition didn't exist in New York at that time—and because Cuban tamboreros who belong to the society have denied it and continue showing their admiration for Chano. There is another story, coming this time from *santería,* according to which Chano broke a promise to the orisha Changó, but this is limited to a strictly religious plane. As for the true version, about drugs and personal resentments, I think it has been told with precision in the aforementioned work of Max Salazar, who relied on the accounts of Machito, Mario Bauzá, Miguelito Valdés, and other trustworthy sources.[26]

The other debated question concerning Chano is strictly musical: There are those who deny that Chano was the best tamborero of his time, an entirely subjective opinion that's not worth discussing. Others, on the contrary, not satisfied with Chano's great talent and indisputable contributions, exaggerate his importance in jazz and bop, affirming that bop was accepted thanks to the presence of Chano in Dizzy's band, and they maintain that the rhythmic variations introduced by bop musicians are because of his contribution, ignorant of the changes introduced on drums (drum set) starting in 1941 by Max Roach and Kenny Clarke, to mention only two musicians among the creators of bop. Also false is the affirmation that Chano "didn't adapt" his form of playing to the requirements of jazz and to the arrangements of Dizzy's band, but rather "imposed" his own style, which everybody else had to follow. Quite the opposite—Chano's great quality was that he adapted the rhythmic patterns of the conga (from traditional Cuban genres) to those that had been established by the creators of bop, changing certain accents to avoid letting the conga part in the Cuban polyrhythm clash with the typical accentuations of bop, particularly on the cymbal. We shouldn't forget that before arriving in New York, Chano Pozo had played with jazz groups in Havana.[27]

There also exists in Cuba the tendency—due to the ignorance about Machito and Mario Bauzá—to believe that Afro-Cuban jazz was born out of the meeting and collaboration of Dizzy Gillespie and Chano Pozo. Once Mario Bauzá's fundamental role in the whole process is clarified, we still have to recognize other jazz musicians who were directly involved with Mario and in the band of Machito and His Afro-Cubans; of extraordinary importance in this process are Charlie "Bird" Parker and Stan Kenton, conductor of the most experimental and controversial white jazz band at that time. In 1947, the year of Dizzy and Chano's historic concert in Carnegie Hall, another explosive encounter takes place in Town Hall: the "battle of the bands" between the bands of Machito and Stan Kenton. The outcome was instantaneous: Kenton was so excited about the Afro-Cubans that he asked Machito to teach him our rhythms and he put his chief arranger, Pete Rugolo, in charge of the composition of the piece "Machito," in tribute to the Cuban. Shortly thereafter Kenton recorded his extraordinary version of "The Peanut Vendor," for which he borrowed Machito's whole percussion section; and this was before the memorable concerts and recordings of Chano with Dizzy's band in 1948. Stan Kenton had already occasionally experimented with the Afro-Latin style, in 1941 with Margarita Lecuona's "Tabú," and then with works of a more experimental character such as "Ecuador," "Journey to Brasil," "Bongo Riff," "Introduction to a Latin Theme," and "Fugue for Rhythm Section," with a band that included the Brazilian guitarist Laurindo Almeida and Italian American bongosero Jack Constanzo. In the Fifties Kenton would increase this tendency, hiring percussionists such as Cándido Camero, Willie Rodríguez, and Carlos Vidal and commissioning Chico O'Farrill for his composition *Cuban Episode*, Johnny Richards for the suite *Cuban Fire*, and different arrangers for other basically Afro-Latin numbers.

Other American big bands, black and white, had experimented with

Afro-Latin material, such as Duke Ellington, Cab Calloway, Woody Herman, and Charlie Barnet, who were joined in the Fifties by Jerry Wald, Harry James, and Gene Krupa, in part thanks to the influence of Machito and His Afro-Cubans. The singer Nat King Cole and different bop groups would also experiment with Afro-Latin music, as we shall see. But without a doubt one of the most transcendental musical encounters was that of Charlie Parker and the band of Machito. Between December 1948 and January 1949 the historic recordings of Parker and Machito were made: "Okidoke," "No Noise," and "Mango Mangüé" (the piece by Gilberto Valdés, not the number by Francisco Fellove of the same name). During these sessions "Tanga," Mario Bauzá's classic, was also recorded, without the participation of Bird. In later sessions, Machito and His Afro-Cubans recorded with three prominent jazz soloists—Bird Parker, Flip Phillips (tenor sax), and the great drummer Buddy Rich—as well as in the *Afro-Cuban Suite* by Chico O'Farrill. In the sessions with Machito, the rhythm section that accompanies Bird's alto solos included René Hernández (piano), Roberto Rodríguez (contrabass), José Mangual (bongo), Luis Miranda (conga), Ubaldo Nieto (pailas), and Machito (maracas).

In that same year, 1948, Machito's recording of "Cubop City" stirred up great interest within jazz circles. Together with the Afro-Cubans the tenor saxophonist Brew Moore (the most loyal white follower of Lester Young's) and the trumpet player Howard McGhee (a bop pioneer on trumpet along with Dizzy, Miles Davis, Fats Navarro, Kenny Dorham, and Red Rodney) performed as soloists. In 1949 Machito recorded another one of his great instrumental hits, "Asia Minor," with the oboist Mitch Miller, who had played with Bird on the albums of *Charlie Parker with Strings*. Other hits of Machito in what had become known as Cubop were "Gone City" and "Hall of the Mambo King." The double album *Afro-Cuban Jazz*, with pieces recorded between 1948 and 1954 (reedited in 1981 with great success), is considered a treasure in its genre, and features three great orchestras and conductors: Dizzy Gillespie, Chico O'Farrill, and Machito. The arrangements are by Chico O'Farrill, Mario Bauzá, and René Hernández, and Machito's rhythm section performs with the three bands. The *Afro-Cuban Suite* by Arturo O'Farrill, with Dizzy as soloist, is today another one of the classics of Afro-Cuban jazz, just as "Mambo Inn" by Mario Bauzá has become a standard not only on the Latin circuit but also of jazz in general.

During the Fifties Machito and His Afro-Cubans received further acclaim with hits such as "Christopher Columbus," "Consternation," "Dragnet Mambo," "Mambo Inferno," "Don't Tease Me," and the album *Kenya,* reedited later under the title *Latin Soul plus Jazz.* On this album the soloists were Cannonball Adderley (alto sax), Joe Newman and Doc Cheatham (trumpets), Johnny Griffin and Ray Santos (tenors), Eddie Bert and Santo Russo (trombones), Cándido Camero and Patato Valdés (congas), and José Mangual (bongo). René Hernández and A. K. Salim handled the arrangements. Another interesting album was *Machito with Flute to Boot,* a collaborative effort with the flutist Herbie Mann, who was attracted more and more to Latin jazz. The arrangements were by Mann, who shares the solos with Johnny Griffin (tenor) and Curtis Fuller (trombone). Other jazz soloists who played with Machito and His Afro-Cubans (although some never recorded with them), aside from those already mentioned, were Dexter Gordon, Jon Faddis, Don Lamond, Lew Soloff, Chico Freeman, Eddie Bert, Richie Cole, Stan Getz, Zoot Sims, Lee Konitz . . . a whole constellation that could be a "Who's Who of Jazz," at least from the 1940s to the 1980s.[28]

Of course the list of jazz greats who were attracted to Afro-Cuban music and rhythms and assimilated many elements doesn't end there. Charlie Parker himself, in his famous quintet with Miles Davis on trumpet and Wynton Kelly on piano, included two Cuban percussionists in 1946: Diego Iborra (conga) and Guillermo Alvarez (bongo); the drummer was Max Roach. And in 1951 Bird included José Mangual (bongo) and Luis Miranda (conga) in a group that had Walter Bishop Jr. (piano), Teddy Kotick (bass), and Roy Haynes (drums). George Shearing, who originated his own style and had a considerable influence on U.S. and Cuban pianists, embraced the Cuban piano style around 1950 and incorporated Cuban percussionists such as Armando Peraza in his group. For his part, pianist Billy Taylor recorded with Cándido Camero. Vibraphonist Cal Tjader, who emerged in Shearing's quintet, became another one of the paladins of Afro-Cuban jazz, employing musicians such as percussionists Mongo Santamaría and Armando Peraza and tenor saxophonist José "Chombo" Silva. The extended résumé of Chombo Silva, whom we mention in several chapters, includes his participation in a variety of groups and orchestras, in Havana as well as in New York and Europe; among the most important were the bands of Isidro Pérez, Beny Moré, Machito, James Moody, César Concepción, René Touzet, Cal Tjader, and Paquito D'Rivera.

There is a case that is quite interesting in this process of fusion and crossover: In 1949 the drummer Cozy Cole, normally associated with the Swing Era, formed a group called Los Cuboppers, which included Cuban percussionists Bill (Guillermo) Alvarez and Diego Iborra, the same ones who played with Charlie Parker and with Dizzy's band. With them, Cozy recorded four numbers for Decca, including two Chico O'Farrill originals: "Botao" and "Mosquito Brain." What's interesting is that in the 1940s, as we have seen, O'Farrill had organized a group called Los Beboppers in Havana. Now the equation is reversed and an American musician forms a group of Cuboppers that includes Chico. This brings to mind another coincidence that I've already pointed out: the creation in Havana of the Cubibop rhythm by Niño Rivera, at the same time that they were beginning to talk of Cubop in New York, completely independent of each other. The fusion of Afro-Cuban music and jazz, particularly at this time, "was in the air." There is no other possible explanation.

6

Havana in the 1950s

*J*ust as it is impossible to make a precise delineation between the 1920s and 1930s with respect to Cuban jazz, such is the case for the 1940s and 1950s. We have maintained this same point of view with respect to the history of jazz in the United States and the blueprint that correlates the 1940s to bop and the 1950s to cool and then hard bop, as there exists an unmistakable continuity between these styles and the many musicians who excelled in all of them, such as Miles Davis, Max Roach, or J. J. Johnson. The Afro-Cuban or Latin influence also left its mark on all of these styles to a greater or lesser degree. In Havana, the Fifties were an extension or a culmination of the musical developments of the previous decade in all aspects: the *conjunto* boom continues, the feeling movement is consolidated, mambo arrives to stay, *chachachá* emerges, and the big jazz bands continue to proliferate.

Starting with mambo, Cuban arrangers develop their own styles of orchestration, and at the same time, among those who master the language of bop and cool jazz, there emerge new and important jazz soloists on all instruments. In Cuban music, the most important development was perhaps the comeback of charangas thanks to the immense popularity of chachachá, with the orchestras América, Aragón, and Fajardo y sus Estrellas as the primary strongholds. Also essential is the beginning of television broadcasts in 1950; Channels 2, 4, and 6, with important musical spots, become a new source of work for Cuban musicians.

Another development that changed the "infrastructure" of Cuban music, this time at the end of the decade, was the construction of new and luxurious hotels such as the Hilton (later the Habana Libre), the Riviera, the Capri, St. John's, the Comodoro, the Copacabana, the Flamingo, the Deauville, and the new Hotel Vedado (the old one was renamed Victoria). Many of these hotels had a gaming room and a cabaret, which increased the musicians' possibilities for work even more. Also, casinos were installed and cabarets were remodeled in old hotels such as the Nacional, the Sevilla, and the Plaza. In addition, under pressure from the musicians union, variety shows were brought back to the capital's main movie theaters: América, Encanto, Fausto, Astral, Warner (then Radiocentro and today Yara), Radio Cine (today Jigüe), and others. Numerous orchestras found a new source of steady work; for example, in the Warner movie theater the "house" orchestra was Adolfo Guzmán's, in Astral it was Armando Romeu's and later Julio Gutiérrez's. As if this weren't enough, small nightclubs multiplied and spread throughout the city to the outskirts, favoring the formation of combos.

Despite the political and economic disorder of this decade, the political corruption of the tyranny, the guerrilla war in the mountains, the violence and bombs in the cities, and the presence of top Mob bosses from Las Vegas, music and show business prospered like never before in Cuba, and musicians found for the first time multiple possibilities for work, without having to fall back on the "guaranteed employment" that the military bands offered or having to supplement work as a musician with other types of work. And while many excellent musicians went back and forth between cabarets or television and military bands, and others studied at the university to become engineers, doctors, or lawyers, many left the military bands or the university to find higher paying jobs at nightclubs or on TV.

The history of music is filled with paradoxes, and in 1950s Havana, music prospered in the shadow of a tourism linked to gambling, which was controlled by Mafiosi from Las Vegas and their Cuban associates. The situation was very similar to 1920s New Orleans where musicians improved their salaries thanks to the Storyville bordellos, or 1930s Chicago and New York where musicians found refuge in the speakeasies, those famous underground cabarets where alcoholic drinks were served in the age of Prohibition, which only served to enrich the families of La Cosa Nostra, although also to turn many jazz luminaries into legends.

𝒞*ultural* ℒ*ife,* 𝒮*hows,* 𝒟*ance . . .*

The cultural panorama in 1950s Cuba was particularly desolate. The Grupo de Renovación Musical, which brought together the symphonic composers of the post-Roldán/Caturla generation (Julián Orbón, Harold Gramatges, José Ardévol, Hilario González) had broken up, and the Havana Philharmonic, which had a resurgence under the direction of Erich Kleiber in 1943–47, was at the point of disappearing around 1953 and barely hung on until 1958. La Orquesta de Cámara de La Habana (the Havana Chamber Orchestra) founded by José Ardévol in 1934, broke up in 1952, and the same fate awaited Alicia Alonso's Ballet a few years later, when Batista withdrew the subsidy it had received up until then. Some choreographers such as Luis Trápaga and Alberto Alonso went into the new field of television and big cabaret productions, as did dancers Leonela González and Elena del Cueto, among others, which favored the world of cabaret shows.

In literature and fine arts the situation was just as somber. Writers had to pay for their own limited book printings or emigrate, as did Alejo Carpentier, unless, with a bit of luck, they could make a living as journalists or teachers. The most important literary magazine of the time, *Orígenes,* founded in 1944 by José Lezama Lima, was going under in 1956 because of lack of resources, as internal dissension arose and its co-founder, José Rodríguez Feo, withdrew his economic support. Just as some writers found refuge in journalism or emigrated, painters and sculptors such as Wifredo Lam, Agustín Cárdenas, Antonio Gattorno, and Felipe Orlando who didn't move to other countries found refuge in the advertising business. The universities—La Habana, Las Villas, Oriente—at one time or another were closed for being strongholds in the struggle against Batista's dictatorship. Another center of cultural activity, the Sociedad Nuestro Tiempo, which was directed by the composer Harold Gramatges, was also persecuted and finally dissolved for its ties with the Partido Socialista Popular. Only two patronage-based cultural focal points remained standing, Pro-Arte Musical and the Lyceum & Lawn Tennis Club, whose important work is today unjustly minimized.

As we've already seen, the rapid growth of television had undermined the attempts to create a national commercial cinema. For its part, theater (classical or experimental) survived with many difficulties and small audiences, but popular theater, with roots in the Cuban comic theater tradition, played during the 1950s at the Teatro Martí and others, and Spanish revue companies continued their traditional visits. In short, entertainment shows, cabarets, radio, and television were the only areas of prosperity in the cultural sphere. Of the four biggest nightclubs, the Casino Nacional had closed its doors, and the Montmartre closed in the mid-1950s, leaving the Tropicana and the Sans Souci, which—starting in 1957—were joined by new hotel cabarets such as the Casino Parisién (Hotel Nacional), the Copa Room (Hotel Riviera), and the Capri, and a little bit later the Havana Hilton's Caribe, as well as the other aforementioned ones.

Along with the biggest and most luxurious cabarets there were others that also offered two shows a night such as the Bambú (on Rancho Boyeros highway), the Night and Day, the Alí Bar, the Sierra, Club 66, La Campana, the Palermo, the Morocco, the Palette Club, the Topeka, the Alloy, and Las Vegas. Some of them had special characteristics: the Alí Bar was one of Beny Moré's preferred venues; many jazz musicians played at the Bambú; the Sierra featured the most popular conjuntos and boleristas; jam sessions were organized once a week at the Las Vegas, and at this cabaret and others, such as the Sierra, there were no casinos, but there were slot machines. But there is another interesting development in this decade: The center of the city, which had been more or less the Acera del Louvre and then the corner of Galiano and San Rafael in the business district, shifts to the Vedado district, until then almost exclusively residential. This movement began when the impresario Goar Mestre built Radiocentro, the new building for radio and TV (on the corner of L and Twenty-third); it continued with the building of the shopping center La Rampa, after which the zone was named, and the construction of new hotels in this same area.

Small nightclubs, most of them with live music, sprang up like mush-rooms throughout Vedado, and not only in the "La Rampa" district. The most popular were Club 21, Club 23, Kasbah, Eden Rock, Mocambo, Johnny 88, Atelier, Karachi, Sheherezada, Pigalle, Havana 1900, Tikoa, St. Michel, Hernando's Hideaway, Maxim's, Sayonara, La Gruta, Rocco, La Zorra y el Cuervo, La Red, Eloy's, Mandy, Le Mans, and the exclusive Monseigneur (also a restaurant). There were also the Pico Blanco (Roof Garden) and the Lobby Bar in St. John's Hotel, the Starlight in the Hotel Nacional, the Hilton's Turquino or the Riviera's Elegante, among other hotel clubs. Nightclubs began to flourish in the Miramar district as well: Le Martinique, Johnny's Dream, Le Rêve, Mes Amis, among others. Many others could still be found in the popular old cabaret district of Playa de Marianao: Pennsylvania, Rumba Palace, Panchín, El Niche. And of course, new places emerged in Old Havana, and even on the nearby roads.

In the red-light districts (the barrios of Colón, La Victoria, and the Havana port area) there were countless bars and clubs whose main attraction wasn't gambling but prostitution, but in which there was also a need for music; and in the brothels themselves drinks were sold and there was something even more important, almost essential: a Victrola with the latest hits. There were bars linked to prostitution that had tables and a dance floor, but only canned music; a unique case was the Victoria, where the jukebox included the latest in jazz, although it would also provide the music of preference in this environment: bolero. Other bars in the same Victoria barrio were the Kumaon, the Brindis, and the Bolero, on Infanta Street, which featured not only live music but also two shows a night. And there was the nearby Blue Moon, where the main attraction was the Bermúdez Brothers duo, who not only sung the latest boleros but also were co-own-ers of the place.

Furthermore, as if to show how "ahead of its time" Havana was in the 1950s—in a manner of speaking—there was even a transvestite cabaret (*transformistas* at that time) where the orchestra accompanied the bolero star, the Spanish dancer, and the "exotic" dancer, the latter usually performing "Caravan," the classic of Juan Tizol and Duke Ellington. This cabaret, the Colonial, was located on Oficios between Teniente Rey and Amargura, across from the Convento de San Francisco (Central Post Office, at that time). Later, they had competition from the Palette Club. Meanwhile, the "academias de baile," such as Marte y Belona or Havana Sport, continued full steam ahead, just as in other areas traditional social clubs continued, from the most aristocratic to the most popular and those "of color." For the inexhaustible Havana dancers, the dance marathon held in the gardens of the breweries La Tropical and La Polar continued to be a "main course"; for Havana dancers, these were the equivalent of the Salón México for dancers in Mexico City and the Palladium for New Yorkers. And while Acerina's danzones were a main attraction at the Salón México as were Machito's Afro-Cubans at the Palladium, at La Tropical the idols were Beny Moré, Aragón, América, Fajardo y sus Estrellas, Melodías del 40, and the Conjunto de Chapotín. Which brings us once again to the topic of the orchestras, and particularly the jazz bands.

Without going into the differences between the bands that had steady work at a cabaret or a television studio and other more or less itinerant ones that focused exclusively on dances in different societies and cities, nor analyzing the advantages and disadvantages of each type of work, I will limit myself to confirming the continuation of jazz bands in the 1950s. The decade's most popular bands were Beny Moré's, not only for the extraordinary personality and charisma of its bandleader and singer, but also for its rhythm, a sort of "perfect fit" between mambo and son; and the Riverside, also in part because of its popular singer Tito Gómez. In the Forties and Fifties there were other quite popular orchestras such as the Cosmopolita, the Havana Swing, (Eddy Lester's) American Swing, the Metropolitana, and the Miramar (led by Ramón Vidal), in addition to others that were mentioned extensively in Chapter 4 and which survived in the Fifties and a few until the Sixties. We can name some orchestras whose personnel consisted primarily of blacks and mulattos, although not to the exclusion of white musicians, such as the Martínez Brothers, which included jazz musicians such as Guillermo Barreto and Rolando Sánchez; the Swing Boys, led by Emilio Peñalver; Néstor Fabelo and Jorge Rojas's Cubamar; or the Havana Melody, led by Roberto Puente. The Continental, led by Ernesto Duarte, was very popular in the 1950s in large part because of the hits composed by its leader. There are also the jazz bands led by Walfredo de los Reyes (senior), Walfredito de los Reyes, Rafael Ortega, Rubén Romeu, Adolfo Guzmán, Rey Díaz Calvet, Carlos Ansa, Armando Pidre, Cheo Valladares, José A. Díaz, Rafael Somavilla Jr., and Bebo Valdés.

Of course, excellent jazz bands could also be found in the rest of the country, although usually they were only known within their respective provinces and were broadcast by local radio stations. This put them at a disadvantage with respect to Havana groups and resulted in the migration of many good musicians to the capital. Among the best known of these jazz bands were Rafael Somavilla Sr.'s in Matanzas; the Swing Casino in Güines; the previously mentioned Avilés Brothers from Holguín; Emilio Salvador's band in Puerto Padre, Oriente; Héctor Mendivel's in Camagüey; and the Monte Casino in Sancti Spíritus, Las Villas.

Excellent improvisers played in all of the jazz bands; for example, the Riverside at its best (led by Pedro Vila) had pianist Pedro Jústiz (Peruchín) and bassist Orlando López (Cachaíto), son of Orestes López and nephew of Cachao, as well as trumpeter Leonardo Timor Jr. Some jazz musicians also worked with Beny Moré, such as trumpet players "El Negro" Vivar and "Chocolate" Armenteros and baritone saxophonist Virgilio Vixama, among others.[1] But the repertoires of the jazz bands—with some exceptions—weren't enough to satisfy real jazz musicians, so some would form combos to work at small places, in addition to taking part in the jam sessions that would be held at different clubs or at somebody's house. Only at the end of the decade was the Club Cubano de Jazz organized, the first and only organization of its kind in Cuba, which produced a significant change for jazz in our country; the Club Cubano de Jazz will be covered in the next chapter.

The Tropicana: Center of the World

Where was the center of jazz in 1950s Havana, if there was one? Without a doubt, at least until 1957, it was the most luxurious and spectacular cabaret of the era: the Tropicana, referred to either as "the largest cabaret in the world" or "a paradise under the stars." The trio Fox-Echemendía-Ardura built the Arcos de Cristal ballroom (designed by avant-garde architect Max Borges Jr.) and remodeled and enlarged the old open-air cabaret, renaming it Bajo las Estrellas, not really a very original name (the Hotel Nacional had a Starlight Terrace). In addition, they opened an enormous gaming room that included a long bar at one end and behind it a platform on which small groups would perform, sometimes jazz groups. When two enormous ballrooms were opened, one outdoors and another one indoors, it was possible to have two cabarets operating at the same time, and on Saturdays orchestras were hired that would play dance numbers in the ballroom that didn't have a show. At the same time, the casino was open until the early hours of the morning, as long as there were clients gambling enough money, and in the casino's bar groups such as Felipe Dulzaides's or intermission pianists of the caliber of Frank Emilio Flynn could be heard.

The Tropicana was the center of jazz in Cuba at this time because of the presence of Armando Romeu and his band, with the most advanced jazz arrangements and excellent jazz musicians, and the jam sessions or *descargas* organized on Sunday afternoons by drummer Guillermo Barreto, from Armando's band. Many American jazz musicians passed through the Tropicana, either hired to play there or simply as tourists or occasional visitors. And it wasn't unusual to see Frank Sinatra, Benny Goodman, or Tito Puente at one of the tables. It's true that the Tropicana featured shows that had little or nothing to do with jazz, such as Josephine Baker, Xavier Cugat, Tongolele, Maurice Chevalier, comedian Harry Mimo, Johnny Puleo and his group of harmonica players, Pedro Vargas, Liberace, the group Tex Mex, and all kinds of celebrities, including Christine Jorgensen. But also performing there were Cab Calloway, Nat King Cole and his trio, Woody Herman with a constellation of jazz stars, and singers such as Jack Prince, Billy Daniels, and Helen Forrest. Not to be left behind, the Sans Souci featured Johnny Mathis, Edith Piaf, Tony Bennett, Dorothy Dandridge, Johnny Ray, and particularly Sarah Vaughan, Tommy Dorsey, and June Christy.

Nevertheless, the first jazz musician of importance at this time was brought to Havana by the Montmartre cabaret, and he was precisely one of the men who were most interested in Afro-Cuban rhythms and in whose band Mario Bauzá and Dizzy Gillespie had played: it was Cab Calloway, the "Hi-De-Ho" man, in 1949. With him came a few top-rank musicians such as Jonah Jones on trumpet, bassist Milt Hinton, and drummer Panama Francis. A great musician—like Dizzy later—Cab was a success not only at the Montmartre but also in his performances at the Campoamor and Warner Theaters. As a result of his trip, Calloway subsequently recorded some songs in Spanish, although while in Havana he had already sung his version of "La múcura," popular at the time, and a "Hey-Ba-Ba-Re-Bop" with inflections of Miguelito Valdés's "Babalú Ayé." His success was such that he returned the following year, hired by the Tropicana. The competition among the big nightclubs would continue until the end of the decade, and with the new hotels and cabarets, particularly the Hotel Nacional's Parisién, would also come Tony Martin, Yma Sumac, Eartha Kitt, Joni James, and Billy Daniels.

Of the American jazz musicians who at different times—and some repeatedly—visited Havana on their own, we should mention Georgie Auld, Lennie Hambro, Zoot Sims, Stan Getz, and Max Roach, who told us personally of the travails of his trip in 1951. Max Roach's visit was very brief and he couldn't associate with Cuban jazz musicians; because he was black, they didn't allow him in the Tropicana or in other cabarets and he ended up traveling on to Haiti, where he familiarized himself with the rhythms of that country. Georgie Auld had been at the Sans Souci in the 1940s and visited us a number of times. Lennie Hambro, who had worked as an alto sax player in the bands of Pupi Campo and Machito, created quite a controversy when he stated that jazz musicians couldn't play Latin music very well because they didn't know the Cuban clave, and that likewise Latin musicians couldn't play jazz, with a few exceptions such as bassist Bobby Rodríguez (with Machito) and Kiki Hernández, another bassist, whom he had met in Havana. Fortunately, it's not necessary to refute his pessimistic opinion, for the history of Latin jazz has already done so quite thoroughly.[2]

Of the renowned stars that came on their own, Benny Goodman seems to have been one of those who enjoyed it the most, particularly at the Tropicana, where he praised Armando Romeu's band very highly and had his picture taken next to drummer Guillermo Barreto, who also received praise and later a contract offer from another famous bandleader, Tommy Dorsey. And Tito Puente, as we have said, was a frequent visitor at the Tropicana and would come often to recruit musicians for his band. Xavier Cugat and Liberace did the same in the 1950s; after performing at the Tropicana with orchestras in which at least half the musicians were Cuban, they hired a number of them for their upcoming tours in the United States. Machito as well recruited musicians in Havana on a regular basis, as did Armando Oréfiche, who after every tour would return to Cuba, which meant that the Havana Cuban Boys were continually renewed. Venezuelan jazz bandleaders, such as Aldemaro Romero, Billo Frómeta, or Luis Alfonso Larraín, were also among the frequent visitors who came to hire musicians.

However, the presence in Havana of an "all star" jazz octet led by Woody Herman in the last months of 1950 turned out to be the most sensational visit that we had had on the island with respect to jazz. Shortly before, Herman had dissolved his big band and had formed this group to fulfill a contract with the Tropicana. It featured Conte Candoli (trumpet), Bill Harris (trombone), Milt Jackson (vibraphone), Dave Barbour (guitar), Ralph Burns (piano), Red Mitchell (bass), and Shelly Manne (drums), with Woody Herman singing and playing clarinet and alto sax. As Horacio Hernández notes, "Never before had there been a constellation of jazz musicians of this caliber" in Cuba.[3] This was a great opportunity for jazz musicians from Cuba to compare what they had been doing with some of the best jazz (and bop) players of the time; and in a way, this was a preview of what would occur at the end of the decade, when this exchange between musicians from the two countries turned into something regular, thanks to the creation of the Club Cubano de Jazz.

At that time among the jazz soloists in the Tropicana band were trumpet player Alejandro "El Negro" Vivar, tenor saxophonist Pedro Chao, pianist Bebo Valdés, bassist Fernando "Yuca" Vivar, and drummer Guillermo Barreto. Of course, the musicians who arrived with Woody met other Cuban jazz musicians, who—like the jazz fans—showed up almost without exception at the Tropicana to see the unique octet. Of the Americans, the ones who got to know our musicians the best were Red Mitchell, Milt Jackson, and Conte Candoli, although Shelly Manne was so excited that he had his wife come to Havana to join him. El Negro Vivar and Pedro Chao, after a few jam sessions at the Tropicana or in private homes, asked Milt, Red, and Conte their honest opinion of the local jazz musicians; the answer was that the Cubans could play jazz just as well as anyone, only that they themselves underestimated their own ability. Almost thirty years later, in 1977, pianist Chucho Valdés (son of Bebo Valdés) received praise from Dizzy Gillespie, Stan Getz, and David Amram during their visit to Cuba, and told me later: "Now I realize that we do underestimate ourselves."

The group that Woody Herman brought with him was quite heterogeneous, for of the musicians of his Third Herd there remained only trombonist Bill Harris and drummer Shelly Manne, who shortly before had left Stan Kenton's band to join Woody's, replacing Don Lamond. None of the saxophonists who gave Herman's band their characteristic "Four Brothers Sound" came with him either. Pianist Lou Levy was replaced by Ralph Burns, who was from Woody's previous band, the Second Herd, and who had become renowned with the composition of the suite *Summer Sequence* and then with the arrangement of "Early Autumn," which had made Stan Getz famous for his tenor sax solo. As for the rest, Conte Candoli had never played with Woody (his brother Pete was in the Second Herd), and another surprise was to see Milt Jackson in place of Terry Gibbs, who was definitely the white version—and leading admirer—of Milt. For his part, Red Mitchell replaced Chubby Jackson, Woody's seemingly irreplaceable bassist. The following year Woody organized a new band in which Bill Harris and Conte Candoli—before moving on themselves—were the only remaining members of this visiting band. The repertoire that Woody brought to Havana was quite diverse, but it included a few numbers recorded by his band, such as George Wallington's bop classic "Lemon Drop."

The most important thing about this group for Cuban jazz musicians was that it included well-known bop soloists for the first time, while musicians such as Georgie Auld or Cab Calloway's group were seen more as typical representatives of the Swing Era. Cubans had the opportunity to hear in person and even play in jam sessions with Jackson, Candoli, Mitchell, and Manne, the four whom the locals got to know the best. Woody Herman impressed everybody, particularly with his contagious enthusiasm. Bill Harris seemed to us to be polite but distant; Dave Barbour continued to be an excellent guitarist, but he had practically left jazz to accompany his wife Peggy Lee, who was at the height of her popularity. Ralph Burns was both laid back and talkative, and would sit in the Tropicana musicians and artists' cafeteria amazing people with his habit of ordering a cup of coffee and milk along with a glass of cognac. Perhaps the presence of these musicians also contributed to creating the right atmosphere to begin a series of historical jam sessions at the Tropicana, long before the previously mentioned "Descarga" recordings took place.

The Tropicana Jam Sessions . . . and the Band

At that time there were a number of spots where jazz jam sessions or "descargas" would take place: cabarets, studios, or private homes. To begin with I should mention the Sunday afternoon jam sessions at the Tropicana, in the early 1950s, organized by our first real bop drummer, Guillermo Barreto, with the support of Alberto Ardura, a jazz enthusiast and co-owner of the cabaret. Entrance to these jam sessions was free and no drinks of any type were sold. The central core of the sessions was a group of "house musicians" made up of members of Armando Romeu's Tropicana band. This base group included Alejandro "El Negro" Vivar (trumpet), Rafael "Tata" Palau (tenor sax), Bebo Valdés (piano), Fernando Vivar (bass), and Guillermo Barreto (drums). This quintet was very tight, not only because its members were musicians who played together every night in the Tropicana band but also because all of them were bop musicians. They had a repertoire of bop classics and standards preferred by musicians of this style, although Tata Palau, who replaced Pedro Chao in Armando Romeu's orchestra, was heavily into the cool style started by Lester Young.

Other musicians who took part in these jam sessions were bassists Orlando "Papito" Hernández and Kiki Hernández, who later replaced Fernando Vivar in Armando's band; tenor saxophonist Gustavo Más, whose periodic visits from the United States were anxiously awaited; pianist Samuel Téllez, a bebopper who was involved in the feeling movement; and drummers Walfredo de los Reyes, having recently arrived from New York, veteran Daniel Pérez, and Guillermo Alvarez, who like Gustavo Más lived in the United States and came periodically. The listeners were for the most part young musicians, of whom the only one who dared to play with the "elder statesmen" was Samuel Téllez; others such as trumpeter Wichy Mercier and me limited ourselves to joining the thirty or forty regular fans, among them a few disc jockeys, singers such as Dandy Crawford, and some members of the feeling movement. The jam sessions might begin with a number such as "Minor Walk," continue with a jazz version of "Cuando vuelva a tu lado" ("What a Difference a Day Makes"), a standard such as "Stella by Starlight" or "Tea for Two," and an Afro-Cuban jazz classic such as "Mambo Inn." And although I don't remember seeing either a *conguero* or a bongosero (except maybe Barreto or Walfredito on a particular number), at times what could be heard was Afro-Cuban jazz, and top quality at that.

In the Tropicana jam sessions we heard tenor player Gustavo Más for the first time; until then we didn't think there was anybody in Cuba who could surpass Chombo Silva or Tata Palau, but Tata himself told me before the jam session began: "It's something like listening to Stan Getz." And that afternoon Tata Palau played alto. For almost the entire decade three excellent musicians took turns as tenor sax soloists in Armando's orchestra: Gustavo Más, Tata Palau, and Pedro Chao. Gustavo lived permanently in Miami and traveled often to New York and Havana; when he would come, Armando Romeu invariably gave him the tenor soloist spot. And rarely were these three tenor players in Havana at the same time, for Pedro Chao frequently traveled to Venezuela with Aldemaro Romero's band, and Tata Palau went to Venezuela with Luis Alfonso Larraín's orchestra and in Caracas in 1956 he helped to organize the Casablanca orchestra. This group included three other Cubans: bass player Kiki Hernández, trombonist and arranger Pucho Escalante, and pianist/arranger Eduardo Cabrera, who had recently left Beny Moré's band, which he had helped to consolidate with his arrangements. In 1958 Tata Palau went to Puerto Rico, where he signed on with Tito Puente, and later continued in the United States, mostly in Las Vegas.

If the Tropicana was the center of jazz jam sessions in the early 1950s, later on these sessions gradually spread to other popular nightclubs such as Club 21, Maxim's, Southland (later Casablanca), Pigalle, and finally Havana 1900, which was the home of the Club Cubano de Jazz. Nevertheless, throughout this decade the Tropicana was the cabaret preferred by jazz lovers, who knew that Armando's band would always perform the latest jazz numbers and arrangements. The orchestra had in its repertoire arrangements by Armando Romeu, Chico O'Farrill, Isidro Pérez, Bebo Valdés, Peruchín Jústiz, Pucho Escalante, and Roberto Sánchez Ferrer. In addition, Armando and drummer Guillermo Barreto would listen to the latest records to arrive in Cuba and transcribe the best arrangements of Stan Kenton, Woody Herman, Count Basie, Duke Ellington, Dizzy Gillespie, Tommy Dorsey, Ted Heath and his British band, and others. They also transcribed numbers from small bop groups, which five or six members of the band played. Jazz lovers could be sure that in each session Armando Romeu would please them with at least two jazz numbers and modern arrangements of Cuban music, and the last sets were dedicated almost entirely to jazz and its enthusiastic fans.

For the first few years of the decade, Armando Romeu's trumpet section included brothers Alberto and Dagoberto Jiménez ("Platanito" and "Rabanito"), as well as El Negro Vivar, who would cover the jazz solos and Cuban *improvisations*. The fourth trumpet was Pedro "El Guajiro" Rodríguez. Later the section increased to five trumpets and there were various changes. The American trumpet and trombone player Harry

Johansson, who had already worked with Armando and led a jazz group at the High Seas club in Havana, returned for a time. And the extraordinary Luis Escalante, co-organizer of the Bellamar with Armando, joined up with him once again at the Tropicana, replacing El Negro Vivar as a jazz soloist when Vivar went on to play in Julio Gutiérrez's orchestra at Channel 4 TV. Later, an extremely talented lead trumpet, "Shorty" Nilo Argudín, who in the 1970s would work with Machito in New York, joined the band. There was a period in which the orchestra went without an improvisational trumpet, but Guillermo Barreto took it upon himself to transcribe solos for Dagoberto Jiménez, who would perform them as if they were improvised, for Barreto pointed out all the subtleties, the breathing, and even the notes that should sound "dirty."

Armando's trombone section changed quite a bit in those days, but one of his cornerstones was always the Spaniard Alberto Martí, who was the only trombone for awhile and then headed sections of three and even four trombones. Another one of the section's indisputable soloists was Leopoldo "Pucho" Escalante, who remained the best Cuban jazz trombonist throughout the decade. The band also featured trombonists Miguel Reina, Modesto Echarte, and Antonio Linares ("Lotario"), who became the best lead on his instrument. The changes in the saxophone section were less noticeable, although more frequent, because the same players would almost always come and go. Among the tenors there was always at least one of the previously mentioned (Gustavo, Tata, Pedro) and often two of them, while Roberto Sánchez Ferrer sometimes filled the fourth chair. Lead alto during this whole period was Rafael "El Cabito" Quesada, while third chair alto was filled at different times by Sánchez Ferrer, Ramón González, or one of the Romero brothers. For years the baritone sax was Rubén Romeu, another one of Armando's brothers, replaced for a time by Tata Palau and then for good by Orlando Fernández Walpole ("Macanta"), when Rubén went on to lead an orchestra at the Sans Souci and then the Banda de la Marina.[4]

The bassists for Armando Romeu at this time were Fernando Vivar, Felo Hernández, and Kiki Hernández, these last two having been members of Armando's bands previously. For quite a long period, Romeu went without a guitar after Isidro Pérez settled for good in Chicago and Félix Guerrero turned to symphonic composition and orchestral conducting. Only around 1956 did the guitar return to the band when Armando hired Pablo Cano, a student of

Isidro Pérez's, and later José Franca, brother of pianist Luis and saxophonist Miguelito Franca. On piano, on the other hand, Bebo Valdés remained for almost a decade, and together with drummer Guillermo Barreto represented the core of the rhythm section, with Kiki Hernández on bass. Barreto, also affectionately called "Barretico," infused this orchestra with a steady rhythmic beat and a swing that no other band of the time in Cuba—or in all of Latin America—could equal. And Barreto was also our first real bop drummer, inspired particularly by Max Roach and Roy Haynes. Bebo Valdés as well as Barreto were replaced by musicians of unquestionable caliber when they decided to leave the orchestra: Barreto was replaced by Armando Zequeira, son of pianist Zenaida Romeu, and Armandito Romeu, son of Armando (whom we will designate from here on as Armando Romeu III). Bebo Valdés had been preceded by such formidable pianists as Peruchín Jústiz and Mario Romeu, and was replaced by Fernando Mulens. But in spite of everything, the band was no longer the same.

Cuban percussion, which had had almost no relevance in the previous editions of Armando's band, was of top quality in this decade. It began with the combination of Rolando Alfonso on conga and none other than Cándido Camero on bongo. Also joining the orchestra was Giraldo Rodríguez, who in addition to playing the conga was among the very best of his time on *batá* drums, along with Trinidad Torregrosa and Jesús Pérez. Working with Armando shortly thereafter was percussionist and future white "showman" Rogelio Darias, who began in Santa Clara as a bongosero in son sextets and then became one of the first to use three congas on a stand and with lighting effects. Darias worked for several years with Armando Oréfiche's Lecuona Cuban Boys, and after his time at the Tropicana he appeared as an attraction in the orchestra-shows of Xavier Cugat and Liberace. Later on Ricardo Abreu ("Papín"), the founder and director of the group Los Papines, was with the Tropicana band. With percussionists like these, I am convinced that Armando Romeu's orchestra of the 1950s would have been able to successfully compete in any battle of the bands with the great Afro-Cuban jazz bands of New York, and it is not coincidental that many of Machito's musicians, as well as Tito Puente's and Tito Rodríguez's, had played with Armando.

Sometimes critics and historians from the United States can be excessively provincial, poorly informed on what occurs in the rest of the world. For this reason many say that Afro-Cuban jazz, mambo, or salsa were created or "invented" in New York. If there is one thing that we have attempted to do in these pages it's to put things in their proper order and show, or at least suggest and offer supporting evidence, that things don't tend to be so simple, and that any history consists of much more than four or five big names. Unfortunately, history has been written by those who live in big metropolises and they have had the benefit of the whole spectrum of mass media to spread their impressions or ideas on this or that development. But I believe that those who don't know what was happening in Havana, and in other parts of the island, during the Forties and Fifties—which has taken us much further back—can never speak with authority on the origins of any of these musical forms. And one of the culminating moments in the history of Cuban music, never mentioned by historians from either the United States or Cuba, took place in the 1950s, with the Tropicana as its epicenter.

Among the great renditions of Armando Romeu's orchestra was the classic "Manteca" by Chano and Dizzy, transcribed by Armando straight from the record. The transcription was exact, but the number sounded different (we don't mean better, but rather that it had its own flavor), in part because of solos by Gustavo Más on tenor and Luis Escalante on trumpet and the combination of three percussionists. Suffice it to say that Luis Escalante started out sounding like Bunny Berrigan and progressed to bop, although it was difficult to say whom he sounded like then. Guillermo Barreto told me: ". . . like *Don* Fagerquist," a little known trumpet player at the time and completely forgotten today, but with a very unique style. One also had to hear tenor player Gustavo Más on an arrangement by guitarist Isidro Pérez of "My Old Flame"; it proved to be very easy for Gustavo to make the transition from his first influence, Lester Young, to the cool style of the "Four Brothers," and in my opinion he sounded like Herbie Steward, except when he would play numbers with a Cuban flavor. We only heard the leader of the band play (on his old Conn tenor) two or three times, and on Ellington numbers such as "Solitude" (Armando was never a bop tenor saxist).

Feeling and Jam
  Sessions in the Fifties

The feeling movement—and style—reached its highest point of expressive development in the 1950s, and its founders were joined by new talents such as pianist and composer Frank Domínguez and Marta Valdés. Nevertheless, the movement's definitive success in the country would not come until the early years of the following decade; there were still many renowned composers, with a lot of influence in the media, who would do everything they could to "block" feeling, using the ridiculous argument that it represented a "foreignizing" or "Americanizing" music. Some feeling greats emigrated, among them José Antonio Méndez and Francisco Fellove, who became real idols in Mexico. In 1956, at the behest of José Antonio, "El King," the composer and arranger Niño Rivera would also travel to Mexico, where he wrote orchestrations for Mario Ruiz Armengol, Sabre Marroquín, Luis García Esquivel, Arturo Núñez, Pablo Beltrán Ruiz, and for the outstanding jazz trumpet player Chilo Morán. Then he worked as an arranger for the record companies RCA Victor, Musart, Columbia, Peerless, and Seeco, but, after a relatively short period of time, he returned to Cuba, where, up to his death in 1996, he didn't have much luck.

Mexico was the country that benefited from the presence of creators and interpreters of feeling, who without a doubt had an influence on the great Vicente Garrido, Alvaro Carrillo, Roberto Cantoral, Luis Demetrio, and so many others who enriched and modernized the Mexican bolero tradition. Meanwhile, the feeling singer Pepe Reyes traveled through Colombia and Peru, and Miguel de Gonzalo went to Venezuela, where he recorded with Aldemaro Romero's orchestra and received the recognition that he was always denied at home (Miguel de Gonzalo committed suicide in his birthplace, Santiago de Cuba, in the 1970s). The instrumentalists linked to feeling and jazz, such as the brilliant blind pianist Frank Emilio, could be found through most of the Fifties in small nightclubs, as soloists, playing accompaniment or as part of a combo. For example, Frank Emilio for years headed a son group at the club Maxim's, and in 1956 a group featuring Frank Domínguez (piano), César Portillo de la Luz (guitar), the Argentine Luis Ortellado (trumpet), Alfredo León (bass), and Gastón Laserie (drums), worked exceptionally at the Sans Souci. But in general, the feeling musicians spent ten years without going much further than small clubs, to which their fans would show up faithfully, as a sort of sect of initiated members, which reminds us again of the bebop scene in the 1940s.

The second wave of the feeling movement, to the extent that it can be separated from the first, was very important at the University of Havana, where regular jam sessions were held in one of its *salones*. Musicians such as pianists Virgilio "Yiyo" López and Samuel Téllez, bassist Reinaldo Mercier, trumpeter Wichy Mercier, guitarist Pablo Cano, and others were university students, as were several members of the vocal group Cuban Pipers (later reorganized under the name Los Cavaliers). One of them, Tony Suárez Rocabruna, would organize frequent jazz and feeling jam sessions at his house on Lealtad Street. These encounters were important for the exchange of ideas and because it was where the younger jazz musicians became stronger through contact with the more experienced ones. Among the participants in these descargas at singer Tony Suárez's house were the following: trumpets: Wichy Mercier and Constantino Clenton ("El Jamaiquino"); tenor saxes: Tata Palau, Pedro Chao, and Leonardo Acosta; pianists: Bebo Valdés, Yiyo López, Samuel Téllez, Frank Emilio Flynn, and Felipe Yánes Pelletier; bassists: Reinaldo Mercier, Fernando Vivar, and Orlando "Cachaíto" López; drummers: Walfredito de los Reyes, Daniel Pérez, and Guillermo Alvarez.

Constantino Clenton, of Jamaican origin, was an excellent bop trumpeter, with great fluidity of ideas and a phrasing that reminded me of Howard McGhee (around 1956 or '57 he left Cuba with Pantaleón Pérez Prado's orchestra). Orlando López, a bassist who worked at the time with the Fajardo y sus Estrellas charanga, was the son of Orestes "Macho" López, composer of the danzón "Mambo," and nephew of the great Cachao, Israel López, who took Orlando to the Philharmonic Orchestra for a rehearsal, which hired him that same day. Having associated him more with Cachao than with Macho, the musicians nicknamed Orlando López "Cachaíto." When Walfredito de los Reyes introduced him to us in a jam session, he impressed us all, playing along on "How High the Moon," which lasted fifty minutes. He showed impeccable technique and a powerful sound. A bit later he would become one of the integral bassists in the jazz sessions and concerts along with Luis Rodríguez and "Papito" Hernández, younger brother of Felo and Kiki Hernández.

Getting back to feeling and the vocal quartets, in this decade the most successful of all emerged: Las D'Aida, led by pianist and arranger Aida Diestro and made up of women, who were initially Elena Burke, Moraima Secada, Omara Portuondo, and Haydée Portuondo. The D'Aida ladies became a main attraction at the exclusive Club 21 (on Twenty-first and N, across from the Capri Hotel) and then they performed in many different nightclubs, from the popular La Campana (on Infanta Street) to the Sans Souci and Tropicana, where the jazz musicians who visited us always wanted to meet the arranger of the quartet, who didn't appear on stage. (We found out later that some of her arrangements were done by Chico O'Farrill). They also became the only group within the feeling movement that performed often on television and went on international tours, which included seasons in the show at the Miami Fontainebleau; on one occasion they shared the stage with Nat King Cole. At the end of the decade two important vocal groups emerged: Felipe Dulzaides's Los Armónicos and Roberto Marín's Los Bucaneros, both inspired by groups such as the Four Freshmen and the Hi Lo's, which we will return to later on.

Among the private homes where jazz and feeling jam sessions were held, I should mention my own place, in the El Cerro barrio. We started out small; all of us were university students and professional musicians at the same time. Virgilio "Yiyo" López was the pianist, Reinaldo Mercier was on bass (he also played piano), Pablo Cano on guitar, and often drummer Bertie Cancio would show up. At that time I played alto sax, and the trumpet player was Wichy Mercier, brother of Reinaldo and of pianist Agustín Mercier, who had already established his residence in the Dominican Republic. (Previously we had been able to get together for jam sessions at the Merciers' house). Joining this group were José Antonio Méndez ("El King") and the great guitarist Isidro Pérez, invited by Pablo Cano. For his part El King brought in Frank Emilio and I spoke with Walfredito de los Reyes and Guillermo Barreto. On one occasion Isidro Pérez played the transcriptions for two guitars that he had made from Lennie Tristano's and Lee Konitz's numbers, with Pablo Cano as second voice. In turn Walfredo told Daniel Pérez about these descargas, and Barreto told the Tropicana's jazz musicians.

So that's how musicians such as Bebo Valdés, Fernando Vivar, El Negro Vivar, and Tata Palau, who in turn brought in Pedro Chao, became involved in these jam sessions. And of course, the number of fans grew, including some from the vocal group Los Cavaliers and pianist Samuel Téllez. It was in one of these sessions that I heard Frank Emilio for the first time in person; one of the Cuban jazz innovators on piano, he had achieved an incredible fusion of Art Tatum, Bud Powell, and George Shearing with Afro-

Cuban rhythms. And although we played standards such as "I'm in the Mood for Love" (from which I was able to transcribe note for note the solo of James Moody's version), "I'll Remember April," "Tea for Two," "Lady Be Good," "Cherokee," "Blue Moon," and others, frequently we would end up improvising on a montuno, as Rafael Somavilla Jr. did on one occasion. The presence of Somavilla was a real surprise, for he had recently arrived from Matanzas and had already found out about these descargas; it was also the first time he had played piano in Havana, and among the audience that listened to him were such notable pianists as Frank Emilio and Bebo Valdés.

As foreign guests, we had the Mexican trumpet players José Solís and Guadalupe Montes, who had arrived in Havana with the band of Dámaso Pérez Prado. Solís was an excellent improviser particularly in the high register, and had replaced Chilo Morán as first trumpet in Dámaso's orchestra. (Years later I happened to meet up with him again in Mexico, in the Rúa cabaret, on Avenida Juárez; in those descargas José Solís played the flugelhorn and Chilo Morán the trumpet). In sum, the following musicians participated in the El Cerro descargas: El Negro Vivar, Wichy Mercier, José Solís, and Lupe Montes (trumpets); Tata Palau and Pedro Chao (tenor saxes); Leonardo Acosta (alto sax); Reinaldo Mercier and Fernando Vivar (bassists); Isidro Pérez and Pablo Cano (electric guitar); Guillermo Barreto, Walfredo de los Reyes, and Daniel Pérez (drums); and the best jazz pianists at that time, with few exceptions: Bebo Valdés, Frank Emilio, Virgilio López, Samuel Téllez, Felipe Yánes Pelletier, and Rafael Somavilla.

The High Point of the Batanga Rhythm

In 1952 the pianist, composer, and arranger Bebo Valdés started what could be considered a musical revolution similar to the one that Machito and Mario Bauzá began in New York or Dámaso Pérez Prado had begun in Mexico. Nevertheless, what would have been the *batanga* rhythm revolution remains as only an interesting historical curiosity and a pleasant memory for those that lived it. Bebo, pianist and arranger of Armando Romeu's band and deeply involved in the feeling movement, seemed the perfect man to bring about a new fusion between jazz and Afro-Cuban music, surpassing the growing commercialization of mambo and the limitations of chachachá. In his musical conceptions, Bebo was very similar to Niño Rivera, and both had spent years experimenting with new rhythmic and orchestral combinations. If El Niño had to his credit numbers such as "El Jamaiquino" and "Atomo," Bebo had composed "Rareza del siglo," "Daiquirí," "Copla guajira," "Ritmando el chachachá," and above all "Güempa," a mambo that became very popular. As usual with mambos, this one had only a sung theme for eight measures and the rest was instrumental, but with no room for soloists. It also didn't offer substantial rhythmic changes. These would come with batanga and the orchestra that Bebo organized to play it.

Two years before, when the band of Pérez Prado was at Channel 4 and the Sans Souci cabaret, one night we took our Mexican friends to hear the Tropicana orchestra. After the set was over we sat down to talk and they asked Bebo Valdés his opinion on Pérez Prado's band. Bebo responded that his ear was telling him that a trombone section would be good to fill the vacuum between the high and low timbres that Damaso's orchestrations created. And this is what he did with batanga from the orchestral point of view, including three trombones and a French horn, an unusual instrument in jazz bands. And there were, of course, new rhythmic combinations introduced in Cuban percussion, where for the first time a *batá* drum was used within a new rhythm. Bebo Valdés along with his orchestra and his batanga rhythm were presented in a special program on the radio station RHC Cadena Azul Sundays in the afternoon and later during evening hours, and recordings were made of some programs, although only on recording tape, which were never made into records to be sold on the market. The orchestra that Bebo formed had a number of musicians from Armando Romeu's band, starting naturally with Bebo himself. The impressive lineup was the following: trumpets: Nilo Argudín, Dagoberto Jiménez, El Negro Vivar, Chocolate Armenteros, and Pedro Rodríguez; trombones: Alberto Martí, Generoso Jiménez, and Miguel Reina; French horn: Víctor del Castillo; saxophones: "El Cabito" Quesada and Roberto Sánchez (altos), Gustavo Más and Ñico Romero (tenors), and Diego "Bebo" Loredo (baritone). The rhythm section featured Bebo Valdés (piano), Kiki Hernández (bass), Guillermo Barreto (drums), Rolando Alfonso and Arturo Linares ("Hueso") on congas, Trinidad Torregosa on batá drum, and the singers "El Indio" Cruz and Ezequiel Cárdenas.

In the orchestra's debut, Bebo Valdés, at six-foot-four, went up to the microphone to explain that batanga came from the African terms *batá* and *tanga*, and he defined the rhythmic design of the percussion. Then the first conga played its basic rhythmic pattern, then the second, followed by the two playing at the same time; then it was the batá's turn, and finally the three drums played together. The reaction from the audience was delirium, and singer Pepe Reyes, a good friend of Bebo's, was shouting: "Bebo, you're crazy!" But the best had only just begun. On numbers such as "Batanga tú bailarás" the band sounded better than we had expected. One of the high points was the trumpet duel between El Negro Vivar and Chocolate Armenteros, which brought the crowd to its feet. If this recording existed, and we could save it, we would have before us a historic milestone of Afro-Cuban jazz: improvising for the first time on the same number were two of the movement's great trumpeters, who would later become renowned in New York, Chocolate after joining Machito in that same decade and El Negro after 1960.

When the program was over, a jam session was held right there in the studio, for the enjoyment of the small group of "initiates" that stayed to listen. Participating were El Negro Vivar on trumpet, Gustavo Más on tenor, Bebo on piano, Kiki Hernández on bass, and Guillermo Barreto on drums, and it was a relaxing "cool" ending to a very intense big band session with Afro-Cuban rhythms. Gustavo Más shone, as was almost customary, especially on a "Pennies from Heaven" worthy of Stan Getz or Lester Young. During the next three Sundays the batanga orchestra continued appearing on RHC, and then at night a few times, but the sponsors didn't seem excited nor was the "new rhythm" given any promotion, and it disappeared almost as soon as it was born. As always, to the promoters, going with what was already popular turned out to be less risky than investing in something new. What had happened to Pérez Prado—which forced him to go to Mexico— and to Niño Rivera with his Cubibop, was happening again. In addition, chachachá had just recently become popular in an almost natural way, first among the dancers, then with the success of Enrique Jorrín's "La engañadora," followed by other big hits of Jorrín's and other songwriters from Orquesta América. And the strength—as well as the weakness—of chachachá was in the simplicity of its sound as well as in the ease with which it could be danced to.

Nevertheless, something more than a simple memory remained of the batanga, since in one of the programs Bebo unexpectedly presented a singer who had recently arrived from Mexico after leaving Pérez Prado's band. It was of course Beny Moré, whose first performances in Cuba after his mambo success in Mexico were on this very program with Bebo Valdés's orchestra and batanga. And the contact with the band and the sonority of batanga had an influence on Beny later on when he formed his own orchestra, which would include some of the musicians from Bebo's band as well.

Beny's band, formed in 1953, featured at different times the two trumpet players from the batanga orchestra, Alejandro Vivar and Alfredo Armenteros, with baritone saxophonist Diego Loredo and trombonist and arranger Generoso Jiménez. Beny Moré's other arrangers were Eduardo Cabrera, the band's pianist, and Peruchín Jústiz. Despite the inevitable influence of Pérez Prado on the arrangers of the time, Beny's band achieved a different sound, perhaps closer to that of Machito's or Bebo Valdés's, despite having only one trombone, like Dámaso (although for recordings he used two). For percussion, unlike Pérez Prado, Beny would employ the classic instrumentation of the Cuban jazz bands—drums, conga, and bongo. Among Beny's percussionists we should mention particularly the bongosero Clemente "Chicho" Piquero, who was a key member of Pérez Prado's band in México and returned to Cuba along with Beny. "Tabaquito" and then Jesusón López, among others, were featured on conga. On drums was Tibo Lee, as well as Rolando Laserie, who also sung in the chorus along with Fernando Alvarez and Enrique Benítez.

Among the jazz musicians or those associated with jazz who passed through Beny's orchestra were, besides Chocolate and El Negro, trumpet players Leonardo Timor Jr., Domingo Corbacho, and the great Jorge Varona (cofounder of Irakere in 1973); trombonist Generoso Jiménez; saxophonists Miguel Franca and Santiaguito Peñalver (altos), Roberto Barreto, José "Chombo" Silva, and Leonardo Acosta (tenors), and Virgilio Vixama (baritone); and drummers Tibo Lee and Rolando Laserie. Although Beny Moré never really played jazz, in his repertoire he had dance numbers of Glenn Miller's and of other American jazz bands, and Beny not only listened to a lot of jazz but also had a whole library of jazz at home. But more important than the presence of jazz musicians in Beny's band was the work of the arrangers, who developed a Cuban way of orchestral composition simultaneously with the "Latin" orchestras of New York. We've already referred to important Cuban arrangers who experimented as much with jazz as they did with our music: Félix Guerrero, Chico O'Farrill, Armando Romeu, El Niño Rivera, Bebo Valdés, and Pucho Escalante, among others. In addition to Beny's arrangers, in the 1950s musicians such as Ernesto Duarte, Rafael Ortega, Adolfo Guzmán, Rafael Somavilla, Rolando Baró, Adolfo Pichardo, and others excelled, without mentioning the arrangers who stood out for their work in the charangas, such as Israel and Orestes López, to mention only the best known.

A peculiar case among the arrangers has been Severino Ramos. Composer of boleros such as "Luna yumurina," Ramos decided to orchestrate classic numbers from the popular Cuban repertoire and those that were becoming popular, all for jazz band format. He ended up orchestrating hundreds of pieces that would be printed and sold in music stores and even at a kiosk at the musicians' union local. Although Ramos was not an exceptional arranger, much less an innovator, he was very skillful, and his arrangements of Cuban numbers for jazz band served as a basic repertoire for more than one beginning orchestra and were of immeasurable value for the development of many new jazz bands and their musicians. But within this brief period of what might some day be labeled the "Cuban school of orchestration," I would like to mention specifically three arrangers of particular importance: Pedro Jústiz, Armando Romeu, and Arturo "Chico" O'Farrill.

Pedro Jústiz, the celebrated Peruchín, began in Santiago de Cuba with the Ideal and Chepín-Chovén orchestras. Upon arriving in Havana he worked with the Casino de la Playa, Mariano Mercerón, Conjunto Matamoros, and saxophonist Emilio Peñalver's Swing Boys orchestra. For a time he worked in Panama with the orchestra of Carlos Boza, who had also hired trumpet player "Coco" Barreto and saxophonists Roberto Barreto and Gustavo Más. Back in the 1940s Peruchín joined Armando Romeu's orchestra at the Tropicana, and in the 1950s he performed superbly with the Riverside. At the end of the decade he decided to form a trio with the typical jazz format (piano-bass-drums), which included at its height drummer Walfredo de los Reyes and bassist Papito Hernández, replaced later by Orlando López (Cachaíto). Peruchín wrote arrangements for the Casino, Mercerón, Armando Romeu, Beny Moré, and the Riverside, and some of his originals were performed by almost all of the Cuban jazz bands and by a few from abroad. His most popular numbers were "Mamey colorao," "Mambo en disminuido," "España en llamas," "Qué equivocación," and the arrangements of "Guantánamo" and "Manzanillo" for Beny Moré.[5]

We have chosen Pedro Jústiz because in a certain sense he summarizes or exemplifies the Cuban style of orchestration, combining mambo phrasing and other Cuban styles and genres with the orchestral legacy of the American jazz arrangers. Something similar could be said with respect to Bebo Valdés, El Niño Rivera, René Hernández, Mario Bauzá, and others, although not all. Arturo "Chico" O'Farrill deserves a special mention, since he has been the only Cuban arranger who has had a big role in jazz orchestration in Cuba and in the United States, for up to the 1950s he traveled between the two countries, while Mario Bauzá, for example, pursued his whole career in the United States, and Armando Romeu remained in Cuba. Furthermore, Chico O'Farrill became the only Cuban arranger to enter directly into jazz history without having to first go through "Latin jazz," when he wrote "Undercurrent Blues" for Benny Goodman's band in the Fifties, whose recording was a hit. O'Farrill began as a trumpet player, as I have already explained, and became known in the Cuban jazz milieu particularly in the orchestras of Isidro Pérez, Armando Romeu, and the Bellamar. Then he studied piano and orchestration (with Félix Guerrero) and organized the first bop groups in Havana (see Chapter 4). In New York he studied with the composer Stephan Wolpe, maestro to several jazz arrangers such as Johnny Carisi and Bob Graettinger.

When Benny Goodman decided to join the bop tendency, he hired soloists such as Doug Mettome (trumpet), Wardell Gray (tenor sax), Buddy Greco (piano), and Sonny Igoe (drums), but he didn't have an arranger who could create the new repertoire, and he organized a sort of audition process in a theater hall where the band would play the submitted arrangements. Discarding various arrangements after only a few measures, he played "Undercurrent Blues" from top to bottom and made the decision to hire Chico O'Farrill. After a year with Benny Goodman's band, O'Farrill received a request from Stan Kenton to write a piece for his new orchestra, which included French horns, a tuba, woodwinds, and up to twenty-two strings, and O'Farrill composed his "Cuban Episode." After that Chico O'Farrill wrote several of the most important works of Afro-Cuban jazz for Machito and Dizzy Gillespie, and afterward he arranged

for his idol Count Basie, who upon meeting Chico expressed his amaze-
ment that a white person had written such arrangements. Besides the LPs
made under his name in the United States (and one in Cuba) during the
1950s, O'Farrill's arrangements were heard—some new and others from
the previous decade, but ahead of their time—at the Tropicana, where they
were performed by Armando Romeu's band, with whom Chico always
remained in contact.[6]

Romeu, with a musical training that is at least three-fourths self taught,
represents an unusual case. He has stated: "I began arranging from practice,
since the traditional harmony that I studied in many aspects doesn't work
for arranging popular music." He would spend a lot of time transcribing
records that had arrangements of the best jazz bands in the world, saying
this was his "favorite hobby in life." He took it in the right direction, analyzing the transcribed works. He continues:

> Transcribing records is the best school that a popular musician can have. . . . You
> learn to manage the voicings correctly, to have a greater understanding of the
> resolution tendencies of the chords, to lay correct harmonic progressions; you
> acquire a good understanding of modulation techniques; you learn to effectively
> write a background, to achieve rich/colorful sonorities through sound combi-
> nations among the sections which make up the orchestral body; you learn about
> musical forms, you gain experience in the techniques of improvisation; you
> acquire a sense of external and internal rhythm, [you learn] to set out logical
> movements in the bass line, to correctly place instruments in their correspon-
> ding registers. . . . In short, the best school that a popular musician can have.[7]

When the Bellamar orchestra was organized to play the Sans Souci, as we
have seen, Armando brought in Félix Guerrero as a guitarist, and Félix in
turn offered courses in orchestration that attracted Chico O'Farrill, Pucho
Escalante, and Armando himself, among others. Later, Armando Romeu
wrote the arrangements for the great Tropicana productions, as well as
"Quizás, quizás" for Nat King Cole, "Bop City Mambo" and "Mambo in
Sepia" for Lionel Hampton's band, and his "Mambo a la Kenton" for
Dámaso Pérez Prado. Other works of Armando Romeu are the *Suite
Varadero,* in three movements; *Variaciones sobre un tema cubano* ("Almendra");
and "Blues in Fourths," to mention only the most experimental. In Armando's

orchestral work we find a certain eclecticism common to all the Cuban arrangers, because of the diversity of sources from which they have drawn. For example, the pianist and arranger Rolando Baró, who had an extensive career, pointed out that his main influences were Niño Rivera, Bebo Valdés, Peruchín, and Pérez Prado; and among American arrangers he mentioned such dissimilar musicians as Thad Jones, Pete Rugolo, Johnny Richards, and Nelson Riddle, which shouldn't surprise us, since Afro-Latin jazz and Cuban music have always been shaped and enriched by such disparate elements.[8]

Jazz in the Nightclubs

Time and again during this decade—as in others—bigger as well as smaller clubs would hire jazz groups, or groups that included jazz musicians and tunes; and these clubs would immediately become hot spots for jazz musicians and eventually centers for jam sessions. One of these cabarets was the Southland, at the centrally located corner of San Rafael and Prado, in the vicinity of the historic Acera del Louvre. This spot had already housed other popular nightclubs, and later it would even be renamed Casablanca and Cabaret Nacional de Prado. Appearing there in the 1950s was a group led by one of the great jazz and alto sax pioneers in Cuba, Germán Lebatard, whose band had finally been dissolved. Rounding out the group were Wichy Mercier on trumpet, Rolando Baró on piano, Megret on drums, and alternating on bass were two of the three Hernández brothers, Felo and Papito. Papito was beginning to shine as the decade's most sought-after bassist.

Germán Lebatard inspired and helped many young jazz musicians. The tenor player Pedro Chao always said that he decided to be a saxophonist when he saw and heard Germán leading the Lebatard Brothers orchestra at the Encanto Theater, playing his theme song, "Star Dust," with a golden instrument and decked out in a white suit. Musicians from different orchestras would frequently show up at the Southland to jam with Germán's group, which for a while turned this club into a new jazz hot spot in Havana. Of medium size and with a variety show, this place—which has been around for more than three-quarters of a century under different names—is one of those that is below street level, although its dimensions are larger than those of a "cave," like many others in Havana or any other big city. One of the regulars was an alto sax player who would become a household name in that decade, Miguelito Franca. In addition to improvising in a style reminiscent of Art Pepper and playing a number of instruments ranging from clarinet to baritone equally well, he was famous for his memory: with one show rehearsal of perhaps an hour and a half he no longer needed to read the music. He was with the Casino de la Playa, Beny Moré, and Julio Gutiérrez. As for the Southland, it changed owners and its name, but years later it would once again become a jazz hot spot when a group led by Pedro Jústiz, our great Peruchín, worked there.

At the beginning of the decade there was another rather unorthodox jazz group, which went almost unnoticed; it played at the Faraón cabaret on Zanja Street about one block from Belascoaín, that is, from the corner occupied by the dance hall of the Sport Antillano society, and across from this the Café O.K., one of the musicians' favorite spots to eat at late hours of the night. Close by was also the Gato Club, a descarga center for the feeling group. The Faraón cabaret had a variety show and two orchestras: the first, which would do the show, was led by Obdulio Morales, a composer and specialist in Afro-Cuban music.[9] The well-known "second orchestra" was a very heterogeneous jazz combo led by the saxophonist Rubén Morales ("Perro Chino") and including four musicians who had been left out of Armando Romeu's orchestra: trumpet player Dagoberto Jiménez ("Rabanito"), bassist Fernando Vivar, conga player Rolando Alfonso, and bongosero (at that time) Cándido Camero; the pianist was Rolando Baró and the drummer Rolando Laserie.

Rubén was one of the three Cuban musicians who survived the Euzkera shipwreck, which included among its passengers the Razzore circus, traveling from Havana to South America. Of the twelve survivors, three were Cuban members of the band: trumpet player César "Piyú" Godínez, the young jazz pianist Felipe Yanes Pelletier, and Rubén Morales. And it was "Perro Chino" who saved the corpulent trumpet player "Piyú" when the occupants of the only lifeboat remaining, in a state of panic, tried to prevent the heavy Godínez from getting into the overcrowded boat. Although Rubén stood out primarily on tenor sax, he was a multi-instrumentalist who played clarinet, alto, flute, trumpet, piano, and percussion with equal skill. His performance on the tenor seems to me of special importance, since in this decade he was practically the only Cuban tenor saxophonist who played in the style of Sonny Rollins, at a time when almost everyone had taken on the cool style, from the veterans Emilio Peñalver and Gustavo Más to Pedro Chao and Tata Palau. And on trumpet he would play with fluidity in the style of the first bop trumpeters. But Rubén had before him a real trial by fire when Obdulio Morales gave up conducting the Faraón's first orchestra and the impresario turned to him as a replacement.

For some time Rubén led the orchestra without leaving the group in which he could "jam," and which to a great extent depended on him. The only other improvising soloist was pianist Rolando Baró, although "Rabanito" had versions of all of the solos written for him by Guillermo Barreto at the Tropicana, and a good part of the group's repertoire came from Barreto. But there was another problem: percussionist Cándido Camero received a contract offer to go to the United States, where almost immediately he achieved a certain level of fame as "Chano Pozo's successor," recording as a soloist with Stan Kenton's band, with Dizzy Gillespie, and with the great pianist Billy Taylor and his trio. During his time at the Faraón, Candito through experimentation would renew the way in which Cuban percussion was played, particularly after Rolando Alfonso had left the group and he remained as the only percussionist. Among other things, he was able to play the bongo and two congas simultaneously, for which he had a special stand constructed, and later he took these techniques to the United States. When he announced his departure, the owner of the cabaret came to "Perro Chino" again and Rubén explained to him that nobody could replace Candito. Finally he came up with an answer: he found a replacement for himself and he personally took charge of playing Candito's two congas and bongo.[10]

When the center of the city shifted to the "La Rampa" zone, in Vedado, there was a complete shift in the musical scene from the Prado zone and its surroundings to the new center, which was situated more or less on the very border between Vedado and what is today called Centro Habana, beginning on Infanta Street. Around 1955 a cabaret that lay precisely on this border became popular: Las Vegas, at Infanta and Twenty-fifth, almost equidistant from the studios of Channels 6 (CMQ) and 4 (P and Twenty-third) and the big hotels in the area (Hilton, Capri, Nacional, St. John's). Finally, across from Las Vegas was Radio Progreso, the "Onda de la Alegría" (oddly, both are still there, and with the same names). The founder and proprietor of the club was an ex-soccer player from the university, equally well acquainted with revolutionary circles, Havana high society, and the Las Vegas Mafia, thus the name. And as he was also a jazz fan, the club became a new center for jam sessions.

On one occasion at this club we recorded a tape with arrangements of mine and of Frank Emilio's; from two to six o'clock in the morning we went from one song to the next, inspired more or less by Lennie Tristano's quintet, with a group that included Frank Emilio (piano), Leonardo Acosta (alto sax), Pedro Chao (tenor sax), Cachaíto López (bass), and Walfredo de los Reyes (drums). Shortly thereafter we held a jam session with Chico O'Farrill, who reminisced on his days as a trumpeter; taking part were Gustavo Más (tenor sax), Leonardo Acosta (alto sax), Frank Emilio (piano), Cachaíto López (bass), and Walfredo (drums). Also participating in these descargas were saxophonist Miguel Franca (playing alto and tenor), drummer Daniel Pérez, trombonist Jorge Rojas, and tenor saxophonist Jesús Caunedo. But the most impressive descarga at the Las Vegas club included the great Sarah Vaughan, who was performing at the Sans Souci. Present at this jam session were the Sans Souci musicians and most of the Cuban jazz musicians, including Bebo Valdés, Guillermo Barreto, and El Negro Vivar, who were not regulars at the Las Vegas jam sessions. Feeling singers such as Elena Burke, José Antonio Méndez, and Omara Portuondo were also present, but that's already another story.

One day the owner of the club proposed that I form a jazz group to work there on a regular basis, and we agreed to begin with some "Jazz Fridays." So I formed a group together with trombonist Jorge Rojas (who had led the Cubamar orchestra) and soon we attracted a very enthusiastic crowd, but they weren't exactly big spenders. The proprietor of the club explained the situation to me: "You know what happens? I don't have anything against blacks, as you know, but they don't spend their money here, and the ones who have money are the whites and they don't like the club filled with blacks." And he added: "Blacks like jazz a lot, and I do too; it would be nice if they had money and would spend it here, so we could have jazz every night." I don't think I've ever heard a better explanation of the problem of jazz in Cuba and the difficulties of the jazz musician.

There were other centers of nightlife where we held jam sessions, sometimes in the afternoon and other times in the late night hours. Among them were places ranging from the exclusive Club 21 and Maxim's to the Gato

Club, a favorite hangout for feeling enthusiasts. One afternoon we even held a jam session at the Mambo Club, on Rancho Boyeros road, where the famous and influential Marina, owner of the most exclusive bordellos in Havana for two decades, had established her headquarters. It was in the afternoon, and there still wasn't much of a crowd. Later on I have thought more than once that on that day, without knowing it, we were returning perhaps symbolically to the days when ragtime pianists would play in the bordellos of the Storyville district, in the legendary years of the birth of jazz in New Orleans.

7
End of the Decade

The Club Cubano de Jazz

A new and decisive factor in Cuban musical life after 1950 was television, and particularly Channels 2, 4, and 6, with their extensive musical programming, big studio orchestras, and the appearance of Cuban singing stars, groups, and top international performers. These artists were often hired exclusively by the channels themselves; sometimes they came to act in cabaret or theater and were also hired by some TV shows. So along with renowned national artists such as Beny Moré, Celia Cruz, Olga Guillot, and many others, the Cuban public could enjoy the performances of Pedro Vargas, Lucho Gatica, Alfredo Sadel, Nelson Pinedo, and many more, some of whom became real idols.[1]

Of the orchestras formed by the television stations, the one with the most jazz musicians was Julio Gutiérrez's, who had organized his band in 1948 to work at the radio station RHC Cadena Azul; although there were a few changes, many of his musicians went with him to Channel 4 TV. Among the trumpet players were Nilo Argudín and Alejandro Vivar; on alto saxes were Edilberto Escrich and Osvaldo "Mosquifín" Urrutia, who then switched to baritone sax, while Amadito Valdés and Miguelito Franca filled the alto sax slots. Among the tenor saxes were Rubén Morales ("Perro Chino"), and when he left the orchestra Emilio Peñalver, Lito Rivero, and Leonardo Acosta alternated. Although Julio Gutiérrez was an excellent pianist and composer, he dedicated himself exclusively to conducting, as he had top-rank pianists such as René Urbino and then Dick Farney, one of the best jazz pianists to come out of Brazil, who also worked in Adolfo Guzmán's orchestra. On bass, Salvador Vivar ("Bol") replaced his brother Fernando Vivar when he went on to Armando Romeu's orchestra at the Tropicana; on drums, Julio Gutiérrez had Daniel Pérez (also known as "Gene Krupa") and then Walfredito de los Reyes; and on Cuban percussion he had for a time Rogelio Darias, who then went on to the Tropicana, and later the exceptional combination of Oscar Valdés (conga) and Marcelino Valdés (bongo), both brothers of the popular bolerista Vicentico Valdés, who was living in New York by then. When Marcelino was hired to work in the United States, his cousin Roberto García replaced him.[2]

Meanwhile, in the world of big cabarets the luxurious Sans Souci remained Tropicana's main competition, and on occasion even surpassed it. Working at the Sans Souci for years was an orchestra of very high caliber led by pianist and arranger Rafael Ortega. At one time this band's trumpet section featured Walfredo de los Reyes Sr., Alejandro "Coco" Barreto, and El Negro Vivar, who played in all the important jazz bands of the time. Also appearing in Rafael Ortega's orchestra were alto saxophonists Juanito Martínez and Orestes Barbachán, tenor saxist Charles Rodríguez, and trombonist Ernesto Romeu. For a time the bassist was José Manuel Peña and the drummer was Guillermo Barreto. These were some of the orchestra's musicians at the Sans Souci when Tommy Dorsey's band arrived, shortly after Woody Herman's performance at the Tropicana. By this time Tommy Dorsey, like other veteran swing bandleaders, had renewed his repertoire with very modern arrangements and a combination of bop and swing soloists. The most notable musicians were the lead trumpet Ray Wetzel, who had recently come over from Stan Kenton's band; trumpeter Doc Severinsen, a marvelous bopper whom we already knew from his solo with Charlie Barnet's band on the number "Cu-Ba"; the tenor sax soloist was the veteran Boomie Richmond, typical representative of the Swing Era; and on drums was the colossal Buddy Rich.

During this band's stay in Havana, all of the jazz fans and musicians switched from the Tropicana to the Sans Souci. Tommy Dorsey—who continued with his sentimental style, playing the trombone solo in his theme song "Marie"—wasn't the main attraction for Cuban jazz musicians; the one who stole the show was Buddy Rich. Then the unexpected happened: Buddy became ill and was hospitalized. Dorsey didn't know what to do and he skeptically accepted the advice that he use Guillermo Barreto as a substitute. Even without previous rehearsal, the Cuban's performance was so perfect that Dorsey couldn't believe it; Barreto knew the right breaks on all the numbers; he had listened to Buddy Rich night after night and memorized everything that he would do; and not only did he memorize the breaks, but also the arrangements. When he left the hospital a short time later, Buddy Rich told Barreto that he had already made the decision to leave Dorsey's band and continue on his own, and he asked Barreto to replace him. Tommy Dorsey offered him a contract, which the Cuban didn't accept at that time because, as he said, he was terrified of flying.[3]

The following year Barreto returned to the Tropicana and found that the latest attraction was Xavier Cugat, who had arrived in Havana with a big Hollywood-type orchestra, with strings and much better arrangements than those of his first stage. A good part of the orchestra consisted of Cuban musicians hired in Havana, among them saxophonist Germán Lebatard and percussionist Rogelio Darias, who would later join Cugat and leave on tour with him. The orchestra of the Catalan musician included some "typical Cuban" instruments made in the United States, such as a set of timbales a bit larger than our pailas. Guillermo Barreto always remembered that Bebo Valdés had prophetically advised him: "Buy yourself a set of those, because that's how you'll make your living, not on the drums." In the following decades Guillermo Barreto acquired international renown more as a timbalero than as a drummer, although in spite of it all, we should say that he was first and foremost one of the most important jazz drummers to come out of Cuba.

With Nat King Cole and Sarah Vaughan

One of the Tropicana's most illustrious visitors in the 1950s was Nat King Cole, who also brought with him a complete trio, that is, one that included a drummer.[4] This group featured John Collins (a guitarist who had worked with Art Tatum); Richie Harvest (bass); Lee Young (drums), brother of the legendary Lester Young; and of course Nat King Cole on piano. It was a significant encounter for both sides, as the famous singer and pianist who had always shown an inclination for Cuban music had also had an influence on Cuban jazz and feeling musicians, as we have seen. We should also remember that Nat King Cole's first "Latinized" LP was *Rumba a la King,* recorded in Cuba with Armando Romeu's band; later he recorded the albums *Papa Loves Mambo* and *Cole Espagnole,* but we should keep in mind that in 1949 Cole had already added Italian American bongo player Jack Constanzo to his trio.[5] We have already referred to Nat King Cole's influence among the feeling singers (particularly Leonel Bravet and José Antonio Méndez) and pianists such as Virgilio López and Samuel Téllez. In addition, a number of Cuban guitarists were followers of Oscar Moore, a member of Cole's first trio: Pablo Cano, for example, started in jazz memorizing all of Moore's solos, and then he did the same with his successor, Irving Ashby.

Just as Cab Calloway had done before and Dizzy Gillespie would do later, Nat King Cole was fulfilling an old wish to come to Cuba and he knew how to make the most of his time in Havana, musically as well as commercially. At that time, to the consternation of jazz lovers, Cole the pianist had been commercially obscured by Cole the singer, who had acquired fame with numbers such as "Nature Boy" and "Mona Lisa," although he also recorded "Lush Life" by Billy Strayhorn about that time. Nevertheless, in his performances at the Tropicana the jazz fans left quite content with his uptempo renditions of "Lover Come Back to Me" and "How High the Moon" and with his piano solos, which reminded us of his years with Lionel Hampton as well as the fact that he was one of the first pianists to assimilate the bop style. And of course, backing up his voice on his latest hits such as "Blue Gardenia" was the band of Armando Romeu. The impression that the Tropicana orchestra made on Cole led to concrete results, and when he decided to record an album with numbers in Spanish he came to Havana to do it with Armando's band; in addition, unsatisfied with the arrangement of "Quizás, quizás" that he brought along, he asked Armando for a new arrangement, which is the one that appears on the record.

While Nat King Cole appeared at the Tropicana, the Sans Souci brought in none other than Sarah Vaughan, not yet so famous, but of greater importance as a jazz singer. With her came her classic trio, perhaps the best she ever had, featuring Jimmy Jones on piano, Richard Davis on bass, and Roy Haynes on drums. Sarah was already involved in pop music, but continued to be essentially a bop singer par excellence, and unlike Cole she joined in various jam sessions with Cuban musicians and singers. One was at Las Vegas cabaret, which I have already mentioned. Another took place right there in the salón-bar of the Sans Souci after the second show. The session began with the trio of Bebo Valdés (piano), Papito Hernández (bass), and Guillermo Barreto (drums); then Sarah's trio played, beginning with a phenomenal "But Not for Me" that featured the piano mastery of Jimmy Jones. Sarah joined in singing on various numbers, among them "How High the Moon" with scat improvisations and new lyrics. At the end Cuban and American musicians played together: Pedro Chao and Leonardo Acosta (tenor saxes), Frank Emilio (piano), Richard Davis (bass), and Walfredo de los Reyes and Roy Haynes alternating on drums. At a certain point we asked Davis to play a song of his preference in which he would be the only soloist; he suggested "The Nearness of You" and asked Frank Emilio whether he knew it. Frank responded with another question, typical of him: "In what key, man?" Richard's bass solo was sensational.

A "monster" jam session was celebrated at a private home in the Country Club zone (today Cubanacán), by a pool, which was attended by about twenty Cuban jazz musicians, Sarah and her trio, and also the members of Nat King Cole's trio: John Collins, Richie Harvest, and Lee Young. The only one missing was Nat King Cole. Among the Cubans was Chico O'Farrill, just back from the United States, who played the piano in the typical "arrangers' style." The first thing he did when he arrived was to ask me about Jimmy Jones, the man whom Sarah Vaughan considered "the best accompanist in the world." Around that time—early 1957—Chico O'Farrill was in Havana with the intention of forming a new band to work at the Sans Souci cabaret, which fell through when he couldn't come to an agreement with the American impresario. Arturo then left for Mexico, where he formed a band that I saw in the Capri cabaret in Mexico City in 1959.

*The Scene before the
Club Cubano de Jazz*

A nightclub that jazz musicians used to visit so they could sit in and jam with the band was the Bambú, on Rancho Boyeros road. The orchestra was led by Cheo Valladares, who would sing guarachas and play the maracas, and the musical director was Rafael Somavilla Jr. This band featured Leonardo Timor Jr., El Negro Vivar, and Evelio "El Manquito" Martínez on trumpets; the veteran Amadito Valdés and Luis "Pinocho" Barreras on alto saxes, and a tenor player from Ecuador by the name of Bastidas played the jazz solos. With Somavilla on piano, bassist Cachaíto López and drummer Walfedo de los Reyes were in the band for a while. When Cachaíto moved on to the Riverside and Walfredito formed his own band in 1957, they were replaced by Fernando "Yuca" Vivar and Daniel Pérez. At times I would sit in and play tenor with this band, and usually I would bring along American drummer Jimmy Betancourt, who worked at that time with a trio on the passenger ship *Florida,* which made a weekly crossing from Havana to Miami. Jimmy was from Chicago, where he had played with Shelly Manne, Georgie Auld, bass player Chubby Jackson, and Lee Konitz. In Miami he used to play with trombonist Eddie Miller, who later visited Havana a number of times with Gustavo Más.

With tenor saxophonist Bastidas we recorded a number of "homemade" pressings in the studio at Monte and Estévez, in a group put together by trombonist Jorge Rojas. With a format that tried to imitate the sound of the Miles Davis-Gil Evans group, one of the numbers recorded was "Venus de Milo," from a transcription done by Rojas. The group included July Rojas (trumpet), Leonardo Acosta (alto sax), Bastidas (tenor sax), Jorge Rojas (trombone), Pepe Herrera (piano), and Gustavo Casal (bass), among others, and in addition to the instrumentals, we accompanied the vocal quartet Los Cavaliers on two numbers (one was "Don't Blame Me"). On another occasion (in drummer Julio Gómez's house) we recorded on magnetic tape the classic "Four Brothers" and other numbers for four saxes (Bastidas, Acosta, Santiago Peñalver, and Pedro Chao), with Orlando "Cachaíto" López (bass), Pablo Cano (guitar), and Julio Gómez (drums). For a few years, every Saturday we would listen to records or jam in Julio Gómez's apartment, located on Twenty-third Street between Eighteenth and Twentieth in Vedado. (Julio was a student of Walfredo's.) Among the regulars, apart from those already mentioned, were pianist Raúl Ondina, percussionist Manolo "Cala" Armesto (a disciple of Chano's), drummer Roberto Cancio, and Jimmy Betancourt, who would arrive every Friday on the ship

Florida. Another visitor was the neighbor and TV actor Enrique Santiesteban, who sometimes would sit in on drums and relive his days with the jazz bands of the 1920s and 1930s. But also frequenting these get-togethers were Horacio Hernández, later a critic and promoter of jazz, and Roberto Toirac, both of whom would be leads in the Club Cubano de Jazz (CCJ).

But places existed that could be considered forerunners of the CCJ, such as the "Sociedad de color" Juan Gualberto Gómez from the bordering Regla district. For a time jam sessions were held there, with the unique characteristic that there was a group of fans who loved to dance to bop music. They were held on Sunday afternoons, as they would be later at the CCJ. The primary organizer and catalyst behind these encounters was Gilberto Torres, an indefatigable dancer with three decades of listening and dancing to jazz, creating another jazz dancing crowd in the barrio Santa Amalia. We should recall that in the late 1940s in the United States some performers who could dance to the most intricate bop numbers, such as Ray Malone, Steve Condos, and Jerry Brandow, would appear on television.[6] In Havana there were those who would dance to bop records or at jam sessions (such as those of this Sociedad), solo or with partners, and out of these dancers I particularly remember Gilberto Torres and Roberto Toirac, later president of the CCJ. And among the diehard musicians at the Regla descargas was trombonist Jorge Rojas, one of its organizers. Others were: July Rojas (trumpet), Leonardo Acosta (alto sax), Pedro Chao (tenor sax), Moisés Alfonso (tenor sax), Roberto Moreira (piano), Raúl Ondina (piano), Gustavo Casal (bass), Cachaíto López (bass), Armando Zequeira (drums), Julio Gómez (drums), and Manolo "Cala" Armesto (Cuban percussion). I met pianist Robertico Moreira there, who was a real find and one of the most promising jazz musicians at that time; unfortunately, he died a few months later of tuberculosis while only in his early twenties.

It's not possible to speak of the jazz environment without referring to the favorite spots of the musicians and fans, aside from cabarets, societies, or private homes. There were other strategic meeting points, two of which were traditional *bodegas* (grocery stores), where food was sold but where there was also a bar and jukebox music. One of these was Celso's, at San José and Gervasio, frequented by jazz musicians and enthusiasts because of the owner's preference for jazz; he always had the latest in jazz to play on his Victrola. There was also the Bodegón de Goyo, at Retiro and Clavel (La Victoria barrio); Domingo, the son of Goyo and the Bodegón's administrator, would travel a lot to Miami and had an impressive collection of jazz 45 rpm records. His records of Cuban music reflected for the most part the latest trends, particularly mambo and feeling. American musicians such as Zoot Sims, Eddie Shu, and Philly Joe Jones were amazed to discover these places, which opened at eight in the morning and in which you could request a specific record: If it didn't appear in the jukebox, they looked for it in the storeroom and the client left satisfied. "In the U.S. there aren't any places like these," they assured us, and they were right. At the end of the decade, the Bodegón de Goyo became the Mecca of hard bop in Havana, where certain numbers such as "Tune Up" by Miles Davis, "The Masquerade Is Over" by the alto saxophonist Lou Donaldson, or "Nica's Dream" by Horace Silver became de rigueur.

If the center of Havana life was the famous Acera del Louvre in the Twenties and Thirties, in the first half of the 1950s the situation hadn't changed much for the musicians. The corner of Neptuno and Consulado, with the bar and cafeteria Los Parados, was the meeting point par excellence and almost a nighttime extension of the Sindicato de Músicos, on San José between Lealtad and Campanario. Catercorner from Los Parados was the restaurant and cafe Fornos, which attracted theater performers. One block down was the historic corner of Prado and Neptuno with the cafe and restaurant Miami just below and the famous dance hall upstairs, and almost straight across from it was the Morocco cabaret, from where you would walk—along the Acera del Louvre—until you passed the Inglaterra hotel and arrived at the Southland cabaret. And, at Consulado and San Miguel we had the Pancho Barata *fonda* (restaurant), where you could eat sumptuously for a few cents. And on Virtudes, around the corner from Los Parados, was the Selmer instrument store owned by Tito Rivera, which stocked accessories and printed music, a gathering spot for musicians where I, along with fellow sax players Tata Palau and Pedro Chao, met a boy who would become the most famous Cuban saxophonist of all time: Paquito D'Rivera.

A lot more could be said of this zone (today practically destroyed), which remained the business center of the city and retained a good part of the attractions of previous decades already described, such as hotels, cabarets, and theaters. We'll limit ourselves to the shops where they sold jazz records, and which had replaced the already outdated one at Humara and Lastra that represented Victor records. Among the new ones was the Goris Shop (Jesús Goris's, who later got into the record business); the Casa Fusté, which sponsored an hour of radio and obtained the exclusive rights to sell Capitol and Mercury records; Musicalia, which distributed MGM records; and particularly André (Galiano and Neptuno), run by Irving Price ("Andresito"), an American Jewish jazz enthusiast and friend of the producer Norman Granz. With Irving one could even order the latest records of our favorite jazz artists, including those from labels such as Prestige, Blue Note, Dial, Epic, Impulse, Verve, Atlantic, and so forth. With the emergence of La Rampa in this same decade record shops appeared in El Vedado, such as the one in the Radiocentro building and the one located in the radio station CMOX (on Tenth between Seventeenth and Nineteenth), which specialized in American music and had announcers who spoke in English. There was even a record shop in the new La Copa (Forty-second Street) shopping area in Miramar called Sammy's; Sammy was another American Jewish jazz fan. Little by little, with the construction of the new hotels in El Vedado and the opening of countless nightclubs in this zone, most of the musicians quit working in the old part of the city, and places like Los Parados had to share their popularity among the musicians with other spots such as the Celeste, a bar and cafeteria on the corner of Infanta and Humboldt, very close to Radio Progreso, the Las Vegas cabaret, and the big and medium-sized new hotels in La Rampa district.

Jazz in the New Hotels

When the new hotels and nightclubs opened and the old ones were refurbished, new groups and bands were formed, and the panorama began to change. Bebo Valdés had separated for good from Armando Romeu's orchestra and created a trio to work at the Sevilla hotel; he took with him drummer Guillermo Barreto and the Philharmonic bass virtuoso Orestes Urfé. The trio played instrumentals and accompanied jazz singer Delia Bravo. In November 1957 the Capri hotel opened and shortly thereafter the Riviera. The Havana Hilton delayed its opening a few months, primarily because of a bomb explosion in its facilities. Previously the Montmartre had closed due to the shooting death of one of Batista's notorious repressive officials, and later the Tropicana would be the target of another bomb. Events such as these reminded us that despite the musical bonanza, the country was at war. Meanwhile, at the Capri two new orchestras were organized: the first one was led by Rafael Somavilla Jr., and along with him were, among others, drummer Guillermo Barreto and bassist Orlando "Papito" Hernández; the second orchestra was conducted by pianist and composer Rey Díaz Calvet, and in that one I remained as first alto for a time, while José Gundín ("El Fiñe") filled first-chair trumpet. However, although there were a number of fine jazz musicians at the Capri, jazz enthusiasts went from the Tropicana to another cabaret: the Hotel Nacional's Parisién.

The Parisién's first orchestra was led by the veteran trumpet player Walfredo de los Reyes; the second, by his son, drummer Walfredo de los Reyes Jr. The first included the "old reliable" Amadito Valdés, Luis Barrera, Triana, Hugo Yera, and Jesús Caunedo (saxes); Walfredo, Jorge Varona, and Evelio Martínez (trumpets); Alejandro Onésimo (trombone); Rubén González (piano); Fernando Vivar (bass); and Luisito Palau (drums). A pillar of this band was the pianist Rubén González, whose son and danzón lineage linked with jazz makes him a typical "Latin jazz" pianist in the mode of Peruchín Jústiz, Frank Emilio, or Bebo Valdés. Also prominent in this orchestra were tenor saxophonist Jesús Caunedo ("La Grulla") and the great trumpet player Jorge Varona, as well as the dependable drummer Luisito Palau, brother of Tata Palau. Many of these musicians went on to the band of Leonardo Timor Jr. around 1960 when the two Walfredos, father and son, left for the United States. As for Walfredo Jr.'s orchestra, it had musicians such as saxophonists Emiliano Gil, the veteran Pedro Guida, and Enrique Palau; on the trumpet, Carlos Arado, exshowman of the Cuban Boys; and a rhythmic section that included Yoyo Casteleiro (piano), Luis Rodríguez (bass), "Rafles" (conga), and Walfredito as drummer.

At that time two great jazz arrangers visited Havana: Johnny Carisi, famous for his "Israel" recorded by Miles Davis, and Johnny Richards, who experimented with Afro-Cuban rhythms and its fusion with jazz in the suite *Cuban Fire,* written for Stan Kenton's band. Among American singers who were brought in by different nightclubs, of special interest to the jazz musicians was the presence at the Sans Souci of Dorothy Dandridge, who had acquired renown through her participation in the film *Carmen Jones* together with Harry Belafonte. This interest was due in large part to two accompanying musicians that came along with her: pianist Marty Paich and drummer Frankie Capp,

both from the West Coast and known by us thanks to their memorable recordings with saxophonist Art Pepper. A few jam sessions with Paich and Capp
were organized at the home of percussionist Rogelio Darias. Meanwhile, at
the Comodoro hotel, in Miramar, they had the composer, pianist, and entertainer Matt Dennis, who owed his renown to high-caliber standard songs such
as "Everything Happens to Me." There, he coincided with a jazz trio that
featured Frank Emilio (piano), Papito Hernández (bass), and Joe Iglesias
(drums), as well as with Felipe Dulzaides's group Los Armónicos.

Surprisingly, an unusual tourist appeared in Havana on his own, in the
winter season of 1957–58: saxophonist Stan Getz. As Lennie Hambro,
Georgie Auld, Benny Goodman, and others before him, Getz came to get
to know Cuba, whose music was already familiar to him from his contact
with Machito, Mario Bauzá, and Dizzy in New York. Getz asked a taxi
driver where he could hear jazz and the driver showed that he knew his
business by taking him to the Tropicana. To Stanley's disappointment,
Armando Romeu's band had that day off, but a musician recommended
that he go to the Capri. There he fraternized with the Cuban musicians,
among them Guillermo Barreto, who always kept a record player in the
dressing room (as he did at the Tropicana) to listen to jazz in between sets;
and of course, there were Getz records. So Stan asked to borrow an alto
sax and he started playing duets with his own tenor sax solos. Then he
asked to play a set with the orchestra, and he did so as first alto, playing
the Somavilla repertoire, which consisted of somewhat modernized "society music," more or less.

At the request of Somavilla himself, the set finished with various jazz numbers in which Stan Getz was accompanied by the orchestra's rhythm section:
Somavilla on piano, Papito Hernández on bass, and Barreto on drums. Later,
in the late night hours, a jam session was organized in the Havana 1900 club,
with other musicians showing up, including pianist Hal Shaeffer, who was
working at the Riviera hotel. Here Stan Getz played the tenor sax, with the
instrument that Braulio "Babín" Hernández lent him, after trying unsuccessfully with Pedro Chao's sax. Accompanying him were Hal Shaeffer on piano,
Papito on bass, and alternating on drums were Guillermo Barreto and singer
(but also a drummer at that time) Rolando Laserie. The following day Stan
Getz left for Varadero, and we didn't see him again until twenty years later (1977),

when he came on the famous "Jazz Cruise" along with Dizzy Gillespie, Earl Hines, and a whole constellation of stars from CBS.[7] The following year he returned for the historic "Encuentro Cuba-USA" sponsored by CBS.

A "Recreation Society" for Jazz

In June 1955 I decided to travel to New York, where I stayed until August, and despite the pessimistic projections for jazz that I had read in the magazines *Metronome* and *Down Beat,* I found myself in a flourishing environment: club Birdland was in full swing, despite the death of Bird three months before, and in the area surrounding Fifty-second Street and Broadway the Basin Street club had opened and the Palladium and the Hickory House were around the same area, not to mention the jazz clubs of Harlem and Greenwich Village. I returned to Havana thinking of the need for a club dedicated exclusively to jazz, but our attempt with the Las Vegas cabaret failed. After some time with the Cubamar orchestra and a smaller group that Jorge Rojas formed, I worked a few months with Beny Moré's band in 1956; Chombo Silva and I filled the tenor sax slots, both of us recruited by Beny's first alto, Santiago Peñalver. After a difficult tour through the eastern part of the country, Chombo informed me of his decision to go to New York, just when I had also decided to leave the orchestra. By the end of the year Beny had dissolved the band, and through Santiaguito I found myself enrolled in the orchestra of the Venezuelan Aldemaro Romero to work for a month in Maracaibo; I had been recommended by the great tenor player Emilio Peñalver—Santiaguito's uncle—who couldn't make the trip because he was busy with union work and his job at Channel 4 TV.

The band that Aldemaro Romero had formed was almost 100 percent Cuban, with twenty-five Chico O'Farrill arrangements (many of which later appeared on the LP *Chico's Chachachá*) and sixteen Cuban musicians out of eighteen (the exceptions were Aldemaro on piano and Mexican singer Oscar Jaimes). In addition to Santiago Peñalver were Osvaldo Urrutia, Ariel Pérez, and Virgilio Vixama among the saxes; the lead trombone was Jorge Rojas; making up the trumpet section were Alberto and Dagoberto Jiménez ("Platanito" and "Rabanito"), César "Piyú" Godínez, and El Negro Vivar; the percussion section included Tibo Lee (drums), Tabaquito (conga), and Marcelino Valdés (bongo), and we had accomplished Cuban singer Miguel de Gonzalo; on bass

Kiki Hernández, who lived in Caracas at that time, joined us. In Maracaibo we won a battle of bands with Luis Arcaraz's great Mexican jazz band, in a unanimous decision by the audience, and made lasting friendships with Mexican jazz musicians then playing with Arcaraz. But when I returned to Havana I was tired of the big bands; I needed to play jazz, and in small groups. But things were not propitious, and in Latin America rock and roll was breaking on the scene, a fad that lasted for just two years in Cuba (1956–57).

Cuban impresarios saw a gold mine in the new type of music and were prepared to exploit it. Gaspar Pumarejo, who had switched from Channel 4 to Cuban TV's Channel 2, organized dance competitions among the young rock and roll fans, on television or in theater halls (for example, Radio-Cine), but they only had canned music, for there were no musicians in Cuba interested in forming a rock and roll group at the time. And as usual in these cases, the first rock and roll group emerged among the youngest: a group of teenagers, almost all amateurs, who were quickly sought after for a television program. At that time I found pianist Raúl Ondina, who always had practical ideas. In 1955, when I returned from New York, it had occurred to him to rent a theater hall to give jazz concerts and save the funds from the admission, and we organized the first one at the locale of the Sociedad Artística Gallega. A lot of musicians supported us, among them pianist Frank Emilio, bassists Papito Hernández and Cachaíto López, saxophonist Miguelito Franca, and drummers Daniel Pérez and Walfredo de los Reyes. Roberto Toirac helped us organize the concert, and after that I spoke with him many times until we finally made plans to find a permanent spot and open a small nightclub for jazz.

When rock and roll and then this youngsters' group appeared, Raúl Ondina convinced me to listen to it. Despite my initial rejection of that music, I had to admit that deep down it was basically "rhythm and blues," and Ondina was a self-taught pianist who began to play boogie-woogies a la Pete Johnson and Albert Ammons, so we took charge of the group. Of the original musicians we kept guitarist Luis Cano—brother of Pablo Cano—and drummer Joe Iglesias, plus pianist Robertico Casas, who moved over to bass while Ondina filled in on piano and I joined in as leader and tenor saxophonist. But the center of the group was young singer Tony Escarpenter, who incredibly could sing ballads, jazz, scat, and rock, and knew by memory all of Elvis Presley's songs. We added another tenor saxophone player, Pedro Chao, then Cuban percussion (Ernesto Calderín and Manolo

"Cala" Armesto), and the dance couple Eneida and Lorenzo, to round out
an act that achieved instant success. We recorded a single that was heard on
Victrolas and on the radio, with "Rip It Up" on one side and an Ondina version of "Oyeme Cachita" that we named "Cachita Rock." We performed
live on Radio Progreso, on television, for dance marathons, and in the theater. Finally the group was signed to perform in Caracas, where we did radio,
television, theater, and cabaret shows, with a few changes (Aníbal González
came on as a drummer). Several months later the group broke up, and a year
later Raúl Ondina and I would put together the first of a series of jazz
groups. Tony Escarpenter began a promising career as a soloist singer until
1961, when he left Cuba. We never even imagined that this group, which
was called Los Hot Rockers, might possibly have been the first to attempt—
however timidly—a fusion between rock and roll and Afro-Cuban rhythms.

Meanwhile the jazz descargas spread, though sporadically, from the Las
Vegas to Club 21, Hernando's Hideaway, Pigalle, the Martinique, and Le Reve.
Roberto Toirac, who studied engineering and had a workshop for repairing
gas stoves in El Vedado, continued with the idea of leasing a small place.
Saxophonist Osvaldo ("Mosquifín") Urrutia succeeded in opening a bar at
Línea and Sixteenth (Vedado), but it folded before we could present our plans
to him. In 1958 I made another trip to New York, and when I returned I ran
into a new jazz enthusiast, the French designer Jacques Brouté, who had been
part of a jazz club in Paris and another one in Rome and was a friend of saxophonist Bobby Jaspar, then with J. J. Johnson. One afternoon we celebrated
a jam session at Club 21 with Pucho Escalante (trombone), L. Acosta (tenor
sax), Chico O'Farrill (piano), Papito Hernández (bass), and Walfredo de los
Reyes (drums), and when the descarga was over I called Roberto Toirac and
Walfredito aside to tell them of Jacques's plan to organize a jazz club. The formula was simple: We would make an agreement with the owner of a small or
medium-sized cabaret to have jam sessions on Sunday afternoon and charge
admittance to gradually raise money. The owner would keep whatever he could
make selling drinks. With the money raised we would be able to pay for the
airfare and expenses of jazz musicians from the United States.

The following day we got together at my house, and then we set up our
"general headquarters" in Toirac's workshop. The first step was to register the
Club Cubano de Jazz as a "recreation society," which was done by pianist
Samuel Téllez, who was also a lawyer. The club's first board consisted of Jacques

Brouté (president), Roberto Toirac (vice president), Samuel Téllez (secretary), Julio Gómez (treasurer), and Horacio Hernández, José Alberto Figueras, and Orlando Pérez (committee members). As with Samuel Téllez, Julio Gómez was selected as treasurer because, besides playing drums, he was also a public accountant. We also decided to name Adolfo Siemans, who was at that time the country's leading jazz disc jockey, "honorary president." Through his Sunday program and through other friends in radio and the press we got the word out of the club's emergence, as we did at a jam session that took place at Maxim's (Tenth and Third streets in Vedado) and consisted of basically a quintet: L. Acosta (alto sax), Pedro Chao (tenor), Frank Emilio (piano), Papito Hernández (bass), and Walfredito de los Reyes (drums). Although he didn't play, Chico O'Farrill was also present that afternoon, and this descarga took on a historic (or perhaps symbolic) connotation by being the first in which an eleven-year-old Paquito D'Rivera played. Then, as at other times thereafter, Paquito was coming on the scene at just the right moment.

Right next to Club 21 a new nightclub had recently opened, the St. Michel, and Jacques spoke with its French owner to start up activities with the Club Cubano de Jazz. The place ended up being too small, but it served to establish, one Saturday afternoon, the quartet that would launch the Club's descargas and concerts and which would do well for a while. It included: L. Acosta (alto sax), Frank Emilio (piano), Papito Hernández (bass), and Walfredo de los Reyes (drums). The following day, Sunday, after speaking with the owner of the Havana 1900 (at Humboldt and P, almost right across from Montmartre), we played with the same quartet for more than a hundred people. The club's owner did well, as did the waiters, who charged twice as much, while Julio Gómez opened the CCJ account. By the following Sunday we had in addition a second group organized by trombonist Jorge Rojas; the place was packed, holding two hundred people or more, from the tables to the bar. The word had spread, and the fans would remain loyal for the almost three years that the Club Cubano de Jazz lasted.

The second group that was added featured Jorge Rojas (trombone and leader), Jesús Caunedo (tenor sax), León Borrell (piano), Luis "Pellejo" Rodríguez (bass), and Germán Gil (drums). The Catalan pianist León Borrell had arrived in Cuba with a Spanish orchestra and settled here on his own. All the members of this group remained enthusiastic during the years of the CCJ, and above all they eased the job that Walfredito and I took on when we organized the club, which consisted of guaranteeing the music, that is, the presence each Sunday of musicians and groups to avoid any break in activities, as well as encouraging other musicians to join us. Little by little the rest of the Cuban jazz musicians would join in on the club sessions; on a number of occasions whole jazz bands were formed consisting of Cuban musicians and sometimes including Americans and Mexicans. A fundamental principle of the club was that all who participated, Cuban or foreign, would play for free, with the goal of using the funds to bring in other jazz musicians. The only exception was for musicians who found themselves out of work, who were paid ten pesos (dollars) per performance.

The CCJ board changed somewhat when Jacques Brouté proposed that a prestigious musician be designated as president, to attract the musicians who still hadn't approached us. On Walfredito's proposal the enthusiastic pianist and arranger Rafael Somavilla was chosen as president; he organized the first big band in these sessions, which turned out to be an "all-star" Cuban jazz ensemble. Shortly thereafter Somavilla had to give up this position because of his workload in cabaret and television. Then Roberto Toirac, the most active and enthusiastic member, assumed the presidency and became the club's main promoter. From his workshop, telephone calls were made and received to musicians in New York or Miami, and more than once his workshop provided funds to cover unforeseen expenditures. Another pillar of the Club Cubano de Jazz, who remained invisible more than half the time, was veteran saxophonist Gustavo Más, who lived in Miami and acted as a direct contact with American jazz musicians. In addition to his participation as a musician on various occasions, Gustavo turned out to be the Club's irreplaceable scout.

From Vinnie Tanno to Philly Joe Jones

The quartet that I formed with Frank Emilio, Papito, and Walfredo, and the quintet that trombonist Jorge Rojas put together, played for six weeks to raise funds to bring in jazz musicians from the United States. In the beginning we would only bring in one musician at a time, to perform accompanied by a Cuban group. One of the first—I think the first—was trumpet player Vinnie Tanno, who shortly before had left Stan Kenton's band, and who heated up the Havana 1900 atmosphere with his interpretation of "The Song Is You," turned into a jazz standard thanks to Charlie Parker.

Vinnie Tanno's stay in Havana wouldn't be his only one, as he returned a number of times at the invitation of the Club. Other visitors were trombonist Lon Norman, trumpet player Harold McNear, baritone saxophonist Dennis "The Menace" Brown, tenor saxophonist Jimmy Casal, drummers Lord Parkinson and Tom Montgomery, pianist Fred Crane, and the renowned guitarist Mundell Lowe. A special guest was the tenor player Zoot Sims, who had already visited Havana on his own, as well as Stan Getz. Occasionally two guest musicians would come and sometimes the Club's scout himself, Gustavo Más, as when he came along with Eddie Miller, who played the valve trombone in a style similar to Bob Brookmeyer's and was an excellent arranger; he later pursued symphonic composition.

Gustavo gradually made more and more contacts, and among American jazz musicians the word spread. Trumpet player Blue Mitchell was ready to come, but he had to postpone his trip at the last minute. Another time Sonny Stitt called Roberto's workshop to say that Dizzy Gillespie wanted to come and that he would as soon as he had the chance (Dizzy couldn't come until 1977, and then returned again in the '80s). The invited musicians were housed at the St. John hotel or at the neighboring Flamingo, both at O and Twenty-fifth (Vedado), only one block from the Havana 1900. By the end of 1958 entire groups could be invited such as those of Eddie Shu, Kenny Drew, and Philly Joe Jones. The multi-instrumentalist Eddie Shu, a former tenor soloist in Gene Krupa's band, made his first trip with a quartet in which pianist Ralph Martin, bassist Sheldon Yates, and drummer Art Schwartz stood out as well. The great bop pianist Kenny Drew also came with a quartet that included tenor saxophonist Bill Miller. After their performance at the Havana 1900 they took part in a jam session with Cuban musicians at the Sheherezada club (Nineteenth and M). As for Philly Joe, the CCJ practically closed its doors with flying colors with his group. But that was in 1960.

The Havana 1900 locale, which up until then had been ideal, in 1959 ended up being too small, and we had to fall back on the Tropicana's Arcos de Cristal ballroom. With the Tropicana the same agreement was made as with the Havana 1900, always reserving Sunday afternoons. The only exception was made in April 1959, when a concert was held in the theater of the Confederación de Trabajadores de Cuba. A band was formed to be led by Chico O'Farrill, who came in from Mexico and brought his wife, singer Lupe Valero, and two Mexican soloists who worked in his orchestra in the

Aztec capital: pianist Raúl Stalworth ("El Güero") and trumpet player César Molina. Arturo employed four saxophones following Woody Herman's format (the so-called Four Brothers sound), with three tenors and a baritone: Gustavo Más, Pedro Chao, and Jesús Caunedo (tenors) and Osvaldo Urrutia (baritone). On trumpet were César Molina, Luis Escalante, and Nilo Argudín, and the trombones included Alejandro Onésimo, Luis González ("El Pibe"), and Alberto Giral; the bassist was Papito Hernández and the drummer Walfredo de los Reyes. O'Farrill wrote "The Bass Family" especially for this concert, for bassists Felo, Kiki, and Papito Hernández.

Big bands had been organized before to perform in the Havana 1900: on two occasions the leader was Rafael Somavilla, and another time a band led by the American pianist and arranger Don Ippolito was organized, with its own arrangements and with Vinnie Tanno alternating with El Negro Vivar on trumpet solos. On another occasion the band served as the background for a sensational drum duel between Daniel Pérez and Walfredo de los Reyes, which ended in a draw. At the risk of leaving out some names, I will attempt to list the members of these diverse CCJ bands: trumpets: El Negro Vivar, Nilo Argudín, Luis Escalante, Chocolate Armenteros, Pedro Rodríguez; trombones: Jorge Rojas, Antonio Linares, Alejandro Onésimo, El Pibe González, Generoso Jiménez, and Alberto Giral (valve trombone); saxophones: Eddy Escrich, Santiago Peñalver, L. Acosta, Enemelio Jiménez (altos), Pedro Chao, Gustavo Más, Jesús Caunedo, Tomás Vázquez (tenors), and Osvaldo Urrutia (baritone); piano: Frank Emilio Flynn, Rafael Somavilla; bass: Papito Hernández, Kiki Hernández, Luis Rodríguez, Orlando López; drums: Walfredo de los Reyes, Daniel Pérez, and Armando Zequeira.

Many jazz groups were organized through the club, almost always to perform exclusively within it, but some stayed together or underwent minimal changes to work outside of the club. The original quartet that I organized together with Frank Emilio, Papito, and Walfredo dissolved when I traveled to New York in 1958, but later we performed together in other settings. Frank then organized various groups that would be direct predecessors of the 1960s' Quinteto de Música Moderna with Guillermo Barreto, Papito Hernández, Tata Güines, and Gustavo Tamayo. But even before that, musicians who had inexplicably kept their distance, such as Barreto, Peruchín Jústiz, and the bassist Israel "Cachao" López, now appeared in the club sessions. For example, in 1959 Peruchín organized a quartet that can be considered a cornerstone in the history of Latin jazz, with Cachao on bass, Guillermo Barreto (drums and pailas), and Arístides Soto ("Tata Güines") on conga. In Peruchín's phrasing on piano the Cuban and jazz styles were fully integrated, and the same can be said of Cachao, whose style and *tumbaos* would have a heavy influence on various generations of bassists. This quartet was, in addition, the immediate forerunner to the recordings that Peruchín, Frank Emilio, and Rubén González made in the 1960s.

Shortly before, I had organized two groups, the first with guitarist Pablo Cano, with unisons of sax and guitar in the style of Lee Konitz with Billy Bauer, or Stan Getz with Jimmy Rainey. The group consisted of alto sax, guitar, Raúl Ondina on piano, Cachaíto López on bass, and Armandito Zequeira on drums. This group split up when Pablo joined Felipe Dulzaides's group. The next ensemble I organized, on the other hand, followed in the style of the groups inspired by Gerry Mulligan, without piano or guitar. It featured: L. Acosta (alto sax), Pedro Chao (tenor sax), Alberto "El Men" Giral (valve trombone), Papito Hernández (bass), and Armandito Zequeira (drums). With this group we alternated with Vinnie Tanno, Dennis "The Menace" Brown, Eddie Shu, and Don Ippolito. With Raúl Ondina and Armandito Zequeira we then organized a group that worked roughly from August to October 1958 at the Plaza Hotel bar, next to the casino. The group included Julio César Fonseca (bass) and Oney Cumbá (guitar), and the Plaza bar turned into a gathering spot for the musicians as they got off work in other centers of nightlife, since our group played until six in the morning.

Furthermore, through the Club Cubano de Jazz and particularly Walfredito de los Reyes, some hotel managers hired two American groups that we had invited. One of them was Eddie Shu's quartet, visiting for the second time (the band would come again in 1960), which was hired to perform for four weeks in the Lobby Bar of St. John's hotel. This time Eddie brought along pianist Teddy Corabi, who had formed part of clarinetist Buddy de Franco's big band and had played for a week or two with the Charlie Parker quintet.[8] He also brought the excellent drummer Art Schwartz. During its time at St. John's the quartet continued to participate every Sunday in the Havana 1900 sessions together with the Cuban musicians and the new visitors. Sometimes when these club sessions ended (around 7 P.M.), some of us musicians would go on to Club Pigalle, along with the most devoted fans. The Pigalle was only a block from the Havana 1900 (at O and Twenty-fifth) and almost right next to St. John's, and the proprietor, "El Gallego" Paco, in addition to playing the accordion for the audience, was always willing to "lend us" the place. Memorable jam sessions with Vinnie Tanno, Eddie Shu, Don Ippolito, and many others took place there.

St. John's—like the Plaza shortly before—became another magnet for jazz lovers and musicians, as Eddie Shu proved to be an ideal musician for any audience because of his virtuosity on different instruments; in addition to playing the tenor sax, he would play part of his repertoire on the trumpet, the clarinet, or the harmonica. Since St. John's was situated in the La Rampa district—as was the Las Vegas, Havana 1900, Pigalle, Club 21, and others—it gradually overtook the Tropicana and the Sans Souci as the focal point of the musicians, who would now come to La Rampa when they got off work. Another favorite spot was the Celeste Bar, with an open air terrace where musicians who worked in that vicinity would get together, and just like Los Parados it turned into a real "office" for a few regulars such as Luis Escalante or Israel "Cachao" López.

In the Eddie Shu quartet's third week of work pianist Teddy Corabi became ill and had to be hospitalized, and Eddie hired Frank Emilio. When the quartet's contract expired, Corabi was still hospitalized with pneumonia. The management of St. John's had paid the expenses and Teddy offered to repay at least a portion of the total if they would hire him to put together a group of Cuban musicians. That's how the Teddy Corabi quintet got started, and it played for about two months right up to December 31, 1958. At that time Teddy was a very difficult pianist because of his harmonic approach, which owed something to Ravel, and he would employ chords in fourths that today are perfectly normal, especially after having heard Bill Evans, McCoy Tyner, Keith Jarrett, and Herbie Hancock. The quintet featured El Negro Vivar (trumpet), Leonardo Acosta (alto sax), Teddy Corabi (piano), Luis Rodríguez (bass), and Walfredo de los Reyes (drums).

Once again the quintet turned the Lobby Bar into a jazz center, where Orlando "Cachaíto" López would show up every night to play at least one set and where Guillermo Barreto and Papito Hernández would often sit in and play. Even Armando Romeu, who could rarely be seen off the premises of the Tropicana, would go night after night after finishing work, quite symbolic of the jazz center shift at decade's end. The Lobby Bar was open until 7:30 in the morning, and after 2 A.M. the group would alternate every half hour with singer Elena Burke and pianist Frank Domínguez (once again, the combination of jazz and feeling). Work schedules would determine the order in which the musicians arrived: first, the performers who worked in the big hotels and finished at 2 A.M., then those from the Tropicana and Sans Souci (3 A.M.), and finally the musicians from the nearby Las Vegas, which closed at six in the morning.

With Eddie Shu's contract at St. John's a precedent was created, which was repeated with Philly Joe Jones in 1960 when he was hired to perform in the Starlight Terrace room at the Nacional hotel, where he alternated with Felipe Dulzaides's group. Philly Joe had recently left Miles Davis's historic quintet to continue on his own, but he couldn't bring all the members of his sextet along as neither the pianist nor the bassist could make the trip. Arriving with him were Mike Downs (cornet), Dave Hillary (alto sax), and Bill Barron (tenor sax), that is, the "front line." On bass and piano were Papito Hernández and Frank Emilio. Their performance in Tropicana's Arcos de Cristal ballroom was sensational. In one of their sets tenor player Gustavo Más joined in to play with the group, and dueled with Bill Barron, both then influenced to a greater or lesser extent by John Coltrane. To alternate with Philly Joe a quartet was formed that included L. Acosta (alto sax), Raúl Ondina (piano), Luis Rodríguez (bass), and Walfredo de los Reyes (drums), who won over not only the audience but also Philly Joe.

Evaluation of the Club Cubano de Jazz

The Club Cubano de Jazz was the only systematic effort with clearly successful results in bringing American jazz musicians to Havana, whether they were renowned musicians such as Philly Joe Jones, Zoot Sims, Kenny Drew, Eddie Shu, Mundell Lowe, or Vinnie Tanno, or musicians who were not so well known but of indisputable caliber such as Teddy Corabi, Eddie Miller, Lon Norman, Ralph Martin, or Don Ippolito. What was most significant is that for the first (and only) time the Cuban jazz musicians had the opportunity to play periodically and share experiences with top American jazz musicians throughout the whole year, not just at annual festivals or occasional concerts, as is the norm around the world except for European countries where there are clubs that operate year-round. Equally important, the

Club functioned in a climate of absolute selflessness and fraternity, at a time when commercialism had come to predominate above all else.

Many musicians who were just beginning at that time started their career as jazz artists thanks to the CCJ, for the club accepted nonprofessional musicians as well as students of music. Among the former were drummers Germán Gil and Julio Gómez, as well as clarinetist Earl Brandon, an American resident of Cuba who together with trombonist Jorge Rojas formed a group to play Dixieland, as a tribute to traditional jazz, which was warmly received by the public. Also on one occasion we presented a group of young musicians—some almost kids—who excelled in the following decade; it included Paquito D'Rivera (alto sax), Kiki Villalta (piano), Luis Quiñones (bass), Amadito Valdés Jr. (drums), and the subsequent guitarist and composer Sergio Vitier on Cuban percussion. Another musician who made a sensational debut in Cuban jazz was the guitarist who would later become number one in the country, Carlos Emilio Morales, who paired up with bassist and drummer Armandito Zequeira and whom we shall see in the following decade in the orchestra of the Teatro Musical de La Habana, in Chucho Valdés's group, in the Orquesta Cubana de Música Moderna, and finally in the 1970s with Irakere. Zequeira himself, who replaced Guillermo Barreto in his uncle Armando Romeu's orchestra at the Tropicana, became known as a jazz musician in the CCJ, as did his cousin Armandito Romeu III, a drummer and vibraphone player, and the bassist Fabián García Caturla, the composer's grand-nephew.

A number of singers performed in the context of the Club, such as the bop and feeling veteran Dandy Crawford and the equally versatile Maggie Prior, the only singer besides Delia Bravo who made a living for more than thirty years dedicating herself to jazz. Likewise there was the outstanding jazz and feeling singer Doris de la Torre, then with Felipe Dulzaides's group, who turned out to be another CCJ pillar. For his part Pablo Cano, guitarist and cofounder of Dulzaides's group, brought in Juanito Márquez from Holguín as a guest of the Club; Márquez appeared for the first time in Havana at one of the Club sessions at the Tropicana, in a guitar duo with Pablo. A few years later Juanito Márquez would become one of the most popular songwriters in Cuba and leader of a jazz band that worked in the Salón Caribe in the Habana Libre (Hilton) Hotel, and he would produce a number of classic recordings of Cuban Latin jazz. But just like veteran Cachao, he became known to the jazz enthusiasts in Havana through the

Club, for despite Cachao's prestige among musicians, his cousin Orlando was better known as a jazz artist.

In the Club's final stage at the Tropicana, the jazz-plus-feeling combination appears once again, and the Sunday sessions took place in a packed ballroom with the participation of singers and trovadores from this movement. Starting in 1959 the activities of the CCJ had wide coverage in the press, especially in the articles for the magazine *Bohemia* and in the *Revolución* newspaper column on music written by the critic and well-known feeling songwriter Giraldo Piloto, from the Piloto and Vera team. Taking part in club sessions were Elena Burke, Omara Portuondo, Leonel Bravet, the duo Las Capella (Marta and Daisy), Dandy Crawford, Ela Calvo, Froylán Amézaga, and others, not counting the tribute to José Antonio Méndez on his return from Mexico in 1960, held this time in the Copa Room of the Riviera hotel. Finally, although we cannot analyze it in detail, there is an element of great importance in the development of the Club Cubano de Jazz: its contribution to the abolition of racial barriers in all aspects, from the makeup of its committee to the admission of the general public to all events and locales, from the Havana 1900 to the Tropicana or the big hotels, which had previously maintained a segregationist policy.

Radio and Records Going into the Sixties

Until now we have concentrated on what was happening in the 1950s with respect to cabarets, television, Victrolas, the "world of jam sessions," and the Club Cubano de Jazz, overlooking other media such as radio and records. This is in part because TV's impact eclipsed national radio, so big in previous decades, and also because radio had very little to do with jazz in this decade, except for Adolfo Siemans's jazz hour. When it comes to records, however, there was a certain awakening toward the end of the Fifties. Jazz always had some space on the radio: In the 1940s disc jockey Ernesto Carricaburu Jr. was successful with his catch phrase "Swing, muchísimo swing," as was Norman Díaz in the previously mentioned spot on Mil Diez; in the 1950s the trio of Orlando del Valle, Tino Castellanos, and Rafael Simón enjoyed success at Radio Artalejo. Then disc jockey Adolfo Siemans's Sunday jazz program, "La hora del jazz" ("The Jazz Hour"), came on the air, which helped to promote the Club Cubano de Jazz. In the 1960s Ovidio

González and Adolfo Castillo would be the main radio broadcasters of jazz, and particularly of hard bop, followed by Horacio Hernández, whose program "El jazz, su historia y sus intérpretes" ("Jazz: Its History and Its Artists"), on CMBF, has succeeded in remaining on the air longer than any other. It's true that in the 1950s there were two stations that broadcast exclusively American music: Radio Kramer and CMOX. The latter had announcers who would speak in English and was intended more for American residents in Cuba. Somewhat older, Radio Kramer came up with a program with performances by pianist Frank Emilio Flynn. But buried in the avalanche of pop music, jazz didn't have much room on either station.[9]

As for records, in the 1950s national record companies such as Panart, Gema, Puchito, Kubaney, Discuba, and Velvet, among others, flourished. But I've already pointed out that the only Cubans able to record jazz did so in the United States (Alberto Socarrás, Machito, Mario Bauzá, Chano Pozo, Chico O'Farrill). In the 1950s tenor player Gustavo Más recorded with Woody Herman's band as a soloist, and then he recorded also in the United States with Tito Puente and Mongo Santamaría. Chombo Silva, tenor player as well, recorded with Cal Tjader, Machito, and other ensembles, and the same can be said of trumpeter Chocolate Armenteros and percussionists Candito, Patato Valdés, and Armando Peraza. But the only jazz recording made in Cuba in the 1950s was the album *Cubano!* on the Mercury label—in 1952— recorded on the initiative of Irving Price, the owner of the record store André and friend of the producer Norman Granz, famous for having organized the *Jazz at the Philharmonic* series of concerts and recordings with the main jazz musicians of the day. The LP *Cubano!* was praised by *Metronome* magazine and classified as B (good). The members of the group were: Alejandro "El Negro" Vivar (trumpet), Gustavo Más (tenor sax), Bebo Valdés (piano), Kiki Hernández (bass), Guillermo Barreto (drums), and Rolando Alfonso (conga). The tunes were in part Latin American standards such as the boleros "Desconfianza" by Julio Gutiérrez and "Duerme" by the Mexican Miguel Prado, and in part originals such as the Afro-bop "Con poco coco" by Bebo Valdés, apparently a tribute to the great pianist Bud Powell, author of "Un poco loco." But overall I don't think that this recording does justice to any of the musicians involved. Bebo Valdés also recorded in 1955 with a group that he called "Bebo Valdés y su Havana All Stars," which included Luis Escalante (trumpet), "El Cabito" Quesada and Gustavo Más (saxes), Kiki Hernández (bass), Guillermo Barreto (drums), and Cándido Camero (conga). And in 1957 he recorded with El

Negro Vivar, Generoso Jiménez (trombone), Cachaíto López (bass), and Tata Güines (conga).

At the end of the decade other recordings were made, among them the now famous "Descargas" or "Cuban Jam Sessions" to which I referred earlier, which Max Salazar has reviewed extensively, and which led to the bit of confusion previously addressed.[10] These recordings by the record companies Panart and Gema attempted for the first time to systematically capture the improvisational virtuosity of a group of Cuban jazz musicians and in the "Cuban style," with montunos, tumbaos, guajeos, and our typical percussion. Despite the avowed commercial intentions of the record companies and also of some of the musicians who promoted these sessions—such as Julio Gutiérrez and Chico O'Farrill—the results were quite positive, with some moments of brilliance and true inspiration on the part of the soloists. A number of the participants— Chombo Silva among them—have stated that they were not aware of the commercial nature of the recordings or even that they were being recorded, and that they were honestly surprised, from an economic point of view. Some of the best Cuban soloists from that period—such as El Negro Vivar, Gustavo Más, Chombo Silva, Peruchín Jústiz, Bebo Valdés, Israel "Cachao" López, and percussionists Walfredo de los Reyes, Guillermo Barreto, Marcelino Valdés, and Tata Güines—took part in making these records, which are today considered classics among the Spanish-speaking community of New York. But in my opinion, the importance of these now "historic" records has been overrated, for the simple reason that they are the only ones in existence. Before and after these recordings much more brilliant and spontaneous descargas have taken place. But of course, this has also occurred with jazz in the United States.

At that time recordings were made with Cuban jazz bands organized just for the occasion, and which today could also be considered historic, such as the one Kubaney produced in 1959 titled *Ritmo,* with "Tojo y su Orquesta," that is, Generoso Jiménez as director as well as the author of all the arrangements. The band lined up Chocolate Armenteros, El Negro Vivar, Armando Armenteros, and Pedro Jiménez (trumpets); Antonio Linares, Luis "El Pibe" González, and Modesto Echarte (trombones); Enemelio Jiménez, Homero Betancourt, Emilio Peñalver, Rolando Sánchez, and Diego Loredo (saxophones); Orestes "Macho" López (bass); Héctor "El Ñato" Alejo (piano); Guillermo Barreto (drums and pailas), Oscar Valdés (conga), and Clemente "Chicho" Piquero (bongo). We see here veterans from the bands of Beny Moré, Bebo Valdés, and Julio Gutiérrez, as well as two great danzoneros (and soneros): Macho López (pillar of Arcaño) and pianist Héctor Alejo. It's an impressive lineup.

Shortly before, three albums had been made with a similar orchestra, although this time the entrepreneurial initiative came from the United States. It was Justico Antobal, son of *Don* Antobal and Aspiazu's cousin, who moved to Havana to record the LPs *Ay Caramba, Día de Reyes,* and *Mango Mangüé* for the London label. The orchestra appeared as Antobal's All Stars, although Antobalito didn't even lead it, for Obdulio Morales was given that job. The writers and arrangers were none other than René Hernández, Alberto Iznaga, Peruchín Jústiz, Chico O'Farrill, Gilberto Valdés, Cachao López, Severino Ramos, and Obdulio Morales. Some numbers had lyrics in English by the great Marion Sunshine.

The all-star band that Antobalito put together included El Negro Vivar, Chocolate Armenteros, and Domingo Corbacho (trumpets); Generoso Jiménez and Antonio Linares (trombones); Amadito Valdés and Santiaguito Peñalver (alto sax), Emilio Peñalver and Pedro Chao (tenor), and Osvaldo Urrutia (baritone); Osvaldo Peñalver (flute); Peruchín Jústiz (piano); Felo Hernández (bass); Guillermo Barreto (drums); Oscar Valdés and Giraldo Rodríguez (congas); Oscarito Valdés *(bongó* and *güiro); * Roberto García *(quinto); * and Justico Antobal (maracas). The singers were Gina Martín and Roberto Cordero.

Meanwhile, Bebo Valdés remained persistent and formed a new orchestra, Sabor de Cuba, in 1958. It included once again five trumpets: El Negro Vivar, Chocolate Armenteros, Nilo Argudín, Dagoberto Jiménez, and Domingo Corbacho. The saxophones were Santiaguito Peñalver, Rolando Sánchez, Emilio Peñalver, and Virgilio Vixama. The rhythm section featured Bebo on piano, Salvador Vivar (bass), Oscar Valdés (conga), Roberto Laserie (drums), and Luis Yáñez (maracas). But the amazing thing about this band was that Bebo had been able to bring together four excellent singers from different styles, all of whom have achieved international success: they were bolerista Fernando Alvarez, the "guapo de la canción" Rolando Laserie, guarachero Pío Leiva, and the great Orlando Guerra, "Cascarita." With this orchestra Bebo performed in Cuba, then traveled to Mexico with only the singers. Shortly thereafter, Bebo established himself in Europe, where he formed a trio and went on tour throughout the Continent until he decided to settle for good in Stockholm, Sweden. Great success would come to his son Chucho Valdés starting in the 1970s with the group Irakere.

8
Musical Transition

1959 and After

$\mathcal{T}$he year 1959 along with the decade that follows can be characterized as a period of musical transition, not only for the island's popular music but for Cuban jazz as well, despite the fact that the revolution that overthrew the Batista dictatorship, from its very inception, dramatically affected almost all aspects of national life. The most notable tendency in the first years of the victorious revolution is the consolidation of styles, songwriters, and performers who had excelled in the previous decade, but who would now "arrive," as the barriers impeding their definitive success were broken. The typical example is the feeling movement, whose primary exponents finally acquire unobstructed access to all media—records, television, and cinema—and many become singing stars in Cuba. In popular danceable music, new rhythms and ensembles will experience sudden—though ephemeral—success *(pachanga, pilón, pacá, mozambique),* while Aragón, Enrique Jorrín, Beny Moré, Roberto Faz, and other renowned artists remain at the top.[1]

Historical periods don't usually end on a precise date, nor do new ones begin on the following day. So it was that the Club Cubano de Jazz, for example, stayed together until 1960 and only dissolved when the United States and Cuba broke diplomatic relations, which led to the suspension of flights between both countries and the interruption of the fruitful contact between Cuban and American musicians. But already in January 1959 an impasse had arisen, not only in the Club, but also in the functioning of all the cabarets. And it was understandable, for there were still armed confrontations in Havana and other cities, and mobs that took advantage of the situation to carry out assaults, with cabarets and casinos being one of their favorite targets. Hotels like the Deauville (on Galiano between Malecón and San Lázaro), the Plaza, and others were assaulted and had their gaming rooms wrecked; others had better luck. For example, the riled-up mob that was heading straight for the Capri ran into actor George Raft at the entrance; he was the boss of the casino and the cabaret, and someone with whom we had worked the year before. To avoid pillage Raft gave a brief speech full of revolutionary slogans, which had the effect of dispersing the mob. It was the best acting job of his career.

The night of December 31 was the last in which Teddy Corabi's quintet played. When I returned to St. John to look for my instrument (we were also paid the last week), I discovered that Angelito González, boss of the casino and the Lobby Bar, had wisely taken the precautionary measure of moving all the gaming paraphernalia to the mezzanine of the hotel in the morning hours; the disappointment of finding the room empty was enough to quell the destructive fury of the crowd and disperse the invaders. A few days later, facing the prospect that the cabarets would remain closed for at least one or two months, we made the decision to dissolve the quintet, and Angelito paid for Teddy's return ticket to the United States. When the situation returned to normal months later, the gaming rooms were opened again, but this only lasted until the moment of the big interventions and nationalizations of 1960. The last time I was in a casino I was in the renamed Habana Libre (ex-Hilton) to hear Peruchín Jústiz and his group.

In times of great change like these, paradoxical events tend to occur. For example, the first jazz concert held in 1959—that is, after the triumph of the revolution—was not organized by the Club Cubano de Jazz, although all of its members showed up; it was organized through the initiative of writer

Guillermo Cabrera Infante, who had recently been named to a seat on a transitional cultural committee. The concert took place in the theater hall of the Museo de Bellas Artes, and for the event we put together a group very similar to the one that opened the activities of the Club Cubano de Jazz, with the addition of Gustavo Más, the man who had been our scout in the United States and who just happened to be visiting. The group (a quintet) included Leonardo Acosta (alto sax), Gustavo Más (tenor sax), Frank Emilio (piano), Orlando "Papito" Hernández (bass), and Walfredito de los Reyes (drums). It played before a packed house with a real joy that united the musicians and the audience, many of whom had been regular attendees at the old CCJ sessions. There was a sort of shared sentiment that the Club had survived, and in effect, shortly thereafter the regular sessions returned with the reopening of the Tropicana, the Havana 1900, and the rest.

Meanwhile, Guillermo Cabrera Infante was preparing a television program on the history of jazz, which would include illustrative photos and a recorded musical selection in addition to a verbal introduction and a live performance by a Cuban jazz group. The television show, "Lunes de Revolución," was produced by the cultural weekly of the same name, which Cabrera Infante directed. And this is where certain officials carried out the first attack on jazz. It has been debated whether or not the revolutionary (and later socialist) government in Cuba prohibited jazz, or whether or not it created obstacles for jazz. As it was, despite sporadic attacks of a certain type, jazz found its way more easily than did other types of music such as Anglo-American rock, which was banned from the media for almost twenty years; or the *toques de santo* (Afro-Cuban religious rituals), officially classified as superstitious witchcraft, and even the *nueva trova*, prohibited on radio and TV in its early stages and then exalted almost as an "official music." But let's return to 1960.

The "Lunes" program on jazz could have been a success, but it was undermined by those whom one would least expect: the Musicians Union, among whose brand new leaders there were some who up until a few months earlier had played jazz, and even some who had been jazz enthusiasts. The boycott of the program consisted of keeping the union musicians from performing, under threat of sanctions. In reality, it was only a skirmish provoked by extremists and opportunists, but we had to prevent them from creating an unfavorable "environment" for jazz.[2] A few months earlier, a group of

Neanderthals had interrupted a jazz descarga at the Capri, in which Guillermo Barreto, Pablo Cano, and other well-known musicians were playing. This kind of agitator, carried away in the anti-imperialist sentiment of the time, was capable of creating an atmosphere of fear and witch-hunting under the pretext that jazz was "imperialist music." There were plenty of examples in the Soviet Union, within the cult of the nefarious theorist of "socialist realism," Maxim Gorky.

I wrote an article in defense of jazz for the Sunday supplement of the newspaper *Hoy,* organ of the Partido Socialista Popular (Communist), directed at the time by the poet and painter Fayad Jamís and in which we had a few friends. Considered the country's most pro-Soviet and "hard line" newspaper, the publication of my article in the cultural supplement turned out to be more effective than if it had appeared in *Lunes.* I based the article on the topic of racism in the United States and the importance of jazz in the struggle by American blacks for their civil and human rights, a question essential to the understanding of jazz and its history.[3] Also at that time, we saw ourselves— as Cuban jazz musicians—benefiting from the Cuban rapprochement with American black civil rights movements and its leaders, one of whom, Robert Williams, lived several years in Cuba and helped us to organize a jazz festival in 1963. Other American black leaders such as Stokely Carmichael and Eldridge Cleaver would later visit the country. Meanwhile, for all of 1959 and part of 1960, the Club Cubano de Jazz maintained its normal Sunday sessions, before increasingly bigger and more enthusiastic audiences. It should be noted that when Philly Joe Jones appeared at the Tropicana, perhaps the Club's greatest success and culminating moment, a situation of maximum tension existed between Washington and Havana.

Although at certain times the "suspicion" with respect to jazz would surface again, this is almost always because of the particular idiosyncrasy of one or another acting bureaucrat, such as the period when students caught playing jazz—invariably the best musicians in the school—would be suspended from the Escuela Nacional de Música (this happened toward the end of the 1960s and on into the 1970s). All of which explains why so many jazz musicians left the country, starting with the first phase of the revolution: Cachao, Bebo Valdés, El Negro Vivar, Pedro Chao, Walfredito de los Reyes, and around 1965 Papito Hernández, Juanito Márquez, and many others. Fortunately, despite the various phases of this exodus that have occurred in the Eighties and Nineties,

Cuba's gold mine of musical talent has always provided a new wave of jazz musicians who have kept this music alive.

The New Atmosphere of the Sixties

In these first years of the decade two American jazz musicians settled in Havana, both light mulattos who interestingly had Latin surnames: the alto saxophonist Eddy Torriente and a little bit later pianist Mario Lagarde, who was born in the Virgin Islands but living in Chicago, where he met Eddy. For years they, with their group Free American Jazz, will represent one of the strongholds of jazz in Cuba. Peruchín Jústiz formed a number of jazz groups around this time, first a trio with Limonta (bass) and Castiñeira (drums), then with Papito Hernández and Walfredito (later Cachaíto replaced Papito). Then Peruchín formed a quartet, which included a singer who was an ex-member of the Cuban Pipers and Los Cavaliers, Regino Tellechea; the bassist was Armando Zequeira and the drummer was Tibo Lee. And we should point out that Armandito Zequeira (son of the pianist Zenaida Romeu) excelled first as a drummer, although he was already playing violin and piano at that time as well; in the end he stuck with the double bass, but soon he was the first Cuban musician to switch to electric bass, way before the rock 'n' roll craze about the Beatles. Shortly thereafter he would form a very popular group, Los Cinco, which produced singer Maggie Carlés and musicians such as Pedro Jústiz Jr. (Peruchín II), an excellent guitarist. Many other jazz groups lasted only briefly, such as the Batchá, Los Fantásticos, and Chucho Valdés's first group, while some stayed around longer, such as the Quinteto Instrumental de Música Moderna, the Noneto de Jazz, the Tres más Uno, the Samuel Téllez combo, and the most constant and long-lasting of all time, Felipe Dulzaides's group.

In this period the close ties between jazz and 'feeling' continued and joint descargas were held at different places, a routine that had taken hold in the last year of the Club Cubano de Jazz. Now these jam sessions would no longer take place in private homes, but rather in small nightclubs of which the Gato Club was the precursor. The most important were El Gato Tuerto, the Sheherezada, the Karachi, La Gruta, Le Mans, Pigalle, the Lobby Bar and the Pico Blanco at St. John's Hotel, El Patio at the Habana Libre, the Salón Rojo at the Capri, La Red, the Flamingo, and the different bars of the Nacional and the Riviera. But there also emerged an important new locale that was called the Descarga Club, which can be considered the symbol of those years 1959–63, and whose importance for the new wave of musicians will be seen when we return to the topic later on. But in all of the places mentioned, the jazz musicians came together with key 'feeling' artists, such as César and José Antonio, Omara Portuondo, Marta Valdés, Elena Burke, the duo Las Capella, Meme Solís, and Miguel de Gonzalo. These years were not just the celebration of 'feeling', but rather its pinnacle.

The arrival of Brazilian bossa nova showed the great affinity between this new international style, feeling and cool jazz, and came to reinforce even more the musical panorama of Havana. Some groups experimented successfully with the bossa nova, among them that of the popular feeling songwriter Ela O'Farrill (no relation to Chico O'Farrill), whom we heard in the La Gruta club (Twenty-third between O and P). The Frank Domínguez and Felipe Dulzaides groups also excelled in the bossa nova. And two Uruguayan musicians from the Symphonic Orchestra organized another group to play bossa nova and some jazz as well; it was called Los Federicos, named after the violinist Federico Britos and the contrabassist Federico García, who recorded an LP. Working with them were pianists Frank Emilio and Chucho Valdés, guitarist Carlos Emilio Morales, guitarist and arranger Abelardo Busch, and percussionists José Luis Quintana ("Changuito") and Manuel "Cala" Armesto; at a certain point the group was known as Los Amigos.

The big bands, which had their highs and lows in the United States but weren't affected too much in Cuba, began in these years a dramatic and almost definitive decline, although a few important ones still remained at the big cabarets. Armando Romeu only stayed at the Tropicana until 1961, while Rafael Ortega was at the Riviera's Copa Room, Rafael Somavilla and then Fernando Mulens were at the Caribe, and Peruchín Jústiz headed an orchestra at the Capri for a while. But it was the trumpet player Leonardo Timor Jr. who fronted the best jazz band of the decade until 1967 at the Hotel Nacional's Parisién cabaret. Many of the musicians who had worked before at the Parisién in the orchestras of Walfredo and Walfredito de los Reyes stayed with him. And performing in the Salón Caribe of the Habana Libre was an excellent band led by the guitarist and arranger Juanito Márquez, who achieved great popularity in those years with his canciones and boleros such as "Alma con alma" and with his *pacá* rhythm. Emerging almost simultaneously were the *pilón* rhythm from the singer Pacho Alonso and his conjunto Los Bocucos and the *mozambique* from the percussionist Pedro Izquierdo ("Pello el Afrokán").[4]

But many of the country's important jazz bands had already broken up, among them the Casino de la Playa, Julio Cueva, Palau Brothers, Lebatard Brothers, Cosmopolita, and Havana Casino. The Castro Brothers band, pioneer of the Cuban big bands, was dissolved in 1960, and a number of its musicians joined the Radio Progreso orchestra, which disappeared a few years later when the orchestra of the Instituto Cubano de Radiodifusión (later "de Radio y Televisión") was organized, following the centralizing tendency of the country and its institutions. Only two jazz bands continued at the height of popularity: the Riverside, with its singer Tito Gómez, and the "tribe" of Beny Moré, which alternated with charangas and conjuntos at dances, on radio, and on television. In perhaps yet another symbolic event, Beny Moré died in 1963, the year of the Beatles explosion in London. The time was approaching when interest in jazz bands would decline, in Cuba and in the entire world. In Havana the large cabarets were all that remained for the big bands, but the small locales were still very plentiful, and it was the combos that were able to find work.

Descargas, Concerts, Recitals

Although the Parisién cabaret, with Leonardo Timor and his band, had turned into a focal point for Cuban jazz musicians, the aforementioned Descarga Club (on Neptuno between Hospital and Aramburu) was for about three years the indisputable successor to the Havana 1900, where many young jazz instrumentalists tested and honed their skills. The Descarga had as its proprietor Raúl Martiatu, a jazz and feeling lover for many years (I've already referred to the jam sessions at the Martiatu family house, not far from the same neighborhood where the Descarga Club took up residence). At the entrance of the place there was a bar with a roof and then you went through to an open-air patio in the style of other cabarets such as the old Edén Concert or La Campana. The shows were generally set up by performers and feeling singers, and on one roofed platform various jazz groups played; a lot of musicians from other ensembles would show up to hold jam sessions, which became regular events. In the beginning the Free American Jazz quartet worked there, with

Eddy Torriente on alto sax and Mario Lagarde on piano; the rest of the members were Cuban musicians, who would change with the different stages of this quartet. But there were also larger groups.

Among the musicians who performed in the Descarga Club, some of whom at different times conducted the club's regular orchestra, were trumpet player Miguel Menéndez, tenor saxophonist Tomás Vázquez, baritone saxophonist Rafael Quiñones, pianist and guitarist Kiki Villalta, pianist and vibraphonist Remberto Egües, guitarists Freddy Muguercia and Ahmed "El Jimagua" Barroso, bassist Luis Quiñones, bassist and guitarist Julio César Fonseca, the multi-instrumentalist Armandito Zequeira, and drummers "Zanahoria" and Joe Iglesias. Among the regular jazz singers, Bobby Carcassés and Maggie Prior stand out. Also participating in the descargas were musicians such as Carlos Emilio Morales, the most important guitarist of the decade, and trumpeter Jorge Varona, legitimate successor to El Negro Vivar and Chocolate Armenteros and one of the most versatile trumpet players the country has ever produced.

Even after the Club Cubano de Jazz was definitively dissolved, a number of its founders, such as Horacio Hernández and Roberto Toirac, continued to organize Sunday jam sessions, concerts, or recitals in different places and theater rooms. For example, in the theater rooms of the CTC (Confederación de Trabajadores de Cuba: Cuban Workers Confederation) and the Ministerio de Relaciones Exteriores concerts with Leonardo Timor's band and Felipe Dulzaides's group were held, with the pianist Samuel Téllez and trumpet player Jorge Varona as invited performers. Appearing at the Havana 1900 (renamed Ensueño) was a sensational quartet with Frank Emilio (piano), Juanito Márquez (guitar), Papito Hernández (bass), and Guillermo Barreto (drums), alternating with a trio led by pianist Chucho Valdés (Bebo's son), with Luis Rodríguez on bass and Emilio del Monte on drums. In turn, at the La Gruta club a Sunday jam session was organized with a quartet of members from Felipe Dulzaides's group, including Paquito Echeverría (piano), Pablo Cano (guitar), José Franca (contrabass), and Nelson Padrón (drums); it alternated with another quartet: L. Acosta (alto sax), Raúl Ondina (piano), Luis Rodríguez (contrabass), and Luisito Palau (drums). Around 1961 we performed with a similar group at the Le Mans club (Fifteenth and B, Vedado).

Even more so than in the previous decade, different combos would form from one day to the next, and after weeks or months they would split up, frequently when they finished a contract at a certain club or some musicians left. Also, a new practice emerged: different institutions or theater rooms would present concerts or jazz recitals, and often various musicians from different ensembles would get together to practice just for these concerts. The main venues were the Palacio de Bellas Artes, the Comunidad Hebrea, the Amadeo Roldán Theater (formerly the Auditorium), the Payret, the Sala Idal, the Hubert de Blanck, and the theater rooms of some of the government ministries. This represented a relatively new development in Cuban jazz, particularly because of its frequency and because the organizations or theaters were the interested party, whereas in previous times it had been the musicians who would take the initiative.

Despite this extensive jazz activity, the ensemble that captured all the attention was trumpet player Leonardo Timor's band. The lineup of this band changed a number of times, and working in it were veterans from past decades as well as new jazz stars who were just coming on the scene. Some musicians who left the country in 1961 or 1962 were still around to perform in the first concerts, aside from their regular work at the Parisién. The first lineup that we know of is as follows: trumpets: Leonardo Timor, César "Piyú" Godínez, Lionel Roseñada, Carlos Arado, and Miguel Menéndez; trombones: Pucho Escalante, Antonio Linares, Alejandro Onésimo, and Francisco García Caturla; saxophones: Jesús Caunedo and Antonio Rodríguez (altos), Pedro Chao and René Ravelo (tenors), and Osvaldo Urrutia (baritone); piano: Samuel Téllez; guitar: Juanito Márquez; contrabass: Kiki Hernández; drums: Luisito Palau or Walfredito de los Reyes. Without a doubt, an all-star band.

The Unique Case of Felipe Dulzaides

Another development of the 1960s was the appearance of numerous vocal groups, from duos and trios to quartets and quintets. Here the scene completely changed; of the groups mentioned in previous chapters only Aida Diestro's quartet remained active, which with various personnel changes was able to survive even after the death of its founder and director. Two quartets that arose at the end of the 1950s, Felipe Dulzaides's group (originally Los Armónicos) and Los Bucaneros, directed by Robertico Marín, were the first to promote the boom of the vocal quartets in the 1960s, this time inspired by the innovations of the Four Freshmen and the Hi Lo's. Guitarist Pablo Cano wrote arrangements for the Armónicos and Roberto Marín for his own group, Los Bucaneros. The difference lay in the fact that Felipe formed a vocal-instrumental quartet and over time abandoned the initial format. He limited himself to including only one singer, and ended up with an instrumental group. Very similar to Los Bucaneros and sometimes with arrangements from Marín himself were Voces Latinas and Los Modernistas, in a line perpetuated by Los Britos and others. Meme Solís, an arranger, pianist, and singer from the feeling movement, had the most popular vocal quartet in the 1960s. In a different line were the Cuarteto del Rey and Los Zafiros. The first has its roots in African American styles such as spirituals, blues, and gospel songs; the quintet Los Zafiros was vocal-instrumental, inspired in part by the Platters, and it was another one of the most successful groups of the decade. It disbanded after the death of two of its members, and the sons of several of them later formed a similar group.

Felipe Dulzaides never thought of forming a jazz ensemble; he just tried to organize a good mixture of voices and instruments to play the best of that period's classic popular repertoire. After his participation in the vocal-instrumental quartet Llópiz Dulzaides (a quite commercial mixture of pop-rock), in which he played accordion and piano, he decided to continue on his own because of his disagreement with the more pop-oriented direction of Frank Llópiz. His primary collaborator in the beginning was the guitarist Pablo Cano, and he relied as well on a vocalist who was ideal for his plans, Doris de la Torre. At a certain point the group increased from a quartet to a quintet, with the addition of clarinetist Lucas de la Guardia or the Argentine trumpet player Luis Ortellado. The instrumentalists performed simultaneously as vocalists in this first stage, when Dulzaides worked in television and in nightclubs such as the Starlight Terrace of the Nacional hotel (where I saw him alternate with Philly Joe Jones) or at the Comodoro hotel, where he alternated with Matt Dennis.

Later on Felipe worked in the Tropicana's casino bar, renamed the Salón Panorámico, where pianists such as Frank Emilio and Adolfo Pichardo also worked. It was there that we heard for the first time singer Doris de la Torre playing the vibraphone, a seemingly insignificant event, but of importance for the group, which was moving away from the format of the vocal-instrumental quartet (or quintet) like the Four Freshman and going in the direction of the famous George Shearing quintet, with its characteristic sound based on the unison melodic line carried by the piano, guitar, and vibraphone. When he ventured into jazz, Afro-Cuban music, and a fusion of the two, Dulzaides couldn't keep the group from occasionally going headlong into what has been called "Latin cocktail music," something George Shearing, Cal Tjader, or Noro Morales had often done. What nobody could imagine or foresee was that Felipe Dulzaides's group (which at some point got rid of the name Los Armónicos) would become one of the primary generators of jazz musicians in Cuba.

Among the guitarists who were members of Felipe Dulzaides's group were Pablo Cano, Kiki Villalta, Ahmed Barroso, Sergio Vitier, René Luis Toledo, and Jorge Valdés Chicoy. On bass: Julio César Fonseca, Armandito Zequeira, José Franca, Roberto Casas, Luis Quiñones, Carlos del Puerto, and Carlos Quintero. On drums: Nelson Padrón, Orestes Barbachán ("Pájaro Loco"), Joe Iglesias, Tony Valdés, Ignacio Berroa, Cristóbal Quesada (and on recordings, veterans Daniel Pérez and Guillermo Barreto). As vibraphonists: Doris de la Torre, Eduardo Dulzaides, Paquito Echevarría (also an excellent jazz pianist), Armandito Romeu III (son of renowned bandleader Armando Romeu), and Rembert Egües. On occasion Felipe included Cuban percussion, with musicians such as Manolo "Cala" Armesto, Carlitos Godínez, and José Luis Quintana, the great "Changuito," as well as wind instruments such as the clarinet (Lucas de la Guardia), trumpet (Luis Ortellado), flute (Rembert Egües) and different saxophones (Rolando Pérez Pérez, Manuel Valera, Javier Zalba).

Not all of the singers who performed with Felipe were jazz singers; generally they were given the Cuban sung part of the repertoire. Singing as soloists with him were Doris de la Torre, Alberto and Nina Pujol, Raúl Acosta, Margarita Royero, Elsa Rivero, and Regino Tellechea. Only the first and the last can be considered jazz singers. The instrumentalists, on the other hand, almost without exception were jazz musicians. With different formats, Felipe appeared at the sessions of the Club Cubano de Jazz, which paid tribute to him in 1960. Many other jazz musicians recorded with him or used to visit the centers of nightlife where he performed, often to jam with the group. In the 1960s and 1970s (primarily) Dulzaides passed through almost all of the Havana venues, in addition to going on tour both in Cuba and abroad and spending eight years in Varadero, where he performed at the Hotel Internacional, the Oasis, and the Red Coach. In Havana he worked at the main hotels (Nacional, Riviera, Capri, Comodoro, Habana Libre) and at clubs such as La Red, Kasbah, and others that were becoming the focal point for jazz lovers, clubs such as the Elegante and the Internacional at the Riviera. Furthermore, Dulzaides was the first Cuban who experimented in jazz-rock and included tunes from the Beatles in his repertoire, which made him a favorite among the youth, who would stand in long lines to hear him or to dance to his music (at places such as the Kasbah and La Red).

Felipe's repertoire represented one of the most complete any Cuban ensemble has ever had. Besides the customary international repertoire of "cocktail music" and intermission pianists (which Felipe had been at one time), or the groups of violins and accordion that played any type of music, he included all the modalities of Cuban music (from son to chachachá and from trova to feeling), along with the Afro-Cuban jazz classics such as Mario Bauzá's "Mambo Inn" or Chano Pozo's "Manteca." He would play modern and jazzed-up versions of Manuel de Falla's "La Danza del Fuego" or Lecuona's "Siboney," as well as tunes of Michel Legrand's and others by John Lennon and Paul McCartney. There were plenty of Broadway and Tin Pan Alley standards (Porter, Gershwin, Kern, Berlin, Rodgers) as well as strictly jazz numbers (Ellington, Parker, Miles, Shearing, Monk) and Brazilian tunes (Tom Jobim, Luis Bonfá, Vinicius de Moraes).

The greatness of Felipe begins with the fact that he was a self-taught pianist who admitted that he didn't read music. Nevertheless, sometimes he made orchestrations for his own LPs with the help of Rembert Egües (son of the flutist from Aragón, Richard Egües). One of the secrets of this pianist was his natural musical ear and a great harmonic training, combined at the same time with a phenomenal memory and an ability to play in any key and improvise on the most complex harmonic progressions. He knew close to a thousand tunes by memory, and he only had to listen to a melody once to memorize it and repeat it immediately on the piano already harmonized, something I witnessed myself. During the trips he took to the United States, whenever Felipe arrived at a bar where there was a piano he would sit down and play, taking requests from those present. Invariably the owner of the place would offer him a job. Felipe suffered a stroke and retired in 1983, although he remained a jazz promoter on the island until his death a few years later because of a second stroke, which happened as he was playing in a jam session with what was by then his only good hand, the right one.

Fortunately, Felipe recorded twenty-two LPs with his groups and with orchestras, and even though there are few jazz numbers on these LPs, we remember his "Tropicana Special" and his version of "The Girl from Ipanema" with a guitar solo by Kiki Villalta.[5]

Free American Jazz and Other Groups

The Capri hotel's Salón Rojo was another one of the spots that served as a showcase for jazz and feeling in the early 1960s; this salón, having almost the same dimensions as the cabaret, was the place where the gaming room had been in the days when George Raft acted as the representative of Meyer Lansky's interests. For a certain period of time, it became a center for 'feeling', and shortly thereafter Felito Ayón, an old jazz and feeling fan, organized "Capri Mondays." Ayón had been founder of the circle of La Bodeguita del Medio, today an overpriced tourist restaurant-bar, a pitiful ersatz exalted to uncertain "fame" thanks to advertising that in no way reflects the truth. During the first half of the 1960s Felito managed various nightlife spots and was the real "spiritual father" of the restaurant, bar, and cabaret El Gato Tuerto (on O between Fifteenth and Seventeenth), for some time the 'feeling' Mecca. He also did the same for the cabaret El Patio, in the Habana Libre hotel, which opened with Meme Solís's vocal quartet and the jazz group Tres más Uno.

It was precisely in the Capri's Salón Rojo where we saw Eddy Torriente for the first time in 1960, during his first visit to Cuba; later he returned to settle for good, and throughout this decade (which ended in 1968, as I will clarify further ahead) his group Free American Jazz, with pianist Mario Lagarde, represented the other pole of jazz in Havana in addition to Felipe Dulzaides. These were the only two groups in those days that were able to make it in nightlife spots where the rest of the musicians went to jam. The other groups of this period either didn't stay around as long or were only interested in recording and giving recitals. In the beginning the Free American Jazz worked at the Descarga Club, and when it closed in 1963 they moved on to La Gruta, in the basement of the La Rampa cinema. Playing with Eddy and Mario early on were Cuban bassists Luis Quiñones and Armandito Zequeira and drummers Salvador "Macho" Almirall and José Luis Yanes ("Pepe el Loco"). Eddy played the alto sax in the swing style and, just like Armando Romeu, was particularly influenced by tenor sax player Paul

Gonsalves, from Duke Ellington's band, whom he knew from Chicago. Mario Lagarde was an excellent accompanying pianist and a soloist halfway between swing and bop, as well as an arranger, to which he dedicated himself exclusively later on, after the death of Eddy in a motorcycle accident in 1968.

Working with the Free American Jazz, in addition to those already mentioned, were the bassists Julio César Fonseca, the Uruguayan Federico García, and the renowned Papito Hernández; drummers Joe Iglesias and Tony Valdés; tenor saxophonist Sinesio Rodríguez; and guitarists Freddy Muguercia and Rey Montesinos. Although I only visited the Descarga Club three times, I was often at La Gruta with a borrowed alto sax, flugelhorn, or baritone sax that Miguel Angel Herrera, member of a combo at the University of Havana, would lend me. Other regular visitors were guitarist Carlos Emilio Morales, trumpeter Jorge Varona, the Uruguayan violinist Federico Britos, and the alto saxophonist and clarinetist Paquito D'Rivera. Around 1965 the Free American Jazz moved on to the Atelier club (at Seventeenth and Sixth, Vedado), bringing jazz lovers and musicians along with them, with the advantage that the Atelier was open until six in the morning. As at the other places I've mentioned, at the Atelier the counterpart to jazz was feeling, and so Omara Portuondo, Reinaldo Henríquez, Elena Burke, and others would go there frequently, often along with Frank Emilio and the guitarist Froylán Amézaga.

Among jazz musicians, the Free American Jazz alternative was preferred even over Felipe Dulzaides's group, for the latter normally had to please the more diverse hotel audience with a varied repertoire, while the former only played jazz, generally at hole-in-the-wall places where neither the manager nor the fans expected anything else, for it was precisely these jazz (and feeling) enthusiasts who kept these nightclubs full. Although Free American Jazz seldom performed in concert and never recorded, it will be remembered for its role as the cohesive base of the Cuban jazz musicians during the years in which, along with Felipe Dulzaides, they kept alive the "spirit of the jam sessions," the ultimate and irreplaceable school for jazz musicians.

As I've already indicated, there were many other combos at that time, some of which we only know by word of mouth. One group called Los Fantásticos featured, as far as we know, Freddy Muguercia (guitar), Armando Romeu III (vibraphone), Armando Zequeira (electric bass), and Joe Iglesias (drums). The group Batchá included Freddy González (piano), Rey

Montesinos (guitar), Roberto Valdés (bass), Joe Iglesias (drums), and Agapito García (conga). This combo, which performed at the Sheherezada, was the seed for the future Tres más Uno, which also featured the vibraphonist Armandito Romeu and was one of the most important and long lasting. I've also alluded to the group formed by pianist Samuel Téllez, which made a number of successful pop recordings of "jazzed up" Cuban numbers. Its biggest hit, which was heard on all the Victrolas and on the radio around 1965, was the instrumental version of the popular feeling song "Aquí de pie," with stimulating changes in tempo and dynamics.

Samuel Téllez's group was made up of Samuel on piano, Jorge Varona (trumpet), Rafael Tortoló (alto sax), Amadito Valdés Jr. or Gilberto Terry ("Lumumba") on drums, and Norberto Carrillo on conga. Around the same time Chucho Valdés would put together his first group, which focused more on recording, for Chucho as well as several of the other members at that time were part of the Teatro Musical de la Habana orchestra. Chucho was able to record some singles that were quite successful in those days, including some boleros converted into "Latin jazz" and sung by the singer Amado Borcelá, better known as "Guapachá." Chucho brought together a combination of veterans and younger players: Paquito D'Rivera (alto sax and clarinet), Julio A. Vento (flute), Alberto "El Men" Giral (valve trombone), Chucho Valdés (piano), Carlos Emilio Morales (guitar), Kiki Hernández (bass), and Emilio del Monte (drums), a student of Guillermo Barreto. The peppery vocalist Guapachá, who brought commercial success to the group, was from the scat tradition started by Francisco Fellove and continued by Bobby Carcassés and Tony Escarpenter, but with his own unique style. This group recorded an instrumental that is today a classic of Cuban jazz, "Mambo influenciado," by Chucho Valdés, based on the twelve-bar blues. At the end of the decade, in 1969, Bobby Carcassés formed a group that performed at the Pabellón Cuba at Twenty-third and N, featuring Julio Vento (flute), Nicolás Reinoso (tenor sax), Raúl Ondina (piano), Bobby Carcassés (bass), and Amadito Valdés (drums).

The Tres más Uno, which made a few personnel changes, lasted a bit longer. Originally it was a quartet, as its name indicates, whose format and style came straight from the Modern Jazz Quartet, and in its early stage it had a number of the MJQ's classic pieces in its repertoire. At that time it featured three of the aforementioned Batchá members: Freddy González (piano),

Roberto Valdés (contrabass), and Joe Iglesias (drums). The fourth but irreplaceable member was the vibraphonist Armandito Romeu, an excellent
improviser inspired by Milt Jackson, whose solos he knew by memory. Tres
más Uno inaugurated Habana Libre's El Patio, alternating with Meme Solís
and his vocal quartet. Through the years Joe Iglesias remained the group's
leader; in addition to playing drums he played the vibraphone, the tenor sax,
and finally the piano, and he had previously been with the Hot Rockers,
Batchá, Felipe Dulzaides, and the Free American Jazz. There were many personnel changes, and among those who passed through the group were tenor
saxophonist Sinesio Rodríguez, guitarist Jorge Valdés Chicoy, bass player
Gustavo Casal, and drummers Amadito Valdés and "Pájaro Loco" Barbachán.
In the 1980s the Tres más Uno was still playing in various clubs, centered
this time on singer Alicia Fraga, ex-member of the quartet Las D'Aida.[6]

The Quinteto, the Noneto, and the Recordings

Two of the most important ensembles of this period were the Quinteto
Instrumental de Música Moderna and Leopoldo "Pucho" Escalante's
Noneto de Jazz, which committed themselves entirely to concerts and
recordings, since their members worked in different places. Most of the
members of the Noneto belonged to studio, radio, and TV orchestras. An
element that favored these groups was that they were able to make recordings on commercial LPs, something unusual in Cuban jazz. The biggest difference between the two, in addition to their formats, lay in the fact that the
Quintet focused on playing popular Cuban tunes with improvised Latin
jazz solos and Afro-Cuban rhythms, while the Noneto was under the influence of the Birth of the Cool sound created by Miles Davis and Gil Evans,
then used by Gerry Mulligan, Shorty Rogers, and other West Coast musicians. These two ensembles have paradoxically gone down in Cuban jazz
history primarily because they were recorded, although their influence on
the country's (or the capital's) jazz scene was much less significant, despite
their sporadic appearances in concerts or recitals, always before a full house.

The Quintet was made up of exceptional musicians on their respective
instruments: Frank Emilio Flynn (piano), Papito Hernández and then
Cachaíto López (contrabass), Guillermo Barreto (drums and pailas), Tata
Güines (conga), and Gustavo Tamayo (güiro). The group achieved its own

unique style, which was difficult to match, because of the ensemble work as well as the solos and the never-failing combination of swing with good taste. But despite the indisputable talent of all its members, what the Quintet needed was perhaps a daily gig in clubs that would have allowed them to "cut loose" more often, for at certain times when they played songs that are today classics (such as "Añorado encuentro") their execution seemed almost too "perfect," as if every note had been written out. For those of us who saw the Quintet live, the studio recordings sound a little bit cold, making up in perfection for what they lack in looseness. Nevertheless, at a recital in the Fine Arts Theater we received a similar impression. Was it self-control on the part of the musicians? Or was it a deliberate effort to avoid ostentations of virtuosity and fits of inspiration? As a way of drawing a comparison, it might be that with the Quintet we can experience what we do sometimes with the Modern Jazz Quartet. I have heard all of these musicians on more brilliant solos. Frank Emilio shows signs of his versatility (as a jazz artist, sonero, danzonero, baladista, songwriter, concert pianist), but I want to hear Frank, Papito, Cachaíto, or Tata Güines, and perhaps Barreto even more. While the latter shines on pailas, on drums he limits himself to accompaniment, very subtle and efficient to be sure. But perhaps I am criticizing precisely the highest qualities of these exemplary recordings.

Pucho Escalante's Noneto de Jazz appeared in concert at various theater halls, with arrangements by Pucho himself. The group focused primarily on their work as an ensemble, although it had good improvisers and dedicated some time to solos. Their music is simply jazz (more of a West Coast style), without the "Afro-Cuban" or "Latin" qualifier. The Noneto consisted of Luis Escalante and then Eddy Martínez (trumpet), Luis Toledo (flugelhorn), Pucho Escalante (trombone), Braulio "Babín" Hernández (tenor sax), Osvaldo "Mosquifín" Urrutia (baritone sax), Rubén González or Rafael Somavilla (piano), Papito Hernández (bass), and Salvador "Macho" Almirall (drums). The Noneto played an important role until the creation in 1967 of the Orquesta Cubana de Música Moderna, in which Pucho Escalante, his brother Luis (who also was first trumpet in the National Symphonic Orchestra), and tenor player "Babín" Hernández were pillars. Just two LP records bear witness to the work of the Noneto de Jazz, but even this is quite an accomplishment considering our circumstances.

The guitarist and composer Juanito Márquez also recorded a few pressings (though singles) of Afro-Latin jazz with a group of stars. Along with Márquez, particularly noteworthy was pianist Luis Mariano Cancañón, whose piano innovations in the Cuban style put him right up there with the greats in this area. Rounding out the group were Nilo Argudín (trumpet), Papito Hernández (bass), Guillermo Barreto (drums and pailas), Oscar Valdés (conga), Roberto García (bongo), and Gustavo Tamayo (güiro). The intricate passages of Juanito's tunes had an unbeatable rhythmic base, with a percussion section that brought together the period's most sought-after musicians, later becoming (except for Tamayo) the percussion section of the Orquesta Cubana de Música Moderna. Luis Mariano Cancañón later returned to his and Juanito's hometown, Holguín, where he organized as many as three jazz bands.

On the other hand, Frank Emilio Flynn and his fellow musicians would get together for a memorable recording of distinctly Cuban music (and descargas), producing the LP *Los Amigos,* another landmark in Cuban musical improvisation that resounded not only on the island but also among exponents of salsa. This unusual group featured: Frank Emilio (piano), Elio Valdés (violin), Miguel O'Farrill (flute), Cachaíto López (bass), Guillermo Barreto (pailas), Jesús Pérez (batá drums), Tata Güines (conga), and Gustavo Tamayo (güiro). The album includes three classic danzones: "Almendra" (Abelardo Valdés), "Tres lindas cubanas" (Antonio María Romeu), and "La flauta mágica" (Romeu and Alfredo Brito). A number of other tunes are categorized simply as "descargas," an international term by then: "Gandinga, Sandunga y Mondongo" (Frank Emilio), "Pa'gozar" (Tata Güines), and "Lázara y Georgina" (Orlando "Cachaíto" López). And in between we have "Como canta el contrabajo" by Orestes "Macho" López, the famed author of the danzón "Mambo" and Cachaíto's father. A noteworthy element of this recording is the combined work of two percussionists of the caliber of the *Olú Batá* Jesús Pérez and Arístides Soto (Tata Güines), masterfully supported by Gustavo Tamayo.

*Leonardo Timor and
    the Transition Bands*

Most of the jazz bands from this transitional period (1960–67) limited themselves to providing danceable music and show tunes for the cabarets, although they are important to us as they helped to professionally train young jazz musicians. When Armando Romeu left the Tropicana, there remained two high quality orchestras: Rafael Ortega's, which went from the Sans Souci (closed in 1959) to the Riviera hotel, and trumpet player Leonardo Timor's band, already mentioned. Ortega always had excellent bands with great arrangements, and with him at that time were trumpet players Dagoberto Jiménez and Félix Prieto, trombonist Francisco García Caturla, pianist Héctor Alejo ("El Ñato"), bassist José Manuel Peña, and the great drummer Fausto García Rivera. Among the saxophonists we find Edilberto Escrich and Rafael Prats (altos), Castillo and Raúl "El Chino" Chiu (tenors), and Osvaldo Urrutia (baritone).[7]

The representative jazz band from this period is Leonardo Timor's, which remained at the Parisién for some seven years and gave numerous concerts, as well as recording a historic album. His band held the spot that Armando Romeu had occupied for the previous two decades, and the Parisién turned into another one of the places where musicians would go to jam after the last show, as we had done before with the orchestra of Walfredito de los Reyes. Also, Timor organized the "Jazz Tuesdays" at the Parisién, in which different guests would play with the band, and he offered several concerts (also with guest soloists), particularly in the Comunidad Hebrea theater (on Línea between J and I, Vedado). In this orchestra we will also find musicians whom we've already seen as members of Armando Romeu's bands and at the Club Cubano de Jazz sessions. And, eventually, in 1967 almost the entire brass section will join the Orquesta Cubana de Música Moderna.

Playing in the orchestra of Leonardo Timor Jr.'s between 1963 and 1967 were the following musicians: trumpets: Timor, Luis Escalante, Nilo Argudín, Andrés Castro, Jorge Varona, Evelio Martínez, and Manuel "El Guajiro" Mirabal; trombones: Antonio Linares, Alejandro Onésimo, Pucho Escalante, Modesto Echarte, and Alberto Giral ("El Men"); saxophones: Amadito Valdés and Luis Barrera (altos), Mario Menéndez and Hugo Yera (tenors), Rolando Triana and/or Osvaldo Urrutia (baritone); piano: Rubén González; contrabass: Fernando Vivar, Luis Rodríguez; guitar: Juanito Márquez; drums: Luisito Palau. The trumpet section was quite impressive; with Timor, Escalante, Argudín, Varona, or Mirabal could play lead. With the exception of Argudín and Martínez, all of them, including

Leonardo Timor, would go on to the OCMM in 1967, and Jorge Varona would be one of the founders of Irakere in 1973. Appearing as a guest, in addition to Juanito Márquez, was another musician who would become internationally famous in the following decades: Paquito D'Rivera (thirteen years old at the time). The band's main soloist was Leonardo Timor, with a trumpet style that owed a lot to Bunny Berrigan and Harry James as well as Count Basie's trumpet players; the orchestra's theme song was "What's New," featuring the leader on a trumpet solo. On the album that this great band recorded, also historic today, we find original numbers by Armando Romeu, Pucho Escalante, Mario Lagarde, and Roberto Sánchez Ferrer, all of whom wrote arrangements especially for Timor, as well as Juanito Márquez, who established himself in this decade as the country's top arranger.

Generally forgotten is the work of an orchestra that was important in this period for the development of its instrumentalists in subsequent years: the orchestra of the Teatro Musical de La Habana, whose home was the old Alkázar theater, which was constructed on the site of the historic Alhambra. The Teatro Musical was founded in 1963 by the Mexican comedian and then film director and actor Alfonso Arau. The orchestra had three highly qualified directors and arrangers: Federico Smith, an American symphonic composer who was very skilled on Joseph Schillinger's composition methods and teacher of two generations of Cuban musicians (he came from Mexico along with Arau); Tony Taño, ex-trumpet player and arranger who studied orchestration and composition with Félix Guerrero and Carlos Fariñas and orchestral conducting with Manuel Duchesne Cuzán; and Leo Brouwer, symphonic composer and classic guitar virtuoso known today throughout the world.

Among the band's sidemen were saxophonists Paquito D'Rivera, Juan Castro, and Horacio Soler, lead trumpet Nilo Argudín, trombonist Antonio Leal, pianist Chucho Valdés, guitarist Carlos Emilio Morales, the veteran contrabassist Kiki Hernández, drummer Juan "Papita" Ampudia, and Roberto Concepción on Cuban percussion. Coming together for the first time in this orchestra were three musicians who would later be among the founders of Irakere, after having also worked together in the Orquesta Cubana de Música Moderna from 1967 to 1973, as well as in the groups (quartets, quintets) formed within the context of this band that took part in international jazz festivals. I'm referring to pianist Chucho Valdés, guitarist Carlos Emilio Morales (whom "we discovered" at the Havana 1900), and the saxophonist who would become the most distinguished Cuban jazz musician internationally in the 1980s, Paquito D'Rivera. These three musicians were also together on Chucho's recordings with vocalist Guapachá, who died prematurely shortly thereafter. And coincidence or not, one of the Teatro Musical actors (who, just like the rest, also had to sing and dance) was Bobby Carcassés, later a well-known singer, multi-instrumentalist, and leader of groups such as the Afro Jazz band.

A Festival, Concerts, and More Descargas

The biggest jazz event after the disappearance of the Club Cubano de Jazz in 1960 occurred three years later with the celebration of a festival at the Payret Theater, where almost forty years before Ernesto Lecuona performed Gershwin's *Rhapsody in Blue* in Cuba for the first time. Attending this festival were ensembles that would later become the most prominent of the decade, such as the Quinteto Instrumental de Música Moderna, Free American Jazz (then with Uruguayan bassist Federico García), and Leonardo Timor's band, which accompanied singers Maggie Prior (on "My Funny Valentine" and "Embraceable You") and Omara Portuondo (on "The Man I Love"). Of particular note in the band was the solo by trumpet player Jorge Varona, not well known at the time, in "Noche de Ronda," with a special arrangement by Armando Romeu. Two vocal groups also took part, Los Modernistas and the Cuarteto del Rey, with their repertoire of spirituals. For this event I organized and led a quintet that featured Leonardo Acosta (alto sax), Carlos Emilio Morales (guitar), Chucho Valdés (piano), Armando Zequeira (bass), and Salvador Almirall (drums), backed up by Manolo Armesto (bongo). The pianist and arranger Adolfo Pichardo organized another group that included Paquito D'Rivera (alto sax), Kiki Villalta (guitar), Luis Quiñones (bass), and Amadito Valdés Jr. (drums).

In charge of putting on the festival was the African American Robert Williams, who opened it with a speech on the transcendence of jazz, its universality, and the role that it has played in the African American struggle for civil rights and black cultural values in the United States. The festival was reviewed extensively by the Cuban press and inspired jazz musicians to give concerts and recitals, such as the one offered in July of the same year by Armando Zequeira with a quartet that included Eddy Torriente (alto sax), Mario Lagarde (piano), Zequeira (bass), and Armandito Romeu (drums), in the Palacio de Bellas Artes theater. In that period Armandito Zequeira also organized his group Los Cinco, which featured Pedro Jústiz Jr. on guitar and Emilio del Monte on drums. The same year another group of very young musicians was created, a septet that would attract a lot of attention, Los Chicos del Jazz, which performed in the Capri's Salón Rojo, at the Olokkú club (Calzada and E, Vedado), La Gruta, La Zorra y El Cuervo, the Omega cinema, and Club 70. The group included Paquito D'Rivera (alto sax), Nicolás Reinoso (tenor sax), Rembert Egües (piano), Sergio Vitier (guitar), Fabián García Caturla (bass), Amadito Valdés Jr. (drums), and Carlos Godínez (conga).

A new stage for jazz was the theater hall of the Ministerio de Industrias, where the jazz critic Horacio Hernández organized a number of recitals. In 1965 we presented a sextet that featured Leonardo Acosta (alto sax and flugelhorn), Chucho Valdés (piano), Carlos E. Morales (guitar), Papito Hernández (contrabass), Emilio del Monte (drums), and Manolo Armesto (bongo). At the Palacio de Bellas Artes that same group appeared (without Cuban percussion), playing mostly numbers by Miles Davis, John Coltrane, and Jackie McLean that I had transcribed. Appearing at Bellas Artes in September 1966 was a quartet consisting of Chucho Valdés (piano), Carlos E. Morales (guitar), Federico García (contrabass), and Manolo Armesto (Cuban percussion). The repertoire, oddly announced as "traditional jazz," was based on classics from the bop period such as "Perdido," "How High the Moon," "Walking," and others. But most of the concerts and recitals of those years featured, as we've already indicated, the Quinteto, the Noneto, and Leonardo Timor's band.

A problem already being felt in Cuba and getting worse as the years passed was the shortage of jazz records and the difficulties in acquiring them. Records have traditionally been the best source of education for young jazz musicians, in the United States and even more so in the rest of the world. Without music shops such as André's or Sammy's or the importation of records (other than those from the Soviet Union or Czechoslovakia) one had to make deals with a few foreign friends living in Cuba who were jazz fans or with Cubans who frequently traveled abroad. Then the records were played on the radio or listened to collectively at a friend's house. Some of us set out to perform the most recent numbers and present the latest trends, from the "modal" jazz of Miles Davis and John Coltrane to free jazz, and including Charlie Mingus with his blues and roots trend. With this idea in mind, in 1966 I formed a quintet with pianist Raúl Ondina to perform in theaters such as the Hubert de Blanck and the Sala Idal. The repertoire included tunes of Miles, Coltrane, McCoy Tyner, Jackie McLean, and a number of our own originals.

The members of the quintet were L. Acosta (alto sax), Raúl "El Chino" Chiu (tenor sax), Raúl Ondina (piano), Luis Quiñones or Cachaíto López (contrabass), and Armandito Romeu (drums). Also performing with the group were bassist Armandito Zequeira, pianist and flutist Rembert Egües, and drummers Blasito Egües, Cristóbal Quesada, and Marcos Larrinaga. Once we recorded at Radio Progreso with Bobby Carcassés (voice and bass), Blas Egües (drums), and Changuito (congas). A number of jazz recitals were held at the Hubert de Blanck Theater, organized by outstanding "feeling" composer Marta Valdés. But the main activity of those years, approximately 1965–67, took place at the jam sessions of the ICAIC (Instituto Cubano del Arte y la Industria Cinematográficos: Cuban Institute of Film Arts and Industry) every Saturday afternoon, renewing in part the tradition of the Club Cubano de Jazz. The organizers were two workers from the film industry: Ricardo Delgado and Ovidio González, the latter codirector with Adolfo Castillo of the best jazz program at that time. The jam sessions were held at the ICAIC union hall, located at Twenty-third and Tenth, Vedado, on the same site where years before the Internacional cabaret (later the Yobana Club) had been.

Although it's almost impossible to remember all of the musicians who took part in these descargas, they include: trumpet and flugelhorn: Jorge Varona; flugelhorn and alto sax: Leonardo Acosta; alto sax: Paquito D'Rivera, Filiberto Alderete; tenor sax: Nicolás Reinoso, Raúl Chiu; baritone sax: Rafael Quiñones; piano: Raúl Ondina, Chucho Valdés, Freddy González, Mario Lagarde, Rembert Egües; bass: Cachaíto López, Fabián G. Caturla, Luis Quiñones, Julio César Fonseca, Bobby Carcassés; drums: Armandito Romeu, Amadito Valdés, Tony Valdés, "Pájaro Loco" Barbachán, Marcos Larrinaga; Cuban percussion: José Luis "Changuito" Quintana,

Norberto Carrillo, Pedrito "Guapachá" Borcelá (brother of the late singer Amado Borcelá).

As one might expect, almost half of the audience consisted of film directors, writers, and technicians, and artists in general, although admission was free. This resulted in a certain coming together of Cuban film producers and jazz musicians. Perhaps the first jazz musician to make the music for a Cuban film was Armando Zequeira, who relied on musicians such as Chucho, Carlos Emilio, and Paquito. In another film Doris de la Torre sang the theme song with only a double bass accompaniment (Papito Hernández) and an alto sax counterpoint (Leonardo Acosta). But it was film director Sara Gómez who systematically brought jazz into Cuban cinema: first she made a documentary on jazz with Chucho Valdés's group, then she had Chucho and Rembert Egües do the music for other documentaries, and she suggested to Tomás Gutiérrez Alea the names of those who made the music for the feature film *Cumbite:* Papito Hernández and Arístides Soto ("Tata Güines"). For my part, I did the music for a documentary of hers, which we made with only three musicians: pianist Emiliano Salvador and drummer and percussionist Leoginaldo Pimentel, with my participation on various flutes. Later on Sara Gómez put Sergio Vitier in charge of the music for her feature film *De cierta manera.* Thereafter other jazz musicians, such as Emiliano Salvador, José María Vitier, Gonzalito Rubalcaba, Eduardo Ramos, and Nicolás Reinoso, would make music for films.

In this decade and into the following, descargas were held in private homes such as those of Enrique O'Farrill (Chico's brother), José Alberto Figueras (one of the founders of the CCJ), bassist Felo Hernández, and others, while Roberto Toirac organized descargas at one of the locales of the Ministerio de la Construcción and, although it may seem strange, at the veterinary clinic of Dr. Caíñas, at Línea and E (Vedado). Playing in these jam sessions were, among others, alto saxophonists Leonardo Acosta and Paquito D'Rivera, tenor saxophonist Nicolás Reinoso, pianists Raúl Ondina and Chucho Valdés, bassists Cachaíto López and Eduardo Ramos, guitarist Carlos E. Morales, and drummers Enrique Plá, Changuito Quintana, and Amadito Valdés Jr. In the office and clinic of Dr. Caíñas there was a space with a piano in which ensembles such as the Tres más Uno and Juan Formell's Van Van orchestra rehearsed as well. That's where singer Maggie Prior and I organized a jam session for the Argentine writer Julio Cortázar, a big jazz fan and trumpet enthusiast, who years later and on another visit had the opportunity to meet and listen to two great trumpet players of ours: Arturo Sandoval and Jorge Varona.

The Orquesta Juvenil and the Orquesta Cubana de Música Moderna

In 1966 an enthusiastic group of young musicians decided to form a jazz band, which they named the Orquesta Juvenil de Música Moderna. It was the forerunner of the "official" jazz orchestra that the Consejo Nacional de Cultura would form a year later at the request of a few of its high officials. The Orquesta Juvenil performed primarily at Radio Progreso, was led by pianist and arranger Adolfo Pichardo, and featured singer Nancy Alvarez. The members of this jazz band, some of whom would become famous in subsequent decades, were the following: trumpets: Arturo Sandoval, Elpidio Chapotín, Octavio Calderón, Adalberto Lara ("Trompetica"), and Víctor Rodríguez; trombones: Juan Pablo Torres, Bruno Villalonga, and Antonio Leal; saxophones: Rolando Tamargo and Rafael Tortoló (altos), Nicolás Reinoso and Sinesio Rodríguez (tenors), and Carlos Averhoff (baritone); piano: Freddy González; bass: Fabián G. Caturla; drums: Amadito Valdés Jr.; Cuban percussion: Bernardo García. The arrangements were by Juan Pablo Torres, Horacio González, and the renowned Pucho Escalante and Pedro Jústiz, the great "Peruchín." Some of these musicians would soon go on to OCMM (Sandoval, Lara, Juan Pablo Torres), and then Adalberto Lara, Sandoval, Bernardo García, and Carlos Averhoff would form part of Irakere, while others (Juan Pablo, Reinoso, Freddy González) organized their own groups.

The then Consejo Nacional de Cultura decided in 1967 to found a jazz-type ensemble that was called the Orquesta Cubana de Música Moderna.[8] The idea was applied to the country's other provinces (six at that time), and the same type of jazz bands were created in Pinar del Río, Matanzas, Santa Clara, Camagüey, and two in the biggest eastern cities, Santiago de Cuba and Holguín, which produced excellent musicians. The great trumpet player Luis Escalante and Armando Romeu, the same two who had formed the Bellamar orchestra almost thirty years earlier, now organized the OCMM, which turned out to be an "all-star" caliber band, like the Bellamar. The OCMM played not only jazz but also "Latin jazz," jazz-rock, and sometimes a certain symphonic (or rhapsodic) jazz along the lines of Stan Kenton's progressive jazz or Gunther Schuller's Third Stream in the 1960s. Veteran Armando Romeu was selected as the orchestra leader, and he also contributed with several compositions and arrangements. Armando himself has stated that this orchestra was "the best of this type that Cuba has ever had."[9] Later on we will return to this opinion—which I don't agree with.

Jazz veterans and musicians of the new generation were combined to form the personnel of this band: trumpets: Leonardo Timor, Luis Escalante, Andrés Castro, Jorge Varona, Manuel Mirabal, Adalberto Lara ("Trompetica"), and then Arturo Sandoval; trombones: Antonio Linares, Pucho Escalante, Modesto Echarte, Luis "El Pibe" González, and Juan Pablo Torres; saxophones: Paquito D'Rivera and Rolando Sánchez (altos), Braulio "Babín" Hernández and Jesús Lam (tenors), and Julián Fellové (baritone); piano and Hammond organ: Chucho Valdés; guitars: Carlos Emilio Morales and Sergio Vitier (who was replaced by José Jaurrieta); bass: Orlando "Cachaíto" López and Carlos del Puerto; drums: Guillermo Barreto and Enrique Plá; Cuban percussion: Oscar Valdés, Roberto García, and Oscarito Valdés. Most of the musicians came from Leonardo Timor's orchestra (including its leader), from the orchestra of the Teatro Musical de La Habana, from the Orquesta Juvenil (which preceded the OCMM), from Pucho Escalante's Noneto, and from the Orquesta Sinfónica Nacional (Luis Escalante, Antonio Linares, Cachaíto López). With this movement of personnel, the Teatro Musical orchestra was left considerably weakened, while Timor's band, the Juvenil, and Pucho's Noneto disappeared. Centralization was becoming the norm once again.

The trumpet section is without a doubt the most perfected that a Cuban jazz band has ever had. Although practically everyone could play first trumpet, the indisputable lead was Leonardo Timor, who also shared the jazz solos with Jorge Varona, Luis Escalante, and then with Arturo Sandoval, who joined the group, replacing his maestro, Escalante. Andrés Castro was the most experienced, going back to the years of the Castro Brothers orchestra that his brother Manolo had led since 1928. "Guajiro" Mirabal, "Trompetica" Lara, and later Arturo Sandoval were in charge of the very high notes. The trombone section was just as impressive, with men of extensive jazz band experience, except for the "young lion" Juan Pablo Torres, who shared the jazz solos with veteran Pucho Escalante. Never before had a Cuban jazz band included two trombone soloists of this caliber, and the presence of Torres reflected the growing popularity of the trombone in Cuban music. Since that time more top trombonists have appeared in Cuba than there were in the previous thirty years.

As for the lineup of saxophones, on lead sax was the onetime "child prodigy" Paquito D'Rivera, who at eleven years of age had played Mozart's clarinet concerto with Cuba's main symphonic ensemble, and who would make a grand entrance into American jazz, nothing less than lead alto in Dizzy Gillespie's band. Of the OCMM's two soloists on tenor sax, the most accomplished was Babín Hernández, perhaps the country's last "cool" tenor player. The role of baritone was assumed by Julián Fellové, a veteran who had excelled as a tenor player; like Chombo Silva, he had played in France with the best jazz musicians, and was returning to Cuba after many years of living in Paris. (A brother, trombonist Guillermo Fellové, had settled in Stockholm, as did Bebo Valdés). In Rolando Sánchez, Armando Romeu had a veteran (from another musical family) who started out in the Martínez Brothers jazz band and had played with innumerable jazz ensembles. He had also played in the Symphonic Orchestra, as did the tenor player Jesús "El Chino" Lam. But the one who stole the show was Paquito, who taught himself to play the flute and the flugelhorn.

In addition to Paquito, this band revealed the existence of other "child prodigies" or "young lions" (as the U.S. jazz critics put it) such as Chucho Valdés, Juan Pablo Torres, Arturo Sandoval, bassist Carlos del Puerto, and drummer Enrique Plá. The orchestra had the luxury, as well, of adding to the guitar of Carlos E. Morales a second guitar (Sergio Vitier and then Pepe Jaurrieta). The same happened with the bass—when Carlos del Puerto joined—and with drums. (Fabián G. Caturla was also for a while on contrabass). On various occasions veteran drummer Guillermo Barreto and the youthful Enrique Plá, who caused a sensation with his Tony Williams kind of style, put on sensational "mano a mano" duels, something that we hadn't seen since the "duel" between Daniel Pérez and Walfredo de los Reyes in the days of the Club Cubano de Jazz. On Cuban percussion, Oscar's son was added to the team that had already proven itself in the orchestras of Julio Gutiérrez and Leonardo Timor, that is, Oscar Valdés on conga and Roberto García on bongo. His son was brought in to play a second conga and other instruments. (I'll call him Oscar II, since today he himself has a son, Oscar III, who is an excellent drummer).

The orchestra made its first appearance on April 12, 1967, at the Amadeo Roldán Theater, the primary venue of its performances in the beginning. Among the tunes they played were "Room 43," "The Man I Love" (with a great solo by Luis Escalante), "One Mint Julep," and "La Guantanamera," an arrangement by Rafael Somavilla. Other concerts included an Armando Romeu adaptation of Leonard Bernstein's *West Side Story,* with solos by trombonist Juan Pablo Torres and altoist Paquito D'Rivera, as well as the drum duel between Barreto and Enrique Plá. In subsequent concerts the orchestra performed new arrangements by Armando Romeu of "Dinah" and the classic Cuban danzón "Almendra." But the band's biggest hit was "Pastilla de Menta," Armando's arrangement on "One Mint Julep," from organist Jimmy Smith's songbook, a jazz-rock piece in which Chucho Valdés was featured on electric organ. Despite the talent of its author (Jimmy Smith) "One Mint Julep" is quite a simplistic and commercial number, and its repetition in every OCMM presentation was a negative sign.

Only a few months after its creation, the OCMM performed at the Cuban Pavilion of Expo-67 held in Canada. The state record company EGREM (Empresa de Grabaciones y Ediciones Musicales) preserved the inaugural concert by recording it, and later recorded the orchestra again in 1971. Meanwhile, Armando Romeu had been replaced by Rafael Somavilla, who would go on to become musical director of the new Ministerio de Cultura in 1977. Somavilla wrote a number of ambitious rhapsodic pieces for the orchestra, such as *Suite en Jazz,* influenced in part by Armando's works, although also by Miles Davis, Gil Evans, and Leo Brouwer. When Somavilla left the orchestra, Paquito D'Rivera, who had studied orchestration with Armando Romeu and became an excellent arranger, was named director. And precisely the best moments of the OCMM were under the direction of Armando and then Paquito, who adopted numbers by Thelonious Monk and of other jazz greats. When Paquito was replaced by Tony Taño—for no apparent reason—and then Tony was replaced by Germán Piferrer, the orchestra entered into a period of unmistakable decline, and a number of its pillars left the band, some to form the group Irakere in 1973. The orchestra survived, dedicating most of its time to working at the EGREM studios, accompanying different commercial singers and taking an occasional trip abroad as Cuban "cultural ambassadors."

Within the same orchestra, jazz groups were formed that were quite possibly of greater consequence than the band itself, for since 1970 they traveled to various countries and contributed significantly to breaking the isolation in which Cuban jazz found itself. In 1970 a Cuban group played for the first time in an international jazz festival, the Jazz Jamboree of Poland. The group featured Chucho Valdés (piano), Paquito D'Rivera (alto sax), Cachaíto López (contrabass), Enrique Plá (drums), and Oscarito Valdés (conga). Attending this festival were prominent jazzmen such as Gerry Mulligan and Dave Brubeck, who were impressed with the Cubans' performance, and influenced *Playboy* magazine to select Chucho shortly thereafter as one of the top jazz pianists in the world, alongside such renowned musicians as Oscar Peterson, Bill Evans, McCoy Tyner, and Herbie Hancock. On various occasions and with different formats a group of OCMM members traveled abroad, under the unimaginative name Cuarteto (or Quinteto) Cubano de Música Moderna. Aside from those mentioned above, taking part in these conjuntos were guitarist Carlos E. Morales, bassist Carlos del Puerto, and later trumpet player Arturo Sandoval, who would reach stardom in the following decade.

Assessment of a Period

The importance that the OCMM had in this period of Cuban jazz history cannot be denied, an importance that is magnified if we take into account that just a year after their appearance (1967), the world of show business and music in Cuba entered into a period of crisis, and this orchestra was the only jazz ensemble that stayed active. We believe, however, that nothing is gained by overestimating it without considering its less positive aspects. It was an ensemble created by the decree of a state institution, and in spite of the (in all likelihood) good intentions of its organizers and the fact that it filled a vacuum in its time, it was faced with the problems that normally afflict any artistic ensemble created somewhat artificially and that finds itself sooner or later wrapped up in bureaucratic issues that represent the polar opposite of what the artistic spirit embodies and even more so of a music such as jazz. For example, the orchestra's leadership changes responded to administrative—and therefore nonmusical—decisions that often gave a footing to intrigues and personal interests. Similarly, the OCMM had to answer to the interests of the latest cultural directors, who gradually were relegating it to the role of an accompanying orchestra for the latest Cuban "pop" singers. These singers were making recordings that generally, despite the fact that they were motivated by plain commercialism, didn't even sell. It was proven once again that excessive "administration" and "planning" in the artistic realm are, in socialism, a calamity similar to commercialism and the emphasis on business in capitalism.

For this and other reasons I don't agree with maestro Romeu's opinion that this was the best Cuban jazz band of all time. It's logical that as a result of selecting from among the country's best musicians a "super-band" would be created (which still, of course, left out many top musicians); it was an orchestra that was conceived so as to eliminate any possible competition, but it has been proven that in this area as well, competition is a plus. I prefer the band that Armando Romeu led at the Tropicana in the 1950s, which was more up-to-date for its time and had more spontaneity and a real desire to play with swing and with expression, particularly in the soloist improvisers, while in the OCMM the desire to "shine," which has hurt so many jazz musicians in recent decades, even in the United States, had taken over. On the other hand, what happens with any "all star" baseball or soccer team whose players lack the cohesiveness that can only be obtained through daily competition, affected the band, in this case the daily contact with the fans (cabaret, theater, dances) and the exposure to other ensembles.

Aside from the fact that comparisons among musicians or artists in general from different periods or historical times are not very convincing, one important event/occurrence to take into account is the already mentioned one on the date on which the OCMM was founded (1967) and its proximity to 1968, the most disastrous year for Cuban popular music and in general for the normal flow of the country's social life, because of administrative measures (a mislabeled "revolutionary offensive") whose negative consequences we are suffering thirty years later, despite all of the real or imagined "rectifications." As part of the measures adopted on a national level in March 1968 there was the so-called Dry Law, never written down, but enforced by opportunist officials who managed to close all of the cabarets (already nationalized by the state), including the Tropicana, the Parisién, and those of any hotel except for one that was reserved for visiting foreign delegations. Closed as well—all of this in one year—were the bars, small clubs, and thousands of bodegas and stands or private "holes-in-the-wall." Nightlife and along with it music and show business were left high and dry. Cabaret models and chorus girls were affected the most, as they were sent to work as employees/assistants in the pizzerias; many left the country; some married foreigners, and others went on to a sometimes successful career as vedettes in western European countries, ranging from France to Sweden.

The musicians had relatively better "luck": some ensembles traveled throughout the country to play in sugar-cane or military camps, others lived off of unemployment subsidies (this was the case with Paquito D'Rivera when he was replaced as director of the OCMM). All of the country's musical activity remained under the control of a bureaucratic monster called the Centro Nacional de Contrataciones Artísticas. At one point 40 percent of the country's musicians were at home on unemployment, to the detriment of music and the national economy. The new bureaucracy didn't know what to do with these thousands of musicians or with the hundreds of locales closed to the public, some of which never opened again. And the popular dances disappeared from Cuban social and musical life, for the first time in history, for almost twenty years, until the end of the 1980s. On December 23, 1968, some centers of nightlife began to function again, only three days a week (Friday to Sunday) and then little by little things started returning to normal, although the damage was irreparable and Havana, famous for its nightlife, its music and musical revues, its shows, and its marathon popular dances, would never be the same again.

Oddly, in this year of silence (1968), after ten years without playing in a nightclub, except for descargas, and turning almost entirely to journalism and organizing jazz events, the circumstances forced me to work for a few months in the only spot that remained open and functioning in Havana, although only for foreign delegations: the one in the Deauville hotel (on Galiano between Malecón and San Lázaro). Two groups worked there, but as luck would have it one of them was basically a jazz group, called Ritmática -7. It was a septet that we had formed: Juanito Costa (piano and musical director), Leonardo Acosta (alto sax and flugelhorn), Nicolás Reinoso (tenor sax and flute), Freddy Muguercia (guitar), Luis Quiñones (electric bass), "Changuito" Quintana (drums and pailas), and Norberto Carrillo (conga). Of course, Ritmática -7 also played Cuban,

Brazilian, and all types of music, but it was known for its jazz soloists. When nightclubs were reopened in December of '68, we moved to the Flamingo hotel (Twenty-seventh and O), with Gilberto Valdés as the drummer. The Flamingo automatically became for a period of months the new jazz center in Havana, where musicians from other ensembles would show up to jam, such as the trumpet player Arturo Sandoval, saxophonist Paquito D'Rivera, vibraphonist and pianist Rembert Egües, drummers Enrique Plá and Amadito Valdés, drummer and percussionist Changuito, and guitarists Sergio Vitier and Pablo Menéndez.

Less fortunate was an excellent group that had been formed in 1966–67, the Sonorama 6, which was led by guitarist and feeling composer Martín Rojas. Initially it consisted of Martín Rojas (guitar and leader), Eduardo Ramos (second guitar), Rembert Egües (piano), Carlos del Puerto (bass), Enrique Plá (drums), and Changuito Quintana (conga), and worked in the La Torre restaurant on the twenty-eighth floor in the Focsa building (Seventeenth and M). When Carlos del Puerto and Enrique Plá left the group to join the OCMM, Sonorama changed its format and became a quintet; Changuito switched to drums, Eduardo Ramos to bass, and tenor saxophonist Carlos Averhoff joined the group. This ensemble took part in one of the biggest jam sessions held in Havana in the second half of the 1960s, organized as a tribute to French caricaturist Siné, who also contributed as a jazz critic in *Jazz Magazine* and wrote at that time an extensive article on jazz in Cuba.[10] Also playing in this "super jam session" held in 1967 in the gardens of the 1830 restaurant was a quartet from the OCMM that featured Paquito D'Rivera (alto sax), Chucho Valdés (piano), Cachaíto López (contrabass), and Enrique Plá (drums), and a group that I organized, given the name Grupo Este by Bobby Carcassés.

We had formed this group for purely experimental reasons and it was the first in Cuba to play free jazz. Coincidentally, we had recorded a tape at the studios of the EGREM a few days before, for noncommercial purposes. On the night of the super jam session in the garden of the 1830 restaurant the group consisted of Leonardo Acosta (alto sax), Raúl Ondina (piano), Carlos del Puerto (bass), Bobby Carcassés (vocals and bass), and Changuito (drums). On this occasion Enrique Plá joined us and Changuito switched to Cuban percussion. On other occasions the tenor player Nicolás Reinoso had also played with the group. When he wrote his chronicle on Cuba for

Jazz Magazine, Siné generously compared us to Ornette Coleman, Archie Shepp, Marion Brown, and John Tchicai, which was quite far from reality, or at least from what we were trying to do. On the other hand, free jazz would not be heard in Cuba again until the 1970s, with the group Arte Vivo, except for the experimental trio consisting of Emiliano Salvador (piano and drums), Paquito D'Rivera (alto sax), and Carlos del Puerto (bass).

Around 1969 there was a rare correspondence of interests between the jazz musicians and the music board of the Consejo Nacional de Cultura, with the creation of a "jazz commission" to organize concerts at different locales. This step reflects the crisis that ran through musical life after 1968; this commission was organized to carry out what in the early years of the decade emerged spontaneously. Among others, Armando Romeu, Paquito D'Rivera, Rafael Somavilla, Horacio Hernández, and I were on this commission. The first concert took place at the Sinagoga at Seventeenth and E, Vedado (today Casa de la Música A. G. Caturla) and had as its main man Bobby Carcassés, who was organizing the first of many groups that would produce young musicians. This time the guitarist Pedro Jústiz (Peruchín II) stood out. Other recitals had as their stage the Casa de la Cultura in the Plaza municipality (old Lyceum & Lawn Tennis Club), at Calzada and Eighth, Vedado. The combination of this place with the initiative and work of Bobby Carcassés would lead to the organization of the Jazz Plaza festivals years later. Also, photographic expositions on jazz and a series of lectures on the history of jazz by Horacio Hernández illustrated with recorded music would be held at the old Lyceum.

Around that time and in that context I organized a recital at the Casa de la Cultura and, in conjunction with Paquito, a series of three concerts at the Amadeo Roldán Theater. For the recital I formed two groups, with two different rhythm sections; originally the group was built around trumpet and alto sax, and we rehearsed with Arturo Sandoval on trumpet, but a few days later he was called up by the military draft (Servicio Militar Obligatorio), and the tenor saxophonist Carlos Averhoff, who was returning from three years of military service, had to sight read the trumpet part. The musicians in this recital were therefore: L. Acosta (alto sax), Carlos Averhoff (tenor sax), Raúl Ondina and Emiliano Salvador (pianists), Cachaíto López and Eduardo Ramos (contrabassists), Leo Pimentel and Marcos Larrinaga (drummers), and Pedrito "Guapachá" Borcelá (conga). We played tunes by

Dizzy Gillespie, Chano Pozo, Charlie Parker, Miles Davis, and Jackie McLean as well as by some of the participants.

But the biggest jazz encounter of that period would take place a bit earlier, February 6–8, 1969, at the Amadeo Roldán Theater. Three groups participated: a quartet featuring Paquito D'Rivera (alto sax), Chucho Valdés (piano), Fabián G. Caturla (contrabass), and Enrique Plá (drums); a quintet with L. Acosta (alto sax and flugelhorn), Raúl Ondina (piano), Eduardo Ramos (contrabass), Amadito Valdés (drums), and Changuito (congas); and a duo of Frank Emilio (piano) with Cachaíto (contrabass). Changuito brought the crowd to their feet with his solo in "Tin Tin Deo." Frank and Cachaíto added a number, "All the Things You Are," backed up by Enrique Plá on drums and Paquito and me on saxes. The same program was presented each of the three nights and it concluded with a number that I called "Maceración," on which the quartet, the quintet, and three contrabasses, a little bit like Ornette Coleman's "Double Quartet," played together.

Soundtrack Experimentation in Cuban Cinema

If in previous years the ICAIC had been the informal stage for jam sessions and encounters between musicians and filmmakers, in 1969 the organization's own management decided to form a group with unusual characteristics, which was called the Grupo de Experimentación Sonora (GES) of the ICAIC. It worked both in cinema and outside of it, with interruptions and personnel changes, until around 1978. The group proposed an innovation and renewal of Cuban popular music, starting with our roots and incorporating all the elements that could enrich it: the Cuban *nueva trova* (related to the American protest song and the Spanish and South American *nueva canción* as well as to the Brazilian *tropicalismo* movement), plus jazz, rock, electro-acoustic music, baroque music, or Hindu ragas. It also strove for the highest levels of artistic, technical, and technological expression. In particular, the GES created and performed music for newsreels, documentaries, and full-length feature films, made a number of LPs, and gave concerts and recitals. But its main objective was to take Cuban music to the level reached by the Beatles and the vanguard of rock, which included Frank Zappa, on the one hand, and Chico Buarque de Hollanda, Gilberto Gil, Caetano Veloso, and the "tropicalist" Brazilian movement, on the other.

Heading the Grupo de Experimentación Sonora was the classic guitarist and composer Leo Brouwer, who, in addition to his experience as a concert guitarist, his studies at Juilliard, and his still limited but excellent symphonic and chamber works, had gained familiarity with popular music during his years with the Teatro Musical de La Habana, and also during these years had successfully experimented in music for the cinema. An only half-articulated goal, but one that was perhaps essential in this project, was to redefine the new Cuban canción (later inserted in the *nueva trova* movement) within a wider context. For this reason the ICAIC included in the GES four of the trovadores from this movement that had emerged around 1967 and who up to this point had been supported by another cultural institution, the Casa de las Américas. Since its inception the nueva trova showed points of contact with the protest song in the United States and with nueva canción, but in Cuba this movement had difficulties and was practically banned by the Instituto Cubano de Radio y Televisión (ICRT) with the consensus of the Consejo Nacional de Cultura. As a result, the "new trovadores" took refuge in the Casa de las Americas and later in the ICAIC.

The Casa de las Americas had organized concerts, "protest and political song" festivals, and a television program, the only musical space in this medium that the leadership of the ICRT couldn't control. The immediate solution to this confrontation between different cultural entities was the assimilation of at least the most representative of this movement by an institution with sufficient resources such as the ICAIC. The trovadores who went to the GES were Pablo Milanés, Silvio Rodríguez, Noel Nicola, and Eduardo Ramos. Eduardo as well as Pablo came from 'feeling' and were connected to jazz: Pablo had worked with the Cuarteto del Rey and Los Bucaneros, and Eduardo Ramos with Martín Rojas's Sonorama 6 group, also from the latest wave of feeling. All of them played guitar, but Ramos was also a contrabassist and he established himself as such in the GES. Sergio Vitier, then in the Orquesta Cubana de Música Moderna, had a solid classical education on guitar, and Brouwer put him in charge of finding the rest of the new group's instrumentalists. It was via this route that the GES included jazz musicians.

Initially the instrumental group featured: Leonardo Acosta (saxophone, flugelhorn, and recorder), Sergio Vitier (guitar), Emiliano Salvador (piano), Eduardo Ramos (bass), Leoginaldo Pimentel (drums), and a little bit later

Genaro García Caturla (flute). But many other musicians collaborated in the first period of experimentation and recordings for cinema. Among them were the composer and keyboard player Armando Guerra, the pianists Raúl Ondina, Remberto Egües, Jorge Aragón, and Alfredo Pérez Pérez, the oboists Amado del Rosario and Ana Vesa, the clarinetist Lucas de la Guardia (founder of the Armónicos de Dulzaides and Los Bucaneros), as well as numerous members of the National Symphonic Orchestra, the OCMM, and students from the ENA (Escuela Nacional de Arte). I remember in particular trumpet players Jorge Varona, Sergio Pichardo, and Lázaro Cruz, trombonist Antonio Linares, flutist José Luis Cortés ("El Tosco"), and even the violinist and principal creator of chachachá, Enrique Jorrín. Collaborating from among the singers were Bobby Carcassés and the vocal quartet Los Nova, two of whose members were Pedro Luis Ferrer, later leader of his own groups, and Carlos Alfonso, who subsequently formed the vocal quartet Tema IV and then the vocal-instrumental fusion group Síntesis.

In the GES's first year it dedicated itself to the studio, rehearsals, experimentation, and recording music for cinema. A system of studies was worked out that consisted of listening to and analyzing all kinds of music, from Bach to John Coltrane, from Xenakis or Webern to the Beatles, from Gilberto Gil to the Mothers of Invention. The courses were designed and directed by Leo Brouwer, who relied on the important collaboration of Federico (Fred) Smith (who also worked with the Teatro Musical) to teach classes on harmony, instrumentation, orchestration, counterpoint, fugue, composition, and musical forms. Also participating as instructors were Juan Elósegui, first viola for the Symphonic Orchestra, as well as Jerónimo Labrada and other sound engineers from the ICAIC who taught acoustic, electro-acoustic, and recording technique classes. Film directors had to overcome certain prejudices concerning the GES, but slowly, after getting over them, they started soliciting the services of the group, which could become a jazz ensemble or play either Cuban music, rock, or samba; it could even extend to cover jazz band, charanga, or chamber orchestra formats, and also provide tunes that were often created as musical theme songs for different movies.

During the first years the GES lived a strange and absurd situation of isolation, because radio and TV, as well as EGREM, maintained an undeclared boycott against the group. It could only be heard on the sound track of Cuban movies or in sporadic performances in theater halls of the ICAIC, particularly at the place that is today the Chaplin movie theater (previously Atlantic) and next door at the 23 y 12 movie theater. Sometimes classical guitar recitals organized by Leo Brouwer and Sergio Vitier were held; more often performances by trovadores, whether it was Silvio Rodríguez, Noel Nicola, Pablo Milanés, or several of them, with or without the entire group; sometimes we formed a jazz quartet with L. Acosta (alto sax), Emiliano Salvador (piano), Eduardo Ramos (bass), and Leo Pimentel (drums), and on one occasion we alternated with the OCMM quintet (Paquito, Chucho, Carlos Emilio, Carlos del Puerto, and Enrique Plá). Later on trovadora Sara González and guitarist Pablo Menéndez, son of the American blues and folk singer Barbara Dane, joined the GES. Then there were various changes in personnel and even in the format. When I decided to leave the group, I was replaced by the saxophonist Carlos Averhoff, who in turn went on to the Moderna, making room for Manuel Valera.

The GES was able to make a few records at EGREM, although Casa de las Américas, which once again came out in defense of particularly the trovadores, produced them. But despite at least partially breaking the "blockade" by the national mass media, the GES faced internal problems, in part economic (lack of sophisticated equipment, low salaries), aggravated by a certain incompatibility with one part of the ICAIC and differences of an aesthetic kind among the members. But the most severe blow to the GES was the absence of its own director, who in this period began in a big way his career as a guitarist, symphonic composer, and director in various western European countries, mainly Italy and Great Britain, with the help of German composer Hans Werner Henze. After a brief lapse in which Armando Guerra, a student of Manuel Duchesne Cuzán's, led the group, there was an impasse of almost two years, until a number of its members got together under the direction of Eduardo Ramos. The following then remained: Pablo Milanés and Sara González as singers, with Emiliano Salvador (piano), Manuel Valera (alto sax and flute), Pablo Menéndez (guitar), Eduardo Ramos (bass), Ignacio Berroa (drums), and the percussionists Norberto Carrillo and Danielito. Included in the repertoire were numbers by ex-member composers of the group, such as Sergio Vitier and Silvio Rodríguez, although most of the numbers and arrangements were by Emiliano Salvador, Eduardo Ramos, and Pablo Milanés. Their performances at the 23 y 12 and the Amadeo Roldán Theater turned out to be a brilliant mixture of nueva trova, Afro-Cuban and Brazilian rhythms, jazz, and rock. Around 1978 it was finally dissolved and some of its members went on to the group that Pablo Milanés formed.

The work of the Grupo de Experimentation Sonora was important in Cuban cinema and for the development of the nueva trova composers, but it also contributed to the education of several young jazz musicians (members of the GES and participants) and had an influence on different ensembles that were put together shortly thereafter based on rock, Afro-Cuban music, nueva trova, or Latin jazz, aside from being a stimulus for the experimentation that has been the core of several Cuban groups in the last few decades. Of course, the GES was never a jazz group strictly speaking, but rather a fusion group (as Irakere, Mezcla, or Síntesis would be). It often experimented with jazz, as well as with works such as *Homenaje a Charlie Mingus* by Leo Brouwer, a condensation of the original score for symphonic orchestra and jazz quintet that was filmed by a French television team (Brouwer's original version had its premiere at the Amadeo Roldán, performed by the National Symphonic Orchestra with soloists from the OCMM).[11] Emiliano Salvador, after a few years as pianist and arranger for Pablo Milanés's group, formed his own Afro-Latin jazz ensembles and became one of the most respected Cuban jazz pianists nationally and internationally, until his unexpected early death in 1992. Sergio Vitier again formed the group ORU (appearing briefly in 1968), centered primarily on Afro-Cuban roots, while Pablo Menéndez organized a fusion group appropriately called Mezcla (Mixture).

We have considered the GES within the period that we've classified as one of "musical transition" in Cuba in the 1960s, although it's obvious that the dates never tend to coincide with mathematical precision. Despite the fact that the GES doesn't break up until well into the 1970s, and that it began in 1969, in essence it belongs to the same period of "grandeur and decline" as the Orquesta Cubana de Música Moderna. In place of both ensembles a third will appear, with a format somewhat intermediate between the GES and the OCMM. We are referring to Irakere, which will represent the take-off of a Cuban jazz that is strongly rooted in all that came before it, but one that has individual characteristics and that will enjoy an international success unprecedented for a Cuban band of "Latin jazz."

9
Irakere and the Takeoff of Cuban Jazz

$\mathcal{W}$ith Irakere, a new era in Cuban jazz begins in 1973, one that will extend all the way to the present. At the same time, this period represents the culmination of a series of individual and collective efforts from our so-called transitional period, which will end with the Orquesta Cubana de Música Moderna and the ICAIC's Grupo de Experimentación Sonora in its early stages. Irakere was, in part, a product of the Moderna, as its founding members completed their musical training in that orchestra and also played jazz in the different quartets and quintets that were created within the OCMM. Among the founders of Irakere were pianist Chucho Valdés, its director since the beginning; saxophonist Paquito D'Rivera, who acted as assistant director; trumpet player Jorge Varona; guitarist Carlos Emilio Morales; bassist Carlos del Puerto; drummer Bernardo García; and percussionist Oscar Valdés II, also a singer. With the exception of Bernardo García, all had been pillars in the OCMM.

From the beginning, Chucho Valdés had three other musicians lined up to form Irakere: tenor saxophonist Carlos Averhoff, trumpeter Arturo Sandoval, and drummer Enrique Plá, who in those days were either completing military service or in the OCMM, which had become an EGREM studio orchestra by then. From the very start Chucho had to deal with bureaucratic obstacles that delayed the formation of Irakere. Many of these obstacles came from the CNC's musical committee, but the one who really made it difficult was Germán Piferrer, then director of the OCMM, who wasn't about to lose the key members of a jazz band that could no longer meet the aspirations of the most talented musicians, as it could in the days when Armando Romeu, Rafael Somavilla, or Paquito D'Rivera led the band. The orchestra languished, spending most of its time in the studio accompanying mostly mediocre singers.

So, for bureaucratic reasons, Carlos Averhoff, Enrique Plá, and Arturo Sandoval did not receive immediate transfers after being released from military service, but they were finally able to join Irakere. In the percussion section, Oscarito Valdés and Enrique Plá were joined by percussionists such as Armando Cuervo, Carlos Barbón, and then Jorge "El Niño" Alfonso, who died tragically in 1987. For a number of years the horns consisted of two saxes and two trumpets; then they increased to three plus three, thereby converting the group into an orchestra of twelve musicians. According to current standards, a group of nine musicians or more becomes an orchestra, just as in the 1920s and early 1930s. In addition to the OCMM, we've referred to other forerunners of Irakere, such as the Grupo de Experimentación Sonora del ICAIC, which assimilated elements from diverse musical traditions: Cuban popular music, jazz, rock, samba, baroque music, and so forth. Saxophonist Carlos Averhoff worked with the GES, and Paquito D'Rivera and Jorge Varona played with the band off and on. For its distinctly experimental character, this group is a forerunner to Irakere, just as Juan Formell's orchestra Van Van is for its innovations in dance music.

For precedents to Irakere's use of the batá drums of Yoruba origin, which until then had rarely been incorporated in professional popular music—with the exception of the Tropicana shows and by the forerunner Gilberto Valdés in 1936—we should keep in mind another innovative group: Grupo ORU, organized by Sergio Vitier in 1968, a year before he joined the GES. As far back as the first ORU recitals, the batá drums and songs in the Yoruba language were fused with elements of classical and contemporary music, from old Spanish romances to jazz, samba, and aleatoric music. With new personnel, ORU appeared at recitals in the 1970s and became a steadily working ensemble in the following decade. Rogelio Martínez Furé, well-known researcher of African and Afro-Cuban cultural heritage, and Merceditas Valdés, the country's all-time best singer of Afro-Cuban music in African languages (who died in 1996), have been among ORU's singers. A number of jazz musicians performed with ORU, among them Guillermo Barreto (drums and timbales), Cachaíto López (bass), Filiberto Alderete (soprano and alto saxes), Leonardo Acosta (alto sax, flugelhorn, recorder, and flutes), Domingo Aragú (piano), and Nicolás Reinoso (tenor sax and flute). The best percussionists in Cuba played with ORU, most of whom were students of the great *olú batá* Jesús Pérez, as well as Jesús himself, an already legendary tamborero.

In 1973 I wrote an article for the youth cultural tabloid *El Caimán Barbudo* on the new and sensational group that was just getting started, Irakere (perhaps the first article on Irakere in the world), and in it I pointed out the qualities that characterized this ensemble: their superb technique, the virtuosity of their soloists, the driving swing that they maintained in any rhythm and at any tempo, and the intelligent recovery of our cultural heritage combined with experimentation. Also significant is the excellent way they fuse Afro-Cuban elements with jazz. At the time this article appeared, Irakere was taking their first trip abroad. The following year they had received quite a bit of attention from the public, from musicians, and from the country's very limited number of critics, and in February 1974 they gave an important concert in the Amadeo Roldán, which was still the most important and renowned theater in Cuba until its almost total destruction in 1979 because of a fire, presumably caused by a criminal act of sabotage (rebuilt in 1999, today it has resumed its role).

Irakere's repertoire was always a controversial topic in the world of Cuban music, because this ensemble actually developed two repertoires: one uniquely jazz oriented, with very well written arrangements and space for soloists, and another one of mostly danceable and sometimes commercial music. For example, in their first concerts they included numbers such as "Juana 1600," "Takatakatá," "Chekeresón," and their first big record hit, "Bacalao con pan," tunes written for dancing. This repertoire contrasted with very advanced versions of Lecuona's "La comparsa" and "Danza de los ñáñigos," Manuel Saumell's "Los ojos de Pepa," and more elaborate and experimental works such as Chucho Valdés's "Valle de Picadura," Paquito D'Rivera's "Suite," or Chucho's "Misa negra." But they also had numbers such as "Yesterday" by Lennon and McCartney; the problem was that Irakere had to play danceable music and produce frequent hits if they wanted to remain at the top in popularity.

In 1977 Irakere gave a concert at the CTC Theater, which is a good illustration of this eclecticism. In it they presented popular hits—"Aguanile," "Bacalao con pan," and "Xiomara"— along with an arrangement of the tango "El día que me quieras" and their first experimentation with "jazzed up" classical music, Paquito D'Rivera's "Adagio," an arrangement based on a fragment of Mozart's music. It was precisely this eclecticism that attracted guitarist and composer Leo Brouwer to the group, to put on a concert together at the Karl Marx Theater that same year. That concert included a wide range of styles that covered the guitar theme song from the French film *Jeux Inderdit*, the Beatles' "The Fool on the Hill," a version of Scott Joplin ragtimes by Brouwer, an arrangement by Chucho Valdés of the classic danzón "Almendra," and a "Bembé" in jazz from Chucho. This mixture of popular languages together with symphonic music wasn't anything new for Brouwer, who in 1967 had given a concert in Bellas Artes with his own works, some by Heitor Villa-Lobos, by Tom Jobim, and by popular Cuban composers, which included the participation of the soprano Yolanda Brito, the flutist Mario Badía, and various jazz musicians: Jorge Varona (trumpet), Rafael Somavilla (piano), Cachaíto López (bass), and Guillermo Barreto (drums). Some years later he would debut his *Homenaje a Charlie Mingus* ("Tribute to Charlie Mingus," the symphonic version) with the National Symphonic Orchestra and five jazz soloists: Chucho Valdés, Paquito D'Rivera, Carlos Emilio Morales, Cachaíto López, and Guillermo Barreto.

A decisive year for Irakere was 1977, when they performed at the Belgrade Jazz Festival and the Warsaw Jazz Jamboree along with such important participants as singer Betty Carter and the band of Mel Lewis and Thad Jones. And traveling to Havana that same year was the jazz cruise, which featured Dizzy Gillespie, Stan Getz, Earl Hines, David Amram, and Ray Mantilla, among others, on board the *Daphne*. It was an excursion that would culminate with a concert at the Mella Theater (Línea and A, Vedado). For the first time since the break in relations between Cuba and the United States we were welcoming a full delegation of American jazz musicians, some of exceptional historic significance. The legendary pianist Earl "Fatha" Hines arrived with a group that included sax and clarinet player Rudy Rutherford, bassist John Orr, drummer Eddie Graham, and singers Marva Josie and Ry Cooder. His best numbers with a Latin flavor were "Tangerine" and "Caravan." Stan Getz brought pianist Jo Anne Brackeen, drummer Billy Hart, and also enjoyed the participation of David Amram and Ray Mantilla. But it was Dave Amram and, of course, Dizzy Gillespie, who stole the show.

The group that Dizzy brought with him included guitarist Rodney Jones, bassist Ben Brown, drummer Mickey Roker, and timbales player Joe Ham, and backing them up were Ray Mantilla on conga and David Amram on any instrument. The spontaneous Amram, in addition to presenting his work "In Memoriam to Chano Pozo," as a tribute to the Cuban tamborero, played the piano, guitar, xylophone, French horn, percussion, and different types of flutes. The concert ended with Irakere playing together with Amram, Dizzy, Getz, and others, including the Cuban percussion group Los Papines. The piece that served as a base for this "jam session" was Chano and Dizzy's historic "Manteca," in a concert that was dedicated to Chano Pozo. We don't know what the historian and critic Leonard Feather wrote or what his impressions of the trip were, but the critic of *Down Beat,* Arnold Jay Smith, wrote an excellent review, and emphasized that music proved once again that it was indeed a common language: "There really is a brotherhood in music which, like love, needs no translation, merely improvisation."[1]

Perhaps more important than the concert itself was the get-together beforehand held in the morning hours in the Habana Libre's Caribe Room, where the members of Irakere were able to jam with Dizzy, Amram, Getz, and the rest of the visitors, all of whom expressed their surprise at the high quality of jazz in Cuba. Dizzy later told the press that he had fulfilled a long-standing wish to visit the island, homeland of his close friend and partner Chano Pozo. In the following years, Dizzy would return to Cuba three more times to take part in the Jazz Plaza festivals. As was to be expected, however, there were also negative aspects behind the scenes of this unexpected encounter between jazz musicians from the two countries.

Unfortunately, most Cuban jazz musicians were not invited either to the informal encounter at the Habana Libre or to the concert; and they didn't even sell tickets to the public at the Mella Theater, as the cultural bureau-cracy, still fearful at the time of anything that came from the United States, resorted to distributing all tickets on an invitation-only basis. The result was that the audience consisted primarily of sons and daughters of officials, while dozens of musicians and hundreds of jazz fans would hear that Dizzy was there, would show up at the theater, and would be turned away at the box office: it was "by invitation only." Horacio Hernández and I were invited only after Rafael Somavilla, at that time the new musical director of the recently created Ministry of Culture, realized that nobody else could prepare the intro-ductory notes for all the visiting musicians, but we weren't invited to the jam session at the hotel. Later on Leo Brouwer defended himself, declaring that "it all happened so fast," and to a certain extent he was right.

The arrival of this jazz cruise was so unexpected that it took everybody in Cuba by surprise, from the Ministry of Culture to the press and the musi-cians themselves. The result was that this jazz event, which culminated with a big concert at a centrally located theater in the capital city, was something like an "underground" event that was never reflected in our cultural press, whereas American jazz magazines gave extensive coverage to the entire voy-age as well as to the encounter with the Cuban musicians. Nevertheless, this visit was a positive one for local jazz, as American musicians and critics had a lot to do with inviting Irakere to the Newport Jazz Festival in 1978, where they were a big hit and received the kind of high praise that had never been given to a jazz group living on the island.

Newport, Montreux, and After . . .

Irakere's main performance at the '78 Newport Festival took place at renowned Carnegie Hall, where they were scheduled to appear alongside the best-known proponents of "acoustic jazz," a somewhat rash programming decision at a time when proponents of electric instrumentation sustained a heated debate with their detractors. On the program were three of the great jazz pianists of all time, all proponents of acoustic jazz: Mary Lou Williams, McCoy Tyner, and Bill Evans. Tyner even took it to the extreme of playing by himself and having the microphones taken away, as a clear gesture of protest against electronics in jazz. After all, hadn't Andrés Segovia, for exam-ple, played at Carnegie Hall without any amplification? On the same program Larry Coryell and Philip Catherine performed as a duo on acoustic guitar, and according to the press reports many fans left when Irakere's electronic equipment started to be set up along with the rest of their stuff. Others stuck around out of curiosity and were glad they did. A number of famous musicians, among them Stan Getz and trumpet player Maynard Ferguson, were present and played with the Cubans. Irakere received praise from both of them and from other musicians who were present such as Walter Bishop, David Amram, Billy Taylor, and also from the critics. After New York the Cubans worked at the Cellar Door in Washington, D.C. Then Columbia Records, the recording division of CBS, signed a recording contract with Irakere and organized a promotional tour throughout the country for June and July; sharing the concerts with Irakere was a performer who was popular at the time, Stephen Stills.

That same year Irakere appeared at another important jazz festival, Montreux (Switzerland), where both the public and the critics loved them. Columbia then edited an album with five of the group's pieces, taken from their appearances in Newport and Montreux: "Juana mil ciento" (Chucho Valdés), "Ilya" (Arturo Sandoval), "Adagio" (Paquito D'Rivera), "Aguanile" (Chucho), and the remarkable live-in-Montreux version of "Misa negra," also by Chucho, 17:36 minutes of Afro-Cuban polyrhythm, brilliant horn passages, and impressive solos, particularly the extended acoustic piano solo by Chucho. Rounding out the group at that time were Jorge Varona and Arturo Sandoval (trumpets), Paquito (alto sax) and Carlos Averhoff (tenor sax), Carlos Emilio Morales (guitar), Carlos del Puerto (electric bass), Enrique Plá (drums), and Oscar Valdés II, Armando Cuervo, and Jorge "El Niño" Alfonso (Cuban percussion).

This first LP titled simply *Irakere* was the result of an agreement between CBS and Cuba's EGREM, and it contains not one but two sets of liner notes with the comments of one American jazz critic and another from Cuba, a job that was entrusted to John Storm Roberts and me. In the text that I wrote back then, I attempted to answer certain questions and statements made by the critics of the *New York Times*, the *San Francisco Examiner*, and *Billboard* magazine. There I emphasized above all these two points: (1) that the fusion of jazz elements and Cuban music has a long history, which is precisely what I am trying to show at least in part in this book, and (2) that the Cuban element, as Irakere illustrates, is not just in the percussion but also in the phrasing, the attack, and the soloists' sense of rhythm, as well as in the ensemble passages. Nevertheless, I made an affirmation that wasn't altogether correct when I said that Irakere had been the first to incorporate elements of Yoruba and Abakuá music into the mainstream of our popular music, which before had drawn primarily from elements of Congo *(bantú)* and Dahomeyanos *(arará)* origin. I should have exercised more caution in expressing myself, since Abakuá and Yoruba music has been incorporated—although in a distilled manner—into various popular manifestations such as the rumba and the son.[2]

In 1979 Irakere received a Grammy award for best "Latin" music recording in the United States. After these great successes, they have participated in the most important jazz festivals in the world (particularly in Europe) and have traveled throughout Africa and Latin America. During this whole time Irakere has made a number of changes not only in personnel but also in format and even in the concept; the changes haven't always been for the better, which is normal. The first and most prominent change was the departure of Paquito D'Rivera; he was the group's assistant director and his liveliness seemed to be the perfect complement to Chucho Valdés's more meditative character. Shortly thereafter, Arturo Sandoval formed his own group, which rivaled Irakere in Cuba until the trumpet player, at a time when he was practically an "official performer" of the Cuban government's, also left, with the help of his *padrino* (godfather) Dizzy Gillespie and to the surprise of his "Socialist padrinos."

The following album of Irakere's, *Tierra en trance,* although without Paquito and Arturo, reflects perhaps a more complete vision and a more direct approach to the band's jazz dimension, with less involvement in the popular danceable types of music. Here the format consists of eleven musicians, with three trumpets and three saxes: Juan Munguía, Jorge Varona, and José Crego (trumpets); Germán Velazco (alto sax, soprano, and clarinet), José Luis Cortés (flute and baritone sax), and Carlos Averhoff (tenor sax and flute). The primary singer is once again Oscarito Valdés. The numbers are Chucho's, except for the tribute "A Chano Pozo" by bassist Carlos del Puerto, with excellent solos by Juan Munguía on flugelhorn, José Crego on trumpet, "El Tosco" José Luis Cortés on flute, and "El Niño" Alfonso on a conga solo.

The tunes on this LP are more strictly jazz than previous recordings, except for "Tierra en trance," a more ambitious piece, a la "Misa negra," only not so well structured. On the other hand, "Las margaritas" is a simple song in ¾ that serves as a showcase for a brilliant solo by Germán Velazco on soprano sax; "Paila" is a ballad previously recorded by Chucho on piano solo, while here the great guitarist Carlos Emilio Morales shines; "Estela va a estallar" is a title that parodies through a phonetic translation of "Stella by Starlight," uses the chords of the latter as a base, and turns out to be one long jam in which Germán Velazco, Chucho, Carlos Emilio, Carlos del Puerto, José Luis Cortés, and Oscar Valdés (on bongo) improvise. "Tierra en trance," more structurally complex, is a full mosaic of styles and moods, with solos by Carlos del Puerto, Germán Velazco, and the director and composer.

In early 1988 Irakere once again made changes in personnel and also in approach. This time Chucho Valdés was looking for more involvement and a more authentic integration with electronic media, including computers, somewhat like what Miles Davis did. Some of the musicians from Irakere's previous edition split off to form an ensemble that has found its way quite successfully, first in "Latin jazz" and then in danceable music or "Cuban *timba*." The name of the group is N. G. La Banda (N. G. for "New Generation"), led by José Luis Cortés ("El Tosco"). The new version of Irakere featured Juan Munguía (trumpet), Manuel Machado (trumpet and trombone), Carlos Alvarez (trombone), César López (alto sax), Javier Zalba (baritone and soprano sax, and flute), and Orlando Valle (flute, sax, and keyboards). Joining the percussion section were Oscarito Valdés III (drums and Cuban percussion) and Miguel Díaz ("Angá") on congas. Rhythmically, they began to speak of Irakere at that time as a standard-bearer for the so-called *songo* rhythm. According to the Dominican jazz pianist Michel Camilo, this rhythm surpasses what the *salseros* were doing, and their primary exponents are "Irakere, and in Puerto Rico a group called Batacumbele; in Santo Domingo, the group 440 and I."[3]

The Scene in the 1970s:
The Río Club and Other Developments

We began this chapter with Irakere because after their success in 1977 and 1978, they paved the way for national and international recognition for other groups and musicians, and since then about ten or more groups have recorded in Cuba for the first time. Generally speaking, the 1970s were not the best of times for jazz throughout the world, and Cuba was no exception. For the most part, in this decade the only groups doing innovative work in Cuban music were the Grupo de Experimentación Sonora, Irakere, and Juan Formell's Van Van, which brought back to the stage the unsinkable charanga and then successfully introduced new rhythmic, timbre, and orchestral elements (electric guitar and bass, trombones, two flutes, and so forth) into this basic format. Essentially, Formell saved our danceable music from the stagnation of that period and succeeded in winning over the public when salsa was thriving in New York and the Caribbean, where they had surpassed us in our own field of expertise. Irakere contributed in part to this renovation of danceable music, when they accepted the challenge to play the Tropicana's Salón Mambí, which was for some time the hot spot for Havana's dancers. As for jazz descargas, there only remained one place: the Río Club (before, Johnny's Dream) in the La Puntilla (Miramar) district by the Almendares River.

Despite the reopening of the big cabarets, none of the orchestras from these centers could fill the vacuum left by the Bellamar at the Sans Souci, Isidro Pérez at the Montmartre, Armando Romeu at the Tropicana, or Leonardo Timor Jr. at the Parisién. And worse yet, jazz not only disappeared from the big nightclubs but many small nightclubs that supported jazz combos in the 1960s began to use canned music. The most popular and stable combo, Felipe Dulzaides's, found a haven for eight years in Varadero. The only exception, thanks to its manager José Molina, a real jazz lover, was the Río Club, where various jazz groups survived for months and even years, and which also held "Jazz Mondays," which attracted three generations of jazz musicians and the same fans as always. A young audience joined in as well.

The main pillar at the Río Club besides Molina was tenor saxophonist Nicolás Reinoso, who led the groups of longer duration. Among the musicians that made up Nicolás's first quartets or quintets were Julito Ramírez (guitar), Luis Adolfo Peñalver (piano), Jorge "Yoyi" Soler (bass), Tony Valdés (drums), and percussionists Pedrito "Guapachá" Borcelá and Víctor Torriente. Later on Nicolás Reinoso organized the first edition of the AfroCuba group and then Sonido Contemporáneo, working with this last group at the same Río Club, with musicians such as guitarist Paul Menéndez (previously in the GES) and the versatile Lucía Huergo (sax and keyboards). Alternating with the Reinoso groups was usually the conjunto formed by guitarist Octavio Sánchez Cotán, an expert in Cuban rhythms with a modern harmonic conception and improviser of very original ideas, whose previous groups had included jazz musicians such as Emiliano Salvador and Juan Pablo Torres. His son Angel Octavio ("Cotancito"), who was one of our first jazz-rock guitarists, excelled with the group.

One of the most enthusiastic organizers of "Río Mondays" and its main promoter was Paquito D'Rivera, then with Irakere, whose members participated on a regular basis in the Monday jam sessions. No less enthusiastic was the singer and multi-instrumentalist Bobby Carcassés. Among the musicians who took part in the Río Club descargas were pianists Luis Adolfo Peñalver, Emiliano Salvador, Raúl Ondina, Chucho Valdés, Pepecito Herrera Jr., Ernán López-Nussa, and Alfredo Gómez; bass players "Yoyi" Soler, Carlos del Puerto, Luis Quiñones, Jorgito Reyes, Cachaíto López, Jorge Macías, and Ray Larrinaga; guitarists Carlos Emilio and Peruchín Jústiz II; drummers Tony Valdés, Enrique Plá, José Luis "Changuito" Quintana (who was also a percussionist), Marcos Larrinaga, and Cristóbal Quesada; percussionists Pedrito Guapachá and Víctor Torriente; flutist José Luis Cortés; saxophonists Paquito D'Rivera and Manuel Valera (altos), José Carlos Acosta (soprano), Fernandito Acosta (alto and soprano), Nicolás Reinoso, Lucía Huergo, and Carlos Averhoff (tenors), Mariano Tena (alto and soprano), Leonardo Acosta (alto, tenor, and flugelhorn), trumpet players Jorge Varona and Arturo Sandoval, and singer Bobby Carcassés, who also played flugelhorn, bass, and Cuban percussion.

Meanwhile, around 1976 there was a brief jazz interlude at the Nacional hotel's Parisién cabaret, with a group that included the two trumpet virtuosos from Irakere, Arturo Sandoval and Jorge Varona, tenor player Jesús "El Chino" Lam, and the singer Bobby Carcassés, among others. And upon his return from "exile" in Varadero, Felipe Dulzaides established himself once again at the Riviera Hotel (in the Elegante bar); his group in Varadero had included Manuel Valera (alto sax), Armandito Romeu (vibraphone), Ahmed Barroso (guitar), Luis Quiñones (bass), and Tony Valdés (drums), with Ignacio Berroa and later on Cristóbal Quesada succeeding Tony. When Felipe returned there were new changes and joining the group were bassist Carlos Quintero, guitarist Jorge Chicoy, and alto saxophonist Rolando Pérez Pérez. Another isolated event, from the early Seventies, was the visit to Cuba by the duo Hilario Sánchez and

Micky, from Mexico, who remained for a few months in Havana. Hilario Sánchez, pianist, trumpet player, composer, and arranger of Mexican jazz, and his wife, the famous French jazz singer Micky, who had been a part of the Swingle Singers, gave numerous concerts, with Orlando "Cachaíto" López on bass and Enrique Plá on drums.

Other than the Río Club, only one thing remained stable in Cuban jazz: the program "El jazz, su historia y sus intérpretes" ("Jazz, Its History, and Its Performers"), which radio station CMBF broadcast nightly, from 11 P.M. to 11:30 P.M., with script and direction by Horacio Hernández; in the late 1980s Horacio retired and Mario Barba (who died suddenly two years later) took his place. Today, José Dos Santos writes the scripts for the show. As for recordings, in the 1970s they were still scarce if we don't count Irakere's and some LPs by one or another of its members, such as Chucho Valdés with a trio or quartet, or Paquito D'Rivera with his own orchestrations, and those of Abelardo Busch; they were jazz records for sure, although with Cuban and bossa nova tunes, sometimes Busch originals. The importance of these records should not be underestimated, however, for they represented a first step toward the "discovery" of Cuban jazz potential, undiscovered for fifty years by the transnational and national record companies.

The year 1978 included another isolated event of relative importance and directly related to the 1977 "Cruise" headed by Dizzy and also to Irakere's success at Newport: we're referring to "Encuentro Cuba-USA" promoted by CBS (and Columbia Records) and held in Karl Marx Theater (previously Blanquita) on First and Tenth Streets in Miramar. This encounter included very diverse styles: jazz, rock, pop, country, jazz-rock, Afro-Latin jazz, rumba, son, salsa, and nueva trova. Among the exclusive artists from CBS who visited Havana were such dissimilar performers as Billy Joel, the Fania All Stars, Kris Kristofferson, Rita Coolidge, and the jazz-rock group Weather Report with its four indisputable luminaries: Wayne Shorter, Joe Zawinul, Jaco Pastorius, and Billy Cobham. Other great jazz stars such as tenor player Dexter Gordon, the trumpet player and arranger Woody Shaw, flutist Hubert Laws, and once again Stan Getz were part of the event. Among the many ensembles and Cuban soloists that participated in the encounter, Irakere was the only one playing jazz. Just as in 1977, the event was "by invitation only," and once again the press didn't cover it. Only Billy Cobham, as a CBS consultant, had the opportunity to play together with Cuban musicians in the EGREM studios. And some American musicians and Nuyoricans—from the Fania All Stars—were able to hear groups such as AfroCuba.

Still another event that has a bearing on 1978 is the celebration in Havana of the XI Festival Mundial de la Juventud y los Estudiantes (XI World Festival of Youth and Students), which brought in thousands of young people from all continents and different musical ensembles, among them various jazz groups or ones whose musicians played jazz. In the middle of this festival Paquito D'Rivera organized the biggest jam session ever held at the Río Club, with the participation of musicians from the United States, Puerto Rico, Cuba, the Soviet Union, Finland, and other countries. Once again the term "symbolic" comes to mind when I think of this occasion, which I witnessed at a table along with guitarist Carlos Emilio Morales, drummer Enrique Plá (both from Irakere), and Russian bassist Yuri Moiseev, who came as a conga player with a group from Leningrad led by violinist and trumpet player David Goloschekin. On the one hand, Paquito performed as master of ceremonies at an overflowing Río Club, reminiscent of the days of the Havana 1900 and the Club Cubano de Jazz, although he forgot to present the group from Leningrad, focusing on the presentation of two New Yorkers, bassist Andy González and alto saxophonist René McLean, son of Jackie McLean (whom I had heard at the Bohemia in New York with George Wallington's quartet exactly twenty years before). Apparently, Paquito could no longer hide his intentions of going to New York, the indisputable Mecca of jazz. But in addition, the end was near for the Río Club as the focal point for Cuban jazz musicians; shortly thereafter, without Molina as the manager, the club started leaning toward rock music with groups such as Los Magnéticos, and in the end it became a dark and impersonal "light dancing" spot, then a discotheque, and later on a mediocre nightclub.

It seemed a sad ending for a locale that had turned out to be almost perfect and which served as our own modest but friendly and democratic "Mecca" for almost ten years. The super-jam of 1978 proved once again that reaching a peak might also signal the beginning of a decline, as had occurred with the Club Cubano de Jazz. But from every decline—or in spite of it—something new and sometimes unexpected always emerges; at that time conditions for a more thorough takeoff of jazz on the island were developing and would crystallize in the formation of numerous groups and in the creation of jazz festivals, first national and then international.

AfroCuba: Divide and Lose

During the period under review, the *Nueva Trova* movement, organized as such in 1972 with the support of the UJC (Unión de Jóvenes Comunistas), reached its high point. The movement evolved through live performances across the country, in schools, military and sugar cane camps, factories, parks, and amphitheaters. Like Irakere, the movement achieved definitive official acceptance after its success abroad, centered on Pablo Milanés and Silvio Rodríguez. The groups linked to the nueva trova, committed initially to the political song and Latin American folklore (Moncada, Manguaré), later on would gradually incorporate elements of rock and popular Cuban music. In this they had been preceded by groups such as 5-U-4 of composer and blind singer Osvaldo Rodríguez, perhaps the first group to get involved in the fusion of Cuban popular music (bolero, son) with rock, if we exclude the Grupo de Experimentación Sonora and the OCMM. Today there are countless groups working within the nueva trova song style that include elements of rock and jazz-rock and feature some jazz soloists.

In this decade jazz musicians had to settle for the Río Club descargas, while they made a living in cabaret and studio orchestras or in groups that played danceable Cuban music. To find a jazz group that could compete with the concentration of "all stars" in Irakere, we have to look to the incredible sonic formation that made up the first edition of AfroCuba, organized in 1976–78 by saxophonist Nicolás Reinoso. At the time when Irakere was winning national and international acclaim, to put together an ensemble with similar characteristics (a fusion of jazz with Afro-Cuban music) was an almost "unpardonable" act of audacity, and there were serious obstacles in the way. Despite everything, Nicolás organized an impressive lineup of young and for the most part unknown musicians, who surprised American and Puerto Rican musicians and critics in 1978. In addition, they won first prize in the competition for popular music groups that was organized by the Unión de Escritores y Artistas de Cuba (UNEAC), in which the second and third prizes were awarded to Osvaldo Rodríguez's 5-U-4 and Pachito Alonso's conjunto (Pachito is the son of the singer Pacho Alonso).

AfroCuba achieved this recognition as a result of the intense work that various members did in composition and orchestration and long practice sessions. But from the start they were at a disadvantage, for reasons that have more to do with Cuban idiosyncrasy than musical factors.

AfroCuba had to fight against one of our deeply entrenched habits: In a basically noncompetitive society, we have and allow only one idol in boxing, one in baseball, one ballerina, one poet, one novelist, one painter, one concert guitarist, and another one on piano, to the exclusion of the all the rest, who will arrive late or never to this imitation of Mount Olympus. AfroCuba discovered that in the minds of all the bureaucratic thinkers there already existed one Afro-Latin jazz group, or "modern Cuban music ensemble" or some such euphemism commonly used by closet jazzists. (Irakere is not a jazz group, as Oscar Valdés and also Chucho, though the latter with less conviction, told me several times). Since Irakere had already achieved such great success throughout the world, why do we need a rival group? This was most probably the bureaucrats' point of view. The logical corollary would be to ask them to do something different, which would make sense if one group was copying the other, but in fact, AfroCuba was doing something different, and in some respects it was more advanced than Irakere.

Nicolás Reinoso came up with a strange combination: one trumpet, three soprano saxes, one tenor sax, piano, guitar, electric bass, drums, conga, miscellaneous percussion, and voice. The musicians were: Roberto García (trumpet and flugelhorn); Germán Velazco, José Carlos Acosta, and Fernando Acosta (soprano saxes), and Nicolás Reinoso (tenor sax); Ernán López-Nussa (piano); René Luis Toledo (guitar); Luis Quiñones (bass); Tony Valdés (drums); Víctor Torriente (conga); and Anselmo "Chembo" Febles (singer and miscellaneous percussion). The arrangements were mostly done by saxophonist José Carlos Acosta and guitarist René Luis Toledo; all the members of the band were jazz soloists, and the percussion had unique characteristics and didn't resemble anything that had been done before. The one responsible for this was Febles, a sculptor and painter who designed and made new instruments that were added to the arsenal of Afro-Cuban percussion, thereby achieving a distinctive sound. In addition, "Chembo" sang in the African dialects that survive in Cuba.

Several AfroCuba numbers achieved a "jungle atmosphere" that could only be compared to pieces by Duke Ellington, though achieved through very different means. The different types of drums, *metalófonos* (metalophones), *raspadores* (scrapers), *sonajeros* (rattles), *kinfuiti* (similar to the Brazilian *cuica*), bells, and other instruments that were played simultaneously by the three percussionists and sometimes other additional musicians, and the use of free and changing rhythms, gave way to the sudden unison of the wind instruments, chord blocks and passages at an accelerated tempo, where the linearity of neobop and the use of modal and pentatonic scales were combined. The rhythmic bass was almost always Afro-Cuban and polyrhythmic, often in $^6/_8$ time, hardly ever using the walking bass in $^4/_4$ time. All the musicians alternated on the solos (like Charlie Mingus's groups), and several showed a unique profile, including José Carlos Acosta, René Luis Toledo, Germán Velazco, and the pianist Ernán López-Nussa. The tunes, in their variety of tempo, rhythm, and timbre changes, presented constant elements of surprise. AfroCuba was able to make an LP (for which I wrote the liner notes) that didn't sell very well, and the worst thing was that before it went on the market, the group had split up.

A great opportunity presented itself to AfroCuba in 1979, when Irakere, winner of a Grammy award and booked with various international commitments, was unable to participate in a jazz festival in Finland. There was only one possible replacement: a group that would have surprised the public as well as the critics, just as Irakere did the year before. But then an obscure official from the agency that handled foreign trips for Cuban performers appeared and, for personal reasons, proposed to the group's representative and manager, Anselmo Febles, that he take over as director and that the ensemble travel abroad under the condition that they get rid of their director Nicolás Reinoso and drummer Tony Valdés. The immediate result was that the group split in two, and the problem went all the way to the courts. With official support, Febles won the right to keep the band's original name, but the trip never happened. Nicolás Reinoso then formed Sonido Contemporáneo, and remaining with him were saxophonist José Carlos Acosta, bassist Luis Quiñones, drummer Tony Valdés, and percussionist Víctor Torriente, who were joined by, among others, the veteran batá tamborero Mario Dreke ("Chavalonga"). With this group they enjoyed phenomenal success at the 1981 Jazz Plaza Festival. Saxophonist Germán Velazco went on to Irakere—to the difficult job of replacing Paquito

D'Rivera—while Anselmo Febles and René Luis Toledo left the country. The rest made up the new AfroCuba and named as their director saxophonist Fernando Acosta; later on flutist Oriente López and then trumpet player Robertico García (son of the bongosero Roberto García) headed the group. In the 1980s Nicolás Reinoso constantly changed personnel and format; José Carlos Acosta moved on to pianist Emiliano Salvador's group and bassist Luis Quiñones joined a cocktail music group, which provided him with steadier work and better pay. Drummer Tony Valdés left for Puerto Rico and then the United States. Nicolás's group became a school for young musicians, among them pianist Gonzalito Rubalcaba, the next Cuban jazz revelation; Peruchín Jústiz II, son of the legendary pianist; the drummer Horacio "El Negro" Hernández, son of the jazz critic and disc jockey, currently living in the United States; bassists Jorge Macías and Angel López Ceballos; keyboard player Jorge Aragón; guitarist Pablo Menéndez; and keyboardist, saxophonist, and arranger Lucía Huergo. In turn the new AfroCuba went through various editions and for a while the flutist Oriente López, who left the country later on, took over as director. Trovador Silvio Rodríguez, who for ten years had been trying unsuccessfully to form a group and had given up in the face of bureaucratic obstacles, performed for several years with AfroCuba, which turned out well for both, until the awaited separation came.

Two Rising Stars: Arturo Sandoval and Juan Pablo Torres

With the departure of Paquito D'Rivera, Irakere had to make changes in midstream to the repertoire, part of which was conceived a la Ellington, around the soloists. But as they say, when it rains it pours, and shortly thereafter Irakere would lose another of it most brilliant soloists, trumpet player Arturo Sandoval (to top it off, in 1988 a brilliant musician who was loved by all died: Jorge Varona). Sandoval had decided to form his own group and make music just as he conceived it. Although he chose to leave at a difficult time for Irakere, his attitude was reasonable: by that time he had already achieved international prominence, and only with his own group would he be able to reaffirm this position. Even though Sandoval still didn't appear among the top trumpet players in the polls by *Down*

Beat, Playboy, or *Jazz Forum,* that was because he lived outside of the United States and Europe, and didn't have a record label such as Columbia or Blue Note to back him. We should keep in mind that these polls are very relative and depend in large part on what has been recorded in the last year, and have very little to do with personal appearances, which only reach a limited audience.

Sandoval started to rehearse and then work with his new group, which in the beginning didn't sound very good because of the haste with which they put together and practiced the repertoire, but step by step he gradually achieved predictable results with musicians such as Hilario Durán (keyboards, musical director, and arranger), Ahmed Barroso and then Jorge Chicoy (guitar), Jorge Reyes (bass), and Bernardo García (drums), who had been Irakere's first drummer in 1973. Reynaldo Valera was then added on Cuban percussion. In their appearances at jazz festivals in Havana as well as abroad, and with the recording of various LPs—some quite commercial—Arturo was making a name for himself as one of the most brilliant trumpet players of the time, with a refined technique and an inexhaustible energy. As an individual artist, Arturo experienced the happiness that most only dream of. From his school days, Dizzy Gillespie was his idol, and Arturo would have the opportunity to play with Dizzy less than ten years later, practically becoming an idol of his own maestro.

As if this weren't enough, on his first trip to the United States with Irakere, Arturo played with Maynard Ferguson—who also had an influence on him—and received the highest praise from the Canadian trumpeter. Ferguson gave him a trumpet as a gift and Dizzy gave him another one, with the famous Dizzy design—one of his trademarks. Arturito then associated with other great jazz trumpet players: Thad Jones, Woody Shaw, Wynton Marsalis, and Jon Faddis. He also met guitarists John McLaughlin and Larry Coryell as well as Billy Cobham, Stan Getz, Michel Legrand, Jaco Pastorius, and Herbie Hancock. He appeared at the Blue Note, the Village Gate, and Ronnie Scott's (in London) and recorded in Finland, Mexico, France, Venezuela, Spain, and the United States (with Dizzy Gillespie). Critics throughout the world were very favorable to him, at least in the beginning, which is not very common if we remember the incomprehension and stupidity with which real geniuses such as Charlie Parker and John Coltrane were greeted in their day. Not satisfied with these achievements, or perhaps precisely because of them, Arturo made the decision to defect and take up residence in the United States, where he recorded with Paquito and with Dizzy before forming his own group. But his music has steadily declined in quality and honesty, as he has gradually dedicated more and more time to circus-style trumpet exhibitionism, the crassest commercialism, and the political machinations of the Miami community.

Another one of the "young lions" from the Orquesta Cubana de Música Moderna was trombonist Juan Pablo Torres. Both drummer Guillermo Barreto and critic Horacio Hernández told me in those days that "Juanito is the best trombonist that Cuba has ever produced," which says a lot considering the expertise and critical expectations of both. Around 1975 Juan Pablo Torres began to experiment with a group that he named Algo Nuevo and which recorded several LPs such as *Super-son* and *Con todos los hierros*, becoming something like a "rival" to Irakere, before the existence of AfroCuba. But Algo Nuevo had two advantages at the time: first, Irakere had not yet consolidated; second, they had official support, above all from EGREM, because the same officials that later torpedoed AfroCuba were at that time bent on hampering Irakere's success, and there could be nothing better for their plans than backing another experimental fusion group and presenting it as a "contender." As for jazz, Algo Nuevo didn't offer anything really new, but it managed to bring together valuable elements from within Cuban popular music, following a line that the GES tried unsuccessfully to develop (mainly because of lack of equipment).

Algo Nuevo was the first group in Cuba to attempt something that Irakere, Gonzalito Rubalcaba's Proyecto, and other ensembles tried to do later on: use synthesizers and other sophisticated electronic components, which EGREM generously provided, to play our traditional rhythms. Juanito Torres, maybe because he came from the eastern part of the island (Puerto Padre, as did Emiliano Salvador), took son as his basic point of reference. He was also able to bring together several musicians who were ideal for his plans; for example, for *Con todos los hierros* he had Jorge Aragón (piano), Fabián García Caturla (bass), Amadito Valdés Jr. (drums), Agapito García (conga), and Ricardo "El Niño" León (bongo). The results were top quality, thanks in part to the orchestrations by Juan Pablo himself. But Algo Nuevo's fundamental problem was that these arrangements were made for the recording studio, at a time when the country lacked the sound equipment necessary for the group to achieve these same effects in a live performance. As a result, the quality of Algo Nuevo's live performances as well as their television appearances remained far below that of their record productions, with the equipment that only EGREM had access to at the time.[4]

The same thing that had occurred with the Grupo de Experimentación Sonora happened to Algo Nuevo: the lack of live-performance contact with the public prevented the creation of conditions for a real takeoff, despite all the cooperation and the official support they enjoyed. Finally Juan Pablo dissolved the group, and in the 1980s returned to jazz and became more deeply involved in his specialty as a trombone virtuoso. At the end of the 1980s he appeared in the Jazz Plaza Festival with a trio that included bassist Rafael Sánchez and drummer Dennis Torres, or with larger groups, but particularly oriented to provide support to the trombone solos. After these brief appearances in public and filling more or less bureaucratic positions, Juan Pablo Torres left the island and settled in the United States.

There was another group, or better yet orchestra (by the number of members), that performed extraordinarily well since its inception in the 1970s through the end of the 1980s and that may have been a more authentic alternative to Irakere's sound: we are referring to Opus 13, which suddenly disappeared after its biggest artistic and public hits. This ensemble emerged from the Escuela Nacional de Arte (ENA) and at first was called Treceto de la ENA, when its musicians were still students. When they finished their studies, and in accordance with the country's school system, each student had to go to the city or town to which they were assigned to work in what is called "social service," generally in musical instruction. After three years, the members of the Treceto got together again and had the patience and tenacity to continue their group work until they achieved a professional level, which was not easy in those days, and much less so considering that they were all unknown youngsters who played experimental fusion music with an unusual orchestral format. But tenacity won out again in this case.

Opus 13 succeeded in becoming one of the most impressive ensembles to appear in the Jazz Plaza festivals between 1980 and 1990. In the last festivals in which they participated we saw them with the same personnel and always under the direction of the talented violinist, arranger, and composer Joaquín Betancourt. Opus 13 featured Joaquín Betancourt (violin and director), José A. Pérez (violin), Frank Padrón and Carlos Betancourt (trumpets), Gerardo Barreto (trombone), Juan Santos and Luis Depestre (saxes), Rogelio Nápoles (guitar), Emilio Morales (keyboards), Carlos del Pino (electric bass), Ernesto Simpson (drums), Miguel "Angá" Díaz (congas), and Carlos Alemán (voice). Its repertoire consisted entirely of Afro-Latin jazz, with brilliant orchestrations, top soloists, and an explosiveness that could keep audiences on the edge of their seats. Then they started to get involved in danceable music within the so-called *salsa cubana,* and for apparently personal reasons the ensemble broke up, with some of its members going on to jazz groups or dance orchestras. Its director, Joaquín Betancourt, has subsequently worked as an arranger for Isaac Delgado's orchestra, which has excelled within the salsa cubana movement, and then for the Cuban recording label Unicornio.

Emiliano Salvador: The Essential Link

Born in Puerto Padre, Oriente, Emiliano Salvador played the piano, accordion, drums, and conga with his father's jazz band starting as a child; Emiliano Salvador Sr. was also his first teacher. In the mid-1960s he studied at the Escuela Nacional de Arte, in Havana, and he was the pianist of the Grupo de Experimentación Sonora from 1969 until its breakup. Then he organized the trovador Pablo Milanés's group, of which he was the musical director and arranger along with two bassists, Eduardo Ramos and Frank Bejerano. In the early 1980s he formed his own group, with José Carlos Acosta (soprano and tenor saxes), Feliciano Arango (bass), and Emilio del Monte (drums), who came back to jazz after having been a member of Chucho Valdés's combo in the 1960s and spending many years practically in hibernation from jazz with the Teatro Martí orchestra, led at that time by the veteran saxophonist and jazz band director Emilio Peñalver.

During his first years in the GES, Emiliano took classes in orchestration, composition, and other disciplines with maestros Frederick Smith and Leo Brouwer, and perfected his piano technique with María Antonieta Henríquez. Around that time he also wrote several movie scores for the film industry, as well as various numbers for the GES. But Emiliano's talent really came out in 1978; he recorded the first LP under his own name, *Nueva Visión,* and despite the recordings and tours on two continents with Pablo Milanés's group, this album gave him international fame as one of the great Latin jazz pianists, particularly in New York and in the Caribbean and Latin American world. This LP showed Emiliano not only as a pianist and arranger but also as the composer of the songs "Nueva Vision," "Puerto Padre," "El Montuno," "Post Visión," and "Angélica," dedicated to his daughter. Here Emiliano Salvador was getting into different genres: son, guaguancó, mambo, all within the limits of Latin jazz and influenced by bop, hard bop, and the modal discoveries of Miles, Coltrane, and McCoy Tyner.

Basically, Salvador used the traditional conjunto format with three or four trumpets, though he also included alto and soprano sax solos that were given to Paquito D'Rivera, as well as an electric guitar (Ahmed Barroso). The singers were Pablo Milanés and Bobby Carcassés, and the trumpet section included three great soloists: Arturo Sandoval, Jorge Varona, and Manuel Mirabal ("El Guajiro"), as well as veteran Andrés Castro, Lázaro González, and Adalberto Lara ("Trompetica"), all of whom alternated on different tunes. The bassist was Jorgito Reyes, then with the OCMM, and the percussion section included Roberto García and Panchito Bejerano (alternating on bongo), Amadito Valdés Jr. (timbales), and Rolando Valdés and Frank Bejerano (alternating on conga). Among other things, this album—with its fusion of jazz, son, and other forms of Cuban music—repopularized the classic bolero "Convergencia" (by Bienvenido Julián Gutiérrez), originally sung by Miguelito Cuní and now by Pablo Milanés with Emiliano's arrangement. Pablo Milanés would later record another version, a duo with Miguelito Cuní himself.[5]

A second LP was recorded in 1980, *Emiliano Salvador 2,* with a great new all-star band that featured the outstanding participation of Changuito, the great percussionist José Luis Quintana. Subsequently, Emiliano formed his group, with which he recorded two more LPs and performed in almost all the Jazz Plaza festivals. The recorded albums were *Emiliano Salvador y su Grupo* (1986) and *Una Mañana de Domingo* (1987), reedited abroad under the title *Con Fé.* Emiliano's group, with a few personnel changes and in which saxophonist José Carlos Acosta (soprano and tenor) and drummer and timbalero Emilio del Monte (student of the great Guillermo Barreto) excelled, went on extensive tours through Europe, Latin America, and

Canada, performing in Italy, Holland, Spain, Switzerland, Belgium, Sweden, Germany, France, Poland, Nicaragua, and Colombia. And they played in numerous jazz festivals, in which Emiliano appeared in the programming guides along with performers such as Art Blakey and His Jazz Messengers, Branford Marsalis, Dizzy Gillespie, Woody Shaw, Jack De Johnette, Larry Coryell, Kenny Kirkland, Freddy Hubbard, Bobby McFerrin, Carla Bley, Jimmy Rowles, Sun Ra, Jimmy Smith, Eddie Daniels, Manhattan Transfer, Steve Swallow, and Joe Henderson.

Among the Latin American musicians with whom Emiliano shared the stage were Ismael Miranda, Andy and Jerry González, Milton Nascimiento, Nana Vasconcelos, Dave Valentín, Louie Ramírez, Airto Moreira, Chico Buarque de Hollanda, and the Brazilian vocal quartet MPB 4, as well as with his compatriot and colleague Gonzalito Rubalcaba. Emiliano played with many of them, bringing back enjoyable memories of the jam sessions in which he played, in different parts of the world, with Andy and Jerry González, Dave Valentín, René McLean, Billy Cobham, Ismael Miranda, Louie Ramírez, Chico Buarque, and MPB 4—whom he accompanied in Havana—Airto Moreira, and Wagner Tisso, pianist and arranger for Milton Nascimiento whom he joined in an unexpected and spontaneous jam session in Paris at the home of singer Christiane Legrand.[6]

Emiliano Salvador's versatility manifests itself in the way he approaches Cuban piano forms such as the contradanza, in his solid son roots, and in his use of rumba or free jazz elements. His music is also characterized by its sense of balance and coherence as it combines traditional and contemporary aspects, as well as by its diversity within an indisputable stylistic unity. There are no virtuoso excesses for the deliberate purpose of dazzling, something so common in today's jazz musicians, but rather sobriety in the conception and the performance. His thorough knowledge of the "standard" tunes—whether American, Cuban, or Brazilian—as well as his innate taste and harmonic insight helped him avoid the monotony that is so common today in solos built on one or two chords or on top of a simple montuno. And with the self-confidence that his background as a percussionist gives him, the rhythmic aspect in Emiliano's style as well as his interplay with the percussion instruments reveal a subtle complexity in his work. It stands in contrast to the lyricism of his melodic lines, in which virtuosity is always subordinated to expressiveness.

In these two decades (1970s and 1980s), in which Cuban jazz "takes off" internationally, three brilliant pianists stand out, although they are not exactly from the same generation: Chucho Valdés, Emiliano Salvador, and then, already in the 1980s, Gonzalito Rubalcaba. This trio could be compared to the one consisting of Frank Emilio Flynn, Peruchín Jústiz, and Bebo Valdés from the 1940s and 1950s. And although Chucho Valdés and Gonzalito Rubalcaba have very different and personal styles, we consider Emiliano Salvador to be the connection or critical link between the Cuban pianists that preceded him and those that will emerge after him, already well equipped with the legacy of Thelonious Monk, Bill Evans, McCoy Tyner, Cecil Taylor, and other piano innovators in jazz, whose contributions were already fully integrated into the evolution of the Afro-Cuban piano by Emiliano Salvador. Hence the importance of this musician, typical representative of the best in "Latin jazz" on piano and in composition. Emiliano was completing the recording of his fifth album when he suddenly died on October 22, 1992, at the age of forty-two.

Jazz Rock, Fusion, and Free Jazz

In the previous chapter we referred to the only group involved in free jazz in the 1960s, a group that was pursuing experimental objectives for the most part. From those days to the present time Cuban musicians have never strongly embraced free jazz. In 1979 the group Arte Vivo was founded. It consisted of recent graduates from the Escuela Nacional de Arte and was led by Alfredo Gómez (French horn, keyboards, and composer); rounding out the group were Mario Daly (guitar), Alfredo Pérez Triff (violin), and Enrique González (drums). Arte Vivo set out to make extremely free and improvised music (not strictly jazz) that would have room for elements from rock and jazz to Renaissance and baroque music. Its only experimentation with free jazz strictly speaking was a long piece dedicated to Angola broadcast by CMBF on Horacio Hernández's jazz program. Arte Vivo had changed somewhat, and on this piece were Mario Daly on guitar and electric bass, violinist Pérez Triff, and pianist Andrés Sendín; rounding out the group were tenor saxophonist Nicolás Reinoso and the then drummer Pedro Luis Martínez, later bassist in the OCMM and director of his own groups. Arte Vivo as such underwent diverse changes and performed in the 1983 Jazz Plaza with a repertoire and style more along the lines of "symphonic rock" or "artistic rock," under the direction of Mario Daly. Then drummer Enrique González directed the group, while Mario Daly organized Monte de Espuma, one of the rock-nueva trova fusion groups.

From the beginning of the 1970s several "underground" rock groups emerged such as Los Dada, a typical ensemble of the period based on guitars and keyboards; Los Barba and Los Magnéticos, which included brass a la Chicago or Blood, Sweat & Tears, and Los Dan, which played a Bee Gees–style soft rock. Also, the singers Raúl Gómez and Osvaldo Rodríguez formed groups with a heavy metal influence. Of course the pioneer in the attempt to come up with a "Cuban rock" was the Grupo de Experimentación Sonora, which achieved good results with the fusion style that took it to its peak in 1976–78. Later on, when various nueva trova singer-songwriters formed their own groups, they were basically rock groups fused with Cuban music; among them we should mention Amaury Pérez and Pablo Milanés in the 1970s, and later on Vicente Feliú and Santiago Feliú with their respective ensembles, which also included jazz soloists. Something similar can be said of the collaboration between Silvio Rodríguez and AfroCuba or between Donato Poveda and Monte de Espuma. The logical explanation is that nueva trova, from the beginning, was influenced by rock.

Many other rock groups have emerged since then, such as Gens, which excelled in the 1980s. Perhaps the most interesting have been two typical fusion groups: Carlos Alfonso's Síntesis, and Mezcla, formed by the ex-guitarist of the GES Pablo Menéndez, son of American blues and folk singer Barbara Dane. Mezcla has experimented with all kinds of fusion, borrowing from traditional Cuban music, jazz, rock, and Latin American music. For his part, Carlos Alfonso, who in the context of nueva trova was a member of the vocal groups Los Nova and later Tema IV—the latter with very advanced vocal arrangements by Carlos Alfonso—created around 1978 the group Síntesis, which featured in the beginning such prominent musicians as José María Vitier and Mike Porcel. Through various stages of experimentation, personnel, and conceptual changes, Síntesis achieved a sound all their own, particularly after their collaboration with Afro-Cuban singer Lázaro Ross, with whom they started a line of songs in the Yoruba language with batá drums and advanced rock sounds, plus a few jazz solos by talented saxophonist, keyboardist, and arranger Lucía Huergo. Also of note in fusion music has been the pianist and composer José María Vitier, brother of the guitarist and director of ORU Sergio Vitier, whose music impressed Michel Legrand during his visit to Cuba in 1983 as much as Arturo Sandoval and Gonzalo Rubalcaba impressed Dizzy Gillespie. In the different versions of his group the saxophonist Javier Zalba (baritone, soprano, and flute) has stood out.[7]

The Jazz Plaza Festivals

In 1979 the indefatigable Bobby Carcassés, singer, multi-instrumentalist, emcee, and showman for many years (particularly in the Hotel Riviera's Copa Room), not satisfied with the Río Club as an only home for jazz musicians and descargas, organized a series of concerts at the theater hall of the Casa de la Cultura in the Plaza district (old Lyceum & Lawn Tennis Club), located at Calzada and Eighth in Vedado. The following year, Bobby and the then director of the Casa de la Cultura, Armando Rojas, were able to organize a national jazz festival that from then on was called Jazz Plaza. An organizing commission was created that included—in addition to Carcassés and Rojas—Horacio Hernández, musicologist Helio Orovio, TV producer and ex-percussionist Ernesto Calderín, disc jockey Mario Barba, TV consultant Rafael Taquechel, as well as several old members of the Club Cubano de Jazz such as José Alberto Figueras, Helen Mitskus, Carlos Fernández, and others. Also on the commission, at least during the first years, were jazz musicians from three generations, among them Armando Romeu, Felipe Dulzaides, Leonardo Acosta, Chucho Valdés, and Arturo Sandoval. The first festival was a bit "all in the family" and featured for the most part groups put together especially for the event, whose members worked in different ensembles; Felipe Dulzaides represented one of the few exceptions, as did Irakere. But the event attracted a full and enthusiastic audience. Admission was free.

The subsequent festivals saw the number of participating groups increase: (Nicolás Reinoso's) Sonido Contemporáneo, Emiliano Salvador, Arturo Sandoval, Pedro Luis Martínez, (Bobby Carcassés's) Afrojazz, Peruchín Jústiz II, and the first "all star" jazz band organized and directed by Armando Romeu for these festivals. In addition, there were ensembles such as Juan

Formell's Van Van and Pablo Milanés's group, which although they didn't play strictly jazz played at least a jazz-inflected music. And this experience would repeat itself years later when "salsa" or dance music orchestras influenced by Latin jazz, such as N. G. La Banda, were included in the festival. The festivals were also successful in attracting various groups formed by students from the fine arts schools and conservatories, among them a Super Sax-style saxophone quintet. And thanks to Armando Romeu's "scouting" work, ensembles from other parts of the country participated: Arará (Holguín), Raíces Nuevas (Santa Clara), and Fervet Opus (Camagüey) showed a surprising quality.

Almost all the Cuban jazz musicians from different generations participated in these first festivals, including some who were partially retired. Armando Romeu not only formed a jazz band to play his own originals and a few jazz classics but also accompanied singers such as Barbara Dane, just as he would later with Flora Purim, Airto Moreira, and Dizzy Gillespie. In 1981 some of us veterans formed a group that included Leonardo Acosta (alto sax), Frank Emilio Flynn (piano), Carlos Emilio Morales (guitar), Julio César Fonseca (bass), Leoginaldo Pimentel (drums), Ernesto Calderín (conga), and Manolo Armesto (bongo). Although Irakere was the biggest attraction at that time, there were festivals in which it didn't participate, although some of its members did perform with different groups, such as the aforementioned Carlos Emilio Morales, drummer Enrique Plá, tenor sax Carlos Averhoff, and Chucho Valdés. Little by little musicians of exceptional historic significance such as Frank Emilio Flynn, Guillermo Barreto, Orlando "Cachaíto" López, and others began to take part in the festivals.

When the festival became international and had world famous musicians on the program, it attracted enough people to fill the main venue (Casa de la Cultura in Plaza) and several additional venues, such as the Mella (old Cine Rodi), Nacional (on Plaza de la Revolución), and Karl Marx theaters, as well as additional locales and the entertainment areas located near the swimming pools of the Nacional, Presidente, and Riviera hotels, Maxim's nightclub, and others. But when the event outgrew its "family" status, there were a number of difficulties of various sorts. The first was the ever-increasing involvement of a bureaucracy whose primary objective was to strip the Casa de la Cultura in the Plaza municipality of the leadership and organization of the event, just when it had acquired the necessary experience to do a good job. They claimed that an international festival should be organized at a higher level, and as a result they committed deplorable organizational mistakes. Often the large number of widely dispersed secondary venues, in a city with a terrible system of transportation and a lack of pianos and amplification equipment, hindered the smooth functioning of the festival and its programming. To make things even worse, the interests of the tourism institutions and businesses started to take over.

The event's initial organizing commission was replaced by officials and turned into an "advisory" commission, thereby stripping it of any decision-making power. And a festival to which admission was initially free and in which the musicians didn't charge anything for their performances was transformed within a few years into a commercial enterprise, with the new "impresarios" forgetting that Havana is neither Montreux nor The Hague. Admission prices were set in national currency and simultaneously in dollars for foreigners, which created unpleasant situations and protests, particularly among foreigners who lived on the island. To top it off, there were years in which bars were set up exclusively to take foreign currency. Nevertheless, with the boom in tourism starting with the "special period" and the country's subsequent "dollarization" (the establishment of Cubans' legal right to possess dollars) in the 1990s, the same tourist promoters have gradually learned to manage these situations more sensibly.

Another source of problems was provoked by the "star system." Instead of having an organizing commission that knew jazz, those in charge decided to name as "director" or "president" of one or another festival a musician who had acquired international recognition. The idea was that this musician, because of his contact with jazz musicians from other countries, could use his connections to attract world-renowned performers, paying tribute to them and honoring them with awards and prizes for their participation, but this created the possibility for this "executive" musician to influence or even determine which national groups would be invited to take part in the festival. The extent to which this mechanism can be abused is obvious. We will just say, however, that to the present this responsibility as top festival executive has been delegated to three Cuban musicians: Arturo Sandoval (who excluded top musicians such as Emiliano Salvador and others from the festival, shortly before defecting with his whole family), then Gonzalo

Rubalcaba and Chucho Valdés. The festivals have improved in spite of all their defects, with a great increase not only in the number of national groups but also in their quality, at the same time that the level of invited artists has been maintained and even surpassed.

Visitors and Hosts

In 1982–83 the ideas and plans to bring soloists and jazz groups from all over the world to the Jazz Plaza began to materialize, and since then jazz musicians from the United States and Canada, Latin America, Europe, and Australia have visited Havana. Of the festivals held, the one in 1986 had perhaps—until the 1990s—the biggest international participation, with the great Dizzy Gillespie and his group (for the second time), the alto saxophonist Zbigniew Namilowski (Poland), the Benders (Australia), Steve McCall (USA), Peter Lipa (Czechoslovakia), and the sensational jazz and blues singer Leon Thomas (USA). Dizzy Gillespie's presence in 1985 and 1986 produced a significant hierarchical jump in the festival, in every sense: artistic quality, participation of national and foreign groups, box office success, transmission through the media, and growing international interest.

Besides Dizzy, in 1985 alto saxophonist Richie Cole was in attendance. A year before (Jazz Plaza 1984) the exceptional Brazilian pianist and vocalist Tania María attended the Jazz Plaza, and she brought her own Brazilian and Afro-Latin style to jazz. In addition to her performance in the Casa de la Cultura, she appeared three nights with her trio at the Karl Marx Theater, and at her request, Brazilian and Cuban musicians were brought together for a big jam session in the same theater. Also present at different Jazz Plaza festivals were flutist Dave Valentín (Puerto Rico); tenor saxophonist Ronnie Scott and his group (Great Britain), on various occasions; American singer Barbara Dane, already mentioned; the formidable Catalan pianist Tete Montoliu; the Czech trumpet player Laco Decsi, with a trio; the Sven Bergerants Orchestra (Sweden); the groups Praxis (Nicaragua), Fulano (Chile), and Cimarrón (Venezuela); the Gut Maljokivic sextet (Yugoslavia); the trio of the outstanding pianist Oliver Jones (Canada); the George Haslam quartet (Great Britain); and the group Mynta (Sweden). Later on, we should mention the presence of Charlie Haden, George Adams, Joe

Lovano, Ray Anderson, Gerri Allen, Max Roach, Don Pullen, Carmen McRae, Chico Freeman, Sammy Figueroa, Roy Hargrove, Steve Coleman, and the numerous visits by the Canadian flutist Jane Bunnett and Ronnie Scott, as well as Airto Moreira, accompanied on his first visit by Flora Purim, and the Czech flutist and saxophonist Jiri Stivin.

Bass icon Charlie Haden deserves a special mention. With his Liberation Orchestra, he practically saved the festival in 1987, arriving one day before his first presentation, when everybody already expected a festival without any guests of fundamental importance. This great musician, who would return a few years later, brought along an impressive lineup: Byron Lynch and Frank Gordon (trumpets), Ray Anderson (trombone), Ken McIntyre (alto sax), George Adams and Joe Lovano (tenors), Alex Brodsky (French horn), Marcus Rojas (tuba), Mike Goodrich (guitar), and Gerri Allen (piano). This year as well as the following, the missing star was saxophonist Branford Marsalis, announced time and again, but always a no-show (once again in 1996 there was talk of him). Meanwhile, the legendary drummer Max Roach, announced in 1988, was finally able to come in 1989, after having wanted to play in Cuba for almost forty years. Max told Mario Barba and me that he had been in Havana in the 1950s, but they didn't allow him to enter the Tropicana because he was black; disappointed, he set off on his historic trip to Haiti to learn firsthand the Afro-Antillean rhythms.

Max Roach came to Havana accompanied only by his student, percussionist Francisco Mora, and performed alone at the Jazz Plaza, although he also did a performance with Arturo Sandoval and several musicians from Irakere (Chucho Valdés, Carlos del Puerto, Enrique Plá). Then he expressed his desire to play with a group of Cuban percussionists, and so he played with Irakere's percussion section, which included Oscar Valdés II, Oscar III, Enrique Plá, and Miguelito Angá. Visiting us that same year was the Czech flutist and alto saxophonist Jiri Stivin, accompanied only by the guitarist Rudolf Dasek, whom I had seen in Prague in 1962 with vibraphonist Karel Velebny's group. We also had once more in the Jazz Plaza tenorist Ronnie Scott, in whose famous London club various Cuban jazz musicians and groups, starting with Irakere, have become internationally known in the last fifteen years. Ronnie Scott's involvement with Cuban jazz steadily increased, to the point that when he entered the country during the "special period" brought on by the economic crisis, he became a promoter and co-organizer of the festival (along with his partner Pete King), and thanks to this collaboration, Jazz Plaza 1993 turned out to be an undeniable artistic success. Nevertheless, economic success did not accompany this enterprise, and the festivals proceeded with great difficulty.[8]

Another stellar moment of the Jazz Plaza Festival took place in 1990 when Airto Moreira and Flora Purim's visit coincided with Dizzy Gillespie's last visit to Havana. For this occasion Armando Romeu had formed a big band with the country's most prominent instrumentalists, including the Irakere musicians, as well as Arturo Sandoval and Juan Pablo Torres, who had not yet defected. Also in attendance was Pawel Brodowski, editor of the Warsaw magazine *Jazz Forum*, organ of the International Jazz Federation with its headquarters in Stockholm, Sweden. In that same year, Carmen McRae, one of the great jazz singers of all time, appeared in the Jazz Plaza. Present as well was percussionist Sammy Figueroa, and a year later, Charlie Haden returned, this time to play together with the pianist Gonzalito Rubalcaba, with whom he was recording an album at that time. As we have said, Ronnie Scott's collaboration livened up the festival in 1993, after two years of uncertainty. By a lucky coincidence, this festival was reviewed for the magazine *Latin Beat* by Deroy Murdock, who visited the island for other reasons.[9] So thorough and enthusiastic is his chronicle of the event that it renders unnecessary any further commentary on the excellent work done by Ronnie Scott, who saved a festival that had been in crisis for two years.

Participating this time, as we've already stated, were Ronnie Scott and his group, in which saxophonist Mornington Lockett excelled; vibraphonist Roy Ayers's group, a jazz-blues-funk fusion; the blues and jazz vocalist Irene Reid; the Shuffle Demons from Toronto, Canada; Triple Heater (Sweden); the Jim Mullen Band (Great Britain); and the piano and sax duo formed by the Swedes Tommy Berndtsson and Johan Borgstrom. The *Latin Beat* correspondent had words of praise for the Cuban groups Cuarto Espacio, AfroCuba, Perspectiva, and, of course, Irakere. In this festival as in all the latest ones there have been dance-music orchestras, such as Elio Revé and Van Van. In spite of all this, the festival lost money, and the Instituto de la Música, in charge of these events now, made the decision to hold the Jazz Plaza only once every two years. It was suspended for a year, and the following year it was held, although there was nothing eventful or noteworthy about it. Then in 1996, in another great year for Chucho Valdés, with his tour of North American universities, Irakere's director was able to bring trumpet player Roy Hargrove to Havana with his group as well as saxophonist Steve Coleman. Meanwhile, another setback was the end of Maxim's as a jazz focal point, which once again left Cuban jazz musicians without an appropriate place to exchange ideas in jam sessions. But there were other positive developments, such as the more frequent holding of recitals and the emergence of a weekly "jazz club" at the Plaza Casa de la Cultura, promoted by Bobby Carcassés, and another one in the tearoom at the Unión de Periodistas, organized by journalist and jazz critic José Dos Santos.

As for the festivals, one of their more positive aspects has been the opportunity they have provided for many new groups and soloists from Cuba to gain exposure and meet renowned musicians, including musicians from abroad that come to visit. Armando Romeu wasn't the only one discovering young talent; in the beginning, the organizing commission was also committed to this job. The best example of a musician emerging from these festivals is Gonzalito Rubalcaba, who attended the first ones (while still a student) with different groups, and primarily as a drummer. Then he appeared as a pianist until he attracted the attention of Dizzy Gillespie and began his rising international career. Another example was the group Raíces Nuevas, from Santa Clara, which traveled to Havana in 1983 on Armando Romeu's recommendation, just as Arará from Holguín had done two years earlier. Raíces Nuevas, which dissolved after recording an LP, produced musicians such as trombonist and scat singer Carlos Alvarez (later with Irakere and other groups) and pianist Pucho López, who has formed different successful ensembles for subsequent festivals and has appeared at festivals in Canada and other countries.

Young drummer Oscar Valdés III (son of the singer-and-percussionist co-founder of Irakere) was another one of the discoveries from these festivals. Similarly I should point out the participation of Fervet Opus, from Camagüey, whose pianist Gabriel Hernández has turned out to be a real find. From 1985 to 1990 more than thirty Cuban groups participated in the Jazz Plaza festivals, groups such as Irakere, Opus 13, Arturo Sandoval, Bobby Carcassés's Afrojazz, Emiliano Salvador, Peruchín and his ensemble, AfroCuba, the Carlos Averhoff Quartet, Ferjómesis, Ireme, Arará,

Pucho López, Babel, Gonzalo Rubalcaba's Proyecto, Juan Pablo Torres, José María Vitier, the Frank Emilio Quintet, Pedro Luis Martínez, Hilario Durán's Perspectiva, the José Jaurrieta Trio, Nueva Dimensión, Grupo Expresión, Sergio Vitier's ORU, the Freddy González Trio, Quinteto Estudio, Quinteto de Saxofones (director Manuel Valera), Quinteto Clásico, Cuarto Espacio, groups from the ENA, ISA (Instituto Superior de Arte), and the Amadeo Roldán Conservatory, big bands formed especially for the festivals, as well as dance-music orchestras. Of course we have not included in this list many groups that appeared in previous or subsequent years, which would increase the count significantly. Never before in the history of our music has there been even half the number of jazz groups as there are today, groups that exist as permanent, established ensembles, independent of these festivals in which they performed.

Rubalcaba's Proyecto and Other Ensembles

The history is already well known, and we have presented at least part of it: Dizzy Gillespie was surprised during the 1985 Jazz Plaza when he heard the twenty-two-year-old pianist Gonzalo Rubalcaba. Dizzy commented, "[He's] one of the best I've heard in many years," a statement that some have gone on to exaggerate, as normally happens. What's important is that a few days later Dizzy gave a concert together with Gonzalito, which was recorded and edited as an LP. At one of its best moments, Gonzalo Rubalcaba's Proyecto featured Rafael Carreño (flute and tenor sax), Lázaro Cruz and Reinaldo Milián (trumpets), Felipe Cabrera (electric bass and bassoon), Horacio "El Negro" Hernández (drums), and Roberto Vizcaíno (miscellaneous percussion). The alto and soprano saxophonist Manuel Valera had been with Proyecto previously.

Starting in 1978, when he formed his first ensemble, Gonzalito caused a sensation among the public and other musicians, as a drummer and a pianist. In 1985 the group Proyecto appeared in the North Sea Jazz Festival (The Hague, Holland), in a salsa festival organized by the London-Havana Friends Society, and at Ronnie Scott's club; in 1986 they returned to The Hague. By 1987 they had already performed in Poland, Japan, Canada, Spain, Brazil, Sweden, Finland, and Nicaragua, as well as in both East and West Germany.

Even as they were just beginning, Gonzalito and his group alternated with jazz greats such as Miles Davis, Dizzy, Pat Metheny, Gary Burton, Joe Pass, Manhattan Transfer, and Kenny Burrell; they had also recorded five albums in Cuba (one for solo piano) and four in Germany. Proyecto showed from the start the same explosiveness as Irakere and the first version of AfroCuba, and thanks to Gonzalito's compositions and arrangements they achieved a very unique and original style and identity. Although individual virtuosity—particularly the director's—was featured, it was subordinated to the search for a language guided by a specific musical conception, based on Cuban roots and incorporating other elements, but avoiding the easy labels Latin jazz, salsa, or electronic jazz. In a second stage, Proyecto consisted of Gonzalo (keyboards), Reinaldo Milián (trumpet), Felipe Cabrera (bass), Horacio "El Negro" Hernández (drums), Roberto Vizcaíno (percussion), and Mario García Haya (guitarist and computer programmer).

One of Proyecto's innovations during this period was their rich and original use of percussion, with Roberto Vizcaíno working with an original combination of instruments, from symphonic tympani to congas, bongo, cowbell, coconuts, and whatever else might produce the right sound. With only two musicians, the combinations achieved in the different Afro-Cuban rhythmic patterns would lead one to believe that more than three percussionists were playing. Gonzalito also combined his pianistic explorations and the Afro-Cuban arsenal of rhythms with synthesizers and computers, creating different sound bases, combining jazz improvisation and the use of very free rhythms in constant change through shifts in tempo, complex counterpoint passages, and flexible structures that would leave more than one composer of aleatory music perplexed. The big challenge that Gonzalito took on was combining two such opposite poles as programmed music and free improvisation, and doing it on recordings as well as in live performances.

According to his own statements, Gonzalo started from the idea that the level of technological development that has made digital recording, stereophonics, and the multiplicity of timbres and sound planes possible should translate into new possibilities for expression, and he stimulated this by thinking differently and conceiving different structures without sacrificing any basic musical parameters. Nevertheless, as the fame of the "young Cuban prodigy" grew, his work as composer with the group gradually gave way to becoming a piano virtuoso, recording for Blue Note preferentially with musicians such as bassists Charlie Haden and John Patitucci and drummer Jack De Johnette. Articles on Rubalcaba have appeared in *Down Beat, Jazz Times,* and other jazz magazines, as have reviews of his latest CDs, although the reviews haven't always been favorable. My opinion is that critiques such as the one by *New York Times* critic Peter Watrous on Rubalcaba's Lincoln Center concert—which characterized his performance as empty virtuosity—are not only wrong but also a typical example of the worst of a certain kind of snobbish and over-bearing jazz critique. In any case, I do criticize Gonzalito's experimentation in that rhapsodic style that has done so much damage to many jazz pianists, starting with Keith Jarrett. On the other hand, when Gonzalito established himself outside of Cuba (now he only performs in Cuba on rare occasions), his jazz career, as that of many other Cubans who no longer live on the island, crosses over from this history into the history of jazz in general, or that of the respective countries in which they live.

Bobby Carcassés's Afrojazz has gone through innumerable personnel changes but has maintained the essential aspects of its style, with frequent passages in which the voice is in unison with the brass and guitar. In 1987 the group consisted of the following musicians: César López (alto sax), Orlando "Maraca" Valle (flute), Manuel Quintero (drums), Antonio Torriente (conga), and Roberto Julio Carcassés, the son of Bobby Carcassés (piano and miscellaneous percussion), with its director per-forming as singer and on flugelhorn. Subsequently alto saxophonists Mariano Tena and Rolando Pérez Pérez and drummer Carlos Salvador (brother of Emiliano), among others, have played with Afrojazz. Like Felipe Dulzaides and Nicolás Reinoso before him, Bobby has shown a special talent in the practical training of many young jazz musicians. Of those mentioned, for example, altoist César López went from Afrojazz to Irakere, as did flutist and keyboardist Orlando Valle (Maraca), who leads his own group today; Mariano Tena was later with Peruchín's group, and Rolando Pérez Pérez went on to the popular ensemble N. G. La Banda. Meanwhile, Roberto Julio Carcassés has stood out as a top-rank pianist and has formed the group Estado de Animo.

That same year the group headed by pianist Pucho López lined up Manuel Machado (trumpet), Rafael Jenks (alto sax), Eduardo Proveyer (tenor sax), Carlos Alvarez (trombone), Raúl Verdecia (guitar), Arturo Basnuevo (bass), Leonel Olivares (drums), and Jorge González (percussion).

In the following years he has completely changed the format on various occasions; some of the aforementioned musicians have gone on to other bands, and trombonist Carlos Alvarez was for a time with Irakere. Pucho López, who comes from a family of musicians, has often experimented in jazz-rock or electronic jazz, and his groups have oscillated between nine and three musicians, performing only occasionally. In recent years he has participated in international jazz festivals in Canada and other countries.

Guitarist Peruchín (Pedro Jústiz Jr.) brought his father's piano style to his instrument, combined with an indisputable influence from Wes Montgomery and George Benson. In various Jazz Plaza festivals he has appeared with his group, which included Mariano Tena (alto sax, soprano sax, and flute), Jorge Benítez (trumpet), Mario Fabián Sardiñas (piano), Jorge Macías (bass), Eugenio Arango (drums), Bernardo Bolaños and Joel Drill (Cuban percussion); he has featured his nephew, pianist Rodolfo Argudín Jústiz (Peruchín III), later with N. G. La Banda, as a guest. In 1988 Peruchín recorded his first LP, *Playa Sirena*, with his own group and various invited soloists, among them trumpet player Jorge Varona, tenor saxophonist Carlos Averhoff, and guitarist Carlos Emilio Morales.[10]

A veteran jazz musician and founder of Tres más Uno from the 1960s, pianist Freddy González (see Chapter 8) organized the group Fusion 3, which also accompanied singer Maggie Prior.[11] The trio consisted of Freddy González (piano), Jesús Fernández (bass), and René Lauzeníquez (drums), but they also performed various numbers in the Jazz Plaza festival with a Cuban percussion group made up of sons and nephews of the famous Papines. This new generation of Los Papines included Lázaro Mengual Abram, Alexander Mengual Abram, Luis Abreu, Orlando Mengual Abram, and Ramón González. For its part, the young group from Camagüey, Fervet Opus, brought the following personnel to Havana: Gabriel Hernández (director and keyboards), Ernesto Simpson (saxophone), Mauricio Rodríguez (bass), Enrique Simpson (drums), and Pedro Porro (percussion). And the Quinteto Estudio, led by the guitarist Ramón Carriera, lined up Luis Depestre (saxophone), David Alfaro (keyboards), Luis Río Rivas (second guitar), Luis Gómez (bass), and Lázaro Poey (drums).

Nueva Dimensión featured Orlando Sánchez (director and piano), Ignacio Arango (guitar), Orlando Barreda, Gerardo Portillo, and Mario Machado (trumpets), Jorge Pérez Fáez (trombone), Amadís Bayard (alto sax), Jesús Lam (tenor sax), Diego Valdés (bass), Isel Rasua (percussion), and, as guests, Maritza Sánchez (piano) and Ramón Rodríguez (bass). Pedro Luis Martínez's group included Rafael Jenks (tenor sax), José Jaurrieta (guitar), Lázaro Poey (drums), and Pedro Luison (electric bass). And the group Expresión lined up Javier Gutiérrez (director and piano), Orlando Valle (flute), Juan Carlos López (trumpet), Jesús Fuentes (tenor sax), Lázaro Reyes (bass), Ramón González (drums), and Miguel Valdés (percussion). Trombonist Juan Pablo Torres, after dissolving Algo Nuevo, reappeared as a jazz musician in 1987 with a quartet that included Enrique Menéndez (bass), Mario Calzado (drums), and Tomás Ramos (percussion). For their part, the ex-members of Arturo Sandoval's group formed Perspectiva in 1991, led by pianist Hilario Durán.

A group formed specifically for the 1987 festival was the Quinteto de Saxofones, which was organized by alto saxophonist Manuel Valera and included Valera and veteran Rolando Sánchez (altos), Carlos Averhoff and Braulio "Babín" Hernández (tenors), and Javier Zalba (baritone), and as guest José Crego (trumpet). The rhythmic section consisted of Frank Emilio (piano), José Luis Martínez (bass), and Guillermo Barreto (drums). Pianist Pucho López also performed with the quintet. This group was in my opinion the best at Jazz Plaza 1987 apart from Charlie Haden's Liberation Orchestra. Bringing together musicians from the OCMM and other ensembles, they played a selection of jazz classics such as "Round Midnight" and Super Sax arrangements. The following year, Jazz Plaza 1988 gave considerable time to the singers, who with rare exceptions had been noticeably absent in Cuban jazz in recent decades. Two of these exceptions were present, Bobby Carcassés and Maggie Prior, as well as Mayra Caridad Valdés (Chucho's sister), Beatriz Márquez, Argelia Fragoso, and the vocal groups Eco and Vocal Juventud, anticipating a certain resurgence of these groups in the coming years. (In 1993 the Cuban vocal group Vocal Sampling, which since then has performed in European and U.S. jazz festivals, participated in the Jazz Plaza.)

Between 1988 and 1989 there were new departures from Irakere and four of its soloists on wind instruments joined N. G. La Banda, which flutist José Luis Cortés ("El Tosco") led from the beginning and which then became a leading band in the so-called timba or Cuban salsa craze. The other three musicians were trumpet player José Crego, tenor saxophonist Carlos Averhoff, and alto and soprano saxophonist Germán Velazco. Before the formation of the band as such, two LPs were made under Cortés's direction with originals and arrangements of his, entitled *Siglo I a.n.e.* and *Siglo II a.n.e.* Cortés (flute and baritone sax), Carlos Averhoff (flute, soprano, and tenor), and Velazco (flute, soprano, and alto) played on these LPs, which were still within jazz parameters. The other participants on these records were Dagoberto González (violin), Juan Munguía (trumpet and flugelhorn), Miguel Núñez and Miguel de Armas (keyboards), Carlos Emilio Morales and Angel Octavio Sánchez (guitar), Diego Valdés and Feliciano Arango (bass), Conrado García and Osmany Sánchez (drums), Juan Noguera and Raúl Oviedo (Cuban percussion), and singers Aymée Nuviola and Anabel López.

No less than sixteen professional Cuban groups and five from the musical schools, which made a favorable showing, attended Jazz Plaza 1989, which as previously mentioned included the presence of Max Roach. And it was only because of bureaucratic reasons that the Santa Clara Orquesta de Música Moderna didn't take part, as they were the best in the country and would later appear in Havana led by maestro Armando Romeu, who was also the band's advisor and wrote many of the arrangements. The lineup of this big band was as follows: official director: Jesús Rodríguez; trumpets: Mario Montalván, Lázaro Hernández, Jorge L. González, Fausto Ledón; trombones: Marcos Peñate, Fausto Vega, Amado González, Francisco Alvarez; saxophones: Melquiades Aparicio and Carlos Bermúdez Jr. (altos), Nelson Peña and Jorge Aparicio (tenors), and Hazario Margañón (baritone); keyboards: Raúl Camilo; guitar: Carlos Bermúdez Sr.; bass: Alberto Rodríguez; drums: Juan Rojas; Cuban percussion: Carmelo Miranda and Guillermo Paredes. The maestro Armando Romeu proved once again to be the most important promoter that the big Cuban jazz bands have ever had.

As a way of making amends, in the following year (1990) Armando formed his own all-star band, which accompanied Dizzy Gillespie on his last visit to Cuba. And if 1989 is remembered for its high participation of national groups with fewer from abroad, 1990 reaches the levels of international participation of 1985 and 1986 again, with those two great draws for the Jazz Plaza, Dizzy and Ronnie Scott, who as we've already seen would return three years later. Also visiting were Carmen McRae; tenor saxophonist Chico Freeman and his group; Canadian flutist and saxophonist Jane Bunnett; the free jazz pianist Don Pullen and the great Brazilian percussionist Airto

Moreira (this time without Flora Purim, although she had been announced as was the boricua percussionist Giovanni Hidalgo). And the festival was dedicated entirely to Armando Romeu. The band that Armando organized featured: trumpets: Juan Munguía, Arturo Sandoval, Edilio Montero, Alfredo Pérez, and Carlos Betancourt; trombones: Carlos Alvarez, Juan Pablo Torres, Antonio Leal, and César Bobalé; saxophones: Manuel Valera and César López (altos), Fernando Acosta and Rafael James (tenors), and Javier Zalba (baritone); piano: Chucho Valdés; guitar: Carlos E. Morales; bass: Jorge Reyes; electric bass: Carlos del Puerto; drums: Enrique Plá; Cuban percussion: Oscar Valdés II, Oscar Valdés III, and Miguel Angá. The festival's culminating moment was when Dizzy and Airto Moreira joined the band to play "Manteca" and other numbers of Dizzy's and Chano Pozo's.[12]

In an interview with Carmen McRae by the Cuban journalist Neysa Ramón, the extraordinary jazz singer confirmed what I have maintained, from the beginning to the end of this book, with respect to the "world of jam sessions": that this "world apart" is the best school for jazz musicians, providing an informal and spontaneous exchange of ideas, experiences, and styles. But it is a world that has been suppressed in the United States as well as in Cuba. In the words of the journalist:

> McRae recalls the places to listen and learn: those jam sessions where the artists—in direct contact with their elders—received an education. These places no longer exist, prohibited by the union that at the start tried to protect the interests of the musicians, who in a spontaneous way and without charging showed up to play while the owners of the locales increased their profits by charging a cover and selling drinks. The rule wiped out the jam sessions.[13]

Whereas in the United States, a bureaucratic union measure and the impresario's eternal greed are to blame, in Cuba, it is just the lack of interest on the part of bureaucrats who manage show business and who aren't even very concerned about profits, but who are possessed by an almost religious fear of everything that they don't understand and by a hardly concealed resentment toward any type of cultural manifestation. And in spite of it all, Cuban (or Afro-Cuban, or Afro-Latin) jazz grew and expanded, even without jam sessions, without jazz clubs, and without festivals during the years when the Jazz Plaza wasn't held because of innumerable difficulties. The number of young jazz musicians increases, as well as the number of groups, even though many have established themselves in other countries, particularly in the United States, as flutist Oriente López, saxophonist Manuel Valera, drummer Horacio "El Negro" Hernández, and many others have done in the 1990s. Of the four Cuban jazz celebrities recognized throughout the world, only Chucho Valdés remains in Cuba, while Paquito D'Rivera and Arturo Sandoval live permanently in the United States and Gonzalito Rubalcaba only visits the island sporadically. Nevertheless, new names are constantly emerging.

Irakere has continued changing its personnel and format. Another one of its founders, the percussionist Oscar Valdés, left the group to organize Diákara, along with his sons Oscarito and Diego. Subsequently, Chucho Valdés has made drastic personnel changes, and according to all indications he will move further and further away from his involvement in dance music to concentrate on Afro-Latin jazz, reducing the group to smaller formats. His latest international successes as a jazz musician seem to support my opinion that Chucho should have devoted all of his energy to jazz and given up "salsa" a long time ago. Meanwhile, other musicians are finding their way; one of them is pianist Ernán López-Nussa, who first stood out with AfroCuba and then with Cuarto Espacio, and now leads his own group. Other excellent musicians that lead their own ensembles are veteran tenor player Carlos Averhoff, the alto saxophonist Javier Zalba, flutist Orlando Valle, and pianist Hilario Durán fronting the group Perspectiva. I should also point out the undeniable maturity that a number of musicians have shown: saxophonist José Carlos Acosta, another AfroCuba cofounder and then with Emiliano Salvador's group; young pianist Ramoncito Valle as well as pianist and percussionist Roberto Julio Carcassés; bassist Carlitos del Puerto Jr., who also was with Emiliano Salvador's group; alto saxophonist Yosvani Terry; pianist Gabriel Hernández, ex-director of Fervet Opus; and many others who would make this an endless list. The important thing is that with so many talented musicians out there, the future of Cuban jazz seems more than assured.

Postscript

$\mathcal{T}$he first version of this book was completed in 1988 or 1989, but because of the unusual publishing problems that we face and the near impossibility of publishing it in a Caribbean country, I decided to make a new reduced version, leaving some theoretical aspects and other anecdotal ones for a future book, and finish it in 1990. Subsequently, I continued to follow the most relevant events with respect to the development of jazz on the island, until I finally decided to finish it, perhaps for symbolic reasons, in 2000. Faced with the same difficulties, I was forced to include here only the most relevant facts that would give readers the basic information, leaving for other texts the corresponding analysis of this period of Cuban jazz, which in general has turned out so fruitful. These facts refer almost exclusively to the Jazz Plaza festivals held in Havana in 1997, 1998, and 2000; in 1999, despite the success of '98, the Jazz Plaza was not held, for reasons and decisions of which I am not aware.

In December 1997 another Jazz Plaza Festival took place, "breaking the routine" of holding the festivals in February. Participating in that festival were Chucho Valdés and Irakere; José Luis Cortés's N. G. La Banda; and Maraca and his group Nueva Vision, so named as a tribute to Emiliano Salvador, and then changed by the group's director and flute virtuoso to Otra Vision. Also taking part were the group Habana Ensemble (a new offshoot of Irakere); saxophonist Javier Zalba's group Temperamento, which is led by the brilliant pianist Robertico Fonseca; Diákara, formed by Oscar Valdés (Irakere's ex-percussion motor); Machete Ensemble; and Bobby Carcassés's Afro Jazz, among others. Those invited from abroad included the Canadians Mutadi Thomas and Jane Bunnett, a big band from Switzerland, the group Mediterráneo from Spain, Sophie Domaich of France, and from the United States were Douglas Ewert, saxophonist of Puerto Rican origin David Sánchez, and trumpet player Roy Hargrove, who since then has been an enthusiast and international promoter of Latin jazz.

Surprisingly, 1998 turned out to be almost sensational with respect to the participation by North American, European, and Caribbean jazz musicians as well as Cuban groups, and a much better than usual festival organization. Particularly pleasing was the second appearance in a Cuban festival by Max Roach, to whom Jazz Plaza '98 was dedicated. Among the outstanding Afro-Latin jazz musicians were Danilo Pérez and his trio, Michel Camilo and his trio, and soloists such as tenor saxophonist David Sánchez, trombonist Steve Turre, and conga player Giovanni Hidalgo. For the second year in a row Roy Hargrove came with his quintet, which consisted of Sherman Irby (alto sax), Larry Willis (piano), Gerald Cannon (bass), and Willie Jones III (drums), although in Havana Hargrove also featured Horacio "El Negro" Hernández on drums, José Luis Quintana ("Changuito") on pailas, and Tata Güines on conga. From Canada Hugh Frazer and the reliable Jane Bunnett showed up.

Other participants were Thiery Eliez, Ramsey Lewis's trio, the Manervio Ensemble (Italy), Nos Square (Switzerland), Liquid Style (Germany), and a full delegation from Spain, whose involvement in every aspect of music has become larger and larger on the island. The 1998 festival saw Chano Domínguez's trio, Dorante Peña and his group, Ximo Tebar, and Miguel Bermejo. From the United States other personalities such as jazz historian Ira Gitler and Blue Note's producer and director Bruce Lundvall attended. The festival venues were once again the Casa de la Cultura in the Plaza municipality and the Teatro Nacional, with secondary venues in the nightclubs Imágenes and La Zorra y El Cuervo, which has been remodeled and dedicated to jazz.

Among the Cuban groups and soloists performing were Chucho Valdés and Irakere, Bobby Carcassés, Frank Emilio Flynn, Mario Romeu, José María Vitier, Yoruba Andabo, Ernán López-Nussa, Giraldo Piloto and his group Klímax, Maraca and Otra Vision, Oscar Valdés's Diákara, the Cuarteto de Saxos de La Habana, the Quinteto de Maderas, Peruchín II and his group, the Havana Ensemble (led by César López), and Roberto Fonseca's Temperamento. The National Symphonic Orchestra also participated, as did Orquesta Iberjazz, led by Braulio Hernández. This orchestra was formed to cover an event that was parallel to the Jazz Plaza, Iberjazz, a contest for jazz composers sponsored by the SGAE (Sociedad General de Autores y Editores) from Spain, in which musicians from any country can enter. Also in 1998 the Jojazz contest for young instrumentalists was held, and the photographic exposition Foto Jazz, which took place annually in the 1980s under the initiative of photographer Elio Ojeda and was continued by Ojeda's colleague, Roberto Bello.

Now we come to the year 2000; just before the end of the millennium, the nineteenth International Jazz Plaza Festival was held. An even larger number of groups and personalities from some fifteen countries attended, something that was never expected even by the most optimistic; I attribute it to the recent worldwide boom in Cuban music and its different styles. The venues were expanded to four: the traditional and emblematic Casa de la Cultura in the Plaza municipality and the Nacional, Amadeo Roldán (which reopened in 1999 after reconstruction), and Mella theaters. The secondary venues included the ballrooms Elegante and Internacional at the Hotel Riviera, La Zorra y El Cuervo, and the Jazz Café, a new locale within the new shopping center built across from Havana's Malecón and Paseo Street, next to the Riviera and Cohiba hotels. There were also encounters with music students from the Instituto Superior de Arte, in Cubanacán.

The list of Cuban groups and soloists extended this time to twenty-two, headed as always by Chucho Valdés and Irakere, followed by Ernán López-Nussa, Bobby Carcassés and Afro Jazz, the Havana Ensemble, Las Canelas, pianist Tony Pérez, Roberto Fonseca and Temperamento, Pablo Menéndez and his group Mezcla, Bellita and Jazz Tumbatá, Frank Emilio Flynn, Changuito, Tata Güines, trumpet player "El Greco" (José Crego) and Top Secret, Diákara,

José Luis Cortés and N. G. La Banda, Giraldo Piloto and Klímax, Jesús Valdés Jr. and his trio, Roberto Julio Carcassés and his group, the veteran singer Lázaro Morúa, pianist Ramón Valle, and the Banda Nacional de Conciertos.

On the list of foreign invitees were: Clarissa and her group (Germany); Hugh Frazer's Quintet along with Jane Bunnett (Canada); Trío Editus (Costa Rica); George Haslam and Steve Waterman (England); Diana Crepaz, Luciano Guarino, Fabrizo Bosso, and Sandro Gibellini (Italy); Havatampa (Japan); Paco Charlery and his quintet (Martinique); Grupo Noga (Panamá); Joel Xavier (Portugal); Hot Siberian Jazz (Russia); and Indira Briceño (Venezuela). From Spain came Alberto Sanz, Mario Rossi, Carlos Benavent, Jorge Prado, Tino Di Geraldo, Ximo Tebar, and pianist Chano Domínguez with his jazz-flamenco fusion. The Spaniards had a special night at the Amadeo Roldán Theater, the "Noche SGAE de Jazz," with a number of Cuban invitees. In addition, in the context of the International Film Festival, which ended two days after the Jazz Plaza Festival started, on December 13 the film *Calle 54* by Spanish director Fernando Trueba was shown. A documentary on Latin jazz filmed in various countries, it is centered on the Sony recording studios on Fifty-Fourth Street in New York City. In the audience were two unexpected visitors: Gato Barbieri, who appears in the film but didn't play in the Jazz Plaza, and Herbie Hancock, who that same night had attended an encounter-workshop with music students and then surprised everybody with his appearance in the Amadeo Roldán Theater along with Chucho Valdés and Chano Domíguez in a joint three-piano performance.

Besides the surprise visit by Hancock, the list of invitees from the United States was impressive: Roy Hargrove, Dave Valentín, Ronnie Cuber, Robin Eubanks, Antonio Hart, Nicholas Payton and his quintet, Kenny Barron's trio, Ronnie Mathews's trio, Ralph Irizarri and Timbalaye, Quinteto Ritmo Caliente, Erick Reed's trio, Donald Harrison & the Armstrong Orchestra, the Wendell Brunius All Stars, the young group Insights, and the Orquesta Juvenil de Jazz led by Mr. Fred Foss. The festival featured, in addition to the traditional Foto Jazz exposition, a painting exhibition, conferences and symposiums that included different personalities, among others photographer and painter Dominique Pianelli from France, Argentine photographer and journalist Jorge Lardone, and the famous jazz photographer William Claxton.

As this brief assessment comes to a close, I feel obligated to remember that in this age of constant change, in the wide world of jazz as well as in music generally—and in any other area of human activity—it's logical that jazz in Cuba finds itself going through a similar stage of change. Every year some musicians leave the country, whether permanently or for a certain period of time, and sometimes they contribute to enriching the history of jazz in other latitudes. Meanwhile, new and younger musicians, and sometimes veterans who had not received the recognition they deserved before, take the place of those that leave. Some groups disappear, others emerge, and a few stick around, and the same thing happens with the places where jazz is played.

The panorama of jazz in Cuba as seen from 2000 or 2001 makes us feel more optimistic than we were a few years ago, basically for three reasons: the better organization of the Jazz Plaza Festival; the interest shown in maintaining jazz clubs on a permanent basis; and the increase in young talent on all instruments, who maintain the characteristic already observed in the musicians from previous generations in mastering jazz as well as Cuban music. In addition to those already mentioned before this postscript, I should mention here a number of the many up-and-coming young musicians at this time: trumpeters Julio Padrón, Mario Félix Hernández ("El Indio"), Basilio Márquez, Yasek Manzano, and Michael González; alto saxophonist Román Filiú and tenor sax players Orlando Sánchez and Irving Acao; flutist Joel Terry; guitarists Ahmed Barroso Jr., Norberto Rodríguez, and Elmer Ferrer; bassists Descemer Bueno, Junior Terry, Alexander Pérez, and José Hermida; drummers Jimmy Branly, Oliver Valdés (Chicoy Jr.), Hilario Bell, Coky García, Ruy López-Nussa, Ramsés Rodríguez, Raúl Pineda, and Julio César Barreto; percussionists Inor Sotolongo and Abel González; and pianists Tony Pérez, Lilia Expósito (Bellita), Rolando Luna, David Virelles, and Osmany Paredes, to mention only about thirty musicians, with the clear understanding that many of equal caliber have been left out.

Before closing I would just like to say that this history, like any other, does not end here and will soon need new chapters, many revisions, and a new perspective. But one has to stop somewhere. Without a doubt other, more qualified historians will emerge and I sincerely hope that this book will be of some use to them.

Notes

1. Cuban Music and Jazz: First Encounters

1. Janheinz Jahn, *Muntu: las culturas neoafricanas*, Mexico, 1963; in this context all of Fernando Ortiz's work is important, as is Melville Herskovits's.

2. Leonardo Acosta, *Música y descolonización*, Havana, 1982. See also Roger Bastide, *Las Américas negras: las civilizaciones africanas en el Nuevo Mundo*, Madrid, 1968; Arthur Ramos, *Las culturas negras en el Nuevo Mundo*, Mexico, 1943.

3. Gunther Schuller, *El jazz: sus raíces y su desarrollo*, vol. 1, Buenos Aires, 1973.

4. Robin Moore, "Minstrelsy in Havana: Music and Dance of the *Teatro Vernáculo*," in his *Nationalizing Blackness: "Afrocubanismo" and Artistic Revolution in Havana, 1920–1935*, Pittsburgh, 1997.

5. Marshall Stearns, *La historia del jazz*, Havana, 1966 (prologue by Leonardo Acosta).

6. On this topic, see my article "Los formatos instrumentales en la música popular cubana," in *Del tambor al sintetizador*, Havana, 1989.

7. His biographic entry appears in Helio Orovio, *Diccionario de la música cubana, biográfico y técnico*, Havana, 1981.

8. John Storm Roberts, *The Latin Tinge: The Impact of Latin American Music on the United States*, New York, 1979.

9. On Machito, see particularly Larry Birnbaum's article, "Machito: Original Macho Man," *Down Beat* (Chicago), December 1980.

10. Alejo Carpentier, *La música en Cuba,* Mexico, 1946. Today some of his points of view on Gottschalk and on Nicolás Ruiz Espadero have become antiquated.

11. Nat Shapiro and Nat Hentoff, *Esto es el jazz (Hear me talkin' to ya),* Buenos Aires, 1957.

12. Schuller, *El jazz;* Solomon Gadles Mikowsky, *Ignacio Cervantes y la danza en Cuba,* Havana, 1988.

13. See Jesús Blanco, *80 años del son y soneros en el Caribe,* Caracas, 1992. Pucho Jiménez, who also played the trombone, was the father of Generoso Jiménez, best known as Beny Moré's lead trombone and arranger. On the topic of the first Cuban musicians to play jazz in a nonprofessional context, that is, in jam sessions, we know very little and there is much uncertainty, and the need for research on the subject becomes ever more urgent, although more difficult.

14. Zoila Lapique, "Habaneras," in *Panorama de la música popular cubana,* Cali (Colombia), 1996; Leonardo Acosta, "La percusión y sus ritmos en la música cubana" (paper presented at the event Percusión 91 in Barlovento, Venezuela, mimeographed).

15. Fernando Ortiz, *Africanía de la música folklórica de Cuba,* Havana, 1965.

16. Roberts, *Latin Tinge.*

17. A summary, although very schematic, can be found in Julio Le Riverend, *La República: dependencia y revolución,* Havana, 1969. On the topic we recommend the bibliography included by Moore, *Nationalizing Blackness,* as well as Moore's text itself.

18. Moore, *Nationalizing Blackness.*

19. Ana Cairo, *El movimiento de veteranos y patriotas,* Havana, 1976; also see Ana Cairo, *El Grupo Minorista y su tiempo,* Havana, 1978, and Oscar Luis López, *La radio en Cuba,* Havana, 1981.

20. The three classic works by Fernando Ortiz on music are *Africanía, Los instrumentos de la música afrocubana* (5 vol.), Havana, 1952–1955, and *Los bailes y el teatro de los negros,* Havana, 1985.

21. The Sociedad de Estudios Afrocubanos included artists such as Nicolás Guillén, Amadeo Roldán, Gonzalo Roig, Juan Marinello, Emilio Roig de Leuchsenring, Elías Entralgo, José Luciano Franco, Regino Pedroso, Ramón Guirao, José A. Ramos, Manuel Navarro Luna, José A. Fernández de Castro, Eusebia Cosme, Marcelino Arozarena, and other national cultural and political personalities.

22. See Cairo's valuable book, *El Grupo Minorista.* Also Alejo Carpentier, *Crónicas,* Havana, 1975 (2 vol.), and Eduardo Robreño, *Como lo pienso lo digo,* Havana, 1985.

23. See Acosta, *Del tambor al sintetizador.*

24. López, *La radio en Cuba.*

25. Blanco, *80 años del son.*

2. The Twenties and the First Jazz Ensembles

1. Horacio Hernández, "El jazz en Cuba: su origen y evolución" (typescript); Maruja Sánchez Cabrera, *Orquesta Filarmónica de La Habana: Memoria (1924–1959),* Havana, 1979.

2. Cristóbal Díaz Ayala, *Música cubana del Areyto a la Nueva Trova,* Puerto Rico, 1981. Another interesting piece of information from that period is the presence in Cuba, in 1922, of the famous march composer John Philip Sousa, performing with his band in the Teatro

Nacional. Souza, in addition, is considered to be of Cuban descent, according to Bobby Collazo, *La última noche que pasé contigo,* Puerto Rico, 1987.

3. Armando Romeu, "Autobiografía" (unpublished); also Leonardo Acosta, "Armando Romeu, maestro de maestros," in *Elige tú que canto yo,* Cali (Colombia), 1993.

4. Stearns, *La historia del jazz.*

5. Cairo, *El Grupo Minorista.*

6. Hernández, "El jazz en Cuba"; also, the author's interview of Amadito Valdés Sr.

7. *Cuba musical* (annual), 1928.

8. Dulcila Cañizares, *Julio Cueva: el rescate de su música,* Havana, 1991.

9. Robreño, *Como lo pienso;* author's interview of Eduardo Robreño; see also Collazo, *La última noche.*

10. Gustavo Robreño, *La Acera del Louvre* (novel, 1925); Gustavo Eguren, *La fidelísima Habana,* Havana, 1986.

11. Eduardo Robreño, *Historia del teatro popular cubano,* Havana, 1961.

12. For more information see Blanco, *80 años del son,* and Collazo, *La última noche.*

13. López, *La radio en Cuba.*

14. Hernández, "El jazz en Cuba."

15. Odilio Urfé, personal communication with the author.

16. Sánchez Cabrera, *Orquesta Filarmónica.*

3. *The Big Bands and the Contradictory 1930s*

1. Joachim E. Berendt, *El jazz: de Nueva Orleans al jazz rock,* Bogotá, 1994.

2. Author's interview of Armando Romeu.

3. Roberts, *Latin Tinge.*

4. Actually the first director and founder of the Hermanos Lebatard was their father, Gonzalo Lebatard, a trumpeter just like his son Gonzalo Jr. Subsequently and until its breakup, saxophonist Germán Lebatard led the orchestra. In 1933, performing at the Montmartre, the orchestra included musicians such as saxophonist and then famous songwriter Gilberto Valdés; pianist René Touzet, also to become a renowned songwriter and bandleader; and bassist Rafael "Felo" Hernández, the oldest of the three jazz bassists of the same name.

5. There is a lot of confusion about the personnel that formed the original Orquesta Lecuona at the Encanto Theater, the one that traveled to Spain led by Armando Oréfiche (later the Lecuona Cuban Boys) and with respect to the Bruguera brothers' participation in the band as well as that of perhaps some musicians from the Lebatard Brothers and Alfredo Brito bands. Bobby Collazo, in his aforementioned book, contradicts himself a number of times; I believe that his most accurate version is found on page 131, where he lists Armando Oréfiche, the Bruguera Brothers, Jorge Domínguez, Daniel González, Bebo Hernández, Barrenechea, Ernesto Vázquez, and "Chiquito" Oréfiche as original members. Manolo Castro, Angel Mercado, Leonardo Timor Sr., Alfredo Sáenz, and other interviewees say that the Lebatard Brothers didn't play in the Orquesta Lecuona. After Oréfiche changed the name of the group to Havana Cuban Boys, the new version of the Lecuona Cuban Boys seems to have been organized by one of the Brugueras.

6. Milagros Monier's interview of Armando Romeu (typed).

7. Carpentier, *Crónicas* (vol. 2). For an approximate list of the Cuban musicians who lived in Paris through the 1950s, see Collazo, *La última noche.*

8. Cañizares, *Julio Cuevas.*

9. Ibid.

10. Díaz Ayala, *Música cubana.* For a more complete list of bands and other female Cuban ensembles, see Collazo, *La última noche.*

11. Stearns, *La historia de jazz.*

12. Hernández, *El jazz en Cuba.*

13. Author's interview of Armando Romeu.

14. Francis Newton, *Une sociologie du jazz,* Paris, 1966.

4. The Forties: Bebop, Feeling, and Mambo

1. López, *La radio en Cuba.*

2. Stearns, *La historia de jazz;* also see the magazines *Metronome* and *Down Beat* from that time, which covered this event thoroughly.

3. The magazine *Swing Makers,* like others already mentioned, did not contribute much to an awareness of Cuban jazz, even though the names of Armando Romeu and Delia Bravo appeared on its editorial board.

4. Hernández, "El jazz en Cuba."

5. Most of these recordings were done in a studio located at Monte and Estévez. Normally they recorded both sides of a single, three minutes each side. Recently I heard one of the recordings on a cassette, which guitarist Carlos Emilio Morales had, and which included the numbers "East of the Sun" and "Take the A Train," performed by Gustavo Más (tenor sax), Isidro Pérez (guitar), Bebo Valdés (piano), Kiki Hernández (contrabass), and Guillermo Barreto (drums).

6. López, *La radio en Cuba.*

7. Bill Coss, "Is Bop Dead? Woody Herman Answers," in *Metronome,* April 1955.

8. López, *La radio en Cuba.* See Collazo, *La última noche,* for more information on Cuban cinema starting in the 1920s.

9. Blanco, *80 años del son;* the use of the conga *(tumbadora)* by the Septet La Llave in 1934 has also been noted.

10. Díaz Ayala, *Música cubana.*

11. Luis Yáñez, Ramiro de la Cuesta, and Rosendo Ruiz Quevedo, *El feeling, un momento estelar en la música popular cubana* (unpublished).

12. Luis Yáñez, personal communication with the author.

13. Max Salazar, "Afro-American Latinized Rhythms," in *Latin New York,* 1986, included in Vernon W. Boggs's book *Salsiology,* New York, 1992.

14. Ortiz, *Africanía de la música folklórica.*

15. See Max Salazar, "La descarga cubana," in *Latin New York,* 1986; I have also expanded on this topic in a recent article, "El mambo, la descarga y el gran Cachao" (still unpublished).

16. Yáñez et al., *El feeling.*

17. Leonardo Acosta, "Pérez Prado: un músico polémico," in *Bohemia* (Havana), September 29, 1989; see also the articles on mambo in the anthology *Panorama de la música popular cubana,* Cali, 1996.

18. Author interviews and conversations with Ninón Sevilla, Osvaldo Urrutia, and Clemente Piquero.

19. In the aforementioned article on Pérez Prado and in others included in the book *Elige tú que canto yo,* Cali (Colombia), 1993.

20. Milagros Monier, interview with Armando Romeu (unpublished).

5. The Explosion of Cubop or Afro-Cuban Jazz

1. On this, see Stearns, *La historia del jazz.*

2. Díaz Ayala, *Música cubana.*

3. Salazar, "Afro-American Latinized Rhythms."

4. Roberts, *Latin Tinge.*

5. Ibid.

6. Ibid.

7. Ibid. Angel Mercado's account comes from the interviews conducted by Ordilio Urfé and Dulce María Betancourt. In *The Latin Tinge* (p. 98) Aspiazu's son is quoted as saying: "My father said, 'That band will go in the front elevator or I don't play here tonight.'"

8. The Latin scene in New York in the Forties and Fifties is described admirably well in Boggs's book *Salsiology.*

9. On the history of Mario Bauzá in the United States, aside from the conversations I had with him in 1991, I've relied almost entirely on work done by Max Salazar, John Storm Roberts, and, in part, Marshall Stearns.

10. Aurora Flores, "Interview with Mario Bauzá," August 28, 1981 (typed copy); see also the booklet *Cubop! The Life and Music of Maestro Mario Bauzá,* edited by the Caribbean Cultural Center, New York, 1993.

11. Accounts by Armando Romeu and Lázaro Herrera.

12. Flores, "Interview with Mario Bauzá"; Max Salazar, "Machito, Mario, and Graciela: Destined for Greatness," in *Cubop!*

13. A conversation between Mario Bauzá and the author.

14. It was precisely at the table that Armando Romeu would reserve for his guests at the Tropicana where I met Tito Puente in the late 1950s (I cannot remember the exact year).

15. Flores, "Interview with Mario Bauzá"; Salazar, "Machito."

16. Vernon W. Boggs, "Salsa's to New York Like an Apple's to Sauce," in *Salsiology* (on a round table discussion in which Max Salazar, Al Angeloro, Steve Blum, and Boggs take part).

17. Choosing certain dates, I've relied on the chronology put together by Mora J. Byrd, "Chronology," in *Cubop!*

18. Stearns, *La historia del jazz;* Berendt, *El jazz.*

19. Personal communication with the author by Rolando Pérez, who is Machito's son, as well as by Odilio Urfé, Ezequiel Rodríguez, and Jesús Blanco.

20. Roberts, *Latin Tinge.*

21. Conversation with Armando Peraza at the Embers Club, in New York, in 1955, in which Peraza also expressed his and Shearing's interest in obtaining recordings by Frank Emilio.

22. Stearns, *La historia del jazz.*

23. Roberts, *Latin Tinge.*

24. Acosta, *Música y descolonización.*

25. Max Salazar, "Chano Pozo" (part 3: Conclusion), in *Latin Beat,* June/July 1993.

26. See Salazar, "Machito, Mario, and Graciela," in *Cubop!*, and the quote in note 25. Also my work "Chano Pozo: el tambor de Cuba," in *El Nuevo Día* (revista dominical), San Juan, Puerto Rico, October 20, 1996.
27. With respect to this, see what Robert L. Doerschuk points out in "Secrets of Salsa Rhythms: Piano with Hot Sauce," in *Salsiology*.
28. Birnbaum, "Machito: Original Macho Man"; Roberts, *Latin Tinge*

6. *Havana in the 1950s*

1. The complete personnel of these bands (Riverside, Beny Moré, Cosmopolita), at least at the time of their greatest popularity, appears in Orovio's *Diccionario;* see also Collazo, *La última noche.*
2. See Bill Coss, "Lennie Hambro, Latin from Manhattan," *Metronome,* April 1955.
3. Hernández, *El jazz en Cuba.*
4. The nickname "Macanta" comes from McIntyre (pronounced in Cuba, it sounds like "Macantaya"), from the time when saxophonist Hal McIntyre, or better yet, his band, was popular. Armando Romeu's brothers, to our knowledge, are Mario (piano), Ernesto (trombone), and Rubén (saxophone and violin), and his sister is Zenaida (piano).
5. Acosta, "La dinastía Peruchín," in *Elige tú.*
6. In Havana, O'Farrill only recorded one LP, *Chico's Cha-cha-cha,* with a big band and his own arrangements of Cuban and Latin American standards, aside from his album of "Descargas." His "Cuban Episode" is on Stan Kenton's album *Innovations in Modern Music.*
7. Monier, interview of Armando Romeu.
8. Author's interview of Rolando Baró.
9. See the biographical information on Obdulio Morales in Orovio's *Diccionario.*
10. There are some discrepancies between my information and that provided by Cándido Camero in interviews. See, for example, Roberto "Bobby" Sanabria, "Candido, Legendary Conguero," in *Hip: Highlights in Percussion,* winter 1988, New Jersey.

7. *End of the Decade: The Club Cubano de Jazz*

1. Díaz Ayala, *Música cubana.*
2. Marcelino Valdés worked for some time with Dizzy Gillespie.
3. Accounts by Guillermo Barreto and Armando Romeu (interviews with the author).
4. Nat King Cole's classic trios consisted of piano, guitar, and bass. Drums were included later.
5. See Roberts, *Latin Tinge.*
6. The emergence of these hipsters was a topic addressed in *Metronome's* Yearly (later discontinued) corresponding to the year 1951: *Jazz 1951, Music USA (The Metronome Yearbook),* New York, 1951.
7. See Arnold Jay Smith, "Jazz Cruise to Cuba," in *Down Beat* (Chicago), August 1977.
8. The only photo that we have of Teddy Corabi, the one in which he appears with Buddy de Franco, accompanies the article "Building a Band," by George T. Simon, in the very same Yearly just mentioned, *Jazz 1951,* p. 55.

9. This information doesn't appear in Oscar Luis López's book, and we are grateful for it, in part, to Horacio Hernández, Jackie de la Nuez, and José A. Figueras.

10. Salazar, "La descarga cubana."

8. *Musical Transition: 1959 and After*

1. See "Problemática de la música y su difusión en Cuba," in *Del tambor al sintetizador.*

2. The only one of these union leaders who participated in the revolution was Carlos Faxas, pianist and director of a quartet; neither saxophonist Celso Gómez nor trumpeter Luis Toledo took part.

3. Leonardo Acosta, "Música y racismo: ¿por qué se persigue al jazz en Estados Unidos?" in *Hoy Domingo* (Havana), September 18, 1960.

4. John Storm Roberts says in the glossary of *The Latin Tinge* that Eddie Palmieri introduced a modified version of the conga called the *mozambique* in the late 1960s, but by about 1964 Pello el Afrokán's *mozambique* (which in effect, contained elements of the conga) was the rage in Havana.

5. Leonardo Acosta, "Dulzaides, un maestro autodidacta," in *Elige tú que canto yo.* See also from the same book "Ñico Rojas: el hombre y la obra." Felipe Dulzaides suffered a second stroke while playing at the Riviera and died on January 21, 1991.

6. I am grateful to musicians such as Amadito Valdés Jr., Nicolás Reinoso, Sinesio Rodríguez, and others for a lot of this information.

7. Account by Amadito Valdés Jr. (author interview).

8. Names such as *Orquesta Cubana de Música Moderna* or *Quinteto Instrumental* reflect a certain reluctance and fear of using or even mentioning the word jazz. Even during Irakere's first stage, its director Chucho Valdés denied that Irakere was a jazz ensemble.

9. Monier, interview with Armando Romeu.

10. "Sinepistolier," in *Jazz Magazine* (Paris), no. 149, December 1967 (the saxophonist Roland Kirk appeared on the cover of this number).

11. For more details see my article "Radiografía del GES," in *El caimán barbudo,* March 1989, and also *Del tambor.*

9. *Irakere and the Takeoff of Cuban Jazz*

1. Arnold Jay Smith, "Voyage of the Jammed," *Down Beat* (Chicago), August 11, 1977.

2. *Irakere,* Columbia 35655, CBS Inc., New York, 1979.

3. Krystian Brodacki, "Michel Camilo: Jazz with a Caribbean Flavor," in *Jazz Forum* 113 (Warsaw), April 1988.

4. In addition to Irakere, I wrote the liner notes for the first AfroCuba record, as well as for Algo Nuevo, Arturo Sandoval, Emiliano Salvador, and many others. Unfortunately, EGREM has never considered itself obliged to provide records to those who contribute to their production, and some of these records have never appeared in Havana stores.

5. Leonardo Acosta, "Emiliano Salvador: retrato desde Cuba," in *Latin Beat* (Los Angeles) 3, no. 5, June/July 1993.

6. Ibid.

7. I wrote an article on José María Vitier that appears in my book *Elige tú que canto yo.*

8. A few days before Ronnie Scott died in London, in December 1996, Chucho Valdés and the other members of Irakere had returned to Havana after performing in his club.

9. Deroy Murdock, "The 14th Annual Havana Latin Jazz Festival," in *Latin Beat* (Los Angeles), June/July 1993. By coincidence, Murdock's piece appears in the same number in which my article on Emiliano Salvador does.

10. On this record of Peruchín's I was in charge of the production and wrote the liner notes. The recording is somewhat deficient, as are almost all of EGREM's recordings from these years. Peruchín has recorded another album more recently.

11. Singer Maggie Prior as well as pianist Freddy González died in the 1990s.

12. In Armando Romeu's participation in the festival with this band, as well as in his 1989 concerts with the Orquesta de Música Moderna from Santa Clara, pianist Freida Anido performed as a special guest, playing Armando's version of *Rhapsody in Blue*. The dance bands of Elio Revé, Adalberto Alvarez, Dan Den, and Juan Formell's Van Van also performed in the 1990 Jazz Plaza.

13. See the magazine *Bohemia* (Havana), vol. 82, no. 11, March 16, 1990.

Glossary

abakuá: Afro-Cuban secret male society derived from those prevalent in the Calabar region (southeastern Nigeria and western Cameroon) of West Africa.

academias de baile: working-class recreational institutions associated with dance and musical entertainment, popular in Cuba through at least the 1940s.

afronegrismo: cultural and political attitude of pride in black African cultural traditions and the attempt to recover these traditions.

afronegrista / negrista: pertaining to or influenced by *afronegrismo.*

arará: Afro-Cuban name for people and their expressive culture originating from the territory of present-day Ghana, Benin, and Togo.

baile de cuna: popular dances of nineteenth-century Cuba, which usually took place in poor neighborhoods and where young white and black people would get together.

baladista: a person who sings ballads.

bandoneón: a musical wind instrument, similar to the accordion, used to play tangos. Also known as the concertina.

bantú: language and culture of people from the area of equatorial and southern Africa.

batá drums: a set of three sacred, double-headed drums used in *santería* ceremonies.

batanga: a rhythm created by bandleader Bebo Valdés in the early 1950s in Havana that incorporated for the first time the use of *batá* drums in popular dance music.

bibosero: Hispanicized term for bebopper.

bodega: a small grocery store.

bolero: a slow rhythmic ballad.

bolerista: a person who sings boleros.

bongó: bongo drums.

bongosero: a person who plays the bongo drums.

boricua: Puerto Rican.

botijuela / botija: a bass instrument made from a ceramic jug associated with Cuban *conjuntos de son* before about 1925.

bugaloo: a fusion of Afro-Cuban dance music with African American styles that flourished in New York City in the late 1960s.

canción: a fundamental vocal genre in Cuban music. The most common setting for this style is voice and guitar, and is often referred to as *trova.*

cabildos (de nación): fraternal mutual aid organizations for slaves in Cuba, first established in the 1500s under the auspices of the Catholic Church. They survived into the twentieth century and became vehicles for the preservation of ancestral African traditions.

cencerro: a cowbell (with the clapper removed), struck with a wooden stick.

chachachá: dance music popularized in Cuba in the early 1950s that developed out of the *danzón, danzonete,* and *son.* It was performed primarily by *charanga* ensembles.

charanga: a specific style of instrumentation, consisting of rhythm section (contrabass, *timbales,* and *güiro*), strings (from two to four violins, or any number of violins with a cello), and one wood flute. The piano was added early in the twentieth century and the conga drums in the early 1940s. This term (and style of instrumentation) evolved from the *charanga francesa,* developed in the early twentieth century.

charanga francesa: the original term for what is now known as the *charanga* instrumentation.

clave: a five-note, bi-measure pattern that serves as the rhythmic foundation for much of Cuban music, salsa, and Latin jazz.

claves: two round, polished sticks that are used to play the *clave* patterns.

combo: an adaptation of the North American jazz combo instrumentation in Cuba during the late 1950s, generally consisting of bass, drums, piano, sax, trumpet, Cuban percussion, and electric guitar.

comparsa: carnaval band that typically performs while marching/dancing down the street.

conga: (1) a conga drum of any type; and (2) a ballroom dance developed in Europe and the United States in the late 1930s that incorporated a simplified version of the *comparsa* or street conga dancing from Cuban carnivals.

conguero: a conga drum player.

conjunto: a specific style of instrumentation developed around 1940, derived from earlier ensembles, consisting usually of piano, guitar (sometimes), *tres,* contrabass, bongos, congas, one or more vocalists (who play hand percussion such as maracas and claves), and two to four trumpets.

contradanza: a nineteenth-century ballroom dance genre derived from the English country dance and the courtly French *contredanse.*

criolla: a vocal genre, similar to the *canción,* usually with lyrics that allude to Cuba's natural beauty and bucolic country themes.

Cubibop: a style developed in the late 1940s by Niño Rivera, a mixture of bebop with the Cuban *son.*

Cubop: The New York-based fusion of Afro-Cuban rhythms with the bebop movement epitomized by the joint work of Dizzy Gillespie and Chano Pozo.

cuica: a small Brazilian friction drum with a tube fastened to the inside of the drumhead that is rubbed to produce a sound.

danza: a nineteenth-century musical and dance form derived from and very similar to the *contradanza.*

danzón: a Cuban musical and dance form developed in the late nineteenth century from the *contradanza* and the *danza;* it is both longer and slower than its predecessors.

danzonera: an orchestra, usually a *charanga,* which plays *danzones.*

danzonero: A performer of *danzones.*

danzonete: a subgenre of the *danzón* that became popular in Cuba in the late 1920s. It differed from the *danzón* only in that it incorporated vocal melodies and also occasionally a *son*-derived *montuno* section.

descarga: "unloading" (lit.); a jam session, as well as an improvised tune.

figle: a deep-toned brass wind instrument consisting of a long tube bent back on itself as well as finger keys. In modern orchestras it has been replaced by the tuba.

fonda: an establishment that provides food, usually at modest prices.

guaguancó: one of three styles of Cuban rumba, featuring a heightened polyrhythmic structure, and danced by male-female couples (in its traditional folkloric setting).

guajeo: the repeated figure played by the string instruments in a particular ensemble, such as the *tres* vamp in a *conjunto* instrumentation, or the violin vamp in a *charanga* instrumentation. Also used to refer to repeated horn lines, such as in a layered mambo section.

guajira: a style associated with rural areas that features a guitar or *tres,* maracas, and cowbell, among other instruments. Its lyrics often celebrate the beauty of the Cuban countryside.

guaracha: Afro-Cuban genre of vocal (and often dance) music that developed in the nineteenth century and was popularized through the *teatro bufo* (Cuban comic opera). In this century *guarachas* have merged with the Cuban *son,* differing from other *sones* in that they are faster in tempo and incorporate bawdy or satirical lyrics.

guarachero: a performer of *guarachas;* also used as a synonym for *sonero.*

guateque: a country party or celebration, where live music is the main ingredient.

güiro: a serrated gourd or calabash, scraped with a stick.

habanera: a Cuban vocal music and dance genre derived from the *danza* that reached the height of its popularity in the late nineteenth century. This genre became popular in Argentina, influencing the development of the tango.

holguinero: a person from the city/province of Holguín.

kinfuiti: a drum consisting of a single head on a wooden box, which is sixty to eighty centimeters high with a diameter of forty centimeters. A string that passes through a hole in the center of the drumhead and extends to the opening of the box produces a sound caused by friction when played. Similar to the Brazilian *cuica.*

mambo: (1) an up-tempo dance style, developed through the Forties and Fifties, that blended several elements of North American instrumentation and harmony with elements of the *son* and other Cuban genres. (2) the section added to the *danzón* form (in the 1940s) that featured an open vamp and instrumental improvisation.

maraca: handheld rattles or shakers, made from gourds, coconuts, wood, or rawhide and filled with beans, seeds, or similar objects.

marímbula: an African-derived instrument used to provide a bass accompaniment in some early *conjuntos de son. Marímbulas* are constructed from large box resonators with a hole cut in them, allowing sound to escape. Near this opening a number of steel metal strips are fastened. *Marímbula* players sit on the box and pluck the strips of metal, each of which has been tuned to a particular pitch.

marquesina: a patio, or atrium, at the entrance of a hotel in Havana.

matancero: a person from the province of Matanzas.

milonga: a popular type of song from Argentina that is sung to a guitar accompaniment, and the dance that is performed to this music.

montuno: the final section of a *son* composition, characterized by a cyclic formal structure, prominent improvisation, and call-and-response interaction between a chorus and a vocal or instrumental soloist.

mozambique: a style of Cuban dance music invented by Pedro Izquierdo (Pello el Afrokán) in the early 1960s. It adapted the rhythms of *comparsa* music to the dance floor.

nueva canción: a Latin American song movement, usually associated with social protest, that arose in the late l96os.

nueva trova: the evolution of the Cuban *canción* or *trova* that appeared in the l960s, closely associated with the Latin American *nueva canción* movement.

olú batá: batá player who can play consecrated *batá* drums in religious *toques de santo.*

orishas / orichas: African ancestor deities. In Cuba, each *oricha* is equated with a particular Catholic saint believed to be a manifestation of the same god.

orquesta típica: an instrumentation used in the interpretation of the Cuban *contradanza*, consisting of woodwinds, brass, strings, *güiro*, and timpani. By the late nineteenth century, the timpani were replaced by the Cuban *pailas* or *timbales*, and the horn section diminished.

pacá: a dance rhythm developed by musician Juanito Márquez that combines elements of Cuban music with the Venezuelan folk style known as *joropo*.

pachanga: a rhythmic style and vigorous dance very popular during the 1950s, and originating in the *charanga* instrumentation.

pailas: a term for a smaller version of the Cuban *timbales.*

pilón: a dance rhythm developed in the early 1960s in Santiago de Cuba by musicians Pacho Alonso and Enrique Bonne.

plena: an Afro-Puerto Rican rhythm, traditionally played on *panderetas* (a form of tambourine), which is an important form of popular music. The *plena* often serves as a vehicle for the expression of social and politically relevant themes.

pregón: musical cries of street vendors used to attract customers, a tradition that comes from Spain and is found throughout Latin America. Beginning in the 1920s, lyrics patterned after the *pregón* also appeared in *sones* and other dance music.

quinto: the highest-pitched drum in a set of three drums used in the styles of rumba, which improvises throughout.

race records: the name given to African American recorded dance music in the United States before the mid-1950s.

raga: (Sanskrit) a Hindu melody that expresses a spiritual state.

revue: a stage spectacle consisting of sketches, songs, and so forth in which parody and satire predominate.

rumba: a heavily African-influenced form of secular entertainment unique to Cuba. Traditional rumba is a complex and highly improvisatory form involving performance on various percussion instruments, song, and dance. It developed in the mid-nineteenth century in the provinces of Havana and Matanzas. Many subgenres and regional variants exist.

rumbero: a male musician or dancer of traditional rumba.

salsa: a musical style that developed in New York City, and other urban centers in Colombia, Venezuela, and Puerto Rico in the early 1970s. The rhythmic foundations of salsa stem from Cuban music genres, such as the *son*, the mambo, and the rumba. But salsa players incorporated certain particular timbric approaches and elements from other Latin American genres from Puerto Rico, Panamá, and so on as well as articulations on melody instruments closer to jazz and U.S. music genres.

salsero: a salsa musician.

samba: a form of Afro-Brazilian dance music popularized in the early twentieth century and closely associated with carnival celebrations in Rio de Janeiro and elsewhere.

santería: the popular name for the Afro-Cuban polytheistic religious tradition that, during the almost four centuries of the slave trade in Cuba, gradually developed by the end of the nineteenth century into a series of religious practices born of mostly West African and some Spanish Catholic roots; more formally known as the *Regla de Ocha* (the law of the *orichas*); focuses on *oricha* worship.

solares: refers to Cuban urban architectural style; usually a small structure that features a patio alongside or at the end of the main rooms; typical of poor working-class neighborhoods, these patios are often the sites for rumbas.

son: a highly syncretic genre of dance music created by Afro-Cuban performers in eastern Cuba towards the end of the nineteenth century. In its form, lyrical content, and instrumentation, the *son* demonstrates the fusion of both African and European elements. It first achieved national recognition in the 1920s. The *son* has become a powerful symbol of Afro-Hispanic cultural fusion and Cuban nationalism.

son oriental: the *son* in eastern Cuba before undergoing transformations in Havana.

sonero: a performer of *sones.*

songo: a contemporary, eclectic rhythm that blends several styles, including the rumba, *son*, conga, and other Cuban secular as well as sacred styles, with elements of North American jazz and funk.

street conga: A street band, same as *comparsa.*

tamborero: drummer.

tango / tango-congo: the rhythmic cell characteristic of the *contradanza,* the *danza,* and the habanera.

timba: contemporary Cuban dance music that is a fusion of *son* and *rumba* with funk and rap music.

timbal: consists of one or two round metal single-headed drums similar in shape to the snare drum. It is played with sticks both on the head and on the shell or *cáscara. Timbales* first gained national popularity in *danzón* orchestras (substituting for the timpani).

timbalero: a performer on the *timbal.*

típica: see *orquesta típica.*

toques de santo: sacred Afro-Cuban musical performances that serve as the liturgical basis of *santería* ritual.

tres: a Cuban stringed instrument derived from the Spanish guitar, consisting of three double-strings and played with a pick. The *tres* is the signature instrument of the Cuban *son.*

tropicalismo: an arts movement in Brazil in the 1960s led by singer-musicians such as Gal Costa and Caetano Veloso.

trova: traditional popular song (also *vieja trova*) performed by street musicians *(trovadores)* and other working-class artists that first became nationally popular at the turn of the century.

The earliest *trova* singers, from Santiago de Cuba, were central to the development of bolero music.

trovador: troubadour, a performer of *trova.*

tumbadora: a conga drum.

tumbao: (bass) The repeated pattern played by the bass, often accenting beats 2+ and 4. The pattern is a mixture of influences from the styles of the *contradanza* and the *son.* (congas) The repeated pattern played by the *tumbadoras* (conga drums), also referred to as *marcha* (march), emphasizing the fourth beat of the measure, as well as beat 4+.

vaudeville: music-hall variety entertainment.

vedette: the lead performer in a variety show, theater, cinema, and so forth.

Yoruba: name given in the early twentieth century to a group of related tribes from southwestern Nigeria, including Iyesá, Oyo, Ijebu, and Egba; said to be the origins of the Lucumí religion, language, and other cultural practices.

zarzuela: a light opera.

Interviews and Conversations

As part of the research for this book, I conducted interviews with the following musicians.

Moisés Alfonso
Froylán Amézaga
Manuel "Cala" Armesto
Rolando Baró
Guillermo Barreto
Roberto Barreto
Mario Bauzá
Dulce María Betancourt
Federico Britos
Ernesto Calderín
Bobby Carcassés
Domingo Corbacho
Felipe Dulzaides
Pucho Escalante
Néstor Favelo
José A. Figueras
Frank Emilio Flynn

Alfredo Gómez
Ovidio González
Felo Hernández Jr.
Horacio Hernández
José Iglesias
Juan Jorge Junco
Pedro Jústiz Jr.
Orestes "Macho" López
Orlando "Cachaíto" López
Inés Martiatu
Gustavo Más
José Antonio Méndez
Rey Montesinos
Carlos Emilio Morales
Jackie de la Nuez
Arturo "Chico" O'Farrill
Raúl Ondina

Luisito Palau
Santiaguito Peñalver
Rolando Pérez
Alfredo Pérez Pérez
César Portillo de la Luz
Luis Quiñones
Rafael Quiñones
Eduardo Ramos
Nicolás Reinoso
Eduardo Robreño
Ezequiel Rodríguez
Luis "Pellejo" Rodríguez
Sinesio Rodríguez
Ñico Rojas
Armando Romeu
Mario Romeu
Rosendo Ruiz Jr.

Gonzalito Rubalcaba
Manuel Saavedra
Ninón Sevilla
José Tabares Palma
Leonardo Timor Jr.
Roberto Toirac

Luis Trápaga
Odilio Urfé
Osvaldo "Mosquifín" Urrutia
Amadito Valdés Sr.
Amadito Valdés Jr.
Chucho Valdés

Gilbertico Valdés
Merceditas Valdés ("Aché")
Jorge Varona
Guillermo Vilar
Manuel Villar
Luis Yáñez

Interviews conducted by Dulce María Betancourt and Odilio Urfé

Atilano Arango
Andrés Castro
Manolo Castro
Pedro Menéndez
Ángel Mercado
Alfredo Sáenz
Leonardo Timor Sr.

Interviews conducted by Horacio Hernández

Luis Escalante
Felo Hernández
Kiki Hernández
Alberto Jiménez Rebollar

Interview conducted by Milagros Monier

Armando Romeu

Index